THE ORGAN

AS A MIRROR OF ITS

THE ORGAN
AS A MIRROR OF ITS TIME

NORTH EUROPEAN REFLECTIONS,
1610–2000

EDITED BY
KERALA J. SNYDER

OXFORD
UNIVERSITY PRESS
2002

OXFORD
UNIVERSITY PRESS

Oxford   New York

Auckland   Bangkok   Buenos Aires   Cape Town   Chennai
Dar es Salaam   Delhi   Hong Kong   Istanbul   Karachi   Kolkata
Kuala Lumpur   Madrid   Melbourne   Mexico City   Mumbai   Nairobi
São Paulo   Shanghai   Singapore   Taipei   Tokyo   Toronto

and an associated company in Berlin

This publication has been created within the European Commission cultural project ORSEV
(The Organ as a Symbol of the European Vision. Raphael Programme 1999)

Library of Congress Cataloging-in-Publication Data
The organ as a mirror of its time : north European reflections, 1610–2000 / edited by
Kerala J. Snyder
p. cm.
Includes bibliographical references, discography and index.
ISBN 0-19-514414-7; 0-19-514415-5 (pbk.)
1. Organ (Musical instrument)—Scandinavia—History.   2. Organ (Musical
instrument)—Germany, Northern—History.   I. Snyder, Kerala J.
ML570.1   .O54   2002
786.5'1948—dc21   2001047643

1   3   5   7   9   8   6   4   2

Printed in the United States of America
on acid-free paper

THIS BOOK INVITES THE READER TO PARTICIPATE IN A TOUR OF SIX CAREFULLY SE-lected organs in North Germany, Denmark, and Sweden. It will be a leisurely trip; we will linger in each place, considering the historical and economic cir-cumstances under which the organ was built, listening to music played on it, and learning how it has fared through the centuries. And we will make some detours as we travel from place to place, pausing for interludes that do not deal directly with our chosen organs.

The geographical limits of our tour are determined by the fact that this book forms one component of a larger project, "Changing Processes in North Euro-pean Organ Art, 1600–1970: Integrated Studies in Performance Practice and Instrument Construction," conducted at Göteborg University and Chalmers Uni-versity of Technology by the Göteborg Organ Art Center (GOArt), with financial support from the Bank of Sweden Tercentenary Foundation, Dan Brändström, Director. This research project ran concurrently with GOArt's building of the North German organ in Örgryte New Church, Göteborg, completed in 2000. This instrument was modeled largely on the Arp Schnitger organ in St. Jacobi, Hamburg (1693), and thus two of our six organs were selected from the very beginning. The other four, each of intrinsic artistic merit and historical interest in its own right, fill in a chronological span through four centuries and form an intricate web of connections, outlined in Chapter 1. The Compenius organ in Frederiksborg Castle (1610) provides a link back to the Renaissance and serves as our only example of an organ built for strictly secular purposes. The Cahman organ at Leufsta Bruk (1728), one of the largest and best-preserved baroque organs in all of Scandinavia, offers a unique example of an elegant instrument built by the owner of an iron mill for the church in his factory town. Because of its isolated location, it is not well known outside of Sweden, and yet E. Power Biggs recorded on it in 1952. Working mainly in Paris, the greatest organ builder of the nineteenth century, Aristide Cavaillé-Coll, built only one organ in Scan-dinavia, in the Jesus Church in Copenhagen (1890). Finally, the Marcussen organ at Oscar's Church in Stockholm (1949) well represents the twentieth cen-tury by mirroring two rather different trends: the organ reform movement and avant-garde composition for the organ.

The stories that these organs have to tell are related here by many different voices, in varying styles, and they can be read in different ways. The twenty-five chapters of this book can of course be read consecutively from start to finish, but they need not be. Information about the organs themselves is found first in the introductory chapter to each part, labeled "Exordium," and in the final chapter, with further details related in chapters 4, 12, 15, and 21. Readers whose primary interest lies in the history of ideas might want to begin with chapters 1, 3, 6, 9, 12, 13, 16, 24, and 25. Discussions of music played on these instruments can be found in chapters 5, 11, and 23, while performance practice is considered in chapters 4, 11, and 22. Organs other than our featured six appear in chapters 7, 10, 17, 18, 19, 24, and 25. The compact disk accompanying this volume contains performances of works that are particularly appropriate to each of the six organs; a short commentary on this program can be found at the end of chapter 1.

Approximately half the authors of this book worked as regular members of the GOArt research team on numerous projects besides this one, coming together periodically for conferences to report on our work and learn from one another. Over the years a sense of cooperation and mutual respect developed that is reflected in the fitting together of the chapters in this book. Without the financial support of the Bank of Sweden Tercentenary Foundation and the wisdom of GOArt's founding director, Hans Davidsson, who assembled and led this team, this book could not have been begun. But even a group as diverse and knowledgeable as this did not possess all the expertise necessary to complete it as we envisioned it. Therefore I am extremely grateful to the invited authors who so richly contributed to this volume. My work as editor was immeasurably assisted by GOArt's resident editorial team: Sverker Jullander, Paul Peeters, and above all Joel Speerstra, who worked tirelessly as my assistant editor and turned my groans into laughter.

With GOArt's support, I was able to become personally acquainted with all six featured organs, and an anniversary trip to the far north of Scandinavia even made it possible to visit the seventeenth-century organ in Övertorneå (see chapter 25). But the actual work of forming diverse contributions into a coherent whole began in a villa overlooking the Mediterranean Sea, at the Ligurian Study Center for the Arts and Humanities, thanks to a fellowship from the Bogliasco Foundation. Back at home, I work in what may be the best of all library worlds for a musicologist, with regular access to both the Sibley Music Library at the Eastman School of Music (Daniel Zager, Librarian) and the Yale Music Library (Kendall Crilly, Librarian). I would also like to thank Karl Schrom at Yale and David Coppen and James Farrington at Sibley for their assistance. But even these fine libraries did not have everything I needed, and I am indebted to a host of colleagues for supplying me with additional information, among them Mats Arvidsson, Göran Blomberg, Hans Fagius, Mark Falsjö, Per Kynne Frandsen, Jørgen Haldor Hansen, Eva Helenius-Öberg, Ibo Ortgies, Andrew Johnstone, Sverker Jullander, Rudof Kelber, Mads Kjersgaard, Robin Leaver, Johan Norrback, Barbara Owen, Paul Peeters, Roger Sherman, Teri Towe, Axel Unnerbäck, Harald Vogel, Joachim Walter, and Munetaka Yokota. Joel Speerstra and Pamela Ruiter-Feenstra provided valuable assistance with translations from Swedish.

The compact disc that accompanies this book brings our featured organs to life, and selecting the music for it was one of my most pleasurable activities as editor. Its production lay in the capable hands of Erik Sikkema and Anna Frisk, to whom I am most grateful.

My final thanks go to Jan Ling, who has acted as a guiding light to all my work at GOArt; to my husband, Richard Snyder, without whose help and moral support I could not have completed the editing of this book; and to those at Oxford University Press—particularly Maribeth Payne, Ellen Welch, and Christi Stanforth—who have brought it so smoothly from vision to reality.

Kerala J. Snyder
New Haven, Connecticut
January 2002

CONTENTS

INTERLUDIUM SECUNDUM

PART III: A FRENCH ORGAN IN COPENHAGEN

INTERLUDIUM TERTIUM

PART IV: REVIVAL AND RENEWAL

POSTLUDIUM

CONTRIBUTORS

Celia Applegate, Associate Professor of History, University of Rochester

Lawrence Archbold, Professor of Organ and Enid and Henry Woodward College Organist, Carleton College

Göran Blomberg, Organist, seventeenth-century organ in Övertorneå, Sweden

Hans Davidsson, Associate Professor of Organ, Eastman School of Music; Research and Artistic Director, Göteborg Organ Art Center

Jesse E. Eschbach, Professor of Organ, North Texas University

Bengt Hambraeus (1928–2000), late Professor Emeritus of Composition, McGill University

Eva Helenius-Öberg, Researcher, National Collections of Music, Stockholm

Martin Herchenröder, Professor of Music Theory, Universität-Gesamthochschule, Siegen

Gisela Jaacks, Director, Museum für Hamburgische Geschichte

Sverker Jullander, Editor, *Orgelforum;* Director of Publications, Göteborg Organ Art Center

Kimberly Marshall, Associate Professor of Organ, Arizona State University

Barbara Owen, Librarian, American Guild of Organists Organ Library, Boston University; Music Director, First Religious Society, Newburyport

Paul Peeters, Librarian and Coordinator of Organ Documentation, Göteborg Organ Art Center

William Porter, Professor of Organ, New England Conservatory of Music

Pamela Ruiter-Feenstra, Associate Professor of Organ, Eastern Michigan University

Kerala J. Snyder, Professor Emerita of Musicology, Eastman School of Music

Göran Söderström, Research Secretary, Committee for Stockholm Research; Executive Secretary, Committee for the Protection of Stockholm's Beauty

Joel Speerstra, Director, Clavichord Workshop; Senior Researcher, Göteborg Organ Art Center

Axel Unnerbäck, Senior Officer and Organ Expert, Swedish Central Board of National Antiquities

Harald Vogel, Professor of Organ, Hochschule für Kunste, Bremen; Director, North-German Organ Academy and the Organeum in Weener

David Yearsley, Assistant Professor of Music, Cornell University

ILLUSTRATIONS

CD CONTENTS

Tracks 1–6: Hans Fagius (Professor of Organ, Royal Conservatory of Music in Copenhagen) playing six dances from the Lublin tablature (c. 1540), on the Compenius organ in Frederiksborg Castle, Hillerød, Denmark. © BBC.

   1. *Corea super duos saltus*. Running time: 1:52
   2. Untitled. Running time: 0:52
   3. *Rocal fusa*. Running time: 1:10
   4. [Passamezzo antico]. Running time: 1:01
   5. *Haÿduczkÿ*. Running time: 1:17
   6. *Jeszcze Marczynye* [Passamezzo antico]. Running time: 1:01

Track 7: Harald Vogel playing Dieterich Buxtehude, *Nun freut euch lieben Christen g'mein* (BuxWV 210), on the Schnitger organ in St. Jacobi Church, Hamburg, Germany. © Musikproduktion Dabringhaus und Grimm. Running time: 15:19

Tracks 8–10: Alf Linder playing Johann Sebastian Bach, Trio Sonata in E-flat Major (BWV 525; recorded in 1971), on the Cahman organ at Leufsta Bruk, Sweden. © Swedish Broadcasting Corporation.

   8. I (untitled). Running time: 3:12
   9. II (Adagio). Running time: 6:13
  10 III (Allegro). Running time: 4:21

Track 11: Sverker Jullander playing César Franck, *Pièce héroique*, on the Cavaillé-Coll organ in the Jesus Church, Copenhagen, Denmark. © GOArt (Göteborg Organ Art Center). Running time: 8:37

Track 12: Erik Boström playing the premier performance of Bengt Hambraeus, *Riflessioni* (1999), on the Marcussen organ in Oscar's Church, Stockholm, Sweden. © Swedish Broadcasting Corporation. Running time: 19:21

Track 13: Hans Davidsson playing Matthias Weckmann, *Es ist das Heil uns kommen her*, versus 7, on the North German organ in Örgryte New Church, Göteborg, Sweden. © GOArt (Göteborg Organ Art Center). Running time: 4:29

ℙRAELUDIUM

I

ORGANS AS HISTORICAL AND AESTHETIC MIRRORS

KERALA J. SNYDER

THE ORGAN, MORE THAN ANY OTHER MUSICAL INSTRUMENT, INVITES US TO REFLECT upon matters beyond music. A chamber organ in the knights' hall of a castle calls us to dance and take pleasure in the movement of our bodies, while a monumental organ in a cathedral draws us into a contemplation of the architecture of the great room itself. Because so much of the mechanism of an organ lies hidden from our eyes, we inquire how it works; and because most organs are so very expensive, we ask who paid for them. As the highest sounds of its mixtures and the lowest tones of its largest pedal pipes drift beyond our capacity to hear them, we contemplate the possibility that they may reflect the unheard music of the spheres. As we gaze at an organ's façade, we see in its varying pipe lengths proportions first discovered by the ancient Greeks. And if we cannot see the organist seated behind the Rückpositiv of a large church organ, we may imagine that the Holy Spirit is playing it. It is the central thesis of this book that organs have stories to tell about the times in which they were built that go far beyond the music that was played on them.

In his *Musurgia Universalis*, published in 1650, the German Jesuit Athanasius Kircher envisioned the organ as God's instrument for the creation of the world (figure 1-1).[1] This organ has six stops, corresponding to the six days of creation, each apparently consisting of a row of seven pipes in the façade. Its six stop knobs to the right and left of the keyboard, labeled Reg[ister] I–VI, are all drawn, allowing wind to issue forth from every pipe, assuming that God, unseen, has depressed some of the keys on the keyboard. Because every pipe is sounding in a grand plenum, this must be the moment of the sixth day that marks the creation of the human being: "But just as an artful organist, when he has previously gone through and tried each of the stops separately, finally draws all the stops of the

---

1. Athanasius Kircher, *Musurgia Universalis sive Ars Magna Consoni et Dissoni* (1650; facsimile reprint, ed. Ulf Scharlau, Hildesheim: Georg Olms Verlag, 1970), 2:366.

Figure 1-1. Athanasius Kircher, *Musurgia Universalis* (1650), plate XXIII.

whole organ together in order to hear the general consonance of all the pipes, so also the eternal Archmusician, after the separate preludes of the six days' work, finally lets the entire great world-organ play, because he has created the human being as the microcosmos, the most perfect creature."[2]

In many respects the illustration of Kircher's allegorical organ resembles an actual organ from about 1650, and an earthly reflection of that heavenly sound of the full organ, the plenum, can be heard in verse 7 of Matthias Weckmann's *Es ist das Heil uns kommen her* (CD track 13). Any keyboard player will instantly recognize, however, that there is something radically wrong with this keyboard: instead of the normal alternation of groups of two and three sharps, Kircher's has only groups of three. One can speculate as to why this is so: each of these six groups of three delineates a set of seven keys that could correspond to the seven pipes of each stop, or perhaps they represent the Trinity, or perhaps it is a device to set this keyboard aside for God; underneath it is written "Thus the eternal Wisdom of God plays in the world."

Kircher's allegorical organ appears in the final section of *Musurgia universalis*, titled "Decachordon naturae," in which the entire universe—including the sing-

---

2. Kircher, *Musurgia* (1650), 2:367.

ing of the angels; the four elements of the world; and the bodily proportions, rhythms, and emotions of the human being—is shown to consist of musical proportions and is organized into ten stops of a world-organ. This may be compared with an earlier section of the book, "Musica Organica, sive Musica Instrumentali," which contains an extensive discussion of musical instruments, complete with many detailed drawings, among them an organ (figure 1-2).[3] Here we see a similar layout of pipes in the façade, but a normal keyboard. Of particular interest is the depiction of the windchest, which Kircher characterizes as the unseen "secret" of the organ. His figure 4 shows a slider chest, whereby when the stop knob is pulled out, the slider (letters M, N, O, and P) moves and its holes line up between those above, on which the pipes sit, and those below, above the key channels, allowing the wind to enter the pipe if the key is depressed. His figures 1 and 2 show how depressing a key (letter L) opens a pallet (M) in the windchest (XY), allowing wind to flow to the key channel and thence to any pipes whose stops are drawn.

Organs in Time and Space

Although the organ lends itself to allegorical interpretations such as Kircher's, most organs are thoroughly grounded, both geographically and historically. The six organs that constitute the focal points for this book are all located in northern Europe: in Germany, Denmark, and Sweden.[4] Thus it is no accident that five of these six stand in Lutheran churches, for it was precisely in Germany and Scandinavia that the Lutheran reformation of the sixteenth century had its greatest impact. Martin Luther himself valued music highly, and the organ figured significantly in orthodox Lutheran worship of the seventeenth century, as we learn in chapter 5. All five of these church organs were intended to provide strong support to congregational singing, which was not the case in Roman Catholic churches until recently.

These five church organs are further grounded not just in a general northern European culture but in specific churches: St. Jacobi in Hamburg; the Leufsta Bruk Church in the Swedish town of the same name; the Jesus Church in Valby, a section of Copenhagen; Oscar's Church in Stockholm; and the Örgryte New Church in Göteborg. Each of these organs was built for the church in which it remains today, and its case was designed to fit into the particular space in which it resides. Nowhere can this be seen more clearly than in Leufsta Bruk, where the organ was installed shortly after the completion of the church (figure 8-1). The ceiling of the church is quite low, so this organ must take advantage of the

3. Kircher, *Musurgia* (1650), 1:512.
4. The geographical restriction to northern Europe is explained in the Preface.

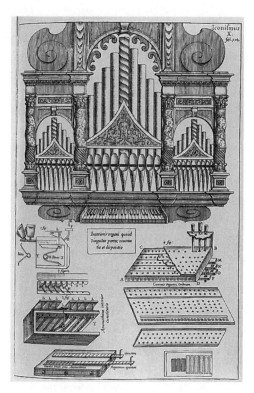

Figure 1-2. Athanasius Kircher, *Musurgia Universalis* (1650), plate X.

available horizontal space. Moreover, the diagonal lines from the inner sides of its pedal towers to the center of the Hauptwerk case mirror the staircases beneath the balcony, creating a total composition in the shape of a diamond (see chapter 9). More than any other musical instrument, an organ tends to remain in one place throughout its working life and to be designed as part of the architecture of that place.

The Compenius organ (figure 2-1) provides a radical exception in this respect. Originally built as a secular instrument for the pleasure palace of a German duke, it was moved shortly after his death to Denmark, where it has stood in three different rooms in two castles—presently in the court chapel of Frederiksborg Castle in Hillerød. Although with 27 stops it is by no means a small instrument, its case is completely self-contained and was never built into any particular place. In fact, it was clearly designed to be transportable; all of the screws are forged with numbers for ease of reassembly, and the case comes apart in pieces that can easily be carried by a single person, except for the solid base. Thus the whimsical-looking iron handles on either side are not only decorative but eminently practical.[5] And the worldly nature of its decoration (see chapter

5. Private communication from Joel Speerstra.

6) serves as an important reminder that throughout its long history, the organ was never intended solely for the church.

The rather narrow geographical circumscription of these six organs has led to some interesting interrelationships among them. The closest is that between the organs of St. Jacobi, Hamburg (1693), and the Örgryte New Church in Göteborg (2000), whose specifications and pipe construction are based almost entirely on those of the Hamburg organ. As a research project at a university, however, the Örgryte organ represents a special case, which is discussed in greater detail in chapter 25.

More surprising is the connection between the Compenius organ (1610) and the Cavaillé-Coll organ at the Jesus Church in Copenhagen (1890). By the time of the building of the Jesus Church organ, Compenius's instrument had fallen into a state of disrepair, and Frederiksborg Castle had become a national museum. Félix Reinburg, Cavaillé-Coll's site supervisor in Copenhagen, was called upon to inspect it, and this led to a proposal from Cavaillé-Coll himself for a renovation, which was carried out by Reinburg in 1895.[6] And the Jesus Church organ leads in turn to the one in Oscar's Church (1949), because the Marcussen firm studied it thoroughly before building their first mechanical-action organ in 1931 (see chapter 24).

A direct familial lineage between builders can be traced between the organs of St. Jacobi, Hamburg, and Leufsta Bruk. Gottfried Fritzsche, who had moved to Hamburg from central Germany, performed a renovation on the St. Jacobi organ in 1635, from which Arp Schnitger retained many pipes in his "new" organ for St. Jacobi of 1693. Fritzsche's son Hans Christoph performed another renovation to the organ from 1655 to 1658 and subsequently became father-in-law to his apprentice Hans Henrich Cahman. Cahman immigrated to Sweden and founded the first important Swedish school of organ building in Stockholm; his son, Johan Niclas Cahman, built the Leufsta Bruk organ in 1728 (see chapter 10). A further relationship exists between the cases of the St. Jacobi and Leufsta Bruk organs. Christian Precht was one of two woodcarvers who worked on the case of St. Jacobi, Hamburg.[7] His younger brother Burchard was born in Bremen in 1651 and got his education in Hamburg from his older brother Christian. In 1674 Burchard moved to Sweden and subsequently became the country's most important baroque wood carver. In the early 1700s he worked together with Herman Buck in the Great Church (Storkyrkan) of Stockholm, and similarities in style suggest that one of them carved the sculptures on the organ, altar, and pulpit of the Leufsta Bruk Church (see chapter 9).

---

6. Cavaillé-Coll's proposal and Reinburg's documentation of this restoration are printed in Povl Eller, "Compenius-orglets historie," *Dansk årbog for musikforskning* 17 (1986): 33–45.

7. Gustav Fock, *Arp Schnitger und seine Schule: Ein Beitrag zur Geschichte des Orgelbaues im Nord- und Ostseeküstengebiet* (Kassel: Bärenreiter, 1974), 59.

The organ of St. Jacobi is also related to the Compenius organ through its wooden 8' Principal in the Brustwerk, which was built by Gottfried Fritzsche. It bears a remarkable resemblance to the 8' and 4' Principals on the upper manual of the Compenius organ,[8] all of whose pipes are made of wood (see chapter 4). Fritzsche might conceivably have seen the Compenius organ in Hillerød, but since both organ builders had originally come from central Germany, it is perhaps more likely that they had a common model there.

A more general relationship exists between the Marcussen organ (1949) in Oscar's Church in Stockholm and the organ in St. Jacobi, Hamburg, as well as that in Leufsta Bruk. As a prime example of the Danish organ reform of the mid–twentieth century (see chapter 24), the Oscar's Church organ returned to the principles of baroque organ construction. One can immediately see this from its case (figure 20-1), which clearly reflects the separate divisions, or *Werke*, of the organ. The large central case contains the pipes of the Hauptwerk, the opening beneath it houses the Brustwerk, and the Ruckpositiv hangs from the balcony behind the organist's bench. Each of these divisions is played from a separate manual, while the towers on either side contain the pipes governed by the pedal. The Danish organ reform followed a similar movement established in Germany during the 1920s, which took Schnitger's organ in St. Jacobi, Hamburg, as one of its chief models. In addition to the *Werkprinzip*, builders influenced by the organ reform movement returned to slider windchests and mechanical key action such as Kircher illustrated in figure 1-2.

Patrons of the Organ

Since large organs are so expensive, the investigation of their financing often reveals historical and economic information about the times in which they were built. Most of them belong not to a single individual but to an institution, such as a church, a concert hall, or a university, and the funds for their acquisition come from a variety of sources. Three of the six organs featured in this book, however, were funded by single individuals: Duke Heinrich Julius of Braunschweig-Lüneburg-Wolfenbüttel, Baron Charles De Geer of Leufsta Bruk, and Carl Jacobsen, the owner of the Carlsberg Brewery in Copenhagen.

Duke Heinrich Julius (1564–1613; see figure 6-4) was himself intellectually and artistically gifted in addition to being an extravagant collector and patron of the arts. From the age of seven he had daily lessons at the keyboard with the court organist Antonius Ammarbach;[9] he also studied painting. At twelve he was

8. Private communication from the organ builder Munetaka Yokota, who has inspected both organs.
9. Wolf Hobohm, "Zur Geschichte der David-Beck-Orgel in Gröningen," in *Bericht über das 5. Sym-*

inaugurated rector of the newly founded university of Helmstedt while simultaneously studying there, and at age fifteen he became bishop of the episcopal
estate of Halberstadt[10] and set up his own household at the bishop's residence in
Gröningen, thirteen kilometers northeast of the city of Halberstadt. Soon afterward he began to remodel the castle, and for its chapel he commissioned a very
large organ, 59 stops on three manuals and pedal, built by David Beck from 1592
to 1596 (see chapter 7). He appointed Michael Praetorius court organist and
later Kapellmeister, and he also tried to hire John Dowland as his court lutenist.

Heinrich Julius's extravagant lifestyle differed markedly from that of his father,
Duke Julius, who lived frugally and whose primary concern had been for the
welfare of his people. By the time of Heinrich Julius's death his duchy was nearly
bankrupt. Among his expensive purchases must be counted the chamber organ
that he commissioned from his court organ builder Esaias Compenius, with its
façade pipes, keyboard and pedals veneered with ivory, solid silver stop knobs
and key arcades, and gilded pipe shades (see chapters 4 and 6).

Charles De Geer (1660–1730) represented the third generation of the De
Geer family to rule Leufsta Bruk (see table 9-1). Very little is known about him
apart from the fact that he was one of the wealthiest men in Sweden and had
both the courage and the means to rebuild the entire town of Leufsta Bruk—
iron foundry, administration building, manor house, church, and workers'
houses—after the Russians burned it all down in 1719 during the Great
Northern War. Furthermore, he supplied the new church with a magnificent
organ by Sweden's best organ builder, Johan Niclas Cahman, though the previous
church had had none. But De Geer died only two years after its completion, so
he had little time to enjoy it; that pleasure would fall to his heir, a nephew, also
named Charles (1720–78), who was only ten years old at the time and living in
the Netherlands. The young Charles received an excellent education there, including the study of science at the university in Utrecht and music lessons,
possibly with the Utrecht organist and composer Karl Gottfried Geilfuß.[11] He
returned to Sweden in 1738 and subsequently moved into the manor house at
Leufsta.

The younger Charles De Geer became one of the pioneers in the field of

posium zu Fragen des Orgelbaus im 17.–18. Jahrhundert, ed. Eitelfriedrich Thom (Blankenburg/Mi-
chaelstein: Die Kultur-und Forschungsstätte, 1985), 51.

10. His grandfather, an ardent Roman Catholic, had secured the appointment to this Catholic episcopal estate for Heinrich Julius, even though he was being raised a Lutheran. In 1591 Heinrich
Julius introduced the Reformation into Halberstadt. See Hilda Lietzmann, Herzog Heinrich Julius zu
Braunschweig und Lüneburg (1564–1613): Persönlichkeit und Wirken für Kaiser und Reich (Braunschweig: Braunschweigischen Geschichtsvereins, 1993), 10–11.

11. Albert Dunning, "Die De Geer'schen Musikalien in Leufsta: Musikalische schwedisch-
niederländische Beziehungen im 18. Jh.," Svensk tidskrift för musikforskning 48 (1966): 190.

entomology, and his work was still valued late in the twentieth century. He corresponded frequently with his more famous contemporary Carolus Linnaeus (1707–78), the Swedish botanist who developed the system for naming organisms by genus and species. Between 1752 and 1778 De Geer published his magnum opus, *Mémoires pour servir à l'histoire des insectes.*[12] On the title page of the first volume he is designated a member of the Royal Academy of Sciences in Sweden and correspondent of the Royal Academy of Sciences in Paris; in figure 1-3 he is seen wearing the Grand Cross of the Order of Vasa, which he received in 1772.[13]

The younger Charles brought with him from the Netherlands an extensive collection of printed and manuscript music, which he augmented during his years at Leufsta Bruk. It consists mainly of chamber music, including sonatas and concertos by Albinoni, Corelli, Handel, Tartini, Telemann, and Vivaldi. There are also a number of opera scores, five of them by Rameau. Keyboard music published in Amsterdam before 1738 by composers such as Johann Conrad Baustetter, F. I. De Boeck, and Jacob Wilhelm Lustig may have been used for Charles's own study.[14] A harpsichord was purchased for the manor house in 1746,[15] and a positive organ from about this time is still there. It thus seems quite possible that Charles might not only have enjoyed listening to music on the organ in the Leufsta Bruk church, but also played it himself. It may even have been the younger Charles, and not his uncle, who ordered the addition of a Rückpositiv to the organ.[16] The original contract calls for an organ with only one manual, and the Hauptwerk contains 5 divided stops, which normally are found only on one-manual organs; they enable the organist to play with a different registration for each hand, as if there were two manuals.

Like Duke Heinrich Julius, Carl Jacobsen (1842–1914; see chapter 15 and figure 15-1) inherited his wealth from a father who had devoted himself to the family business, be it governing a duchy or brewing beer, and who disapproved of his son's extravagant involvement with the arts. Carl's appreciation of sculpture, painting, and architecture was awakened at the age of nine, on his first trip

12. Charles De Geer, *Mémoires pour servir à l'histoire des insectes*, 7 vols. (Stockholm: L. L. Grefing, 1752–78).

13. Per Inge Persson, Adrian C. Pont and Verner Michelsen, "Notes on the Insect Collection of Charles De Geer, with a revision of his species of Fanniidae, Anthomyiidae and Muscidae (Diptera)," *Entomologica Scandinavica* 15 (1984): 90.

14. Catalog in Dunning, "Die De Geer'schen Musikalien," 192–210.

15. Tomas Anfält, "Offentlighet och privatliv: Om livet på Leufsta herrgård på 1700-talet," in *Herrgårdskultur och salongsmiljö*, ed. Erik Kjellberg (Uppsala: Uppsala University, Institutionen för musikvetenskap, 1997), 6.

16. This idea was first suggested to me by Göran Blomberg. Carl-Gustaf Lewenhaupt proposed the organ builder Daniel Stråhle as the builder of the Rückpositiv (*Dokumentation av Cahmanorgeln i Leufsta bruks kyrka* [Uppsala: Länsstyrelsens meddelandeserie, 1998], 7). Stråhle died at Leufsta Bruk in 1746.

Figure 1-3. Baron Charles De Geer (1729–78).

to Germany and Italy, and he studied the history of art at Copenhagen University, along with the mathematics, physics, and chemistry that he would need to manage the brewery. He assembled an enormous collection of sculpture, which he displayed at first in a museum at the brewery; when it outgrew that space, he established the Ny Carlsberg Glyptotek in 1897, which is still one of the glories of Copenhagen. By 1879 he had funded a trust for procuring sculptures with which to embellish public squares and gardens in Copenhagen.

Carl Jacobsen devoted a quarter of his inheritance and even more of his own funds to the building of the Jesus Church in Valby, the Copenhagen suburb where the brewery is located. Its architecture reflects that of churches in southern Europe that had so impressed him, notably in Ravenna and Poitiers. For its organ he chose the best builder in Europe, Aristide Cavaillé-Coll. Jacobsen cut the size of the organ down from its originally planned 40 stops to 20, however, probably for financial reasons; even the 20-stop organ was extremely expensive by Danish standards. But a glance at the interior of the church (figure 15-2) shows that the organ does not play the prominent role in the decorative scheme that it does in Leufsta Bruk; the complete design of its façade (figure 14-1) is in fact obscured by the columns supporting the small arches within the chancel. Carl Jacobsen's greater interest in art and architecture than in music seems to be clearly reflected here.

Each of these three patrons inherited enormous wealth; Heinrich Julius's was based almost entirely on land, Charles De Geer's on a combination of land and industry, and Carl Jacobsen's entirely on industry. The level of extravagance with which these wealthy patrons endowed their organs seems to have diminished with each passing century. Also, both Heinrich Julius and Charles De Geer the younger may well have played their organs themselves, while it is unlikely that Carl Jacobsen did so. And whereas Heinrich Julius commissioned his chamber organ purely for his own pleasure, for Charles De Geer the elder and Jacobsen the organ formed part of the furnishings of churches that they built for the welfare of their workers, even if De Geer also regarded the Leufsta Church as his baronial chapel and Jacobsen used the Jesus Church as a family shrine.

In the old Hanseatic cities, such as Hamburg and Lübeck, a different form of patronage manifested itself. There a group of wealthy merchants formed an oligarchy, not unlike that of Venice, and these men communally supported the Hamburg opera, the Lübeck Abendmusiken, and the building of organs. After the city hall, churches offered the best opportunity for cities to display their prosperity, and the monumental organ façade on the west wall, as the most prominent furnishing within the church, commanded the attention of all those entering the building. Organists were the best-paid and most highly respected musicians in these cities, and they often entertained visiting trade delegations with an organ recital. At the beginning of the seventeenth century each of Hamburg's four main churches had a three-manual organ; by the end of the century the number of manuals had risen to four. No other city in northern Europe could compare with that.

The Organ and the Physics of Sound

Just as the organ prompts us to consider its geographical and historical placement, it also demands that we understand something about the physics of sound. One can play the piano for a lifetime without ever giving much thought to the length of its strings, but one cannot sit down at an organ bench without being immediately confronted with the lengths of its pipes: 8′ stops produce normal pitch, 4′ stops sound an octave higher, and 16′ stops sound an octave lower; the ratio for the octave is 2:1 for pipe lengths, string lengths, or frequencies (see figure 4-3). In the case of organ pipes, these measurements represent the sounding length of the lowest pipe (usually C) of an open flue stop. The discovery of the proportions for the octave, fifth (3:2), and fourth (4:3) are attributed to Pythagoras.

The proportions of an organ are not just heard; they can often be seen in its case as well. In Schnitger's organ for St. Jacobi, Hamburg (figure 2-2), for example, the pipes of the 16′ Principal stand in the façade of the Hauptwerk, and those of the 8′ Principal in the Rückpositiv. Both cases consist of a central round tower for the longest bass pipes, with C in the middle; pointed towers on the sides that contain the pipes in the tenor range; and flat fields between them for the highest pipes, with the upper flat fields of the Hauptwerk and the lower ones of the Rückpositiv consisting of dummy pipes for the sake of appearance. The Hauptwerk thus stands in a 2:1 proportion to the Rückpositiv, both aurally and visually. The pedal towers on either side contain in their façades the fourteen pipes from F to f♯ of the 32′ Principal; the rest of its pipes are on the windchest inside. The largest pipe is the 24′ F in the center of the right tower (with F♯ in the left tower); thus the round towers of pedal, Hauptwerk, and Rückpositiv stand in the ratio 3:2:1.

Schnitger's case for St. Jacobi may be compared with the case, similar in arrangement but with different proportions, that he designed just six years later for the Lübeck Cathedral (figure 1-4). Here the height of the arch did not permit a 32′ Principal in the pedal, so the longest pipe is the C of the 16′ Principal in the middle of the right pedal tower. The Hauptwerk is also based on a 16′ Principal, but in order to create a harmonious relationship with the pedal towers, its façade pipes begin not with C but with F, a fourth higher (12′); the Rückpositiv again contains the 8′ Principal in its façade. Thus the round towers of this organ stand in the ratio 4:3:2. Because the ceiling height of Örgryte New Church in Göteborg is similarly restrictive, the new North German organ there (figure 25-1) took the Lübeck Cathedral façade as its model.

The physics of sound confronts the organist in another manner that can be less harmonious. The beautiful 3:2 ratio of the perfect fifth, when multiplied around the circle of fifths to produce the chromatic scale, does not close the circle but ends on a pitch approximately ⅛ tone, or 23.46 cents,[17] higher (after seven octaves have been subtracted) than the point of departure; this difference is known as the Pythagorean comma. Flexibly intoned instruments, such as voices and violins, can compensate for this problem quite easily, but keyboard instruments, whose pitch is fixed, must be tempered in some way so that their octaves will be in tune. And of all keyboard instruments, the question of temperament is most critical for organs, both because their tone is so sustained and because they are the most difficult to tune.[18]

Since about the middle of the nineteenth century, nearly all keyboard instruments have been tuned in equal temperament, whereby each fifth is diminished by 1/12 Pythagorean comma, or approximately 2 cents. The organs of Leufsta Bruk, the Jesus Church, and Oscar's Church are all tuned in equal temperament.

17. Cents are logarithms of ratios; one cent is 1/100 of an equally tempered semitone.
18. For a good discussion of temperaments for organs, see Charles A. Padgham, *The Well-Tempered Organ* (Oxford: Positif Press, 1986).

Figure 1-4. The Arp Schnitger organ (1699) in the Lübeck Cathedral. Courtesy of Museum für Kunst und Kulturgeschichte der Hansestadt Lübeck.

Although its fifths are quite good, this temperament produces major thirds that are about 14 cents sharper than the pure interval (see table 1-1). We generally accept these out-of-tune thirds as the price that we must pay to have enharmonic equivalence and every key equally in tune.

During the Renaissance another system of temperament that did produce pure major thirds was in widespread use for keyboard instruments: quarter-comma meantone. The comma meant here is the slightly smaller syntonic comma, 21.5 cents, which represents the difference between four pure fifths (less two octaves) and a pure major third with the proportion 5:4. Both the Compenius and the Örgryte organs are tuned in quarter-comma meantone. In this temperament, eleven fifths are each diminished by ¼ syntonic comma, but the circle does not close, because the cumulative result is a shortening by 2¾ commas, where only one was needed. The twelfth fifth is called a "wolf," because it howls at an interval 41 cents sharper than the others. Organs tuned in meantone generally begin the succession of fifths with E♭ and end with G♯, producing eight pure major thirds and four diminished fourths that are unusable (41 cents sharp) as major thirds: C♯–F, F♯–B♭, G♯–C, and B–E♭. Since there is no enharmonic equivalence, it is not possible to play in keys calling for thirds such as A♭–C or B–D♯. The range of usable pitch classes can be extended, however, by the provision of subsemitones, or split keys, so that the keys (and the corresponding pipes) for both E♭ and D♯, as well as G♯ and A♭, and occasionally also B♭ and A♯, are present. The Örgryte organ has subsemitones; the Compenius organ does not. Gottfried Fritzsche installed them in the Rückpositiv of the St. Jacobi, Hamburg, organ in 1635, but Arp Schnitger did not retain them in 1693.

The period from the late seventeenth century until the early nineteenth witnessed the discussion of many new temperament systems, as theorists and organ builders grappled with the fact that composers were writing music that ventured well beyond the old meantone limits, while equal temperament remained unacceptable to most organ builders and musicians. Various modifications of meantone were tried; one of these, using a fifth-comma division, is currently in use at St. Jacobi, Hamburg. There the diatonic keys sound almost as pure as they do in quarter-comma meantone, while the howling of the wolf fifth has been diminished considerably and the sharpness of the third B–D♯ reduced to the syntonic comma. The thirds A♭–C, F♯–A♯, and C♯–E♯ are still larger (24 to 28 cents) and virtually unusable.

Two German theorists of this period wrote extensively on temperament: Andreas Werckmeister (1645–1706) and Johann George Neidhardt (c. 1685–1739). Werckmeister closed the circle of fifths in 1681 with two unequal circulating systems (also known as "well tempered"), one for use with more far-ranging keys

TABLE 1-1.
Tuning Systems Compared

Pure intervals, reckoned from C

	C	C#[Db]	D	[D#] Eb	E	F	F#[Gb]	G	G# [Ab]	A	[A#] Bb	B	C
proportions:	C		M2, 9:8	m3, 6:5	M3, 5:4	P4, 4:3		P5, 3:2		M6, 5:3			
cents:	0		204	316	386	498		702		884			1200

Quarter-comma meantone:

11 fifths 1/4 syntonic comma, or 5 cents, flat; 1 unusable ("wolf," = 36 cents sharp), normally G#–Eb on organs.
8 major thirds pure; 4 unusable (41 cents sharp), normally C#–E#, F#–A#, G#–B#, and B–D# on organs.

	C	C# [Db]	D	[D#] Eb	E	F	F# [Gb]	G	G# [Ab]	A	[A#] Bb	B	C
	0	76 · 117	193	269 · 310	386	503	579 · 620	697	773 · 814	890	965 · 1007	1082	1200

Modified meantone of St. Jacobi, Hamburg (1993)

7 fifths (F–C–G–D–A–E–B–F#) 1/5 syntonic comma, or 4.3 cents, flat; 3 fifths (F#–C#, C#–G#, Bb–F) pure; Eb–Bb 1/10 Pythagorean comma sharp; G#–Eb 1/5 syntonic comma sharp.
Major thirds on C, D, F, and G close to pure (4 cents sharp); major thirds on C#, F#, G#, and B still extremely sharp (21–28 cents).

	C	C#	D	Eb	E	F	F#	G	G#	A	Bb	B	C
	0	88	195	296	391	502	586	698	790	892	1000	1088	1200

Neidhardt's 1724 Temperament for a Village (Neidhardt I)

4 fifths (C–G, G–D, D–A, A–E) 1/6 Pythagorean comma, or 4 cents, flat; 4 fifths (E–B, B–F#, Ab–Eb, Eb–Bb) 1/12 Pythagorean comma, or 2 cents, flat; remaining fifths pure.
Major thirds vary from 6 cents to 18 cents sharp; all usable; no "wolf" fifth.

	C	C#/Db	D	D#/Eb	E	F	F#/Gb	G	G#/Ab	A	A#/Bb	B	C
	0	94	196	296	392	498	592	698	796	894	996	1092	1200

Equal temperament

All fifths 1/12 Pythagorean comma, or 2 cents, flat; all major thirds 14 cents sharp.

	C	C#/Db	D	D#/Eb	E	F	F#/Gb	G	G#/Ab	A	A#/Bb	B	C
	0	100	200	300	400	500	600	700	800	900	1000	1100	1200

Syntonic comma (21.5 cents): the amount by which 4 pure fifths less 2 octaves exceed a pure major third.

Pythagorean comma (23.46 cents): the amount by which 12 pure fifths exceed 7 octaves.

To evaluate any interval, subtract the smaller cents value from the larger and compare the difference with the cents value of the pure interval.

and the other for use with the old diatonic keys.[19] The first, later known as Werckmeister III following the numeration in his *Musikalische Temperatur* (1691), divides the Pythagorean comma equally among four fifths (C–G, G–D, D–A, and B–F♯) and tunes the rest pure. In the title of a 1706 publication, Neidhardt called equal temperament the "best and easiest,"[20] but in 1724 he proposed a more sophisticated collection of three unequal circulating temperaments for use in a village, a small city, and a large city, reserving equal temperament for use at court.[21] All three of these unequal temperaments produce four major thirds that are better than equal temperament, two that are the same, and six that are worse. The good thirds become slightly better from the large city to the small city to the village (where presumably the diatonic keys are more in use), and the bad thirds worse, but all three favor the old meantone keys to a lesser degree than does Werckmeister III. The advantage of unequal temperaments such as these is that the differences between keys can be clearly heard and exploited for affective purposes.

The organ at Leufsta Bruk is presently tuned in equal temperament, but one must question whether it has always been that way, even in the absence of clear evidence that the temperament has been changed.[22] And if Neidhardt's categories had been applied to this organ, built four years after his 1724 publication, into which of them would Leufsta have fit—the village or the court? If Charles De Geer had been asked this question, he might well have replied that it was a court organ; indeed it contained considerably more stops than the organ that was built for the royal court in Stockholm in 1753.[23] But Cahman himself seems to

19. Andreas Werckmeister, *Orgelprobe . . . Benebenst einem kurtzen jedoch gründlichen Unterricht, Wie . . . ein Clavier wohl zu temperiren und zu stimmen sey, damit man nach heutiger Manier alle modos fictos in einer erträglichen und angenehmen harmoni vernehme* (Frankfurt: Calvisius, 1681), 35.

20. Johann George Neidhardt, *Beste und leichteste Temperatur des Monochordi, vermittelst welcher das heutiges Tages bräuchliche Genus Diatonico-Chromaticum eingerichtet wird, daβ alle Intervalla, nach gehöriger Proportion, einerley Schwebung überkommen, und sich daher die* Modi regulares *in alle und iede* Claves, *in einer angenehmen Gleichheit, transponiren lassen . . .* (Jena: Johann Bielcken, 1706).

21. Johann George Neidhardt, *Sectio canonis harmonici, zur vollen Richtigkeit der generum modulandi* (Königsberg: Christ. Gottfr. Eckart, 1724), 12–15, 20. The first, for the village, is given in table 1-1; this is the temperament "Neidhardt I" in Padgham, *The Well-tempered Organ*, 71–72. Neidhardt designated this same temperament as best for a small city in 1732; see his *Gäntzlich erschöpfte, Mathematische Abtheilungen des Diatonisch-Chromatischen, temperirten* canonis monochordi (Königsberg: Christoph Gottfried Eckart, 1732), 38, 40.

22. The organ was in equal temperament before the Marcussen restoration of 1963–64, and no discussion of temperament during the 1933 restoration by John Vesterlund has been preserved (private communication from Axel Unnerbäck, 29 March 2001). However, the Moberg brothers, who assisted Vesterlund at that time, told Göran Blomberg that Vesterlund had changed the organ to equal temperament (private communication from Göran Blomberg, 29 April 2001; on the Moberg brothers, see chapter 12).

23. This organ had 17 stops on two manuals and a pull-down pedal. It was reconstructed by Mats Arvidsson and Carl Gustav Lewenhaupt in 2000.

have favored an unequal circulating temperament at this time. In 1732 he wrote to Bishop Erik Benzelius Jr.:

> Thus to divide the twelve intervals which make up an octave on a keyboard like a clock which counts out the day's twelve hours equally, for that I can find no reasonable excuse or reason, for the harmonies would be just as true, or rather just as false in one key as in another and thus just as wrong whatever note the composer wished to use and the musician played. . . . For my part, I think it has gone far enough when all the twelve intervals of the octave can be tempered and adjusted so that all the fifths are beating rather little when all the thirds are tolerably helped, so that one can enjoy playing in all keys, as well in C♯, F♯ and G♯ major as in C, D, and F major.[24]

If indeed the temperament of the Leufsta organ has been changed, it is not alone; most historical organs have been altered in this respect over the years, including the Compenius organ. When it was moved in 1791, its tuning was changed to what the organ builder C. F. Speer described as "the best temperament." But in his proposal for the renovation, Cavaillé-Coll, who tuned his own organs in equal temperament, specified that the Compenius should be "tuned as originally, in an unequal temperament (with the wolf fifth)."[25] In his report on the renovation, Reinburg described the entire tuning process in detail, noting that he had taken it from Dom Bédos.[26] And indeed he followed Dom Bédos's "old" tuning system, in which "eleven fifths are diminished by a quarter of a comma."[27]

The Organ as Aesthetic Mirror

Tuning systems provide excellent reflections of the musical aesthetics prevailing at the times of their most widespread use. Medieval composers and theorists considered thirds to be dissonances and accepted only unisons, fourths, fifths, and octaves as consonances. This aesthetic is mirrored in the Pythagorean tuning of the medieval organ, in which all the fifths (except the wolf) are tuned perfectly, making most of the thirds one syntonic comma sharp.[28] When thirds and sixths

24. From a letter of 15 April 1732 about the scientist Christopher Polhem's suggestion for an equal-beating temperament (Linköpings stiftsbibliotek, handskriftssamlingen, N 12). Translation, with slight modifications, from Mats Åberg and Herwin Troje, "The Choir Organ in the Kristine Church, Falun," *British Institute of Organ Studies* 7 (1983): 53–54.

25. Eller, "Compenius," 34.

26. Eller, "Compenius," 44–45.

27. Francois Bédos de Celles, *L'art du facteur d'orgues* (1770; facsimile reprint edited by Christhard Mahrenholz, Kassel: Bärenreiter, 1965), 2:429.

28. For an excellent discussion of Pythagorean tuning, within the context of an anthology of medieval organ music, see Kimberly Marshall, ed., *Historical Organ Techniques and Repertoire*, vol. 3, *Late-Medieval before 1460* (Colfax, N.C.: Wayne Leupold Editions, 2000).

were admitted as consonances during the fifteenth century, the tuning system followed with meantone temperament, which was first discernible in Bartholomeo Ramos de Pareia's *Musica pratica* (Bologna, 1482) and later defined more precisely by Giosefo Zarlino, Michael Praetorius, and others. Meantone temperament brings Renaissance music to life, as can be heard in Hans Fagius's performance of dances from the Lublin tablature (c. 1540; CD tracks 1–6) on the Compenius organ. As is the case with most music of the period, these pieces have signatures only for *cantus durus* (no flat) or *cantus mollis* (B♭) and do not exceed the set of meantone pitch classes ascending by fifth from E♭ to G♯. The harmony of these dances, which is almost totally dominated by what we would call root-position triads, is definitely enhanced by the perfectly tuned thirds of meantone temperament. This aesthetic, glorying in full-bodied consonance, can still be heard in Matthias Weckmann's *Es ist das Heil uns kommen her* (CD track 13) from the mid–seventeenth century, played by Hans Davidsson on the full plenum of the Örgryte organ.

New forces were also at work during the seventeenth century, however, and they are reflected in the concurrent experimentation with temperament. Dieterich Buxtehude's *Nun freut euch lieben Christen g'mein*, like most of his chorale-based works, rarely exceeds the meantone limits; it is well suited to the modified-meantone tuning of Hamburg's St. Jacobi organ. One of the properties of meantone—and of unequal circulating temperaments as well—is the presence of unequal semitones, which impart much greater pathos to a chromatic melodic line than is possible with equal temperament. At the entrance of the last chorale line (CD track 7, at 09:39), whose text refers to the passion of Christ, Buxtehude introduced a chromatic countermelody, whose affective impact is enhanced here by the uneven semitones. A number of Buxtehude's free organ works cannot be played on an organ tuned in meantone, however, and there is reason to believe that the temperament of the organs in St. Mary's Church in Lübeck, where he served as organist, was changed to Werckmeister III in 1683.[29]

Unequal temperaments continued to be in favor throughout the eighteenth century, chiefly because they enhanced the differentiation of keys. As Neidhardt wrote in his final publication on temperament, "Most do not find in [equal temperament] what they seek. They say it lacks the changes in the beating of the major thirds, and consequently in the movement of the various affections."[30] And since most baroque composers would have agreed with Johann Mattheson that the proper goal of all melody is to move the affections,[31] this was a serious issue.

---

29. See Kerala J. Snyder, *Dieterich Buxtehude: Organist in Lübeck* (New York: Schirmer, 1987), 84–85, 354.

30. Neidhardt, *Gäntzlich erschöpfte, Mathematische Abtheilungen*, 40.

31. Johann Mattheson, *Der vollkomene Capellmeister* (1739; facsimile reprint edited by Margarete Reimann, Kassel: Bärenreiter, 1954), 207 [part 2, chapter 12, section 31].

In 1776 Johann Philipp Kirnberger, a student of J. S. Bach, presented a system of key classification in volume 2, number 1 of *Die Kunst des reinen Satzes in der Musik* that depended on unequal temperament. Of the connection with the affections, he wrote:

> It can be taken as a basic rule for judging scales that the major keys whose thirds are completely pure possess most strongly the quality of the major mode, and that the greatest roughness and finally even something like ferocity enter into those major keys farthest removed from this purity. The same must also be assumed of minor keys: Those whose thirds are purest have the most gentle and pleasing tenderness and sadness, but those that are farthest removed from this purity blend the most painful and adverse qualities into this character.[32]

Bach himself played organs in various temperaments—most of them unknown to us—ranging from meantone through unequal temperaments to equal temperament. His preferred tuning was most likely his own personal variant of unequal temperament.[33]

Equal temperament suits perfectly the theory and aesthetic of twelve-tone music, such as Bengt Hambraeus's *Permutations and Hymn*, in which tone rows are transposed to many different levels and absolute equality of tones is sought (see chapter 23). Hambraeus's *Riflessioni* (CD track 12) is not a twelve-tone work, but it is nonetheless rooted in the chromatic scale. The music of Franck, with its chromatic harmony and enharmonic modulations, likewise depends on equal temperament for its proper effect. The sections in B major of *Pièce héroique* (CD track 11, at 03:01 and 06:55) provide first an oasis of calm and later a triumphant conclusion in contrast with the agitated opening section in B minor. But B major, with its key signature of five sharps, is one of the keys that are most removed from purity in an unequal temperament and that Kirnberger might have chosen to express roughness or even ferocity. This is surely not what Franck intended here.

The design and specifications of organs also reflect the musical aesthetics of their times, of course. The compact disc accompanying this book offers a recording on each organ of a composition from its own era that draws upon the particular characteristics of the instrument. Registrations are given in the "Exordium" chapter for each organ.

The Compenius organ, with its human scale and distinctly secular decoration,

32. Johann Philipp Kirnberger, *The Art of Strict Musical Composition*, translated by David Beach and Jurgen Thym (New Haven: Yale University Press, 1982), 340. See also Rita Steblin, *A History of Key Characteristics in the Eighteenth and Early Nineteenth Centuries* (Ann Arbor: UMI Research Press, 1983), 86.

33. See Mark Lindley, "A Quest for Bach's Ideal Style of Organ Temperament," in *Stimmungen im 17. Und 18. Jahrhundert: Vielfalt oder Konfusion?* ed. Günter Fleischhauer et al. (Michaelstein: Stiftung Kloster Michaelstein, 1997), 45–67.

invites us to dance to music copied down by the Polish organist Jan of Lublin in the mid–sixteenth century (tracks 1–6). These anonymous dances represent an international repertory, including two examples of the passamezzo antico. Hans Fagius has chosen registrations that call to mind the consorts of instruments that might have played for an evening of dancing in Hessen Castle: flutes, crumhorns, and mixed consorts with viols.

Dieterich Buxtehude (c. 1637–1707) offers in *Nun freut euch lieben Christen g'mein* (BuxWV 210; track 7) one of the finest examples of the chorale fantasy, a genre that flourished only briefly in North Germany, in which each phrase of the chorale (example 1-1) is developed extensively in highly differentiated sections. Harald Vogel's performance in St. Jacobi, Hamburg, demonstrates the various ways in which this genre exploits the clearly delineated divisions of the large Hanseatic organ: by playing a highly ornamented solo line on the Rückpositiv, as at the beginning and end (13:38), or with echoes—between two manuals (04:12), three manuals (08:34), and even four manuals (12:57). Buxtehude had only three manuals on his Lübeck organs, but we can be sure that when he visited Hamburg he found ways to use all four manuals that were available on the organs there.

Johann Sebastian Bach (1685–1750) composed his Trio Sonata in E-flat Major (BWV 525; tracks 8–10) at about the same time that Johan Niclas Cahman built the Leufsta Bruk organ, although this piece may not have been played there until the twentieth century. Alf Linder (see chapter 22) made this recording for Swedish Radio in 1971. Bach's sonata, with its contrapuntal texture of three independent lines for two manuals and pedal, also reflects the *Werkprinzip* of the baroque organ, but in a single sustained way, as is typical for the eighteenth century, as opposed to Buxtehude's constantly varying textures. The aristocratic elegance and clarity of this organ provide a most appropriate vehicle for this masterful composition.

César Franck (1822–90) played the premiere of his *Pièce héroique* (track 11) in a recital on October 1, 1878, on the organ that Cavaillé-Coll had built for the five-thousand-seat auditorium in the Palais du Trocadéro, the central building for the Universal Exposition in Paris that year.[34] That instrument had 66 stops on four manuals and pedal, but Sverker Jullander demonstrates here that a much smaller Cavaillé-Coll organ can still convey the French symphonic style. One immediately notices the subtle dynamic shadings that are possible with the use of the swell pedal, as well as the dramatic entrance of the prepared reeds (at 06:14). Another characteristic Cavaillé-Coll sound is the *flute harmonique*, which enters in the upper voices at 03:04. The slower speech of the pipes, as compared

34. Rollin Smith, *Playing the Organ Works of César Franck* (New York: Pendragon Press, 1997), 165–67.

Example 1-1. Nun freut euch lieben Christen g'mein (Archiv der Hansestadt Lübeck, Marienkirche, Musik, MS 13, c. 1675

Nun freut Euch lie - ben Chri - sten g'mein,   und laßt uns fröh - lich sprin - gen,
Daß wir ge - trost und all in ein   mit Lust und Lie - be sin - gen,

Was Gott an uns ge - wen - det hat   und sei - ne sü - ße Wun - der - tat,   gar teur hat ers er - wor - ben.

with a baroque organ, suits the homophonic texture, particularly its repeated chords.[35]

Concerning his *Riflessioni*, Bengt Hambraeus (1928–2000) states:

> *Riflessioni* was written in the spring of 1999 as a commission from Oscar Parish in Stockholm, Sweden, for the 50th anniversary of the 1949 Marcussen organ (partly renovated in 1980 by Bruno Christensen & Sønner, when 240 combinations, and a Register-crescendo, were added). The title of the work—*reflections*—is directly inspired by the great organs in Oscar's Church. . . . As the title indicates, there are numerous reflections, in this case from [Alf] Linder's repertoire as I remember it—but transformed in many ways; music of Bach, Reger, Bruhns, Reubke, Buxtehude. . . . [36]

Hambraeus composed this work in memory of Alf Linder and dedicated it to Linder's successor as organist of Oscar's Church, Erik Boström, who played the premiere on 5 September 1999, which we hear on track 12. Hambraeus himself specified the registrations in his score, which definitely reflect the post-1980 aesthetic; his use of the new register-crescendo is so pervasive (at 0:28–35; see chapter 20 for others) that one could hardly guess simply from hearing it that this instrument was built as a *Werkprinzip* organ.

Matthias Weckmann (c. 1616–74) served as organist at St. Jacobi, Hamburg, during the years 1654–74, before Arp Schnitger built the organ that we now know, which served as the chief model for the North German organ in Örgryte New Church. But the organ that Weckmann played in Hamburg already had four manuals and 59 stops, with subsemitones in its Rückpositiv that indicated without a doubt that it was tuned in pure quarter-comma meantone. Also, Schnitger incorporated into his new organ 25 stops by Hans Scherer and Gott-fried Fritzsche from the organ that Weckmann played, which have been repli-cated in the Örgryte organ. Thus, hearing the final versus of his set of variations

35. See Kurt Lueders, "Reflections on the Esthetic Evolution of the Cavaillé-Coll Organ," in *Charles Brenton Fisk, Organ Builder: Essays in His Honor* (Easthampton, Mass.: Westfield Center, 1986), 1: 128–30.
36. Bengt Hambraeus, *Riflessioni* (photocopied manuscript, 1999), verso of title page.

Example 1-2. Es ist das Heil uns kommen her (*Melodeyen Gesangbuch*, Hamburg, 1604)

Es ist das Heil uns kom-men her, von Gnad und lau - ter Gü - te,
Die Werck die hel - fen nim - mer mehr, sie mü - gen nicht be - hu - ten,

Der Glaub sicht Je - sum Chri-stum an, der hat gnug für uns all ge -

tan, er ist der Mit-ler wor - den.

on the chorale *Es ist das Heil uns kommen her* (track 13) played by Hans Davidsson on the full plenum of the Örgryte organ, with its pure meantone tuning, brings us as close to the aesthetic of Weckmann's time as we can now get. In this movement, the chorale (example 1-2) appears as a cantus firmus in the tenor, surrounded by five other voices of dense counterpoint, two of them in the pedal.

The Örgryte organ is the only one of our six that was built specifically to play the music of a bygone era—the seventeenth century—and thus it might appear that it does not reflect its own time. But in fact it does, in several important respects. To the aesthetic of our own time belongs the recognition that no one organ, no matter how large or eclectic, is adequate to the task of performing every part of the vast repertory for the instrument, which extends over seven centuries. We know that the music of César Franck is not at home on a neo-baroque organ, and we have learned that pieces from the sixteenth and seventeenth centuries that appear uninteresting on a modern instrument spring to life when played on a mechanical-action organ with a short octave and the proper stops, tuned in meantone. Furthermore, like its neighbor in Stockholm, the Örgryte instrument has demonstrated that an organ that looks back to the past can also inspire composers of the present. On 6 August 2000 Hans-Ola Ericsson (born 1958) played the premiere of his mass for organ and tape, *The Four Creatures' Amen*,[37] which had been commissioned for the new organ by the Swedish Concert Institute. The tape incorporates a vast array of sounds—including those of the bellows, action, stop knobs, and wind system of the Örgryte organ and recordings of the Schnitger organs in Hamburg, Stade, and Norden—which Ericsson combined artfully with his live performance. Finally, it is not only the completed instrument itself, but even more the process of its building, recounted in chapter 25, that makes the Örgryte organ truly a new organ for a new millennium.

---

37. Ericsson's recording of this work on the Sauer organ of Bremen Cathedral has been released by Hochschule für Künste, Bremen.

ℙART I

COURT AND CITY

2

EXORDIUM: ORGANS BY COMPENIUS (1610) AND SCHNITGER (1693)

WHEREAS THE OTHER PARTS OF THIS BOOK REPRESENT CIRCLES RADIATING FROM single instruments, Part I may be compared to an ellipse with two foci: two German organs from the seventeenth century that are radically different from one another. Esaias Compenius built his exquisite chamber organ for the Wolfenbüttel court, although it was soon moved to Denmark; Arp Schnitger's imposing church organ stands in St. Jacobi Church in the Hanseatic city of Hamburg. These instruments can thus symbolize opposing realms of society: court and city, nobility and bourgeoisie, secular and sacred. But in reality these realms are not always as distinct as we might suppose. Gisela Jaacks sets the stage in chapter 3 with a discussion of the intricate political connections between the courts and cities of northern Germany during this tumultuous century. In chapter 4 Harald Vogel focuses on the Compenius organ, bringing it forward from its origins to its influence on organ playing in the twentieth century. William Porter's essay in chapter 5 gives us new insights into the composition methods of the Hamburg organists of the generation before the Schnitger organ, and in chapter 6 Hans Davidsson juxtaposes the two instruments within a much broader context that goes beyond both court and city.

The Compenius Organ, Frederiksborg Castle, Hillerød, Denmark

Esaias Compenius (d. 1617) belonged to the second generation of an organ-building family from central Germany. He built the chamber organ that now stands in Frederiksborg Castle (figure 2-1) for Duke Heinrich Julius of Braunschweig-Lüneburg at Wolfenbüttel and installed it in his pleasure palace, Hessen, located between Wolfenbüttel and Halberstadt, Germany. Following Heinrich Julius's death in 1613 it was given to his brother-in-law King Christian IV of Denmark, and Compenius installed it in the chapel of Frederiksborg Castle, Hillerød (outside of Copenhagen), in 1617. In 1692 it was moved to the Knights'

Figure 2-1. The Esaias Compenius organ (1610) in Frederiksborg Castle. Photograph by Annelise Olesen, 2001. Courtesy of Musikhistoriskmuseum, Copenhagen.

Hall above the chapel, where it was used for dinner music and dancing. In 1791 it was moved again, this time from Frederiksborg to the Frederiksberg Castle Church in Copenhagen, and at that time its tuning was changed from its original quarter-comma meantone to what the organ builder C. F. Speer described as "the best temperament." It remained in Copenhagen until 1868, thus avoiding the 1859 fire that gutted the Hillerød castle, and was returned to the chapel of Frederiksborg following the restoration of the castle as a museum. Aristide Cavaillé-Coll—or at least his site supervisor, Félix Reinburg—became acquainted with the instrument during the building of the Jesus Church organ in Copenhagen (see Part III), and Cavaillé-Coll recommended in 1894 that it be thoroughly restored, including a return to its original temperament, "with the wolf fifth." Reinburg carried out this restoration in 1895. The organ was most recently renovated in 1985–88 by Mads Kjersgaard and is played in a public concert every Thursday afternoon.

Specification 2-1.

Frederiksborg Castle, Hillerød, Esaias Compenius, 1610

Boldface type represents abbreviations on stop knobs, expanded by Mads Kjersgaard; compare with Michael Praetorius's published specification in figure 4-2.

Upper Manual	Lower Manual	Pedal
CDEFGA-c'''	CDEFGA-c'''	CDEFGA-d'
Gross **P**rincipal 8'	**Q**uinta**D**ehna 8'	**G**edact**F**löiten **B**ass 16'
Klein **P**rinci**P**al [façade] 4'	**G**edact**F**löite 4'	**G**ems**H**orn **B**ass 8'
Gross **G**edact Flöite 8'	**G**ems**H**orn 2'	**Q**uinta**D**ehn **B**ass 8'
Gems**H**orn 4'	**N**a**S**att 1–1/2'	**Q**uer**F**löiten **B**ass 4'
Nacht**H**orn 4'	**Z**imbel I	**N**acht**H**orn **B**ass 2'
Plock**F**löite 4'	**P**rincipal **D**iscant Cantus	**P**aur**F**löiten **B**ass 1'
Gedact-**Q**uint 3'	(from f) 4'	**S**ordunen **B**ass 16'
Kleine **F**löite 2'	**B**lock**F**löite Cantus	**D**olzian **B**ass 8'
R. Rancket 16'	(from f) 4'	**R**egal **B**ass 4'
	Krumb**H**orn 8'	
	Klein **R**egal 4'	

Bagpipes (three Rankett pipes)

Drum

Bumblebee

All pipes are made of wood.

Coupler: Lower manual–upper manual

Tremulants for lower manual/upper manual and pedal

Mechanical action with slider chests

Temperament: quarter-comma syntonic meantone

Pitch: a' = 468 Hz

Recording and Registrations

CD tracks 1–6: Hans Fagius (Professor of Organ, Royal Conservatory of Music in Copenhagen) playing six dances from the Lublin tablature (c. 1540)

1. *Corea super duos saltus*
Upper manual: Gedacktflöte 8', Nachthorn 4', Gedackt Quint 2⅔', Supergedacktflöitlin 2'

2. Untitled
Lower manual: Klein Gedacktflöte 4', Krumbhorn 8'

3. *Rocal fusa*
Upper manual: Nachthorn 4', Supergedacktflöitlin 4'
Lower manual: Klein Gedacktflöte 4', Nasatt 1⅓'

4. [Passamezzo antico]
Upper manual: Gedacktflöte 8', Klein Principal 4'

5. *Haÿduczkÿ*
Upper manual: Blockpfeifen 4'

Figure 2-2. The Arp Schnitger organ (1693) in St. Jacobi Church, Hamburg, prior to World War I. Courtesy of Museum für Hamburgishche Geschichte.

6. *Jeszcze Marczynye* [Passamezzo antico]
Upper manual: Gedacktflöte 8′, Klein Principal 4′, Rankett 16′
Lower manual: Quntadena 8′, Super Gemshörnlein 2′, Nasatt 1⅓′, Klein repetiert
Zimbel 1′

Selected Literature

Eller, Povl. "Compenius-orgelets historie." *Dansk årbog for musikforskning* 17 (1986):
7–51.
Den Danske Orgelregistrant, Frederiksborg Slotskirke, Esaias Compenius: <http://
www.kulturnet.dk/homes/mhm/reg/Frederiksborg_Compenius_Ramme.htm>

The Schnitger Organ, St. Jacobi Church, Hamburg, Germany

Arp Schnitger (1648–1719) was the foremost North German organ builder of
his generation and rose to prominence again during the twentieth century, when
his instruments were rediscovered and served as models for the organ reform
movement. He moved his workshop to Hamburg in 1682 to build his largest
organ, at St. Nicolai, which was destroyed by fire in 1842; the organ in St. Jacobi
(figure 2-2), completed in 1693, was his second largest. In it he retained 25 stops
from the preceding instrument that had been installed by the eminent Hamburg
organ builders Hans Scherer the Elder (active c. 1571–1611), Gottfried Fritzsche
(1578–1638), and Gottfried's son Hans Christoph Fritzsche (d. 1674). The two
world wars of the twentieth century damaged the organ severely; its façade pipes
were requisitioned in 1917 for their tin but were restored between 1926 and
1930, largely through the efforts of the expressionist playwright and organ enthusiast Hans Henny Jahnn. During World War II the organ's pipework and
windchests were safely stored away, but its case, bellows, and console were
destroyed in the bombing of 1944. From 1989 to 1993 Jürgen Ahrend carried
out a complete restoration, based on written and photographic evidence from
the original instrument and using details in other Schnitger organs as models.
Despite all these intrusions, the St. Jacobi organ has the largest extant collection
of pre-1700 pipes of any single instrument in the world, and it served as the
principal model for the new North German organ in Örgryte New Church, Göteborg.

SPECIFICATION 2-2.
St. Jacobi Church, Hamburg, Arp Schnitger, 1693 (after 1993 restoration)

Werck (Manual II)	Rückpositiv (Manual I)	Oberpositiv (Manual III)
CDEFGA-c‴	CDE-c‴	CDEFGA-C‴
Principal 16′	Principal 8′	Principal 8′
Quintadehn 16′	Gedackt 8′	Rohrflöht 8′
Octava 8′	Quintadehna 8′	Holtzflöht 8′
Spitzflöht 8′	Octava 4′	Spitzflöht 4′
Viola da Gamba 8′	Blockflöht 4′	Octava 4′
Octava 4′	Querpfeiff 2′	Nasat 3′
Rohrflöht 4′	Octava 2′	Octava 2′
Flachflöht 2′	Sexquialtera II	Gemshorn 2′
Rauschpfeiff II	Scharff VI–VIII	Scharff VI
SuperOctav 2′	Siffloit 1½′	Cimbel III
Mixtur VI–VIII	Dulcian 16′	Trommet 8′
Trommet 16′	Bahrpfeiffe 8′	Vox humana 8′
	Trommet 8′	Trommet 4′

Brustpositiv (Manual IV)	Pedal	
CDEFGA-C‴	CD-d′	
Principal 8′	Principal 32′	
Octav 4′	Octava 16′	
Hollflöht 4′	Subbaß 16′	
Waldflöht 2′	Octava 8′	
Sexquialtera II	Octava 4′	
Scharff IV–VI	Nachthorn 2′	
Dulcian 8′	Rauschpfeiff III	
Trechter Regal 8′	Mixtur VI–VIII	
	Posaune 32′	
	Posaune 16′	
	Dulcian 16′	
	Trommet 8′	2 Cimbelsterne
	Trommet 4′	Totentrommel
	Cornet 2′	2 tremulants

Couplers: Brustpositiv-Werck, Oberpositiv-Werck
Haupt-Ventil; 5 ventils for the individual divisions
Mechanical action with slider chests
Pitch: a′ = 495 Hz
Temperament: modified meantone (⅕ syntonic comma; see table 1-1)

Recording

CD track 7: Harald Vogel playing Dieterich Buxtehude, *Nun freut euch lieben Christen g'mein* (BuxWV 210)

TABLE 2-1.

Harald Vogel's Registration for Dieterich Buxtehude, *Nun freut euch lieben Christen g'mein*

Schnitger Organ in St. Jacobi, Hamburg

Time		Action
00:00	RP	Dulcian 16', Principal 8', Octava 4', Octava 2', Siffloit 1½', Sexquialtera
	W	Principal 16', Octava 8', Octava 4'
	P	Octava 16', Octava 8', Octava 4'
00:50	RP	Principal 8', Octava 4', Octava 2', Sexquialtera
	OP	Trommet 8'
	P	Trommet 8'
02:39	RP	Bahrpfeiffe 8', Blockflöht 4'
	OP	Vox humana 8', Spitzflöht 4'
04:06	BP	Trechter Regal 8', Hollflöht 4'
04:37	BP	Principal 8', Octava 4'
	P	Octava 8'
04:58	RP	Principal 8'
	OP	Principal 8'
	P	Octava 8'
06:31	RP	Quintadehna 8', Querpfeiff 2'
07:32	OP	Holtzflöht 8', Gemshorn 2' (off for echo at 07:51)
07:47	BP	Principal 8', Waldtflöht 2'
08:34	W	Spitzflöht 8', Flachflöht 2'
	BP	Principal 8', Waldflöht 2'
	OP	Holtzflöht 8'
	P	Octava 8'
09:39	OP	Vox humana 8'
	W	Spitzflöht 8'
	P	Subbaß 16'
11:14	P	Octava 8'
11:21	RP	Bahrpfeiffe 8', Blockflöht 4'
11:28	BP	Dulcian 8', Hollflöht 4'
12:09	BP	Octava 8'
12:15	RP	Trommet 8', Octava 4', Octava 2'
	OP	Principal 8', Octava 4', Octava 2'
13:04	W	Spitzflöht 8'
13:07	BP	Principal 8'
13:38	RP	Principal 8', Octava 4', Octava 2', Sexquialtera
	W	Octava 8', Octava 4'
	P	Octava 8', Octava 4'
13:56	RP	Dulcian 16', Principal 8', Octava 4', Octava 2', Sexquialtera
	W	Principal 16', Octava 8', Octava 4'
	P	Dulcian 16', Octava 8', Octava 4'

Selected Literature

Fock, Gustav. *Arp Schnitger und seine Schule: ein Beitrag zur Geschichte des Orgelbaus im Nord-und Osteekustengebiet*. Kassel: Bärenreiter, 1974.

———. *Hamburg's Role in Northern European Organ Building*. Edited and translated by Lynn Edwards and Edward C. Pepe. Easthampton, Mass.: Westfield Center, 1998.

Reinitzer, Heimo, ed., *Die Arp Schnitger-Orgel der Hauptkirche St. Jacobi in Hamburg*. Hamburg: Christians Verlag, 1995.

3

DUCAL COURTS AND HANSEATIC CITIES: POLITICAL AND HISTORICAL PERSPECTIVES

GISELA JAACKS

SEVENTEENTH-CENTURY CULTURAL LIFE IN NORTH GERMANY WAS SHAPED BY DUCAL courts and Hanseatic cities. For this period, the definition of these two terms is not as clear as it may seem at first glance. Owing to the turmoil of the Thirty Years' War, the North German duchies surrounding the Hanseatic cities were politically unstable. Numerous dynastic changes occurred, and some of the old familial and cultural ties dissolved, while relationships with foreign sovereigns were consolidated.

The Hanseatic Cities

The term "Hanseatic city" is especially problematic; in effect, the Hanseatic League disintegrated over the course of the seventeenth century. The previous century had already ushered in the economic and political decline of the Hanseatic League's obsolete medieval trade structures that the events of the Thirty Years' War now accelerated.[1] During the peace negotiations conducted between 1645 and 1649, the individual towns and cities pursued their own interests above all else. Apart from Lübeck, whose economic base was, to a large extent, dependent on the continuance of Hanseatic structures, pan-Hanseatic concerns played only a small role for the delegates of the Hanseatic cities. In fact, only three of them were left: Lübeck, Hamburg, and Bremen. Their sequence here is determined by a historical point of view, for it was in this form that in 1629 the Hanseatic assembly had charged them with protecting the interests of the Hanseatic League as a whole. A year later, the three cities formed a further alliance to pursue common political goals. Owing to the involved property laws

1. Philippe Dollinger, *Die Hanse* (Stuttgart: Alfred Kröner, 1966), 462–78.

ruling the relationships between its city, its episcopal estate, and the surrounding area in the second half of the seventeenth century, Bremen had very little political or economic leeway.[2] Hamburg and Lübeck alone were able to maintain an independent position in the North German region.

Former Hanseatic cities were the only ones that proved able to preserve a certain autonomy, even if they did not—like Lübeck, Hamburg, and Bremen—have the status of free imperial cities. Braunschweig, for example, remained an "autonomous city" until 1671 and was thus legally and constitutionally independent of the local sovereign. Such autonomies of course intensely annoyed the princes concerned. The dukes of Braunschweig-Lüneburg-Wolfenbüttel therefore repeatedly attempted to take the city, and in 1671 Duke Rudolf August finally succeeded.

According to an inscription discovered during its restoration from 1984 to 1988 (see chapter 4), one of the earlier failed attempts, the siege of Braunschweig by Duke Friedrich Ulrich in 1615–16, occasioned the removal of the Compenius organ from Hessen Castle (Schloss Hessen) to Frederiksborg Castle. We may assume that it was a gift of thanksgiving from the duke to King Christian IV of Denmark, who had sent troops to the failed siege. Located about halfway between Wolfenbüttel and Halberstadt, a Protestant episcopal estate in the duke's property, the estate of Hessen had been furnished as a hunting lodge by Friedrich Ulrich's grandfather, Duke Julius. Shortly after 1600, during the reign of Duke Heinrich Julius, it was converted into a pleasure palace. Its splendid gardens were modeled on the imperial gardens in Prague, which Heinrich Julius had enjoyed when at court as a friend and advisor of Emperor Rudolph II. An order he placed with the organ builder Esaias Compenius reflected his imperial-courtly taste: he commissioned an organ that would also serve secular uses. A harmless comment in itself, it still gives a hint of the dukes' imperial claims to power, which the towns and cities would soon have to face at the level of practical politics.

Even the two free imperial cities of Lübeck and Hamburg had to defend themselves against sovereign attempts on their independence. The duchy of Holstein surrounded the cities and was tied in personal union to the Danish crown, which refused to acknowledge Hamburg's status as an imperial city. To make things worse, both cities housed within their walls cathedral chapters endowed with the title "Undoubted Imperial Estate." The 1555 Peace of Augsburg and the territorial decisions of the Peace of Westphalia determined that neighboring Protestant dynasties would alternately rule the episcopal territories, including town chapters. Legal conflict was inevitable. In 1555 the recess of the Imperial

2. Herbert Schwarzwälder, *Geschichte der Freien Hansestadt Bremen*, vol. 1, *Von den Anfängen bis zur Franzosenzeit (1810)* (Hamburg: Hans Christians, 1985), 283–412.

Diet decreed the division of the empire into ten administrative districts known as imperial circles. Each of these circles was headed by a local sovereign, who watched over the implementation of the decrees of the Imperial Diet and the judgments pronounced by the Imperial High Court of Justice. He was also responsible for keeping the peace; in case of war he had to provide the relevant contingent of the imperial army. His authority extended to all estates, including the free imperial cities, in whose internal concerns the sovereign holding this office could now intervene on this pretext. For the cities, continuous exchange with their noble neighbors therefore became a political necessity. Though regular contact could lead to open conflict, it also had positive effects on their cultural life.

Lübeck and Hamburg belonged to the circle of Saxony and in a later division to that of Lower Saxony, which also included the duchies of Braunschweig and Mecklenburg as well as the duchy of Holstein. Their family ties to each other and to outside powers at best offered the two Hanseatic cities a rich web of international relations; at worst, an invincible foe. It was therefore imperative for the cities to pursue a well-balanced diplomacy. The greatest threat was the king of Denmark, feudal lord to the dukes of Holstein-Gottorf, who were descendants of a younger branch of the Danish royal family. Their own political significance within the Danish state as a whole was small, and throughout the seventeenth century, they kept coming into conflict with their royal relations in Copenhagen. The Danish royal family—and with it the dukes of Holstein-Gottorf—was connected by marriage with the kings of England and Sweden, the dukes of Braunschweig and of Mecklenburg, the electors of Saxony, and the landgraves of Hessen. Further relations with the imperial family in Vienna, the czars of Russia, the electors of Brandenburg and the Palatinate, and the governors of the Netherlands evolved along these ties of kinship. A tight mesh of dynastic family relations thus surrounded the cities. Therefore, starting around the end of the sixteenth century, it was no longer a viable strategy to play off the interests of one local sovereign against the other, tactics that the Hanseatic cities had successfully pursued in the late Middle Ages. Too dense was the web the noble families had woven around the free cities.

The cities knew very well, however, that these princes depended on them. The cities had merchants well versed in international trade, and it was here that the greater financial resources lay. At the peace negotiations in Osnabrück, the Hanseatic cities had been able to affirm the stable neutrality that had been their political guideline in the war. As a result, they—or more precisely, Hamburg—naturally developed into the diplomatic center of northern Europe.[3] Throughout

3. Joachim Whaley, *Religiöse Toleranz und sozialer Wandel in Hamburg, 1529–1819* (Hamburg: Friedrich Wittig, 1992), 51.

the seventeenth century, nearly all larger sovereign states of Europe and the extensive territories of the empire maintained permanent embassies in Hamburg.

On the one hand, this type of cosmopolitanism brought economic advantages and was therefore encouraged. On the other hand, it caused internal problems. Legally speaking, the envoys' residencies in the city represented extraterritorial ground; what happened in them and whoever found refuge there lay outside the jurisdiction of Hamburg's laws. This is where the question of the religious or denominational ties of the embassy came in. In its constitution of 1603, Hamburg had declared orthodox Lutheranism, as defined in the 1580 Book of Concord, the foundation of Hamburg's political system. The city council was thus committed to protect its burghers from all pernicious religious influence and to ensure that no other religious practice would threaten the city's pure Lutheran doctrine. At the same time, the embassies had to be permitted to hold non-Lutheran services in their grounds. For economic reasons, it was also highly advantageous to encourage wealthy non-Lutherans—such as Dutch Calvinists, British Anglicans, French Huguenots, and Sephardic Jews—to settle in the city. The baroque era, however, adhered to the medieval custom of defining human beings primarily by their religion, and this is what determined their standing in the community. The strictly Lutheran city of Hamburg could therefore admit non-Lutherans as temporary guests but would not grant them full citizenship. Restrictions with regard to law and religion, then, seriously handicapped the city's dealings with outsiders.

In Lübeck, which after the Thirty Years' War finally proved the economically weaker partner, the settlement of foreigners met with even more difficulties than in Hamburg. Lübeck, too, was committed to the Book of Concord. The religious reservations were therefore the same. More strongly than in Hamburg, however, local merchants and artisans feared the competition of immigrants, who might benefit from further-reaching connections or superior craftsmanship than the locals could command. Under certain conditions, what the authorities of the cities welcomed as a potential for additional tax revenues could represent a very real threat to the economic survival of the individual burgher. It was no coincidence that these decades saw an increasing severity in the admission regulations of merchant and craft guilds, nor that in the second half of the seventeenth century both cities witnessed serious internal strife that at times reached the brink of civil war. Economic and religious factors alternately incited the townspeople to rebel against the council, whose generous policy toward outsiders provoked the burghers' wrath.

Princes of the Region

It was the open or latent prejudice prevalent in the cities that the neighboring duchies now turned to their advantage. Even in the late sixteenth century, Duke

Julius of Braunschweig-Lüneburg had furthered the extension of his town of residence, Wolfenbüttel, by granting generous privileges to foreigners willing to settle there: exemption from military service and certain taxes, free loans for building houses and setting up workshops, free religious practice, and so on.[4] In contrast, the burghers of Braunschweig pressed their city council, which had to fear Wolfenbüttel as a potential economic competitor, to require settlers to use their expertise and wealth exclusively for the benefit of the native townspeople while refusing to grant them full citizenship. The Danish king and the duke of Holstein-Gottorf also used the guarantee of religious and economic tolerance to entice foreigners to their new foundations at Glückstadt, Friedrichstadt, and Altona. All pursued a single aim: to leave the metropolitan capital of Hamburg high and dry.

However, the princes' plans remained unsuccessful in the end, for in spite of religious prejudice, native obtuseness, their insistence on obsolete guild structures, and local egotism, the great former Hanseatic cities were still more attractive. They had superior ports, and they were the main junctions of North Europe's trade routes, thus providing the best opportunities for buying raw material. Good conditions for the various manufacturing trades had evolved from centuries of experience, and a market turning over large sums of money attracted affluent buyers. Since 1558 and 1605 respectively, Hamburg and Lübeck also had stock exchanges, and finally, with fortifications renewed at the beginning of the Thirty Years' War and the neutrality they had negotiated in the peace treaty of 1648–49, both cities still offered more peace and security than the rulers of the neighboring duchies ever could.

The local princes themselves benefited from the safety of the cities when political necessity forced them to seek refuge near their hereditary estates. When the imperial general Wallenstein occupied their lands from 1629 to 1632, the dukes of Mecklenburg fled to Lübeck. Between 1676 and 1689, Duke Christian Albrecht of Holstein-Gottorf, ousted from his territories by his Danish cousin, spent several years of exile in Hamburg. Incidentally, his stay gained Hamburg a further attraction: the opera, whose foundation is indebted to his initiative. After her abdication in 1654, Sweden's Queen Christina chose Hamburg as a base from which to negotiate her financial settlement with the Swedish crown and repeatedly honored the city with her visits.

When in 1650 Christine Margareta of Mecklenburg-Güstrow, widow of Duke Franz Albrecht of Saxony-Lauenburg and sister of Duchess Sophie Elizabeth of Braunschweig, married her cousin Duke Christian Ludwig of Mecklenburg-Schwerin, the couple needed neutral ground for the wedding ceremony. First,

---

4. Andrea Theissen, "Die Neubürgerpolitik der Stadt Braunschweig im Rahmen ihrer Finanz-und Wirtschaftspolitik vom Ende des 15. Jahrhunderts bis zum Dreißigjährigen Krieg," in *Stadt im Wandel: Kunst und Kultur des Bürgertums in Norddeutschland 1150–1650*, vol. 4, ed. Cord Meckseper (Braunschweig: Braunschweigisches Landesmuseum, 1985), 119–29.

the wedding was undesirable from the dynastic point of view: the bridegroom's father had refused his consent because he was hoping for a more advantageous match for his son and his country. Secondly, it was a denominational scandal: the bride was a Calvinist, the groom Lutheran. Their highnesses therefore availed themselves of Hamburg's latent denominational plurality and its political neutrality, which permitted a private Calvinist ceremony to be conducted in the home of Andreas Berenberg, a wealthy merchant who originally hailed from the Netherlands.

The bride's nephew, Duke Ferdinand Albrecht of Wolfenbüttel, was present at the wedding celebrations in Hamburg. His diary tells us which places counted as sights worth visiting.[5] Social institutions such as the prison and the orphanage were praised for their progressiveness. St. Catharine's provided artistic highlights. Hamburg's most distinguished sculptor at the time, Maximilian Steffens, who had immigrated from Brabant in 1628, had created its chancel and baptismal font. St. Catharine's also housed the equally famous perspective painting of Solomon's temple, a work of Hamburg's resident artist Gabriel Engels. The young duke then went on to admire the carillon of St. Petri, the stalls of booksellers and vendors of fashion accessories in the cathedral cloisters, and of course the harbor. The following days' excursions were dedicated to the splendid gardens in the vicinity of the city.

Courtly Influence in the Cities

The young duke's record also gives an idea of the diplomatic balancing acts such noble visits demanded of the city council, especially where the circumstances were as delicate as in the case of the scandalous wedding, or with exiled and abdicated princes with whose enemies or successors the city wanted to remain on friendly terms. As far as protocol was concerned, the question was mainly which member of the council waited on a visiting prince. While the Mecklenburg wedding had been attended only by a legal adviser, two of the city's aldermen waited on the abdicated Queen Christina.[6] The council musicians were at the disposal of all guests, and Duke Ferdinand Albrecht praised them as being "of wide renown." They were paid extremely well on these occasions, for their highnesses liked to brighten their stays in the city with splendid festivities in the courtly style. However, the escapades of some, like the self-willed Christina of Sweden, sorely tried the diplomatic finesse of the city authorities. The skill of

5. See Jill Bepler, *Ferdinand Albrecht Duke of Braunschweig-Lüneburg (1636–1687): A Traveller and his Travelogue*, Wolfenbütteler Arbeiten zur Barockforschung, vol. 16 (Wiesbaden: Otto Harrassowitz, 1988), 134–39.

6. Dorothea Schröder, *Christina von Schweden in Hamburg: "Die Stunden dauern hier Ewigkeiten . . ."* (Hamburg: Kurt Saucke, 1997).

governors as experienced as the council members belonging to Hamburg's Meu-rer and Moller families was required to deal with such situations. Before they joined law firms at home, these lawyers had often been abroad in the service of noble houses. The most eminent politician Lübeck had in that century, the lawyer David Gloxin, had also started his career as a councilor in noble employ—the city probably owes him the engagement of Franz Tunder as organist for St. Mary's, and therefore the rise of the imposing style of church music he repre-sented.[7] They knew how to cope with the capricious wishes of their guests, and they possessed the courtly refinement indispensable for such tasks.

Their familiarity with court life, however, also brought the ruling classes the censure of the other burghers, who accused them of indulging in aristocratic tastes and behaving like small princes.[8] Contemporary records illustrate how the burghers' judgment on the aristocratic luxury paraded before their eyes vacillated between fascinated admiration and moral indignation. The close contact between the two lifestyles led to an increased emphasis on civic respectability and work ethic, but aristocratic license and extreme forms of courtly etiquette also flour-ished. According to the traditional allegorical interpretation so popular in the baroque age, this was the conflict between the princely virtue of *magnificentia* (splendid display) and the civic virtue of *modestia* (modest restraint).[9]

Magnificentia held an undeniable allure. But even apart from that, it was considered one of the princely virtues; the city authorities almost felt it their duty to join the ranks of its followers. As long as their magnificence was restricted to an official context and increased the city's prestige, it was considered seemly enough. However, the burghers were wary of council members who adopted habits of luxury in their private lives. In the final quarter of the seventeenth century, similar misgivings, combined with repeated suspicions of embezzlement of public funds and nepotism on the part of the council, triggered fierce civic strife in Hamburg

Hamburg's Five Parishes

The social tension erupting here was largely a product of Hamburg's constitution, which was based on parochial statutes. In the 1690s, Hamburg had a population of approximately 74,000. The ruling power lay in the hands of the council, and

7. Antjekathrin Graßmann, "David Gloxin," in *Lübecker Lebensläufe aus neun Jahrhunderten*, ed. Alken Bruns (Neumünster: Karl Wachholtz, 1993), 160–63.

8. Gisela Jaacks, *Hamburg zu Lust und Nutz: Bürgerliches Musikverständnis zwischen Barock und Aufklärung (1660–1760)*, Veröffentlichungen des Vereins für Hamburgische Geschichte, vol. 44 (Hamburg: Verein für Hamburgische Geschichte, 1997), 15–18, 118–20.

9. Nicolas Delamare, *Traité de la police*, vol. 1 (Paris, 1705), 380–81; see Karl Möseneder, *Zeremoniell und monumentale Poesie: Die "Entrée solennelle" Ludwigs XIV. 1660 in Paris* (Berlin: Gebr. Mann, 1983), 69.

its members had the right to elect further members, so that power was concentrated in a small number of upper-class families related by marriage. The remaining burghers were represented by delegates in what was then called the citizenry. Each parish, no matter how large its area or population, returned the same number of delegates. A glance at the population figures of the individual parishes shows where the deeper reasons for the political tension of these years lay: St. Petri, at 5,900 inhabitants, had no more than 8 percent of the entire population; St. Nikolai had 5,200, that is, 7 percent; St. Catharine's had 13,900, making 19 percent; and St. Jacobi had 19,000, or 26 percent of the entire population. Finally, the new parish of St. Michael's, incorporated into the city as late as 1685, counted 30,000 inhabitants, a full 40 percent of the population.

St. Petri, St. Nikolai, and St. Catharine's were considered wealthy parishes. This was where well-to-do merchants and council families had their homes, though St. Catharine's included a number of streets near the harbor where lower-class dockworkers lived with their families. In contrast to the other two wealthy parishes, then, its population figures were quite high. These three parishes made up no more than about a third of the population as a whole, but, owing to the fixed allotment of seats each parish commanded, they had three-fifths of all delegates in the citizenry and therefore always dominated it. In contrast, only two-fifths of the delegates in the citizenry and almost no councilors came from the two less-affluent parishes, which between them had 66 percent of the entire population.

St. Jacobi and St. Michael's were not only poorer parishes, but because of their history of settlement, newcomers more easily found a home here. This implied that there was a considerable innovative potential, but at the same time entailed the danger of imperfect integration into Hamburg's rather exclusively minded native population. These housing patterns also prevented the newcomers, financially successful merchants though they might be, from gaining access to the ruling class. A high degree of transience inevitably characterized these parishes. St. Michael's, having been settled at a later date, furthermore provided sufficient space to accommodate the houses of foreign delegations, most of which were located here. The legal vacuum surrounding them and the aristocratic luxury distinguishing them were more strongly in evidence in this parish, and the "threat" posed by different denominations seemed more immediate. It was these two parishes, then, that repeatedly clashed with the council, which increasingly emulated the model of absolutist princes and considered itself to rule by divine right.

The struggle between Pietist and Orthodox Lutherans did nothing to improve the situation. The Pietist movement found most of its Hamburg following among the underprivileged classes. By a strange twist, the poorest parish, St. Jacobi, was then headed by the fiercest opponent of Pietism to be found among the city's clergy, Johann Friedrich Mayer. Now the orthodox believers above all fostered the promotion of music (see chapter 5), which was considered one of the characteristics of *magnificentia*, and Mayer also embraced this view. Thus it was that in these difficult years, the poor parish of St. Jacobi acquired one of the finest new organs built at the time.

When Mayer was appointed pastor, St. Jacobi's organist could begin to think of replacing the old organ; although it had been thoroughly refurbished by Gottfried Fritzsche in 1635–36 and his son Hans Christoph from 1655 to 1658, it was again falling into decay. Judging from contemporary sources, Mayer was a skilled rhetorician of near-demagogic eloquence who wielded considerable influence over his parish council. Thanks to his commitment, the commission went to Arp Schnitger, the most able and distinguished organ builder of his day. Schnitger in turn seems to have had a high personal regard for the controversial pastor of St. Jacobi, for in 1694, he presented Mayer with a small organ of 8 stops for his private use. The organ in St. Jacobi's filial church, St. Gertrude, actually lay within the responsibility of Johann Kortkamp, a Weckmann disciple important as a chronicler but evidently less than brilliant as a musician. It needed Mayer's initiative to engage Schnitger to carry out its reconstruction in 1699. Whether his parishioners really appreciated the new musical grandeur of their services is a matter of some doubt: the funds expended on the instrument were unavailable when it came to social concerns, and the congregation would have found little consolation in the fact that in their church at least they possessed an organ which no prince far and wide could equal. On the whole, the rivalry between the parish churches for the biggest and best organ—not only in Hamburg, but also in Lübeck or Lüneburg—is strongly redolent of the way the local princes vied with each other in displaying their prestige.

Building Projects in Court and City

In another field, however, the burghers were on no account able to compete with the ducal courts. The Hanseatic cities, with their medieval web of narrow streets, simply lacked the room for great architectural innovations. In the North German duchies, by contrast, this period witnessed the creation of splendid buildings of wide renown and outstanding importance for the history of architecture. At the beginning of the seventeenth century, Wolfenbüttel's main church, St. Mary's, was the world's first important Protestant church building and a fine product of the German Renaissance;[10] Duke Heinrich Julius had commissioned it to prepare a tomb worthy of himself and his house. At the end

---

10. Friedrich Thöne, *Wolfenbüttel: Geist und Glanz einer alten Residenz* (München: F. Bruckmann, 1963), 61–68.

of the century, Duke Anton Ulrich of Braunschweig-Wolfenbüttel created the most lavish North German residence of its time, Schloss Salzdahlum—"an earthly paradise," as his admiring cousin, the Hanoverian electress Sophie put it.[11] Although intra-dynastic strife greatly restricted them financially, the dukes of Gottorf had elaborate plans to refurbish their Schleswig residence.[12] What was actually built—for instance, the ducal pew in the palace chapel—still stands testimony to the family's urge to enhance their prestige. Battered by the Thirty Years' War, the dukes of Mecklenburg faced similar restrictions. Their palaces in Schwerin and Güstrow had to be content with redecoration and some extensions.

Originally, the counts of Schaumburg, distant relatives of the Gottorf family, had ruled the Holstein territories. They were now recompensed with Schaumburg-Lippe, where their buildings transformed the residential city of Bückeburg into a center of architectural mannerism. A leading patron of music, Count Ernst was also a prominent patron of architecture who in 1601 commissioned the magnificent palace chapel and the Golden Hall. It is thanks to him that Bückeburg has North Germany's second notable genuinely Protestant church, surpassed only by Wolfenbüttel's St. Mary's. The mausoleum built as a tomb for his family in Stadthagen, one of the finest works of the early baroque in Germany, confirmed the count's princely magnificence in death.[13] Stylistically, the mausoleum points to Italian baroque classicism, which in North Germany could thrive only in the environment of princely courts with extensive dynastic ties. They oriented their taste toward new artistic trends coming in from the south and southwest of Europe. The burghers of the Hanseatic cities, in turn, uniformly rejected neoclassicism, considering it an aristocratic and absolutist style and tainted by its Catholic provenance. In the towns, the Renaissance style known by the name of the Flemish Floris family who had coined it prevailed throughout the seventeenth century, and only a few neoclassical ornaments of the Palladian tradition relieved the façades of public and private buildings.[14]

In the furnishings of their rooms, however, town houses demonstrated the same trend toward the internationally predominant style as the seats of the ar-

11. Gerhard Gerkens, *Das fürstliche Lustschloß Salzdahlum und sein Erbauer Anton Ulrich von Braunschweig-Wolfenbüttel*, Quellen und Forschungen zur Braunschweigischen Geschichte, vol. 22 (Braunschweig: Geschichtsverein, 1974).

12. Ernst Schlee, *Das Schloß Gottorf in Schleswig*, Kunst in Schleswig-Holstein, vol. 15 (Flensburg: Christian Wolff, 1965), 20–59.

13. Monika Meine-Schawe, "Neue Forschungen zum Mausoleum in Stadthagen," in *". . . uns und unseren Nachkommen zu Ruhm und Ehre": Kunstwerke im Weserraum und ihre Auftraggeber*, Materialien zur Kunst-und Kulturgeschichte in Nord-und Westdeutschland, vol. 6 (Marburg: Jonas, 1992), 69–132.

14. Jörgen Bracker, ed., *Bauen nach der Natur—Palladio: Die Erben Palladios in Nordeuropa* (Ostfildern: Gerd Hatje, 1997).

istocracy. Emulating their noble models, wall paintings in Lübeck and Hamburg[15] reveled in luxuriant florid arabesques, illusion-filled pastoral scenes, and series of allegorical figures. Burghers also pursued the princely pastime of collecting art and curiosities, though on a smaller scale. In this, many were inspired by an immediate acquaintance with ducal collections of strange natural objects, whose scholarly custodians often hailed from burgher families. Once they returned to the Hanseatic cities to work as lawyers, theologians, or schoolteachers, they discussed the contents and meaning of these collections with former fellow students, thus spreading the fashion. Baroque scholars at court and in town venerated the ideal of "Polyhistor," or universal scholar. It may thus be assumed that the construction of Hamburg's famous model of Solomon's temple, inspired by the early baroque reconstruction by the Jesuit Villalpando, arose from a scholarly debate between the court at Wolfenbüttel and the Hamburg lawyer who had commissioned the model, Gerhard Schott. In late-seventeenth-century Hamburg, a city shaken by public unrest, the ideal of aristocratic rule expressed here also had immense political significance. The citizenry considered the hegemonic pretensions of the ruling upper classes with wary mistrust and harbored similar doubts about the founding of Hamburg's opera, another project in which Schott played a decisive part. Opera as such was a courtly luxury—pleasure without profit—and therefore, according to civic standards, immoral. In the face of a powerful mercantile bias, Schott was hard put to render his operatic enterprise palatable or even bearable to the burghers.[16]

A Shared Love of Gardening

There was one partiality, however, that seventeenth-century dukes and Hanseatic dwellers fully shared. Where the pleasure of gardening was concerned, the burghers unrestrainedly emulated the princes, though on a smaller scale. In 1663 Johann Rist, a pastor living in Wedel, near Hamburg, praised the city's horticultural splendors without the least moral reservation.

> Some say: I have been at the court of a great potentate, and there I saw an uncommonly beautiful Royal Garden. But, how's that? If it do please you to admire a garden as has royal beauty, then come to Hamburg, where they will show you not one, not five, not ten, nay thirty, forty, fifty, which are almost,

15. *Ausstatungen Lübecker Wohnhäuser: Raumnutzungen, Malereien und Bücher im Spätmittelalter und in der frühen Neuzeit*, ed. Manfred Eickhölter and Rolf Hammel-Kiesow, Häuser und Höfe in Lübeck, vol. 4 (Neumünster: Karl Wachholtz, 1993). See also Gisela Jaacks and Silke Beiner-Büth, *Decken-und Wanddekoration in Hamburg vom Barock zum Klassizismus*, Hamburg-Porträt, vol. 28 (Hamburg Museum für Hamburgische Geschichte, 1997).

16. See Jaacks, *Hamburg zu Lust und Nutz*, 114–18. For the model of the temple see Gisela Jaacks, *Abbild und Symbol: Das Hamburger Modell des Salomonischen Tempels*, Hamburg-Porträt, vol. 17 (Hamburg: Museum für Hamburgische Geschichte, 1982).

nay wholly equal to the fine princely gardens, and where, when they lead you through the gates, not eyes alone, but mouth and nose will gape, to swallow all the beauties, follies, walks, fountains, pools, figures, strange and foreign plants, and a thousand pleasant rarities, contained therein.[17]

It was above all regarding the unknown and foreign plants grown and carefully tended in these gardens that the garden lovers of the city strove to outdo both each other and the local princes. The trade links available in a port city undoubtedly gave them the advantage over the noble estates in the hinterland. Neither the princes nor the usually thrifty Hanseatic burghers spared any expense; they even had painters immortalize their favorite blooms on large panels. It is no coincidence that of the four florilegia that have come down to us from the horticultural painter Hans Simon Holtzbecker, who lived in Hamburg during the mid–seventeenth century, two volumes are dedicated to the gardens of the Hamburg merchants Barthold Moller and Albert Anckelmann, while the other two codices depict the gardens of the dukes of Gottorf at Schleswig and Husum.[18]

The Hanseatic love of gardening also reflects the fact that city dwellers were beginning to develop a taste for country life around this time. They acquired rural properties in order to indulge their taste and set out to imitate the lifestyle of the neighboring lord of the manor. The establishment of upper-class families of Hamburg and Lübeck in the ducal territories surrounding their cities also had tangible economic implications. The economic and religious tolerance of the dukes' mercantile policies convinced many a burgher to swear fealty to the duke and join the landed gentry. In the villages belonging to their estates, they could settle craftsmen who were able to work independently of the strict urban guild regulations. It was no coincidence that the first factories founded by Hanseatic citizens in the eighteenth century were on estates outside the city limits.

Strategies for Circumventing the Medieval Guild System

In the towns and cities, only a master craftsman enrolled with the guild was permitted to run his own workshop and take on jobs. Most were "closed guilds"— that is, the maximum number of masters was fixed from the outset. In times of economic decline, as in the war-torn seventeenth century, still further-reaching

---

17. Johann Rist, *Das AllerEdelste Leben der gantzen Welt / Vermittelst eines anmuthigen und erbaulichen Gespräches / Welches ist dieser Ahrt Die Ander / und zwahr Eine Hornungs-Unterredung* (Hamburg: Johann Naumanns Buchhandlung, 1663), 160–61.

18. Helga de Cuveland, *Der Gottorfer Codex von Hans Simon Holtzbecker* (Worms: Wernersche Verlagsgesellschaft, 1989). See also *Das Moller-Florilegium des Hans Simon Holtzbecker*, ed. Dietrich Roth, Kultur Stiftung der Länder-Patrimonia, vol. 174 (Berlin and Hamburg: Kulturstiftung Ossietzky, 1999).

restrictions on the number of members were occasionally introduced.[19] The guild regulations stipulated the equality of all guild masters; individual workshops were not allowed to expand by employing additional apprentices or journeymen, or by buying raw material beyond an agreed limit, even when mounting demand required it. This meant that successful master craftsmen often had to share large orders with their less successful colleagues. In these cases, the customer could be sure only that the master with whom he had placed the order would supervise and control the work—not that it would be fully and entirely carried out in his workshop. It was possible for town councils to grant individual craftsmen permission to work as "free masters" who did not have to obey the guild's statutes. However, the advantages this privilege brought the craftsmen were few. For one thing, they were not allowed to employ apprentices or journeymen, and since most crafts depended on teamwork within the context of a large workshop, this restriction considerably reduced their production capacity. Furthermore, they were cut off from the distribution of raw material, which was managed by the guilds. Only a craftsman who had alternative resources and contacts could afford the status of a free master. In some trades, moving to a village seemed a lucrative escape: the landowner guaranteed freedom of trade and, in his capacity as a city merchant, might even be able to obtain the required raw materials at a lower cost.

Freedom, however, had its price. Rural craftsmen were effectively cut off from the urban market. The markets of the two big Hanseatic cities represented the hub of international trade. It was here that trade representatives and agents of noble estates met. Here they tested the skills of individual workshops. Here alone did guild regulations guarantee reliable quality controls ensuring that the agreed amount of raw material was worked according to standard. And here a continuous flow of foreign visitors and itinerant journeymen combined with strong competition to minimize the danger of lapsing into the kind of parochial backwardness that threatened craftsmen in the village, where exchange was limited and stylistic innovation depended on the taste of the landowner.

These disadvantages affected above all the applied arts, which therefore preferred the cities and made Hamburg and Lübeck the northern European centers of their trade. Nevertheless, they were often the ones that suffered most from restrictive guild regulations. Particular materials were reserved for particular guilds, but the work of artists depended on the use of many different materials. This the guild regulations prohibited.

In this context, episcopal property and the grounds that foreign envoys occupied within the cities because of their exceptional legal and tax status proved

19. Johannes Warncke, *Handwerk und Zünfte in Lübeck* (Lübeck: Gebrüder Borchers, 1912).

extremely favorable for craftsmen working in the applied arts. The areas concerned were practically extraterritorial: those who stayed there enjoyed immunity from city law. Many of the distinguished painters and, above all, the sculptors of this period thus avoided the guild regulations while at the same time working in close contact with the urban market.[20] Such a decision removed them from the legal system of the city, meaning that there are of course no archival documents to bear this observation out. However, it is a fact that most of these artists are not listed in guild rolls and apparently did not even apply for membership.[21] Archival evidence does show that there were further options, as for example the path chosen by the Hamburg sculptor Ludwig Münstermann,[22] who is assumed to have worked in close cooperation with the organ-building Scherer family. He was admitted to Hamburg's turner guild in 1599 and ran a lathe workshop there. Originally trained as a stonemason, he ought to have applied for admittance to that trade. His decisive and artistically significant work, however, lay in carvings, most of them in wood, although this type of work was actually reserved for the joiner trade. His works were evidently created for noble customers from outside the city, especially the counts of Oldenburg; no documents prove that Münstermann also took orders from within Hamburg. We may conclude that he had joined the Hamburg turner's guild, then not yet closed, to benefit from the advantages this association would bring—for example, contacts with raw-material suppliers for wood. As a sculptor, he was thus forced to exchange his habitual material, stone, for the material that was favored at the time, wood. But according to the guild regulations of Hamburg, he would not have been permitted to work wood as a sculptor. Only the princes' outside orders could provide this possibility, for which he was apparently granted noble privileges.

Such privileges were much sought after among artists, for they obliged the city council to protect their holder from the persecution of the guilds. This explains the almost manic obsession with noble privileges we can observe in Arp Schnitger.[23] Organ builders especially had to work with a wide variety of different materials and tools and were therefore continually coming into conflict with a number of guilds. If they wanted to settle in the cities, which doubtless offered the best prospects where sales and orders were concerned, they needed privileges to protect them. We may assume that the Scherer family found itself in a similar

20. See Cuveland, *Der Gottorfer Codex*, 5–12.

21. Karin Eckhardt, *Christian Precht: Ein Hamburger Bildhauer in der zweiten Hälfte des 17. Jahrhunderts*, Beiträge zur Geschichte Hamburgs, vol. 32 (Hamburg: Verein für Hamburgische Geschichte, 1987), 31–41.

22. Holger Reimers, *Ludwig Münstermann: Zwischen protestantischer Askese und gegenreformatorischer Sinnlichkeit*, Materialien zur Kunst-und Kulturgeschichte in Nord-und Westdeutschland, vol. 8 (Marburg: Jonas, 1993).

23. Gustav Fock, *Arp Schnitger und seine Schule: Ein Beitrag zur Geschichte des Orgelbaues im Nord-und Ostseeküstengebiet* (Kassel: Bärenreiter, 1974).

situation, whereas Gottfried Fritzsche went straight to the duchy of Holstein, whose less stifled atmosphere he much preferred. The situation of free imperial cities set in principalities with a taste for grandeur offered many a skilled strategist numerous advantages, for they could combine the liberties granted by the one with those of the other, and use both to their benefit.

In addition, the council and citizenry knew all too well that it was the artistic resources assembled in their cities that attracted visitors and orders from outside and thus strengthened their economic power. Gerhard Schott argued in a similar vein when defending his opera against its opponents. The purpose of its founding, he claimed, had been "to provide various persons of high standing and other wealthy people staying there [i.e., in Hamburg] with a pastime that is as lawful as it is decent." He further emphasized that its performances would mainly be attended "by strangers, and would thus not only give the city a good reputation among foreigners, but also support the food and lodging business. Apart from this, so many poor students would find a livelihood here and for the most part earn so well that thereafter they would be able to subsist at the university several years longer, not to mention many needy craftsmen and poor burghers who could draw income and food from this."[24]

Art as a Commercial Asset and Tourist Attraction

These terms outline a large part of the direct exchange between ducal courts and Hanseatic cities. Schott's opera offers one of the best examples. Regular cooperation with Braunschweig and Schleswig determined the first decades of its existence—finding and exchanging singers, instrumentalists, compositions and composers, libretti and librettists, sets and set painters. The aristocracy traveled to town for the opening nights, and envoys commissioned gala performances at the Hamburg opera to celebrate the political or dynastic festivals of their respective countries. Hamburg's music looked back on a much longer history in the service of diplomacy. Throughout the seventeenth century, the quality of Hamburg's and Lübeck's council musicians was considered remarkably high, and the criteria for selecting new members were extremely demanding. The surrounding courts regularly engaged instrumentalists of the council's music consort, as soloists or as a body, for special festivities. The city council was happy to grant permission, for the appearance of council musicians invariably increased the fame of the city employing them. The fact that a city could engage and keep distinguished musicians furthermore counted as a sure sign of financial soundness and internal harmony and—to put it in modern terms—promoted its polit-

---

24. See the introduction by Schott to *Vier Bedencken Fürnehmen Theologischen und Juristischen Facultäten, Wie auch Herrn Doct. Johann Friedrich Mayers / P.P. und Königl. Schwedischen Ober=Kirchen=Raths / Was doch von denen so genandten Operen zu halten* (Frankfurt/M, 1693).

ical image as a trustworthy ally and partner. The cities in turn liked to employ musicians who had already proved their mettle at court, for this guaranteed that they were familiar with new international styles and could meet the demands of prestige patronage. William Brade, Nicolaus Bleyer, Gabriel Voigtländer, Franz Tunder, and Georg Österreich provide only a few examples of the continuous flow of musicians between court and city.

The most famous violinist to join Hamburg's council consort in the seventeenth century, Johann Schop, and his friend Heinrich Scheidemann, organist at St. Catharine's, were regularly engaged for gala performances in Gottorf and Wolfenbüttel.[25] The climax of northern European courtly spectacle in those years was the wedding of Crown Prince Christian in Copenhagen in 1634.[26] For several weeks the Danish court enjoyed the best of the artistic resources that North German courts and Hanseatic cities could command. Johann Schop was of course among them, and according to archival notes he shared the responsibility for musical events with no less a figure than Heinrich Schütz himself.

But this was not the only field of courtly spectacle where the duchies engaged the assistance of the cities. In the seventeenth century, Hamburg was considered a stronghold of expertise "in the art of directing noble funerals," even though sumptuary laws barred the burghers themselves from indulging in too much funereal pomp.[27] But crafts and trade provided Hamburg with sufficient resources to produce and deliver on short notice any amount of mourning clothes, mourning decorations for palace and church rooms, coaches and horses, black and silver mourning trumpets, black-edged dinnerware, and coffin plaques. Regarding the memorial plaques and tombs that the occasion of death required, influence seems to have traveled in the opposite direction. The monuments of the North German residencies followed the international style coined in Italy and France, which met the standard of decorum suitable for a ruler's grave. This was the model the urban upper class oriented themselves toward, introducing a hint of the despised princely luxury into their own parish churches. On moral grounds, the city clergy ought to have opposed such practices, but licensing epitaphs, chapels, and memorial stones proved to be a good source of income, an argument that refuted all moral reservations.

25. Kurt Gudewilt, "Die Gottorfer Musikkultur," in *Gottorfer Kultur im Jahrhundert der Universitätsgrundung: Kulturgeschichtliche Denkmäler und Zeugnisse des 17. Jahrhunderts aus der Sphäre der Herzöge von Schleswig-Holstein-Gottorf*, ed. Ernst Schlee (Kiel: Christian-Albrechts-Universität, 1965), 223–31. See also Karl Wilhelm Geck, *Sophie Elisabeth Herzogin zu Braunschweig und Lüneburg (1613–1676) als Musikerin*, Saarbrücker Studien zur Musikwissenschaft, vol. 6 (Saarbrücken: Saarbrücker Druckerei, 1992), 43–44.

26. Mara Wade, *Triumphus nuptialis Danicus: German Court Culture and Denmark: The "Great Wedding" of 1634*, Wolfenbütteler Arbeiten zur Barockforschung, vol. 27 (Wiesbaden: Harrassowitz, 1996).

27. Gisela Jaacks, " 'Eitler Pomp' oder 'Hamburger Anstand'? Zu Kleidungssitten im hamburgischen Toten-und Trauerbrauchtum des 17. Und 18. Jahrhunderts," *Beiträge zur deutschen Volks-und Altertumskunde* 24 (1985): 19–30.

With these links and commissions, the tastes of the court influenced the artistic style of Hanseatic craftsmen and their civic customers. The agents of ducal courts stayed in town to supervise their lords' orders. The skill of Hamburg's goldsmiths, for example, transmitted the fashion of silver altars from Italy and South Germany to the Danish and Swedish realms.[28] The role Lübeck had played as a center of northern European art dealing during the late Middle Ages and even at the beginning of the sixteenth century now fell to Hamburg. The cities' native artists pursued the trends established at the courts in order to secure their share of the profit from lavish orders, thus changing the taste of the burghers.

A significant example of this development is the fashion for still lifes and especially trompe-l'oeils that evolved in Hamburg and Lübeck in the second half of the seventeenth century. Originally fostered by aristocratic amateurs, it derived from the new interest in optical phenomena and illusion and reflected the political-absolutist aspect of the science of sensory perception. In the Netherlands it had become one of the preferred genres of painting. Unaware of the power that politics wielded, the burghers enjoyed such representations for purely aesthetic reasons, at most seeing some sort of moral point in them. This is where the interpretation of art at court and in the city diverged, even though both admired the same paintings. But it was the local princes who commissioned the masterpieces of this genre, created by two painters who intermittently worked in Hamburg: Cornelis Norbertus Gijsbrechts and Georg Hinz.[29] Some works, however, remained in burghers' hands.

Where artistic expression and aesthetic sensibility are concerned, the courts and Hanseatic cities of the late seventeenth century were clearly converging. The urban upper class had begun to emulate an aristocratic model. The remaining classes enjoyed the efforts of the Hanseatic councils to equal their ducal partners at official functions and profited through lavish orders from the city authorities. Economically and politically, the cooperation of Hanseatic cities and ducal courts benefited both partners. These benefits convinced even the most puritanical burghers, and created the conditions for their relatively peaceful coexistence in the following century.

Translated by Nina Hausmann

---

28. Witness the silver altar made by the Hamburg goldsmith Jacob Mores in 1606 for Frederiksborg Castle; also probably by Jacob Mores, the silver altar from 1620 for the Castle of Husum; the silver altar made by the Hamburg goldsmith Eustachius Erdmüller for the Great Church (Storkyrkan) in Stockholm in 1650; and the silver altar by the Hamburg goldsmith Hans Lambrecht III for Gottorf Castle in 1666.

29. Christoph Heinrich, *Georg Hinz: Das Kunstkammerregal* (Hamburg: Hamburger Kunsthalle, 1996).

4

THE GENESIS AND RADIANCE OF A COURT ORGAN

HARALD VOGEL

Esaias Compenius and the *organo di legno*

The Esaias Compenius organ in Frederiksborg Castle belongs to a category of organs whose pipes are completely—or almost completely—made of wood and which was widespread in Italy. Its subtle sound was particularly appreciated around 1600, and Claudio Monteverdi called for it in the score of *Orfeo* in 1607.[1] The Italian *organo di legno* consisted of a *ripieno* based on a Principale 8′ with the corresponding overtone ranks of octaves and fifths. All these stops were built as open principal pipes with a square cross section, usually from thin cypress wood. A well-preserved example of an organ of this sort in Italy stands in the church of Santa Maria delle Grazie in Montepulciano, Tuscany.[2] Another example of this style is the famous wooden organ in the Silver Chapel in Innsbruck.

On its way northward, the conception of the *organo di legno* made an interesting transformation: organ builders began to experiment with the construction of different forms of wooden pipes and expanded the Italian ripieno with every imaginable consort sound, attempting with these stops to imitate the sounds of actual musical instruments, particularly woodwinds and brass instruments. The most significant wooden organ from the sixteenth century in northern Europe stands in Wilhelmsburg Palace in Schmalkalden, Thuringia.[3] Count Wilhelm IV of Hessen commissioned it in 1586 from the Göttingen organ builder Daniel Meyer. The 4′ façade pipes are veneered on three sides with thick ivory. An 8′

1. It sounds for the first time in act 2, at the appearance of the messenger who announces Euridice's death with the words "Ahi! Caso acerbo."

2. For specifications see Barbara Owen, *The Registration of Baroque Organ Music* (Bloomington: Indiana University Press, 1997), 53.

3. See Gunter Hart, "Daniel Meyer, Orgelmacher zu Göttingen," *Acta Organologica* 11 (1977): 119–34.

Figure 4-1. Keyboards of the Compenius organ, Frederiksborg Castle. Photograph by Annelise Olesen, 1976. Courtesy of Musikhistoriskmuseum, Copenhagen.

Gedackt functions as the foundation; a conical stop, Spitzoktave, sounds at the 2′ level; and crowning the ensemble is a high one-rank Zimbel; in addition, there are two Regals.

From an instrument such as that in Schmalkalden, in which the vocally oriented sound of the Italian Principal is present only in the 4′ Principal of the façade, it was but a small step to the Compenius organ, with its concept of tonal diversity and refined construction. Following the musical tendencies of his time, Compenius attempted to present a *summa* of the organ sounds of his day in the smallest possible space. He apparently worked under no financial constraints, and thus he used only the finest materials in its construction. Its pipes are variously built of maple, oak, walnut, satinwood, birch, and ebony. The façade pipes are veneered with ivory, with the upper and lower lips constructed of ebony. Its pure silver stop knobs are absolutely unique, fashioned as women's heads for the upper manual, men's heads for the pedal (in the middle of the upper row), and as lions' heads (on either side) for the lower manual. On the forehead of each face is engraved the abbreviation for its stop name. Four more silver knobs are situated on the cornice above the key desk: an owl, which activates a low humming tone on C; two roses, for the two tremulants; and a fool's head for the bagpipe (see figure 4-1). The manual keys are veneered with thick ivory, and their arcades are decorated with silver; the pedal keyboard slides in and out like a drawer, and its keys are also covered with ivory.

Compenius and Michael Praetorius

Compenius built his wooden organ at the court of Braunschweig-Lüneburg at Wolfenbüttel, where he served as the official organ builder and instrument maker to Duke Heinrich Julius. At this same time, Michael Praetorius (c. 1571–1621) was the court *Kapellmeister*, and it appears that the two men collaborated quite closely in developing their knowledge of the organ and of other musical instruments. In 1619 Praetorius published volume two of his monumental *Syntagma Musicum*,[4] titled *De Organographia*, a comprehensive treatise on all musical instruments, followed a year later by the supplemental *Theatrum Instrumentorum*, containing forty-two famous woodcuts of musical instruments and organ pipes. Volume three of *Syntagma Musicum*, also published in 1619, contains a list of his compositions and writings, among which he announced a forthcoming treatise that did not appear before his death, *Orgeln Verdingnis*, whose complete title may be translated *Contracting for Organs, Construction and Delivery, Covering Both New Construction and the Rebuilding of Older Organs. Made Available in Order to Provide Reliable Advice and Counsel for All Christian Congregations, Pastors, Church Elders, Church Supervisors, Organists, and Other Interested Parties.*[5] This title closely resembles a manuscript treatise at the Herzog August library in Wolfenbüttel that is ascribed to Compenius: *Kurzer Bericht . . . or Brief Account of What Must Be Observed upon the Delivery of a Small and Large Organ, and How the Fundamentals Must Be Examined, Diligently Inspected, and Judged by the Ear. Left By Esaias Compenius, Organ and Instrument Maker to the Duke of Braunschweig, and Promised by Michael Praetorius in the Preceding Treatise, fol. 160.* Compenius had left Braunschweig and gone to Hillerød to deliver his wooden organ to King Christian IV of Denmark and install it in Frederiksborg Castle, and he died there in 1617. Friedrich Blume published the *Kurzer Bericht* in 1936 as the work of both men.[6]

If Compenius and Praetorius collaborated on the writing of this small treatise, then it would follow that Compenius contributed to the enormous fund of information on organs in Praetorius's *De Organographia* and that Praetorius in turn had some influence on the building of the chamber organ. Indeed, a lost inscription from inside the organ, dated 7 October 1610 and preserved in a later copy, documents their collaboration: "By the design [*inventione*] and financing of the most honorable Lord Heinrich Julius, Bishop of Halberstadt and Duke of Braunschweig and Lüneburg; with the guidance [*directione*] of Michael Praetorius, chapel master and organist; through the talent and hand [*ingenio et manu*] of Esaius Compenius, this organ was happily elaborated and built [*elaboratum et*

4. Michael Praetorius, *Syntagma Musicum*, 3 vols. (1615–19; facsimile reprint, ed. Wilibald Gurlitt, Kassel: Barenreiter, 1958–59).

5. Praetorius, *Syntagma Musicum* 3:224; translation from Vincent J. Panetta Jr., "Praetorius, Compenius, and Werckmeister: A Tale of Two Treatises," *Church, Stage, and Studio: Music and Its Contexts in Seventeenth-Century Germany* (Ann Arbor: UMI Research Press, 1990), 68.

6. Michael Praetorius and Esaias Compenius, *Orgeln Verdingnis*, ed. Friedrich Blume, Kieler Beiträge zur Musikwissenschaft, vol. 4 (Wolfenbüttel: Kallmeyer, 1936). See also Vincent Panetta, "An Early Handbook for Organ Inspection: the 'Kurzer Bericht' of Michael Praetorius and Esaias Compenius," *Organ Yearbook* 21 (1991): 5–33.

189   DE ORGANOGRAPHIA.

5. Rancket	8
6. Regal	8
7. Zimbel Regal.	2

In der Bruſt auff beyden
Seiten zum Pedal.
6. Stimmen.

1. Quintflöiten Baß	12
2. Bawrflöiten B.	4
3. Zimbel B.	3
4. Rancker B.	8
5. Krumbhorn B.	8
6. Klein Regal B.	84

XXI.
Zu Heſſen vffm
Schloſſe.

Das hölgern/ Aber doch ſehr herrliche Orgelwerck ſo von M. Eſaia Compenio An. 1612. gemacht. Jetzo aber de König in Dennemarck verehret/ vnd Annn 1616. doſelbſten zu Friedrichsburg in der Kirchen geſetzt worden/ iſt ſtarck von 27. Stimmen/ Coppel zu beyden Manualn. Tremulant. Groſſer Bock. Sackpfeiffe. Kleinhümlichen.

Jm obern Manual
9. Stimmen.

1. Principal	8. fuß
2. Klein Principal von Elffenbein vnd Ebenholtz.	4
3. Gedactflöite	8
4. Gemßhorn oder klein Violn	4
5. Nachthorn	4
6. Blockpfeiffeu	4

7. Gedact Quint	3
8. Supergedactflöitlin	2
9. Rancket.	16

Jm Unter Manual / vnten
an ſtatt des Poſitiffs
9. Stimmen.

1. Quintadehna	8. fi.
2. Klein Gedactflöite	4
3. Super Gemßhörnlein	2
4. Nafart	anderthalb
5. Klein repetirt Zimbel einfach.	
6. Principal Discant	4
7. Blockpfeiffen Discant	4
8. Krumbhorn	8
9. Geigend Regal.	4

Jm Pedal
9. Stimmen.

1. Groſſer Gedactflöiten Baß	16. fuß
2. Gemßhorn B.	8
3. Quintadeen B.	8
4. Querflöiten B.	4
5. Nachthorn B.	2
6. Bawrflöiten Bäßlein	1
7. Sordunen B.	6
8. Doltzian B.	8
9. Jungfrawen Regal Baß.	4

XXIII.

Die Fürſtliche Widtwe zu Braunſchweig vnnd Lüneburg leſt jetzo in jhrer F. G. Schloßcapell durch den Churf. Sächſiſchen Orgelmacher M. Gotfried

Aa iij   Fritz

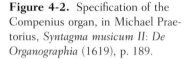

Figure 4-2. Specification of the Compenius organ, in Michael Praetorius, *Syntagma musicum II: De Organographia* (1619), p. 189.

exstructum]."[7] Thus it is to be expected not only that *De Organographia* contains the full specifications for this instrument (figure 4-2), but also that descriptions of its stops and possibilities for registration can be found elsewhere in the volume. Above the specifications, he describes the organ as "the wooden, but very magnificent organ made by Master Esaias Compenius in the year 1612. But now it has been given to the King of Denmark, and in the year 1616 has been placed there in Frederiksborg in the church."[8] Praetorius's date of 1616 may reflect the time when the organ was removed from Hessen Castle, for a recently discovered source in Compenius's hand states that he installed the organ in Frederiksborg in 1617:

> I have begun this work in Wolfenbüttel, with the help of God, and put it together in Hessen, where it stood for more than five years, and during the second siege of Braunschweig it was presented by my gracious Prince and Master, Duke Friedrich Ulrich, to His Royal Majesty. Thus, I have brought this work, through the Providence of God, into the Kingdom of Denmark, and here I have once again put it together and finished it in the year 1617. Eternal praise be to God.[9]

7. The copy was made by Peter Botzen in 1692; see Povl Eller, "Compenius-orglets historie," *Dansk årbog for musikforskning*, 17 (1986): 8; facsimile on p. 46.

8. Praetorius, *Syntagma Musicum* 2:189.

9. Eller, "Compenius," 50. It was found by Mads Kjersgaard on the stopper of a Subbass pipe during the 1988 restoration. (On the siege of Braunschweig, see chapter 3.)

Every one of the 27 stops on the Compenius organ appears in the descriptions of the voices of the organ that Praetorius gives in part four of *De Organographia*, from pages 126 to 148. There, however, the pipes described are those more typically made of metal. Concerning pipes made of wood, he states:

> The wooden form of organ pipes ought to be discussed here; since, however, the layout of their [various] proportions (which I personally have observed with great diligence) as well as their [resultant] tone color requires an altogether different description [from that given here]; they are hardly to be compared in tone and construction to [the examples found in] other instruments. These facts are [adequately] proven by the aforementioned instrument in the palace at Hessen.
>
> This strange, mild, delicate, and lovely tone cannot really be described in writing; so, for the sake of brevity, I have considered it unnecessary to go into further detail concerning these [wooden] stops. Perhaps Compenius himself will in due time issue a report concerning these and other matters in a more comprehensive and thoroughly mathematical manner, since this is really not my profession.[10]

But Praetorius refers directly to the Compenius organ when he describes the Querflöte:

> This species of Querfloete [i.e., the Querfloete Gedackt], to be sure, is a good [voice] and of recent invention. But another species, [constructed of] open [pipes] and in double length, pleases me more. This is the one placed into the princely new wooden organ of 27 voices and 3 claviers enclosed in a decorative case and described in section V, which the Right Reverend, Illustrious, and Honourable Sovereign and Lord, Lord Heinrich Julius, Postulated Bishop of Halberstadt, Duke of Braunschweig and Lüneburg, my gracious Sovereign and Lord of most blessed memory, had constructed by Master Esaias Compenius, distinguished organ and instrument builder, for His Sovereign Grace's beloved spouse, and erected in her palace at Hessen. Here [the Querfloetes] are made of wood, although other builders had previously constructed them also of metal. For it is more natural that [the pipes] should transpose into the octave than go beyond and fall into the twelfth. These [open ones] resemble the tone color of the [mouth-blown] Querfloete more closely than do the covered ones.[11]

He relates this organ stop to the natural sound of the transverse flute, which he discusses in part two, devoted to the families of wind and string instruments. Here he introduces the concept of the consort (*Accort*), which he defines as "an entire family of pipes, curtals, or whatever, which contains every size in order

10. Praetorius, *Syntagma Musicum* 2:141–42; translation from Paul G. Bunjes, *The Praetorius Organ* (St. Louis: Concordia, 1966), 664.

11. Praetorius, *Syntagma Musicum* 2:138–39; Bunjes translation, 649–50.

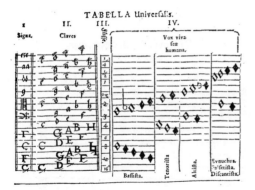

Figure 4-3. Universal range chart, in Michael Praetorius, *Syntagma musicum II, De Organographia* (1619), p. 20. The numbers in column III, "Füsse," represent the length of an open organ pipe for the lowest key, C.

from the largest pipe at the bottom to the smallest at the top."[12] This concept is amplified by numerous charts and by the woodcuts in the *Theatrum Instrumentorum*. In his charts he shows the range of each instrument in the consort, using both staff lines with clefs and organ tablature. In the introductory "universal" chart, showing the ranges of human voices, he also introduces a column for organ foot lengths, because "organ builders use 'feet' to give a precise designation to individual notes and stops, and to distinguish the various upper and lower registers: it makes for clearer thinking and clearer expression."[13] In this chart (figure 4-3) the numbers in column three, "Füsse," represent the length of an open pipe that produces the corresponding pitch from the lowest key on an organ keyboard, normally C.

In the corresponding chart for the transverse flute (figure 4-4), he shows three sizes: a bass, with a bottom note of g, one in the alto-tenor range, extending from d' to d''' (or possibly higher), and a discant flute with a range of a' to a'''. These three transverse flutes are then illustrated in plate IX of *Theatrum Instrumentorum* (figure 4-5), under number 3 on the lower right side, with the letters g, d', and a' indicating the lowest finger hole that marks the bottom of their respective ranges. The ruler at the bottom of the plate gives the scale to which the figures are drawn, using the Brunswick foot, which is equivalent to 28.5 centimeters. Plate XXXVII (figure 4-6) then shows the corresponding organ pipe, "Offen Querfloit 4 Fuss" as number 13, near the top. Although a round metal pipe is pictured, this is the same stop found in the pedal of the Compenius organ. One can see from the scale that even though it sounds at 4' pitch, an octave higher than normal, its lowest note is over nine feet long, even longer than the Principal 8 Fuss, number 1, at the bottom of the plate.

12. Praetorius, *Syntagma Musicum* 2:12; translation from Michael Praetorius, *Syntagma Musicum II, De Organographia: Parts I and II*, trans. and ed. David Z. Crookes (Oxford: Clarendon, 1986), 30.
13. Praetorius, *Syntagma Musicum* 2:19; Crookes translation, 34.

Figure 4-4. Range chart for the transverse flute family, in Michael Praetorius, *Syntagma musicum II: De Organographia* (1619), p. 22.

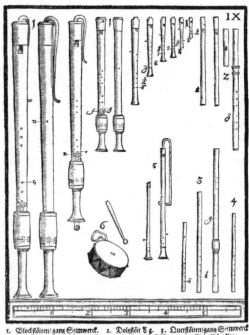

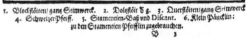

Figure 4-5. Michael Praetorius, *Syntagma musicum II*, "Theatrum Instrumentorum" (1620), plate IX, showing three transverse flutes with the letters *g, d′,* and *a′* as number 3.

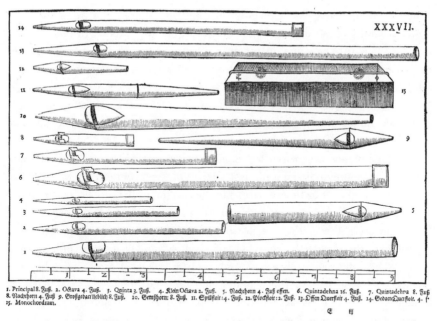

1. Principal 8. Fuß. 2. Octava 4. Fuß. 3. Quinta 3. Fuß. 4. Klein Octava 2. Fuß. 5. Nachthorn 4. Fuß offen. 6. Quintadehna 16. Fuß. 7. Quintadehra 8. Fuß 8. Nachthorn 4. Fuß 9. Grofgedact lieblich 8. Fuß. 10. Gemßhorn: 8. Fuß. 11. Epißfloit:4. Fuß. 12. Plockfloit:2. Fuß. 13. Offen Querfloit 4. Fuß. 14. Gedacte Querfloit. 4. f 15. Monochordium.

Figure 4-6. Michael Praetorius, *Syntagma musicum II,* "Theatrum Instrumentorum" (1620), plate XXXVII, showing the organ pipe "Offen Querfloit 4 Fuss" as number 13, near the top.

In other instances—Blockflöte and Dulzian—Praetorius specifically compares the sound of the organ stop with that of the similarly named instrument. Most of the instruments that he describes in part two of *De Organographia* and illustrates in *Theatrum Instrumentorum* are shown in families of different-sized instruments, later termed a "whole" consort when they are played together, as in a consort of viols or crumhorns. An organ stop encompasses the range of an entire family of similar instruments, extending downward almost to the lowest A_1 of Praetorius's bass crumhorn and upward well beyond the d' of his smallest. By playing polyphonically on a single stop, the organist can emulate an entire consort. As Praetorius wrote, "In sum, the organ alone contains all other musical instruments, large and small, whatever their names, within itself. If you would like to hear a drum, trumpet, trombone, cornett, recorder, transverse flute, bombard, shawm, dulcian, rackett, sordun, crumhorn, violin, lyra, etc., you can have all of these and many other wonderful delights in this ingenious piece of work."[14]

In volume three of *Syntagma Musicum*, Praetorius actually uses the English word "consort" to refer to a broken or mixed consort: "It is also very pleasant to hear when one sets up this *Capella Fidicina* in the English manner, with a complete *Consort*, so that a strong harpsichord, two or three lutes, a theorbo,

14. Praetorius, *Syntagma Musicum* 2:85.

pandora, cittern, bass violin, recorder or transverse flute, quiet trombone, viola bastarda, and a small discant violin, tuned purely and sweetly to one another, play together."[15] In practice, many organ registrations represent mixed consorts. Praetorius did not use the term "consort" with reference to organ registration, but since he had imported it into the German language, I have found it a very useful term, in both German and English, for registrations, particularly those with reed stops, that do not employ the normal plenum of principals and mixtures.[16]

The Compenius organ and the organ aesthetic of Michael Praetorius have become very influential since the last quarter of the twentieth century. One of the most important new instruments built according to the models of its various stops is Charles Fisk's wonderful chapel organ at Wellesley College (near Boston, Massachusetts). It was the last instrument Charles Fisk voiced himself and a milestone of the twentieth-century organ-building trend of reviving antique models for the performance of seventeenth-century music in our time. I had the privilege of being part of the planning and building process. The Brustpedal, located next to the console, contains 4 stops, 3 of them copied from the Compenius organ (Doltzian Baß 8′, Jungfrawen Baß 4′, Bawrflöiten Bäßlein 1′). A similar Brustpedal was built by Charles Fisk in the large dual-temperament instrument at Stanford Memorial Church in California—another major achievement of historically oriented organ building in the twentieth century. One of the most elaborate house organs in the last decades was built by Paul Fritts in 1989 for the residence of Jeff Smith in Seattle, Washington. Here the renaissance front of Compenius's masterpiece has been recreated, together with many stops in the typical wooden construction.

Compenius, Praetorius, and Finn Viderø

During the 1940s Finn Viderø (1906–87), the leading Danish organist of his generation, began to play concerts on the Compenius organ in Frederiksborg, which were recorded and broadcast by Danish Radio. I remember hearing these broadcasts in North Germany as a child during the early 1950s. What a stunning impression they made on me! Early in the 1950s, Odeon issued a recording of Viderø playing works of the sixteenth and seventeenth centuries on this organ.[17] The registrations that he used on this recording agree almost perfectly with those

15. Praetorius, *Syntagma musicum* 3:137 [*sic*; should be 117].

16. See Harald Vogel, "North German Organ Building of the Late Seventeenth Century: Registration and Tuning," in *J. S. Bach as Organist: His Instruments, Music, and Performance Practices*, ed. George Stauffer and Ernest May (Bloomington: Indiana University Press, 1986), 31–40.

17. Finn Viderø, *Music on the Historic Compenius Organ in Frederiksborg Castle* ([Denmark]: Odeon, MOAK 9, n.d.). It was reissued in 1959 by Valois (MB 17) as *Musique pour orgue sacrée et profane des XVI et XVIIèmes siècles*.

he gave for the Compenius organ in volume two of his edition of these works, with Fin Ditlevsen, *Orgelmusik*.[18] Although this edition was not published until 1963, the registrations had been set in 1944, as he states in the foreword: "The collection of organ music which follows, dating from before 1650, was arranged for the Compenius organ in the summer of 1944 and the suggested registrations are those, which, in our opinion, seem to suit the character and individuality of each piece."[19]

The foreword gives a complete description of the organ, including the layout of its keyboard with short octave and the abbreviations for each stop that are found on the silver stop knobs. These same abbreviations are used throughout the edition. Although the Compenius organ had been played regularly since its restoration by Félix Reinburg in 1895, it was through Viderø's radio broadcasts, recordings, and edition that it became more widely known, and with them he set a standard for registration practice of early baroque organ music.

The repertoire that one can play successfully on the Compenius organ is very limited. It is not a church organ; it is a consort organ, and it has no plenum. The Hanseatic repertoire of praeludia and chorale fantasias was composed for very large organs in very large churches; this is a chamber organ built for a smaller space. Viderø made excellent choices of pieces to play on the recording—works by Jan Pieterszoon Sweelinck, Samuel Scheidt, Paul Siefert, Antonio de Cabezón, and Juan Cabanilles, as well as some anonymous dances—and that was a reason for its success. People were amazed at how well this music worked on that organ. Of course, the quarter-comma meantone tuning contributed significantly to the wonderful impression the music made. Also, this organ has a more spectacular effect on the player than on the audience—it actually sounds too soft from the seats of the castle chapel where it now stands—so the recording process itself added to the radiance of the organ, because the microphones were placed close to it.

Viderø's registrations for the Compenius organ reflect a careful study of Praetorius. In verse three, "Fecit potentiam," of Samuel Scheidt's *Magnificat secundi toni*, a bicinium with the cantus firmus in the right hand, he specifies Gedact Flöite 4′ and Nasatt 1½′ [actually 1⅓′] on the lower manual for the right hand and Blockpfeiffen 4′ on the upper manual for the left hand. Of the Nasatt, Praetorius wrote: "Otherwise, [the Klein Gemshornquinte of 1½′ pitch] is, not unjustly, called *Nasat*, since because of its diminutive size, the tone is somewhat nasal in effect when compared to other voices, especially when it is properly

18. *Orgelmusik*, Bd. II, ed. Fin Ditlevsen and Finn Viderø (Copenhagen: Engstrøm & Sødring, 1963). The works that appear both in the recording and in this edition are Antonio de Cabezón, *Tiento del primer tono* and *Diferencias sobre el canto llano del Caballero*; Jan Pieterszoon Sweelinck, *O lux beata trinitas* and *Fantasie op de manier van een echo*; and Samuel Scheidt, *Magnificat secundi toni*.
19. Ditlevsen and Viderø, *Orgelmusik*, Bd. II, n.p.

voiced and not too intense. It provides also a fine discant in the right hand when used in combination with other voices."[20]

The running notes of the left hand sound as if they are being played on a recorder, as Praetorius said they should:

> Some still call the Gemshorns, *Blockfloetes.* This is not a proper designation because Blockfloetes have a different shape and tone color. The Spitzfloetes of 4' pitch (of which we shall speak presently), if they are given the proper scale (i.e. somewhat wider than [the scale] of Gemshorns), can, because of their tone color, more justly be called Blockpfeifes or Blockfloetes. When so constructed they produce a tone color which resembles, in a natural way, the tone of the [mouth]-blown instruments known as Blockpfeifes.[21]

Praetorius refers to the German practice of playing a soprano or alto cantus firmus on the pedal in his description of the 1' Bawrflöiten Bass: "Here in Germany we lay great store by this voice, especially when one wishes to lead the chorale in the Pedal. The Italians, however, despise all such small bass voices of 2' or 1' pitch, because to them they sound like empty octaves."[22] Viderø specifies this stop in the pedal, together with the Querflöiten Bass 4', for the alto cantus firmus in verse three of Scheidt's *Magnificat tertii toni.* He also employs this technique with Antonio de Cabezón's *Diferencias sobre el canto del caballero,* using the 4' Regalbass in the pedal for the soprano melody. The fact that this would not have been possible on a Spanish organ of that time does not seem to have concerned him.

Another registration that appears to have come right out of Praetorius is the "mixed consort" registration that Viderø uses for Cabezón's *Tiento del primer tono*: Gross Gedact Flöite 8', Klein Principal 4', Gedact Quint 3', Kleine Flöite 2', and Rancket 16'. Praetorius wrote that "it is a pleasure to hear [the Super Gedackt 2' played] together with a Gross Rankett or Sordun of 16' pitch, with which it provides an unusual registration resulting in a strange tone color."[23]

This second volume of Ditlevsen's and Viderø's *Orgelmusik*—with its repertoire drawn entirely from before 1650 and with each piece registered specifically for the Compenius organ in Frederiksborg—represents a completely different concept from that of their first volume, which had been published in 1938.[24] Although subtitled *Preludes and Chorale Settings from the Seventeenth Century,* the repertoire of the first volume reaches well into the eighteenth century. Its

---

20. Praetorius, *Syntagma Musicum* 2:134; Bunjes translation, 624–25.

21. Praetorius, *Syntagma Musicum* 2:135; Bunjes translation, 625.

22. Praetorius, *Syntagma Musicum* 2:140; Bunjes translation, 655.

23. Praetorius, *Syntagma Musicum* 2:140; Bunjes translation, 654–55.

24. *Orgelmusik,* Bd. I, *Praeludier og Koralbearbejdelser fra det 17de Aarhundrede;* udgivet til gudstjeneste-og studiebrug af Fin Ditlevsen og Finn Viderø (Copenhagen: Engstrøm & Sødring, 1938).

individual pieces contain no registration information whatsoever. A foreword, "Om Registrering," gives general information about the character of Italian, French, and German organs and suggests various possibilities for *organo pleno* and *canto solo* registrations based on neo-baroque specifications of the 1930s. In one respect, however, the first volume employs better editorial practice than the second: it presents most of its works in a more neutral notation on two staves, leaving it to the performer to decide whether to play them *manualiter* or *pedaliter*. In the second volume, most of the works are presented *pedaliter* on three staves, including obligatory pedal lines in works of Cabezón and Sweelinck that would now be considered inappropriate.[25] We see here a very individual approach to the artistic quality of the Compenius organ by a twentieth-century performer—Finn Viderø—trying to use a very colorful sound for this repertoire and to employ the pedal as much as possible. Thus this volume is an interesting and important historical document in itself.

Consort registrations similar to those that characterize the Compenius organ are also obtainable on the large Hanseatic organs; for example, Arp Schnitger's 1693 organ for St. Jacobi, Hamburg, contains numerous stops that imitate natural instruments, such as Blockflöht, Querpfeiff, Dulcian, Cornet, Trommet, and Posaune. The multisectioned North German praeludia work very well on these organs when their fugues are played with consort registrations as a foil to the plenum of their opening and closing free sections. In my recording of Dieterich Buxtehude's Praeludium in D Minor (BuxWV 140) at St. Jacobi,[26] for example, I use a mixed consort of Principal 8', Dulcian 8', Octava 4', and Waldflöht 2' on the Brustpositiv for the first fugue (mm. 20–45).

The organ at St. Jacobi, unlike the Compenius organ, is presently tuned not in quarter-comma meantone, but in a modified fifth-comma tuning. I got my first intimation of what a large meantone organ might sound like in 1971 when I put on the first performance in the twentieth century of the large multiple-choir works of Michael Praetorius for Radio Bremen. For the Praetorius recording we had all the consort instruments that he specified in *Polyhymnia Caduceatrix*, with the keyboard instruments—regal, harpsichord, positive organ, and the reeds of the Ahrend organ in St. Martin's Church in Bremen—all tuned in quarter-comma meantone. When I heard this performance, it was clear to me that this was the same idea of sound that we would hear in a large organ tuned in quarter-comma meantone—"Praetorian tuning," as it often was called in the seventeenth century. And now, thirty years later, with the North German organ in Örgryte Church, Göteborg, we finally have it.

25. Modern editorial practice has returned to a notation that allows the performer to decide where to use the pedal; see Samuel Scheidt, *Tabulatura nova*, ed. Harald Vogel, vol. 2 (Wiesbaden: Breitkopf und Härtel, 1999).

26. Dieterich Buxtehude, *Orgelwerke, vol. 7* (DG Musikproduction, MD + GL 3427, 1993).

5

HAMBURG ORGANISTS IN LUTHERAN WORSHIP

WILLIAM PORTER

May the faithful, dear and true God help us as in this transitory life we tune our wagging tongues in taking up with alternating choirs the heavenly songs of prayer and praise of the holy patriarchs, prophets, and apostles and other holy and blessed Christians. . . . May it be thus also in the approaching eternal and heavenly life, at the joyful marriage of our heavenly bridegroom, Jesus Christ, with heavenly singers and most perfect musicians holy angels and archangels, to stand before the throne of the Lamb and hold an eternal chorus with them in our praise and shouts of joy, to praise and honor God the Lord . . . singing together with the cherubim and seraphim this most solemn and precious song in concert, the triple Sanctus . . . and together with the elders in the Revelation of John with their harps and cymbals, singing the Song of the Lamb.

MICHAEL PRAETORIUS, *SYNTAGMA MUSICUM* VOL. 2

ALTHOUGH THERE IS NO MENTION OF THE ORGAN IN THIS PASSAGE FROM THE introduction to the second volume of Michael Praetorius's *Syntagma Musicum* (1619), it is noteworthy that it appears in a volume dealing not with vocal music, but with musical instruments, especially organs. The implication is clear: the songs of praise offered in earthly life are a form of participation in the divine life of heaven, and musical instruments are included. This is more than the attitude of an inveterate lover of music; it is a theological position that was in full bloom within Lutheran circles in the early seventeenth century, one that developed Luther's own views concerning the role of music in creation and the importance of music in the liturgy of the church and the education of the young.[1] The institutionalization in Lutheranism of these views ushered in what can only be described as a "golden age" of music for the Lutheran churches. The combination of a stable and fertile liturgical practice and an established musical curriculum in the Latin schools,[2] supported by a well-articulated theological perspective, allowed principal centers of Lutheran orthodoxy to develop a tradition of liturgical music on a very high professional level, involving singers, instrumentalists, and—above all—organists. By the second half of the sixteenth century, Hamburg had become one such center.

Hamburg as a Center for Lutheran Music

A key figure in the establishment of this center was Hieronymus Praetorius, not only through his organ playing, but also through his vocal and instrumental compositions, as well as his role in codifying the repertoire of liturgical song in the Hamburg churches. Praetorius's *Cantiones Sacrae Chorales* (1587), along with Franz Eler's *Cantica Sacra* (1588) and the somewhat later *Melodeyen Gesangbuch* (1604), provided hymns for congregation and choir that also served in the development of a new practice in the use of cantus firmus in organ playing. It was Hieronymus Praetorius who laid the foundations of the great North German organ school, which was later brought to full bloom by his immediate successors.

Early in the seventeenth century, four young organists from Hamburg traveled to Amsterdam to study with Jan Pieterszoon Sweelinck. Following their return, one by one they eventually became the organists for all four of Hamburg's main churches. Jacob and Johann Praetorius—both sons of Hieronymus Praetorius, and not related to Michael Praetorius—served at St. Petri and St. Nicolai; Heinrich Scheidemann—also the son of a Hamburg organist, David Scheidemann—and Ulrich Cernitz worked at St. Catharine's and St. Jacobi respectively. Their average length of tenure was thirty-nine years. As a group they dominated the art of organ playing in Hamburg to such a degree that a century later Johann Mattheson would describe Sweelinck as the *hamburgischen Organistenmacher* (creator of the Hamburg organists).[3] Their studies with Sweelinck consisted of both composition and performance, and their surviving repertoire suggests that they combined these skills in a rather specific way, which will be explored later in this chapter.

1. For instance: "For music is a gift and largesse of God, not a human gift. . . . After theology I accord to music the highest place and the highest honor." Quoted in Walter Buszin, "Luther on Music," *Musical Quarterly* 32 (1946): 88. The quotation is taken from a thesis entitled "Concerning Music."

2. John Butt, *Music Education and the Art of Performance in the German Baroque* (Cambridge: Cambridge University Press, 1994), 2.

3. Johann Mattheson, *Grundlage einer Ehren-Pforte* (1740; facsimile reprint, ed. Max Schneider, Kassel: Bärenreiter, 1969), 332.

Since 1556 Hamburg's liturgies for the Mass and for the offices of matins and vespers had followed an order established by Johannes Aepin that remained in use until the end of the seventeenth century[4] and gave the organ a significant role. The Mass began with a German psalm, for which the organist played once or twice between the verses. On feast days, a Latin motet was performed. The organist also played at the Kyrie and Gloria. Either an Alleluia or a German psalm was sung just before the Gospel; in the case of the latter, the organist played between the verses. At the end of the sermon the *Vater Unser* was sung, and the organist played afterward. The organist also played between the verses of the communion hymn. Matins and vespers followed a similar pattern; he played at the responsories, the hymns, the Benedictus and Magnificat, and the Benedicamus.[5] Aepin's liturgy in general allots more duties to the organist than the previous order, including increased opportunities to play between the verses of more German psalms. Even so, Aepin's prescriptions for the Mass, taken at face value, seem not to reflect the fullness of actual practice in Hamburg at the beginning of the seventeenth century. When one looks to the extant repertoire connected with Hamburg at this time, a fuller picture begins to emerge. The large collection of organ works known today as the *Visby Tabulatur*—which includes not only a complete Magnificat cycle by Hieronymus Praetorius, but also hymns (German psalms and Latin hymns) and music for the Mass, probably by the same composer[6]—shows that the organ was used extensively in alternation with the choir for the entire Ordinary of the Mass. The four principal churches in Hamburg had only one choir among them, so the role of the choir in singing the motet (for the proper) was taken over by the organist whenever the choir was not present.[7] The large repertoire of motet intabulations for organ preserved in a variety of sources testifies to the importance of this tradition, not only in Hamburg, but throughout the region.[8] Finally, the extensive repertoire of praeludia in the North German tablatures is indicative of the essential role that such pieces played in Hamburg's liturgical practice. The praeludium, or praeambulum, was often played before the beginning of a vocal or concerted piece in order to

4. Liselotte Krüger, *Die hamburgische Musikorganisation im XVII. Jahrhundert*, Sammlung Musikwissenschaftlicher Abhandlungen, vol. 12 (Strassburg: Heitz, 1933), 21.

5. Since it has been documented that the playing of "Ein paar feine Stuck oder Motetten" after the Benedicamus was a practice in Lüneburg at the time, it may be assumed to have taken place in Hamburg as well. See Krüger, *Die hamburgische Musikorganisation*, 112.

6. Jeffrey T. Kite-Powell, *The Visby (Petri) Organ Tablature: Investigation and Critical Edition* (Wilhelmshaven: Heinrichshofen, 1979), 1:60–79.

7. Krüger, *Die hamburgische Musikorganisation*, 112.

8. Cleveland Johnson, *Vocal Compositions in German Organ Tablatures, 1550–1650: A Catalogue and Commentary*, Outstanding Dissertations in Music from British Universities (New York: Garland, 1989).

establish the mode for what was to follow.[9] While exploring the implications of the mode, it also developed a clear rhetorical structure, often employing the various techniques of fantasia; by the later seventeenth century it had assumed such substantial proportions that it took on a life of its own, apart from its original liturgical function.

The extant repertoire combined with Aepin's liturgical prescriptions gives us a picture of immense richness, in which the organ, together with choir and congregation, weaves a musical tapestry that unites and connects the different elements of the liturgy. In Hamburg the organ played alone, as well as with choirs and professional instrumentalists and with the congregation.[10] Orthodox Lutheranism had focused the broad sensual appeal of Roman Catholic worship almost entirely on music, as we see in Lucas van Cöllen's description of the rededication of St. Gertrude's Chapel in Hamburg in 1607: "I want to recall . . . how this dedication was conducted with singing and preaching, so that anyone could know, even if not present, what kind of ceremonies were used and in what a Christian manner this dedication took place, not in a popish way, with crosses, banners, incense, holy oils, and the like, but with hymns, [musical] instruments, prayers, after the manner of Solomon."[11]

The order of service included chant, hymnody, organ music, and much polychoral music, including the Te Deum of Hieronymus Praetorius for four choirs with instruments. It is clear that the sense of hearing was given rich fare. The lavishness with which the worshiper's ears had such splendor bestowed upon them rivals anything to be found in the contemporary Catholic tradition. The Lutheran understanding of what it means to "hear the word of God" allowed for the possibility of delight in hearing, without which the organ never would have assumed such a position of honor within the church, nor could the choral tradition have continued to develop as it did. The musicians in the church, especially organists, came to be seen as having a role not unlike that of the preacher, and music played upon the organ was scrutinized in a similar way, both for rhetorical procedures and for evangelistic content.

9. See Praetorius, *Syntagma Musicum* 3:25, 151–52.

10. *Melodeyen Gesangbuch, darinn D. Luthers und ander Christen gebreuchlichsten Gesenge, jhren gewöhnlichen Melodeyen nach, durch Hieronymum Praetorium, Joachimum Deckerum, Jacobum Praetorium, Davidem Scheidemannum. Musicos und verordnete Organisten in den vier Caspelkirchen zu Hamburg in vier stimmen ubergesetzt begriffen sindt* (Hamburg: Samuel Rüdinger, 1604), 5.

11. Lucas van Cöllen, *Dedicatio Templi S. Gertrudis Hamburgiensis* (Hamburg, 1609); cited and translated in Frederick Gable, *Dedication Service for St. Gertrude's Chapel, Hamburg, 1607* (Madison: A-R Editions, 1998), viii; CD recording: *Gertrudenmusik Hamburg 1607*, Ulrike Heider and the Göteborg Baroque Arts Ensemble, Intim Musik, IMCD 071.

Jacob Praetorius, Heinrich Scheidemann, and Matthias Weckmann

No surviving keyboard compositions can be ascribed with certainty either to Johann Praetorius or to Ulrich Cernitz, but the large corpus of surviving works of Jacob Praetorius and Heinrich Scheidemann confirms the high regard in which both were held during their lifetimes and well into the next century. Johann Mattheson draws a comparison between both men in his *Grundlage einer Ehren-Pforte* of 1740:

> These two [Praetorius and Scheidemann] were taught by one master, and they had daily contact with each other; the inclinations of their personal temperaments, however, were not at all the same. Praetorius always assumed a quite grave and somewhat odd manner; he took on the refined ways of his teacher; and he loved the highest degree of neatness in everything that he did, as is usual with the Dutch. Scheidemann, on the other hand, was more friendly and genial, he mixed with everyone freely and joyfully, and did not make much of himself. His playing was just that way; nimble with the hand; spirited and cheerful: well grounded in composition; but mostly only as far as [the limits of] the organ would reach. His compositions were easy to play. . . . Praetorius's works were more difficult to play and showed more workmanship, in which he had the advantage above all others. Rist referred to the young Scheidemann alone as the excellent Arion of the city of Hamburg.[12]

Mattheson's biographical sketch of Matthias Weckmann, the organist at St. Jacobi, Hamburg, from 1655 until his death in 1674, further testifies to the contrast between the personal styles of these two men. He mentions that Weckmann "had the good fortune to hear the agreeable Scheidemann at St. Catharine's, and to attend Vespers there, [which] gave him the opportunity to moderate the Praetorian seriousness with a Scheidemannian gracefulness, and therefore to introduce [into his playing] many galant ideas."[13] The "Praetorian seriousness" referred to by Mattheson had been mentioned earlier by Johann Kortkamp in his *Organistenchronik*,[14] a document dating from the early eighteenth century. Writing near the end of his life, Kortkamp recalls how his father, who had studied with Jacob Praetorius, remembered the master:

> Like the preacher, he could awaken and move the hearts of the congregation to prayer; for example, when he played a penitential hymn such as "Erbarm Dich mein o Herre Gott," how devoutly and prayerfully he played, how he knew how to use the registers of the organ with regard to their particular

---

12. Mattheson, *Ehren-Pforte*, 329.

13. Mattheson, *Ehren-Pforte*, 395.

14. Liselotte Krüger, "Johann Kortkamps Organistenchronik, eine Quelle zur hamburgischen Musikgeschichte des 17. Jahrhunderts," *Zeitschrift des Vereins für Hamburgische Geschichte* 33 (1933): 188–213.

character so that one had to admire not only the playing, but also the organ. One cannot describe with what joyfulness he adorned high feast days with his organ playing. My dear father, Jacob Kortkamp, may he rest in peace, also learned from H[err Jacob] Praetorius, as did my own blessed master, Matthias Weckmann, and all throughout my youth advised and recommended that I follow this method.[15]

Kortkamp, the organist for forty-seven years at St. Gertrude's, a chapel of its parent church of St. Jacobi, was very much a part of the St. Jacobi tradition. He took care to portray his beloved teacher, Weckmann, as having carried on the tradition of Praetorius, personally as well as musically. His description of Weckmann's audition for the post of organist at St. Jacobi in 1655 mentions that while Weckmann was waiting for his turn to perform, "he walked around the church listening and praying to God, which was observed by two pious women, who predicted that he would be [the choice], because he reflected such prayerfulness [*Andacht*]."[16]

This anecdote identifies the young Weckmann with the older Praetorius, to show that the mantle of "Praetorian seriousness"—and therefore also the authority to fulfill the liturgical function of organist-as-preacher—was now to be placed upon Weckmann's shoulders, at a time when traditional orthodox ideas concerning organists and organ playing had already been subject to challenge from within more Pietistic circles. Perhaps it was also intended that this role, particularly associated with Jacob Praetorius at St. Petri, was now to be claimed for the organist at St. Jacobi (whose chapel Kortkamp served), rather than for the more worldly Johann Adam Reincken, Scheidemann's successor at St. Catharine's.

The quality of piety to which Kortkamp refers is not simply one of personal bearing; rather, it is manifested in particular ways of performing and of registering the instrument, analogous to the ways in which rhetorical principles governed a pastor's composition and performance of the sermon. Kortkamp gives an indication of these characteristics elsewhere in the *Organistenchronik*, where he refers to his study with Weckmann:

> In those days my father, Jacob Kortkamp, was also a disciple [of Jacob Praetorius along with Weckmann], and these two sons of Jacob were united in brotherly love to the end. I enjoyed the fruit of that love, for my master [Weckmann] loved me as his own child and faithfully instructed me, withheld nothing from me that I was capable of comprehending. . . . When he performed, I stood behind him and drew the stops that he requested. Also, if I wanted to know how Jacob Praetorius played, he would play the chorale, in vespers the Magnificat, on Sundays a psalm, so that I listened with great delight and shed tears

15. Krüger, "Kortkamps Organistenchronik," 199.
16. Krüger, "Kortkamps Organistenchronik," 205.

of joy. Afterward he would explain his thoughts and ideas. By this means he enlightened me.[17]

In moving the hearts of the faithful, the art of registration was perhaps as important as other aspects of performance style. Such praise of Weckmann's expertise in the matter (as with similar contemporary statements about Johann Sebastian Bach) should be understood not so much as a praise of individual artistry, but rather as an indication of the organist's skill as poet and preacher, reflecting his role as the inheritor of a practice handed down from his forebears. It is not surprising, then, that Kortkamp's description of Weckmann's audition at St. Jacobi should include reference to Weckmann's registrations. The following is a summary of Kortkamp's detailed and vivid account:[18]

1. He played a fantasia on the full plenum upon a given fugue, in the first tone, which he mixed with the third tone that was wonderful to follow.
2. He played a work upon a given chorale, "An Wasserflüßen Babylon." Here he used the registration frequently used by Jacob Praetorius at St. Petri, namely (in the Oberwerk), Trommete 8′, Zincke 8′, Nasat 3′, Gemshorn 2′, Hohlfleute 4′; in the Rückpositiv, Principal 8′ and Octave 4′ for the soft and middle parts. In the pedal, Posaune 16′, Principalbass 24′, Trommete 8′ and 4′, Cornet 2′. He first played the chorale simply, so that an ordinary person could understand it, and then treated it fugally through all the transpositions, so that he went through the semitones and it was to be wondered at how he found the original tone again.
3. He displayed his thoroughbass skills by accompanying Johann Schop in a violin solo.
4. He intabulated, from the bass, a motet by Hieronymus Praetorius in six voices, using two manuals.
5. He played a "merry fugue" on the full plenum.[19]

Orthodox and Pietist Views on Church Music

The evolving role and function of the organist as applied in Hamburg may have been well supported by traditional Lutheran thought concerning art music in the church, but the growing influence of Pietistic thought in the seventeenth century did not allow this practice to go unchallenged. In 1661, Theophil Grossgebauer, a theologian at Rostock, published a treatise, *Wächterstimme aus der verwüsteten Zion*, in which he launched an all-out attack on the use of art music in the

---

17. Krüger, "Kortkamps Organistenchronik," 208.
18. For a full translation, see Kerala J. Snyder, *Dieterich Buxtehude: Organist in Lübeck* (New York: Schirmer, 1987), 227.
19. Krüger, "Kortkamps Organistenchronik," 206–8.

church. Grossgebauer, who was influenced by Calvinistic thinking within Lutheranism, believed that the use of organs and other instruments should be limited to the support of the singing of psalms and hymns by the congregation. His attack on organ playing was particularly vituperative: "There sits the organist and plays and shows off his art: in order that one man's art should be displayed, the congregation of JESUS CHRIST sits there and hears the racket of pipes, whereupon the congregation becomes sleepy and indolent: some sleep, some gossip, some look where it is not seemly. . . . Some would gladly pray, but are prevented from doing so as they are so captivated by all the noise and clamor."[20]

Grossgebauer believed that the current practice had abrogated the principles of the Reformation and reflected the habits of a corrupt Catholicism. His belief that the influence of Italian music was becoming more pervasive only confirmed his position that an urgent reform was necessary, through a renewed emphasis upon the spiritual power of congregational singing. This reform would permit musical instruments in the church, but not the artful music that was being made upon them. For Grossgebauer, the problem was not simply the misuse of art music in the church, but rather its presence there in the first place.

As one might expect, Heinrich Scheidemann took considerable offense at this position and sent a copy of the book to his brother-in-law, Hector Mithobius, the pastor at Otterndorf, inducing him to write a response. Mithobius's *Psalmodia Christiana*, perhaps the fullest exposition of an orthodox Lutheran position on church music in the seventeenth century, appeared in 1665.[21]

Mithobius drew upon the writings of earlier Lutheran theologians, particularly Conrad Dannhauer and Conrad Dieterich, who earlier in the century had sought to develop a theological basis for the use of church music. Mithobius's concern was not to construct a defense on aesthetic grounds, but to articulate a theological position that supported the development and use of art music. In doing so, he was careful to distinguish his position from a "papist" one and echoed the position of Lucas van Cöllen, referred to above, which is not papist but nonetheless rather broadly catholic in affirming the goodness of creation and the created. Mithobius held to the traditional view of music as *adiaphora*, things neither required nor forbidden by Scripture, but which one is free to use; according to this view, organ music can be said to represent freedom from the strictures of Old Testament law and from papist ceremonial. He adopted a classically orthodox Lutheran position in appealing to Scripture as a justification for

20. Quoted in Arnfried Edler, *Der nordelbische Organist: Studien zu Sozialstatus, Funktion und kompositorischer Produktion eines Musikberufes von der Reformation bis zum 20. Jahrhundert*, Kieler Schriften zur Musikwissenschaft, vol. 23 (Kassel: Bärenreiter, 1982), 42.

21. For a detailed discussion of this controversy, see Christian Bunners, *Kirchenmusik und Seelenmusik: Studien zu Frömmigkeit und Musik im Luthertum des 17. Jahrhunderts* (Göttingen: Vandenhoeck & Ruprecht, 1966).

current musical practice, particularly with regard to the use of instruments. Mithobius used Scripture to support a theocentric spirituality in which humanity is obligated to praise God using the gifts of creation.

Mithobius's thinking ventured beyond the concept of music as *adiaphora*, however; if music, as one of the gifts of God's creation, was to be used in the praise of God, then the use of the musician's highest skills was also to be seen as rightfully belonging to the realm of praise,[22] making composition and performance of art music an inevitable expression of piety rather than merely a secular endeavor. For a traditional Lutheran, the kind of music played by Scheidemann and his contemporaries functioned as a mark of a faithful church, and the development of high levels of musical skill was an expression of piety. This theological-cosmological function of music is no less important than the practical-liturgical and the devotional functions; an appropriate understanding of the development of the organist's art must take into account all these functions.[23] The ability of music to move the soul to devotion, important to both Pietist and orthodox, was nonetheless dependent upon skill, the development and expression of which was supported by orthodox thinking but held in suspicion within some Pietist circles.

The Compositional Process of the Hamburg Organists

So far I have focused upon the various ways in which organ playing functioned in Hamburg's culture; in order to understand these functions more fully it is necessary to consider the relationship between composition and performance, and the interaction between composing music on paper and improvising it. Here it is easy to get bogged down in conceptual frameworks more appropriate to music of later times.

The compositional process by which this repertoire was created was more multifaceted than we commonly imagine today. The act of creating a piece of music, particularly within the keyboard tradition, was not simply a matter of writing it and then performing it. Written composition was one aspect of how a work could be created, but the hallmark of the organist's art was the ability to create a composition in his mind, *a mente*, while performing it. We call this "improvisation" today, and that is not a bad term to describe what the organists of Hamburg did when they played the organ, as long as we can rid ourselves of two modern notions about what the word means when applied to organ playing in seventeenth-century North Germany. The first of these is the belief that their improvised music making was totally spontaneous, without preparation; the second is the idea that improvisational "style" is somehow different from what is

22. See Joyce L. Irwin, *Neither Voice nor Heart Alone: German Lutheran Theology in the Age of the Baroque* (New York: Peter Lang, 1993), 89–90.

23. Bunners, *Kirchenmusik*, 15.

preserved in the written repertoire. These two assumptions are related and can easily cause misunderstanding about the relationship of performance to composition that characterized this tradition.

We may assume that *a mente* performance constituted the normal activity of the organist in the liturgy. If we look at how an organist was trained, however, as opposed to simply what he did, we see that improvisation as such was not a special field of study. An organist studied composition; this, in addition to the study of technical aspects of performance, appears to have been the primary emphasis, for instance, in the pedagogy of Sweelinck.[24] It was in the context of these compositional studies that the Hamburg organists learned the art of quasi-spontaneous music making. The term "quasi-spontaneous" is appropriate here because the idea that improvisation was an art that produced totally "free" music making without respect for conventions of genre and style was utterly foreign to the thinking of the time. Rather, the organist's training enabled him to compose in performance the same kind of music that we find preserved in the repertoire. There is no evidence to suggest that the improvised music produced was in any substantive way different from the surviving repertoire; there is some evidence, however, that there was a close correspondence between music composed in performance and music written down. Throughout the repertoire there are recognizable patterns of the improviser's art; chief among these patterns are those of fantasia, diminution practice, and thoroughbass.

Although the seventeenth century saw the rise of a new, monodic organ style, the ability to craft counterpoint at the keyboard remained central to the organist's art. The "merry fugue" improvised by Weckmann during his audition at Hamburg's St. Jacobi was the result of a long tradition of improvising keyboard polyphony, and we can find some indications from earlier sources that illuminate how this skill could have been learned. No treatise on improvisation in the Hamburg circle from this time is extant. However, Sweelinck's own rules for composition survive and were circulated as theory manuscripts among the Hamburg organists well into the seventeenth century.[25] Drawing heavily upon Zarlino's *Insitutioni Harmoniche* (1573 edition), Sweelinck's composition rules are essentially instructions in the art of counterpoint in the learned tradition and as such formed the basis for the development of compositional skill. A closer look, however, reveals that while they would have served as the basis for learning com-

24. For information on Sweelinck's performance pedagogy see William Porter, "Sweelinck's Fingering?" *Courant* 1 (1983): 34–36; and Harald Vogel, "Zur Spielweise der Musik für Tasteninstrumente um 1600," in Samuel Scheidt, *Tabulatura Nova*, ed. Harald Vogel, vol. 2 (Wiesbaden: Breitkopf und Härtel, 1999), 145–180.

25. See Hermann Gehrmann, ed., *Werken van Jan Pieterszoon Sweelinck*, vol. 10, *Die Compositions-Regeln* (Leipzig: Breitkopf und Härtel, 1901); and Paul Walker, "From Renaissance 'Fuga' to Baroque Fugue: The Role of the 'Sweelinck Theory Manuscripts,'" *Schütz-Jahrbuch* 7–8 (1985–86): 93–104. See also Paul Mark Walker, *Theories of Fugue from the Age of Josquin to the Age of Bach* (Rochester: University of Rochester Press, 2000).

Example 5-1. Tomas de Santa María, "Fuga a tres vozes," from *Libro llamado: Arte de tañer fantasia*, f. 68, mm. 13–24

position, the repertoire of Sweelinck, his students, and their immediate successors reflects an approach to the crafting of keyboard polyphony that is to a large extent missing from these treatises. The approach in the repertoire involves the practice of improvised counterpoint (*contrapunto alla mente*), which is documented in Renaissance sources, and although relevant passages from Zarlino were included in the composition rules, one must look elsewhere for a clear description of the practice, since the rules themselves deal largely with strict written counterpoint. This is perhaps not surprising in view of the fact that skill in the crafting of strict counterpoint was considered to be a prerequisite to learning how to improvise keyboard polyphony.

The particular qualities of keyboard polyphony practiced by Sweelinck and passed on to his students reflect the concept of fantasia; this involves the use of short patterns of contrapuntal movement, often used sequentially, which could be variously embellished.[26] The most extensive discussion of fantasia is to be found in Tomas de Santa María's *Libro llamado: Arte de tañer fantasia* of 1565.[27] Here the aspiring keyboardist is systematically instructed in the art of improvised keyboard polyphony, and the elements of compositional technique described in the treatise can be clearly seen in the works of Sweelinck and the Hamburg organists.[28] The following example, found in Santa María's chapter on forming imitations,[29] shows a portion of a canon that is entirely constituted by one of the common patterns of sequential imitation, alternating descending fourths and ascending thirds, at the level of the semibreve (example 5-1).

26. See Pieter Dirksen, *The Keyboard Music of Jan Pieterszoon Sweelinck* (Utrecht: Koninklijke Vereniging voor Muziekgeschiedenis, 1997), 329; and Gregory Butler, "The Fantasia as Musical Image," *Musical Quarterly* 60 (1974): 602–15.

27. Thomas de Santa María, *Arte de tañer fantasía* (1565; facsimile reprint, ed. Rudesindo F. Soutelo, Madrid: Arte Tripharia, 1982). See also Fray Thomas de Sancta María, *The Art of Playing the Fantasia 1565*, trans. Almonte C. Howell Jr. and Warren E. Hultberg (Pittsburgh: Latin American Literary Review Press, 1991).

28. For a discussion of the relevance of Santa María's treatise to the keyboard works of Sweelinck, see Dirksen, *Sweelinck*, 521 ff.

29. Santa María, *The Art of Playing the Fantasia*, 220.

Example 5-2. Jan Pieterszoon Sweelinck, Fantasia in g, mm. 20–26

Example 5-3. Heinrich Scheidemann, Praeambulum in d (WV 33), mm. 28–31

An interesting link between contrapuntal patterns found in the pedagogically oriented examples given by Santa María and their incorporation into the larger-scaled works of Sweelinck and the Hamburg pupils can be observed in Swee-linck's Fantasia in g.[30] This unusual piece, in two voices, is virtually a little compendium of the most common patterns of sequential imitation discussed by Santa María, each following in rapid succession in the compact space of only forty-four measures; example 5-2 shows the pattern of descending fourths and ascending thirds. Such patterns permeate Sweelinck's other keyboard works in a less compressed manner, particularly the fantasias and toccatas. In the fantasias they are used most often either as counterpoint to a subject or in passages where a subject is not present. In the toccatas the patterns are found primarily as a contrapuntal frame for brilliant passagework.

The techniques of fantasia were not limited to polyphonic textures. Especially in the praeludium, with its increasing use of highly declamatory and dialoguelike passages, patterns of sequential imitation play an important role; the same patterns that produced a flowing polyphony during the time of Sweelinck were now adapted to modern tastes. Example 5-3 shows how a sequential pattern that appears in a polyphonic work may generate a quite different kind of music in a praeludium, in this case a praeambulum by Scheidemann.

The term "generating principle" denotes this simple pattern of descending fourths and ascending thirds in one voice imitated canonically in another. It is the "internalized" pattern that can be used to generate a passage of music in a variety of outward manifestations. This pattern of sequential imitation, and others like it, is part of the essence of *fantasia* in the sixteenth and seventeenth cen-

30. Jan Pieterszoon, Sweelinck, *Opera Omnia*, 2d rev. ed., fasc. 1, ed. Gustav Leonhardt (Amsterdam: Vereniging voor Nederlandse Muziekgeschiedenis, 1974), 68.

turies, but is by no means limited to the genre called "fantasia," as we have just seen. It is of course found in all kinds of vocal and instrumental music, but it was a technique specially cultivated in keyboard composition because of the way it lends itself to the practice of music composed in performance. But the generating principles of *fantasia* were not the only ones used by the Hamburg organists and their colleagues throughout Europe. A generating principle is any simple procedure or pattern that can be internalized by the performer to produce a variety of realizations, *a mente*. For example, the development of thoroughbass provided an important generating principle for creating music: the harmonic bass. Every organist was expected to know how to create at sight a coherent musical texture from a bass progression; in addition to being a fundamental skill for accompaniment, it provided the principle for creating the exordium for a *praeambulum* or *praeludium*. The bass progressions themselves are remarkably similar from one piece to another, but their realization shows considerable variety, often with the use of various *figurae* to animate the texture. Similarly, the way in which chorale melodies are harmonized increasingly shows a tendency toward the expression of thoroughbass practice. Likewise, the practice of diminution, through which keyboard intabulations of vocal models are crafted, is present in virtually every genre in the extant repertoire, from secular song variation to Magnificat *fantasia*.

Such generating principles tend to be formulaic in nature and include characteristic melodic patterns and gestures, contrapuntal relationships and movements, and procedures for developing a whole musical texture from just one element of it (as in the harmonic bass). The important thing is that a given generating principle can be realized in a variety of ways, in varying degrees of complexity. Frequently more than one generating principle may be operative at any given moment: while the principle of the cadence pattern may generate the end of a praeludium, a cadence pattern combined with an echo principle generates the internal sections of many such pieces. In the seventeenth century, generating principles such as echo, cadence patterns, suspension chains, and parallel sixth chords took their place along with fantasia and other older principles, such as *fuga* and the art of diminution, as essential parts of the composer-organist's compositional vocabulary.

Written composition, for the Hamburg organists, drew upon patterns of musical craftsmanship that can be shown to have their roots in composition-in-performance, a term that is now associated with studies of oral and written transmission within certain traditions of poetry. This is perhaps a better term than "improvisation," as it takes account of the close relationship between creation through writing and creation through performing that characterized the tradition, and it avoids some of the common misconceptions held today about improvisation as an essentially different kind of activity from composing. That there can be a close correlation between written and oral composition of poetry from a given period is no longer considered impossible, largely because of the work of Milman Parry and Albert Lord.[31] Their pioneering study of oral transmission of south Slavic epic poetry was instrumental in the formation of a theory of how Homeric poetry was created and has led to a new perspective about the close relationship that can exist between written and oral poetry from a given tradition. Parry and Lord's concept of "formula,"[32] while conceived with reference to epic poetry, has nonetheless stimulated analogous approaches, with varying degrees of success, to the study of certain musical traditions, particularly Western chant,[33] jazz,[34] and certain kinds of popular music.[35]

For the North German keyboard tradition one can regard the generating principles of *a mente* performance described earlier as general—but not absolute— parallels to the Parry-Lord concept of formula. The pervasive presence of such principles as basic elements of the written repertoire's vocabulary points to the repertoire's being a reliable reflection of what composition-in-performance was like at this time. Did they write an improvised work down exactly as they had played it? Perhaps the most one can say is that what we see written down is largely material that can be documented as belonging to the sphere of *a mente* music making, material that is not limited to a particular genre but is found throughout the keyboard repertoire, albeit realized in different ways.

The Hamburg organists of the seventeenth century may thus be viewed as belonging to a tradition of composition that links them with other traditions in which a close correlation between oral (composed in performance) and written practice exist.[36] For the tradition of the North German organists, the written work can serve as a means of transmission between performances, and even as a means of "practicing" for performance. At the same time, the grounding of composition in principles of internalized formula allows for each performance to be, to some extent, an original creation. Viewed from this perspective, the complexity of the written work, far from arguing against a close correspondence between the written work and the work composed in performance, rather argues for the high level of artistry of the performing composer.

31. See Albert Lord, *The Singer of Tales* (Cambridge: Harvard University Press, 1964), 13–39.

32. For a discussion of the concept of formula in such traditions and a summary of Parry and Lord's earlier work, see Albert Lord, *Epic Singers and Oral Tradition* (Ithaca, N.Y.: Cornell University Press, 1991), 6–7, 25–27, 76–77.

33. Leo Treitler, "Homer and Gregory: The Transmission of Epic Poetry and Plainchant," *Musical Quarterly* 60 (1974): 333–72; and Peter Jeffery, *Re-Envisioning Past Musical Cultures: Ethnomusicology in the Study of Gregorian Chant* (Chicago: University of Chicago Press, 1992).

34. Gregory Eugene Smith, "Homer, Gregory, and Bill Evans? The Theory of Formulaic Composition in the Context of Jazz Piano Improvisation" (Ph.D. diss., Harvard University, 1983).

35. Lars Lilliestam, "On Playing by Ear," *Popular Music* 15 (1996): 195–216.

36. See Gregory Nagy, *Poetry as Performance* (Cambridge: Cambridge University Press, 1996), 7–38.

Part of the genius reflected in the North German repertoire of this time is that the same generating principles could be used to create music that was either highly complex or quite simple. The often complex and deep works of such luminaries as Scheidemann, Jacob Praetorius, Reincken, and Weckmann were simply the most sophisticated expressions of a musical language that allowed more modest musicians to create music of fine craftsmanship that, like the works of their more famous counterparts, illuminated the kaleidoscopic qualities of the organs of the time.

It is well to keep in mind that the organist, like the poet, "sang his own song," however traditional the components of the song were required to be. Unlike the liturgical singer of the seventeenth century, the organist's art in performance was not simply embellishment but the creation of a whole work. The emerging concept of *musica poetica*, with its emphasis on the rhetorical dimension of performance and of composition, required, among other things, that a musical performance have the power to persuade and move the listener. The ability to communicate the sense of a musical text through figure and embellishment that was required of singers also formed part of the organist's skill. The difference between the singer (and ordinary instrumentalist) and the organist was not only that, for the organist, such embellishment was part of the compositional practice as well, but also that, unlike the singer, the organist created his own "text," albeit within the strictures of ritual practice. The only other person in the Lutheran liturgy who was entrusted with composing a text and "performing" it with a view toward persuasion of the listener was the preacher.

It is therefore not surprising that the organist should begin to take on certain aspects of the role of the preacher in the Lutheran service. Mithobius's direct reply to one of Grossgebauer's sharpest remarks (quoted above) reflects this role:

> The organist is not sitting up there just to show off his Art but rather to praise God artfully with a lovely harmony, and to move himself as well, but primarily the whole congregation, into "the rest of God," to a passionate devotion, to spiritual thoughts, and to joy in the Lord. By this he should awaken the spirit of the congregation and make them attentive, joyful and willing to join in the service.[37]

The fulfillment of this role is to be seen particularly in the development of what is usually now called the "chorale fantasia," beginning with Scheidemann. In this large-scale genre the organist brings the vocabulary of generating principles, including fantasia, to the chorale itself to serve the purpose of making music that is, in the words of Mithobius, "a beautiful intonation moving the heart to

---

37. Mithobius, translated and quoted in Hans Davidsson, *Matthias Weckmann: The Interpretation of his Organ Music*, Skrifter från Musikvetenskapliga Institutionen, vol. 22 (Göteborg: Gehrmans Musikförlag, 1991), 17

the praise of God."[38] In the case of Scheidemann, this meant primarily a synthesis of techniques of fantasia and intabulation. By the second half of the seventeenth century, it meant—to organists such as Buxtehude, Weckmann, and Bruhns—sensitivity as well to the portrayal of text through *figurae* and an expansion of the techniques by which this could be accomplished. Buxtehude's *Nun freut euch, lieben Christen g'mein* (BuxWV 210; CD track 7), for example, uses gigue rhythms to accompany a joyful text and chromaticism to invoke the pain of Christ on the cross. This new approach included not only the generating principles of composition-in-performance, but also—especially in the case of Weckmann—the incorporation of a theological perspective expressed in number and symbol.[39] In the chorale-based music of Weckmann we find the limits of composition-in-performance being reached as older principles of keyboard improvisation give way to ones based upon proportional, cosmological, and theological considerations. Out of this a new kind of music emerged, a different genre altogether from the chorale fantasia of Scheidemann's time. With Weckmann, the role of organist as preacher may be fully realized, but the analogy of the organist as oral poet begins to break down in the face of additional compositional considerations that no longer reflect the principles of composition-in-performance seen in the earlier part of the century. The older tradition continues more fully in the "free works": praeludia, toccatas, and canzonas.

It is ironic that by the time the "preaching" function of organ music reached its peak, the traditional theological underpinnings of the art, which had been derived from Luther himself, were increasingly coming under attack from the Pietists. We have seen how Grossgebauer's tract was received by those loyal to an orthodox view of music's role in the church; what is clear from the interchange is that not only art music was under attack, but also its supporting theological framework. While some composers, such as Weckmann, were able to some extent to adapt to these new currents, the influence of pietistic thinking was one factor that contributed to the weakening of the role of the organist in Hamburg in the succeeding generations.

The image of the nightingale, which figures so prominently in the troubador and classical traditions, also has its place in the tradition of the Hamburg organists. In the troubador repertoire the nightingale frequently represents the poet himself as he "moves" his song.[40] The poet Johann Rist, a friend of Scheidemann's, was among those who held that music had its origins in the songs of birds, especially that of the nightingale. Grossgebauer characterizes the singing of art music as "an ambitious howling, [to see] which of the birds can sing the

---

38. Mithobius, quoted in Bunners, *Kirchenmusik*, 109–10.

39. Davidsson, *Weckmann*, 87–89, 105–9.

40. Nagy, *Poetry*, 15–17.

best." There is poignancy to Mithobius's refutation of Grossgebauer when one thinks of the Hamburg organists as latter-day nightingales and, like their predecessors, masters of composition-in-performance. Mithobius writes that one can "not only imitate, but rather surpass the nightingale; and this is praiseworthy and not to be condemned, . . . for we can learn something of value from the birds."[41]

One reason for the prominence of the nightingale in various poetic and musical traditions has to do with the belief that the nightingale never sings its song exactly the same way twice; the processes of composition-in-performance work against a work's absolute fixity. How remarkable that one of the supreme nightingales of his tradition, Matthias Weckmann, should have introduced compositional principles in works such as *Es ist das Heil uns kommen her* (CD track 13) and *O lux beata Trinitas* that move the tradition in the direction of a greater tendency toward fixity. While making music *a mente* did not die out in the succeeding generations, it gradually came to represent a particular kind of music making, distinct from composition in general, so that an independent "improvisational style" emerged in the eighteenth century.

This stylistic change can be observed in the works of the last great exponent of the Hamburg school, Vincent Lübeck, organist at St. Nicolai from 1702 until his death in 1740. Lübeck presided over the largest organ built by Arp Schnitger, a four-manual organ of 67 stops, dedicated in 1687. His only chorale fantasia, *Ich ruf zu dir, Herr Jesu Christ*, cannot in any way be characterized as a late expression of the role of organist as preacher, although the overall character of the piece is not antithetical to the sense of the text. Here Lübeck draws instead upon the keyboard suite as a basis for casting the different sections in the style of various dance types, in alternation with fugato and echo passages. In this respect he looks not to Weckmann the contrapuntalist and preacher, but rather to Weckmann's friend Froberger, the *claveciniste*, as a model for compositional procedure. Lübeck's own musical formation lay somewhat outside the orthodox Hamburg tradition, and he worked—with great success—in a climate increasingly indifferent to its cultivation.

The monumental organ that Arp Schnitger built for Hamburg's St. Jacobi Church was completed in the twilight years of the great tradition of composition-in-performance, enjoyed in that city through the organ playing of Sweelinck's students and their immediate successors. One wonders to what degree the traditional preaching and theological functions of organ playing in Hamburg would have been further shaped had the position of organist there been awarded to Johann Sebastian Bach in 1720. Bach's journey to Hamburg in connection with this matter was also the occasion of the famous concert at St. Catharine's. It is recorded in Bach's obituary that during this concert he played an extended im-

---

41. Bunners, *Kirchenmusik*, 110.

provisation on the chorale *An Wasserflüssen Babylon*, following the manner and practice of the Hamburg organists of the seventeenth century in their perform-ances at the Saturday vespers.[42] Reincken's response is well known: "I thought that this art was dead, but I see that in you it still lives." The reference to the vesper tradition in this context is significant, because it suggests that Reincken was referring not simply to the art of improvisation, which was by no means dead in Hamburg in 1720, but rather to the way in which Bach's particular manner of playing reflected the traditional functions of the art of the Hamburg organists. Would Bach's continued presence in Hamburg have contributed to a revival of the tradition? Or had the sociological and theological shifts of the previous generation been so great that, despite the rich musical culture that Hamburg continued to enjoy, they precluded any further development of the tradition, even at the hands of Bach?

---

42. English translation in *The New Bach Reader: A Life of Johann Sebastian Bach in Letters and Documents*, ed. Hans T. David and Arthur Mendel, rev. Christoph Wolff (New York: W. W. Norton, 1998), 302.

6

THE ORGAN IN SEVENTEENTH-CENTURY COSMOLOGY

HANS DAVIDSSON

AT THE BEGINNING OF THE SEVENTEENTH CENTURY, THE IDEA THAT THE UNIVERSE worked like a clockwork machine pervaded society. In 1611, when Hieronymus Praetorius was teaching on the recently restored organ in St. Jacobi and Esaias Compenius had just finished the organ that now stands in Frederiksborg Castle, a contemporary Scandinavian scientist, Sigfrid Aronus Forsius, wrote in his encyclopedic work *Physica*:

> As the almighty creator has made and ordered everything wisely, so has he truly wondrously arranged the orbits of the heavens and the stars, like an artful clock work, where one of the gears touches and drives the others and this all with great skillfulness, perfection, harmony, and congruence. Like an artful Organ work or a stringed instrument, where the one pipe or string coincides in hidden voices with the other, and makes a lively melody and Consonance of thirds fifths octaves etc.: In this way there is also a lively Harmony and Consonance between the heaven and its planets. For that reason the Pythagoreans and Platonists have wondrously said that heavens' circles several orbits should make a sweet and lively sound among them.[1]

This clockwork universe was almost universally called the macrocosm. It encompassed everything outside the human experience, including the planets and the stars and the angels, and it surrounded and penetrated the human world, the microcosm. Hovering over both was the unseeable and incalculable presence of God.

The Harmony of the Planets: Kepler and Kircher

At this same time, Johannes Kepler (1571–1630), imperial mathematician to Emperor Rudolph II at his court in Prague, was making great strides in under-

---

1. Sigfrid Aronus Forsius, "Physica 1611" (cod. Holm. D 76), ed. Johan Nordstrom, *Uppsala universitets årsskrift 1952*, no. 10 (Uppsala: Lundequistska bokhandeln, 1952), 88.

standing how the planets actually move. He delayed the publication of his *Harmonice Mundi* (The Harmony of the World) from 1599 to 1618 because in the interim it became clear to him that Mars was moving not in a perfect circle but in an ellipse, and this changed everything.[2] The elliptical orbits of the planets meant that the ancient Greek idea of the harmony of the spheres needed to be completely rethought. Each planet produced a range of speeds depending on whether it was at its perihelion (the point of the orbit closest to the sun) or its aphelion (the point farthest from the sun). The range between these two points for each planet was expressed by Kepler as a proportion, and each proportion could be represented by a common musical interval. For instance, if you were standing on the sun and timing Saturn, it would seem to move at a rate of one minute and forty-six seconds a day across the sky at its aphelion, but at two minutes and fifteen seconds a day across the sky at its perihelion. This range of movement is in a relationship of 4:5, so Kepler considered the orbit of Saturn capable of expressing that motion as musical tones over an interval of a major third.[3] Taken together, the planets could create consonant chords with each other, but only at certain times in history, and then only for a brief moment of alignment.[4] Kepler's view of the harmony of the spheres was revolutionary because it created a system that was polyphonic and affirmed the contemporary view of thirds and sixths as consonances rather than dissonances, as they were in the old Pythagorean system.[5] Contemporary polyphonic music could thus be understood as an imitation of the celestial harmony:

> Therefore, the motions of the heavens are nothing but a kind of perennial harmony (in thought not in sound) through dissonant tunings, like certain syncopations or cadences (by which men imitate those natural dissonances) and tending towards definite and prescribed resolutions, individual to the six terms (as with vocal parts) and marking and distinguishing by those notes the immensity of time. Thus it is no longer surprising that Man, aping his Creator, has at last found a method of singing in harmony which was unknown to the ancients, so that he might play, that is to say, the perpetuity of the whole of cosmic time in some brief fraction of an hour, by the artificial concert of several voices, and taste up to a point the satisfaction of God his Maker in His works by a most delightful sense of pleasure felt in this imitator of God, Music.[6]

2. Johannes Kepler, *The Harmony of the World*, trans. E. J. Aiton, A. M. Duncan, and J. V. Field (Philadelphia: American Philosophical Society, 1997), vii.

3. Kepler, *Harmony*, 424. The term *minute* is used here as a measurement of distance: 1/60 of a degree of an arc.

4. Willie Ruff and John Rodgers have produced a compact disc containing a computer-generated realization of Kepler's data, titled *The Harmony of the World: A Realization for the Ear of Johannes Kepler's Data from Harmonices Mundi 1619* ([Branford, Conn.]: Kepler, 2000).

5. D. P. Walker, "Kepler's Celestial Music," *Journal of the Warburg and Courtauld Institutes* 30 (1967): 235.

6. Kepler, *Harmony*, 447–48.

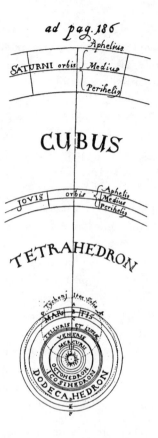

Figure 6-1. The elliptical orbits of the planets, as illustrated in Johannes Kepler, *Harmonices mundi libri V* (1619), p. 186.

This idea of cosmic harmony was applied by many authors to the study of music, among them the Jesuit writer Athanasius Kircher. The remarkable life of this polymath spans almost the entire seventeenth century. Born in Germany in 1600 or 1601, he had a remarkably long and productive active career as a Jesuit scholar in Rome, a career that produced thirty-two books in forty-six years before his death in 1680. One of his best-known works, the thousand-page *Musurgia Universalis*, published in Latin in 1650,[7] was disseminated in Germany more widely than usual for such a work because of a partial translation into German by the Lutheran pastor Andreas Hirsch, in 1662.[8] Kircher presented Kepler's theory of the elliptical orbits of the planets and included tables and diagrams taken directly from *Harmonice Mundi*; figure 6-1 shows Kepler's original illustration of the orbits of the planets and figure 6-2 Kircher's replication of it. Kepler's system is clearly heliocentric, and on the facing page he writes that "readers

7. Athanasius Kircher, *Musurgia Universalis sive Ars Magna Consoni et Dissoni* (1650; facsimile reprint, ed. Ulf Scharlau, Hildesheim: Olms, 1970).

8. Athanasius Kircher, *Musurgia Universalis*, abbreviated German translation by Andreas Hirsch (1662; facsimile reprint, ed. Wolfgang Goldhan, Kassel: Bärenreiter, 1988).

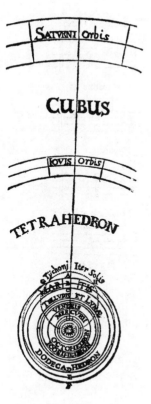

Figure 6-2. Copy of Kepler's illustration in Athanasius Kircher, *Musurgia universalis* (1650), Book II, p. 376.

should take it as absolutely settled today among all astronomers that all the planets go around the Sun, with the exception of the moon, which alone has the Earth as its center." As a Jesuit writing in Rome so soon after Galileo had been forced in 1633 to recant his heliocentric views, Kircher could not accept Kepler's theory. The German version sums up Kircher's position succinctly: "This is certain: all heavenly bodies were created for the sake of the earth as the center, which the divine Majesty itself has walked with human feet."[9]

Kepler's harmonies of all the planets, which he computed both in cantus durus (with B♮) and cantus mollis (with B♭), extend from bass G for Saturn upward to Mercury, more than six octaves above middle C, in the order of the solar system.[10] In adapting these to the ranges of human voices for the "artificial concert of several voices," he kept this order, so that Mercury became the soprano, Earth and Venus the alto, Mars the tenor, and Saturn and Jupiter the bass. He even found analogies between the eccentricities of the planets and the character of these vocal parts: "And as the bass makes harmonic leaps, so Saturn and Jupiter

9. Kircher, *Musurgia* (1662), 276.
10. Kepler, *Harmony*, 444–45.

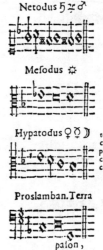

Figure 6-3. Athanasius Kircher's harmony of the planets, in *Musurgia universalis* (1650), Book II, p. 383. (Tenor clef is misplaced.)

cover harmonic intervals. . . . And as the treble is most free, more than all the rest, and the same is also the fastest, so also Mercury can range over more than a diapason and back again very quickly."[11]

Kircher developed his own system for adapting the harmony of the planets to human vocal polyphony. In tune with his geocentric worldview, the earth functions as the bass, the *proslambanomenos*, the lowest pitch in the ancient Greek system of music theory. He orders the traditional seven planets above it, with the soprano and tenor each consisting of groups of three alternating consonant and dissonant planets and the sun between them in the alto, which "directs the other planets, making them lively and sounding with its rays." The dissonant planets Saturn and Mars are mediated in the soprano by the consonant Jupiter; likewise, dissonant Mercury comes between consonant Venus and Moon in the tenor: "So it is with the grim planets Saturn and Mars; what evil would they cause in the lower world with their poisonous cooperation, if the good Jupiter did not stand between them, conciliate, and temper them; what are Mars and Saturn other than dissonances?"[12] The musical example that he offers (figure 6-3, example 6-1) indeed consists of an alternation of consonances and suspended dissonances.

The Organ as Allegory

Kircher's discussion of celestial harmony is embedded in a much larger framework that occupies all of book ten of *Musurgia Universalis*. It is subtitled *Orga-*

11. Kepler, *Harmony*, 450.
12. Kircher, *Musurgia* (1650), 383; Kircher, *Musurgia* (1662), 272.

Example 6-1. Athanasius Kircher's harmony of the planets, in *Musurgia Universalis* (1650), Book 2, p. 383

num Decaulon, in reference to an organ of ten registers, each of which corresponds to some portion of the macrocosm or microcosm. The first chapter describes how "God is compared to the greatest of organists and the world to an organ" (see chapter 1). The allegorical organ that Kircher depicts here (figure 1-1) has six registers, one for each day of creation, and is thus not the same as the other "world organ" that provides the structure for book ten (or book six in the German edition), where it is shown that "nature and the whole world are nothing other than a perfect music and musical harmony." The ten registers of this world organ extend from the symphony of the four elements as the first to the music of God as the tenth; the second, the symphony of the heavens, includes the discussion of Kepler and the music of the planets. Of particular interest is the fourth register, "Symphonicus microcosmi cum Megacosmo, sive de Musica humana," in which he speaks of the proportions of the human body; registers five and six belong to the microcosm as well, as they concern the rhythm of the human body and the symphony of human affects. Kircher's use of the organ as an allegorical tool must have been rooted in his respect for the actual instrument. Earlier in *Musurgia*, in his discussion of musical instruments, he had written: "The organ is the most perfect of all the pneumatic instruments, the *compendium* and the *epitome*, the most beautiful and most perfect. . . . Who will deny that the art of organ building has been brought in our time to its pinnacle of perfection?"[13]

Numerous literary examples show the symbolic meaning that was firmly encoded for the organ in society. It was something larger than life—certainly it was physically larger than human scale—and its ornamentation and proportions were meant to be appreciated, like a theatrical stage set, from a great distance. The organ was also capable of inspiring awe and reverence. These instruments represented the highest level of music, art, science, technology, and craft of their time.

The Hamburg organs were, of course, also important symbols of the prosperity and power of the free Hanseatic cities, but they too were symbols of the presence of the macrocosm in the daily life of their citizens. They were a symbol of the congregation and of Christian life as a whole, and even creation itself, all of

13. Kircher, *Musurgia* (1662), 115, 135.

which can be seen in their allegorical use as a subject for sermons and other writings of the period. We find organ allegories, for example, in a sermon preached in 1662 by Johann Münstermann, the Lutheran superintendent of Hadeln:

> We may make ourselves into living, spiritual, sensible, and steadfast organs: Our body shall be the Corpus of such an organ, our mouth shall be its pipes and our tongue the little tongue of the pipe; the breath or wind that is blown into it shall be the word of God; the keyboard and pedal of this our spiritual organ shall be our heart; its stops shall be the affections and desires of the emotions of our heart; the organist is the Holy Spirit, who is there with his sevenfold gifts, and the finger in God's right hand . . . shall play the keyboard of our heart with his godly and powerful fingers.[14]

Such writings, in which the instrumentalist is likened to an image of the Heavenly Organist, must have provided an inspiring metaphor for church organists of the time. Indeed, the organist's role within the service was often larger than it is today. Between the two musical pillars of the prelude and the postlude, the organist frequently played solo variations in alternation with the choir and provided short intonations before chanted parts of the liturgy and interludes to mark musically otherwise silent liturgical movements. When the choir was not present, the organist replaced it entirely with intabulated motets. The organ thus continued to take the role of the heavenly commentary in a dialogue with the human act of the liturgy (see chapter 5).

The intention during this period was not to showcase the organist as a performer but to create the illusion that the organ was playing itself. The organist was hidden behind the ornamented façade of the Rückpositiv, completing the illusion that the instrument spoke in the allegorical voice of the Creator himself. It played solo pieces that polyphonically surrounded and elaborated the plainchant melody notes in extremely long note values. Using his art in registration, the organist made the solo notes, the cantus firmus, shine out from the polyphonic texture. He played with his hands on different keyboards and often played the cantus firmus with his feet, using, for example, a solo trumpet stop in the pedal. The style of these compositions set into motion tenors and countertenors and also quicker divisions, circling around one another like planets at stately predetermined speeds in proportional relationships, reflecting in music the turning gears of Forsius's clockwork universe.

14. Quoted in Arnfried Edler, *Der nordelbische Organist: Studien zu Sozialstatus, Funktion und kompositorischer Produktion eines Musikberufes von der Reformation bis zum 20. Jahrhundert*, Kieler Schriften zur Musikwissenschaft, vol. 23 (Kassel: Bärentreiter, 1982), 357. See also Christian Bunners, *Kirchenmusik und Seelenmusik: Studien zu Frömmigkeit und Musik im Luthertum des 17. Jahrhunderts* (Göttingen: Vandenhoeck and Ruprecht, 1966).

The Organ in St. Jacobi, Hamburg

The organ in St. Jacobi represents the macrocosmic extreme, based as it is on the older medieval tradition of the Blockwerk organ, in which cylindrical pipes representing all the harmonics of the overtone series play simultaneously, producing a plenum of principals and mixtures that could not be separated. Although as early as 1611 the Hamburg instrument was musically much more flexible than the Blockwerk organ, with a multitude of varying solo and contrasting choir sounds, the organ was still capable of creating the majestic power of the full plenum sound that listeners would have associated with the image of the heavenly choirs (cf. CD track 13). The organ is placed in the largest space of the community, a building that somehow attempts to grab an earthly image of heaven and freeze it in architectural proportions. These proportions are made manifest by the sounding music of the organ. The organ, placed above the west entrance, functions also figuratively as a musical port into this space, leading from the time of everyday life into the timelessness of the heavenly spheres. As people entered the church, they mentally and physically prepared themselves to enter a sacred space. They literally left their weapons at the door in the weapon house (*Wappenhaus*), and as they took their seats they prepared themselves to experience a greater degree of equality with one another than existed in Hamburg culture outside the church. When the organ started to play the prelude, normal time stopped, and the sacred time of the High Mass began. Similarly, the postlude served as a musical doorway for the congregation, an inspiration to help them go out into the world. The music of the organ literally created liturgical sacred space, and the harmonies of the organ could also physically affect the four humors of the body and move the hearts of the congregation to promote spiritual and physical health.

One of the consequences of the Thirty Years' War was that a leading organ-building family of the time, the Fritzsches, left Dresden for Hamburg, which was more stable and prosperous, and took on a thorough rebuilding of several instruments there, including the organ in St. Jacobi. From 1635 to 1636 Gottfried Fritzsche added many new elements to the organ. He added subsemitones with split keys in the Rückpositiv in order to enable the organist to play basso continuo, accompanying the instrumentalists and singers in remote keys in the latest musical styles. The Rückpositiv was also the manual for toccatas and other harpsichord-idiomatic writing because of the lighter character of its action and more elegant and refined sound world. Together with the Trumpet 16' on the Hauptwerk, added in 1635, the organist could play the bass line with the left hand, two parts with the Principal of the Rückpositiv in the right hand, and the melody line on a Trumpet 8' in the pedal. This registration yielded a completely new and transparent combination of sounds, reflecting the new orchestral ideals emerging from the instrumental sonata tradition that combined strings with trombones and dulcians.[15] Fritzsche also added a completely new Brustwerk division that included the delicate sounds and novelties of the world of the Compenius organ—for example, the Holz Principal.

Arp Schnitger in St. Jacobi

Despite the fact that St. Jacobi was the poorest of the main congregations in Hamburg (see chapter 3), they managed to finance a truly monumental new instrument by Arp Schnitger, completed in 1693. It must have been the head pastor at the time, Johann Friedrich Mayer, who managed to raise the funds to have the organ built for St. Jacobi, despite the restrictive economic situation and the rising wave of Pietism against church music and large organs. Yet the sculptures and woodcarvings were never completed. There were not even any carved pipe flats in the pedal towers; from the beginning they were only painted. It may have been that the Jacobi congregation was too poor to consider such luxurious decoration, but a dispute between the two woodcarvers is also recorded.[16] In this sense St. Jacobi is not a representative example of the normal Schnitger façade, but a mirror of the very particular situation of the local congregation. Schnitger's Lübeck Cathedral organ, completed with all its carvings in 1699 (figure 1-4), is more typical as a representative of the North German seventeenth-century city organ.

The angels and the statue of King David on the Lübeck Cathedral organ as well as the elaborately carved wings on the sides of the pedal towers and the Rückpositiv create the fully realized illusion that the organ is a baroque stage set, extending the instrument out into the space of the church beyond the confines of the instrument case. The decoration is also clearly a way of drawing the eyes to the geometrical proportions of the large parts of the case as they relate to one another. The main thing is not the details, but the heavenly proportions, emphasized by the four magnificent angels and King David at the top of the main organ case, two angels on the wings jutting out from either side of each pedal tower, and one large angel below the Rückpositiv.

The Compenius Organ in Frederiksborg Castle

The organ built by Esaias Compenius in 1610 brings us to the other end of the spectrum of seventeenth-century organ building. Unlike the Blockwerk organ in

15. Hans Davidsson, *Matthias Weckmann: The Interpretation of His Organ Music*, Skrifter fråan Musikvetenskapliga Institutionen, vol. 22 (Göteborg: Gehrmans Musikförlag, 1991), 55

16. Gustav Fock, *Arp Schnitger und seine Schule* (Kassel: Bärenreiter1974), 59.

northern Europe before Compenius, with its grandiose physical and musical proportions, this little experimental organ has nothing but wooden pipes and is soft enough to be listened to and appreciated by someone standing right next to it. With its incredibly refined and luxurious case, it invites the listeners and the player alike to approach. The front pipes are inlaid with ivory; the stop knobs are tiny, incredibly detailed figural heads cast in silver; and the instrument has other ingenious mechanical details to enjoy close up, such as a pedal board that can be slid into the front of the case and completely hidden from view.

The Compenius organ is the best-preserved example of a wider trend toward introducing new musical sounds and intimate acoustic environments to the organs of northern Europe. This *organo di legno* represents a new kind of organ and organ repertoire on a human scale, unlike the architectural stage set of the large Hanseatic organ that seems to play itself. Like the new opera singers in Italy at the dawn of the seventeenth century, the performer at the Compenius organ is a visible individual musician. According to an inscription once found inside the organ, it was built according to the design (*inventio*) of Duke Heinrich Julius of Braunschweig-Wolfenbüttel (1564–1613).[17] What "inventio" means in this context could be debated, but it certainly suggests that Heinrich Julius was personally involved in the concept of the instrument.

Heinrich Julius (figure 6-4) was an unusual and colorful figure, one of the first German baroque princes. His interests were extremely broad, although he never seems to have concentrated on any one of them for long. For instance, in 1590, while courting his second wife, Elisabeth, sister to King Christian IV of Denmark, he saw his first troupe of professional actors from England, who were then visiting the Danish court. He went home with his new bride, installed Europe's first permanent troupe of English actors at his own court, and became the first serious German dramatic poet, producing eleven plays in only two years and then never writing again. Like his brother-in-law James I of England, he burned witches at the stake, but he also seems to have dabbled in alchemy himself, a trait that may have stood him in good stead at the alchemy-obsessed court of Emperor Rudolph II in Prague, where he spent much of his time during the latter part of his reign.[18]

Unlike the Gröningen organ that Heinrich Julius also commissioned (see chapter 7), which truly expressed the macrocosm in organ sound, the Compenius organ represented the microcosm. Its decoration too, was secular rather than sacred. The sculptures in the upper right- and left-hand corners of its façade

17. Povl Eller, "Compenius-orglets historie," *Dansk årarbog for musikforskning* 17 (1986): 8. For a translation of the text, see chapter 4.

18. The biographical information on Heinrich Julius for this paragraph comes from the opening essay of A.H.J. Knight, *Heinrich Julius, Duke of Brunswick* (Oxford: Basil Blackwell, 1948), 9–16.

Figure 6-4. Duke Heinrich Julius of Braunschweig-Lüneburg, portrait by Elias Holwein, 1603. Printed with permission of Herzog Anton Ulrich-Museum, Braunschweig.

have drawn a good deal of attention in the most recent literature.[19] In the upper left-hand corner a male figure with a winged cap, generally accepted as Mercury, plays a cornett. The figures in the upper right-hand corner were misread in the nineteenth century as an old man leaning over the woman in the foreground[20]; however, the small figure is clearly a child, making the most likely reading Venus and Amor, although Amor does not have his characteristic bow. Other depictions of Venus, Mercury, and Amor together include one with a musical theme.[21] Could the figures of Mercury and Venus refer to Duke Heinrich Julius and his new wife, Elisabeth, and their love for one another?

But there is an iconographical puzzle, too. Mercury's relationship to music is normally associated with the lyre, not the pipe or flute. Michael Praetorius himself writes about Mercury, but only in conjunction with the lyre and the cithara.[22] The Compenius organ provides a very unusual instance of a coupling of Mercury as a piper with Venus and Amor. Not only do the images of the pagan gods lead us firmly into the realm of the secular, but Mercury playing a pipe is always associated in the seventeenth century with the slaying of the giant Argos, an allegory for the alchemical process, and it is possible that Heinrich Julius's *inventio* for the organ included a detailed plan for the design of the façade to reflect his interest in alchemy.[23] At the very least, the figures create a personal frame around music that focuses not on the public arena of the church but on the private sphere of human emotions. This instrument surely was meant to function as a symbol of the pinnacle of good taste and refinement achieved by the duke's court: a political and worldly microcosm, not the macrocosm of the church's heavenly choirs.

In designing an organ that would produce as many sounds as possible from wooden pipes, Esaias Compenius stretched the limits of the *organo di legno* tradition in what can only be described as a scientific experiment in collaboration with Michael Praetorius. If Praetorius is taken at face value, they began this project with the ambition of trying to imitate all other instruments. This vision led to the invention of completely new stops as well as the reinventing of tra-

19. Eller, "Compenius," 12.

20. Eller reports that C.-M. Philbert, the French consul in Helsingør and organ expert, published the idea in Le monde musical in 1891. It was copied by other writers ("Compenius," 12).

21. Mercedes Rochelle, *Mythological and Classical World Art Index* (Jefferson, N.C.: McFarland, 1991), 137–40, lists two instances with this grouping and one with Venus and Mercury poring over a musical score together, with Eros in the background, in a painting by Nicolas Poussin, c. 1628, Dulwich College Picture Gallery, London.

22. Michael Praetorius, *Syntagma Musicum*, vol. 1 (1615; facsimile reprint, ed. Wilibald Gurlitt, Kassel: Bärenreiter, 1958), 396. Praetorius quotes Homer, who links Mercury with the cithara and with the invention of a kind of lyre.

23. Joel Speerstra, "The Compenius Organ: An Alchemical Wedding of Sound and Symbol" (paper presented at the June 2001 meeting of the Swedish Society for Musicology).

ditional stops in a new acoustical environment and a new material: wood. Radically new registration ideas also emerged, as well as evolutionary ideas that are taken, in this instrument, to a radical extreme, and described with utmost care by Praetorius in *De Organographia* (see chapter 4). The reed instruments, which were popular, even dominant, during the first half of the seventeenth century, were well represented, and the "strange and soft, subtle sound" of the wooden flue stops might have been an attempt to imitate the gamba consort sound beloved in England and Germany.

The instrument must have primarily been used to play dance music for entertainment (CD tracks 1–6). This is not the music of the spheres; rather, it is full of all-too-human shifting rhythmical meters. There were also sets of variations on well-known tunes that would be embellished by diminutions (faster and faster figuration in the same amount of time) and rhetorical gestures, creating small-scale emotional vignettes of everyday secular life in the microcosm.

The Two Organs Compared

We have focused here on two of the most important organs of northern Europe that have been preserved from the seventeenth century: the colossal organ in Hamburg, St. Jacobi, built in the last decade of the century, and the intimate ducal court organ by Esaias Compenius built in its first. St. Jacobi's organ, with 60 stops on four manuals and pedal, is the largest surviving organ of Arp Schnitger and was the second largest organ he ever built (after the one in Hamburg's St. Nicolai, which was destroyed in the great fire of 5 May 1842). Schnitger's organ for Hamburg St. Jacobi in fact contains some pipework from two previous generations of the best Hamburg organ builders, as was fairly common in large church organs, while the Compenius organ was the product of a single person's patronage and a single builder's construction.

These two instruments represent two very distinct building traditions that correspond to seventeenth-century northern European concepts of the sacred and the secular, the macrocosm and the microcosm. And yet, in Arp Schnitger's organs these two worlds do come together to a certain extent. The development from macro- to microcosm, the shift from purely theoretical to more practical concepts that are also reflected in literary sources, art, and architecture, seem toward the turn of the century to reach a certain degree of balance, an integration of new and old perspectives, such as we also see in the juxtaposition of free and fugal sections in the North German toccata and praeludium. Arp Schnitger also finally integrated in the tonal design of his instruments powerful fundamental reeds for the bass and the large, brilliant mixtures required for the accompaniment of congregational singing. In the examination report of the Jacobi organ, three well-known organists—Vincent Lübeck, Christian Flor, and Andreas

Kneller—praised Schnitger for his excellent work and are careful to mention how absolutely necessary the Posaunen 32′, Principal 32′, and Octave 16′ of the Werk and Pedal were for a congregation so rich in inhabitants.[24] This dimension of Schnitger's concept, then, is a response to the higher level of integration of all members of the church within the liturgy. It mirrors the political development from feudal to more democratic structures in which more and more power was transferred from the courts to the city, and to some extent from the noble class to the merchants and tradespeople. Now all voices of the citizens were not only able but expected to sing with the choirs, musicians, and heavenly choirs in hymns and songs in their own native language. This development allowed and perhaps even became the catalyst for the building of large-scale, late-baroque organs by Arp Schnitger and his contemporaries, monuments that witnessed the culmination of a new, dynamic, and somewhat mannered style. This was to be followed by the *galant* style, which marked the final emancipation from medieval to modern concepts generated by the Enlightenment.

24. Fock, *Schnitger*, 58.

7

AN IDEAL ORGAN AND ITS EXPERTS ACROSS THE
SEVENTEENTH CENTURY

DAVID YEARSLEY

WITHOUT THE CONCEPT OF A GOLDEN AGE, THE HISTORY OF THE ORGAN AND ITS music in seventeenth-century North Germany would be fragmentary, partial, prone to contradiction, often vexed and contentious, and in the end, inconclusive. It is not surprising, then, that the notion of centuries of seamless progress culminating in the instruments of Arp Schnitger and his school and the music of Dieterich Buxtehude and his contemporaries forms the basis for the history of the North German organ and its literature. Just as indispensable as growth is the inevitable decline that follows, for without decay there can be no subsequent rejuvenation, no renaissance, which takes its inspiration from that same history and its construction of a golden age.[1]

This idea of continuous progress has an obvious intuitive appeal. Builders and players learn through apprenticeship, consolidating and innovating as time moves on. To be sure, there are fits and starts, punctuations and reversals, controversies and compromises; nonetheless, there is steady advance. On reflection, however, the grand sweep of these narratives begins to seem rather frail. Soon we find ourselves so far removed from our predecessors that connections become harder to establish: the births of Franz Liszt and Gustav Leonhardt are separated by little more than a century, yet they are more than an age apart. But it is worth remembering that a belief in relentless improvement is not specifically modern. Writing in 1619, Michael Praetorius could claim in his *De Or-*

---

1. "The development of the North German organ proceeded in an unbroken line from the late Middle Ages to the 'golden age' of Arp Schnitger and his school." Harald Vogel, "North German Organ Building of the Late Seventeenth Century: Registration and Tuning," in *J. S. Bach as Organist*, ed. George Stauffer and Ernest May (London: Batsford, 1986), 31–40, at 31. For a classic statement of progress, culmination, decline, and rebirth see Vogel, foreword to Gustav Fock, *Hamburg's Role in Northern European Organ Building*, trans. and ed. Lynn Edwards and Edward Pepe (Easthampton, Mass.: Westfield Center, 1997), ix–xii, esp. xii.

ganographia (the second volume of *Syntagma musicum*) that while the differences between modern and old organs were not as significant as one might imagine, "the art of organ-making has grown astoundingly with every year."[2] Though proud of these innovations, Praetorius shows a profound respect for the accomplishments of the past, arguing that contemporary builders could still learn from the construction and scaling of antique pipes as much as two hundred years old.[3]

Yet it is probably fair to say that most, if not all, writers on the organ have represented themselves as living in or near a golden age. For Praetorius the organ had reached its zenith a century after the Reformation. Just as Lutheranism had freed the meaning of the Scriptures from the suppressions of popish secrecy, so too this spirit of liberation had extended to organ design, spawning the sparkling developments of the hundred years separating Praetorius's *De Organographia* and the posting of Luther's Ninety-five Theses. Through this process of discovery and improvement the organ had achieved such heights "that it henceforth will hardly be able to go any higher."[4] Praetorius thus invokes the primacy of Lutheran Germany in advancing the art of the organ and links it with divine revelation and public enlightenment. Nearly a hundred years later, no less a figure than Arp Schnitger would marvel with similar enthusiasm at the state of his art. In his dedicatory poem printed in the preface to the important treatise on organ examination *Orgel-Probe* (second edition, 1698) by his friend Andreas Werckmeister, Schnitger can certainly be forgiven a discernible complacency regarding the progress of organ building: "Should the long-departed now awaken and be resurrected / They would be astounded at what human genius has invented."[5] At both ends of the century organists and builders harbored little doubt that they had secured an unsurpassable level of technological and aesthetic perfection.

But "culmination" is surely the wrong word and "golden age" the wrong idea with which to make sense of the history of the organ over the course of the seventeenth century in Germany. These twinned concepts are, in any case, hardly useful for confronting such a severely attenuated historical record. In this essay I examine a single organ—now vanished, except for its case—and the events surrounding the instrument's dedication just before the close of the sixteenth

---

2. Michael Praetorius, *Syntagma Musicum*, vol. 2, *De Organographia* (1619; facsimile reprint, ed. Wilibald Gurlitt, Kassel: Bärenreiter, 1958), 117.

3. Praetorius, *Syntagma musicum*, 2:107.

4. Praetorius, *Syntagma musicum*, 2:114.

5. Arp Schnitger, dedicatory poem, in Andreas Werckmeister, *Erweiterte und verbesserte Orgel-Probe* (1698; facsimile reprint, ed. Dietz-Rüdiger Moser, Kassel: Bärenreiter, 1970), unpaginated prefatory matter.

century, as well as its renovation in the first years of the eighteenth century. I hope to triangulate between the "original instrument," the conception of it offered one hundred years later, and our own more remote historical position. Equally important here is our role in interpreting and, as the contents of this book demonstrate, implementing that history. I propose an approach to this organ's history that both respects and challenges the competing views of the instrument offered from either side of the seventeenth century. The result will be open-ended, but perhaps the more rewarding for resisting the seductive notion of a golden age.

The Gröningen Organ as an Ideal of Germanness

One of the greatest events in the history of organ building and playing took place at the end of July 1596 in the castle church at Gröningen, thirteen kilometers northeast of the central German town of Halberstadt.[6] It was here, in his favorite residence, that Duke Heinrich Julius of Braunschweig-Lüneburg convened a gathering of leading organists from across Germany to dedicate the newly finished organ by David Beck, a well-known builder resident in Halberstadt. The participants called by the duke represented a huge geographical spread running the length and breadth of Germany, from Augsburg, four hundred kilometers south of Gröningen, to Danzig, some six hundred kilometers to the northeast. Several of the players came from cities near the mouth of the Elbe (two from the famous organ center of Hamburg), and others came from their homes near the Baltic coast (Lübeck, Rostock, and Schwerin). Directly to the east, Brandenburg and Leipzig were represented as were many central German towns— Wolfenbüttel, Braunschweig, Halberstadt, and Helmstedt, among a dozen others. From these far-flung locales the participants journeyed to the meeting place to test a massive and daringly innovative instrument in an atmosphere of celebration, collegial exchange, and, one suspects, competition.

The lavishly appointed organ, its stunning case richly decorated with elaborate carvings and gold leaf, was a striking adornment to an already resplendent church. The building had been renovated and expanded under Duke Heinrich Julius's auspices in a project he began almost immediately on his accession in 1589; work on the organ started just three years later. For almost two centuries after its inauguration the Gröningen organ was recognized as a

6. Wolf Hobohm, "Zur Geschichte der David-Beck-Orgel in Gröningen," in *Bericht über das 5. Symposium zu Fragen des Orgelbaus im 17./18. Jahrhundert*, ed. Eitelfriedrich Thom (Michaelstein: [n.p.], 1985), 50–70, at 55. For another account of the Gröningen meeting see Frederick Gable, "The Polychoral Motets of Hieronymus Praetorius" (Ph.D. diss., University of Iowa, 1966), 29–33.

landmark; its extraordinary disposition was reprinted in several important treatises from the seventeenth and eighteenth centuries, including *De Organographia* by Michael Praetorius, himself a participant at the congress, and the *Musicalische Handleitung* (1721) by F. E. Niedt, whose compendium of organ
specifications was collected and collated by the book's editor, Johann Mattheson. On his way to Leipzig for diplomatic purposes in 1706, the young Mattheson made it a point to visit the Gröningen Castle church and play the organ.[7] Noting both the beauty of the instrument and the differences from the
stop list as printed in *De Organographia*, Mattheson deemed it especially
worthwhile to include the Gröningen disposition among the "Sixty (mostly) Famous Organs" of his day.[8]

Of the twenty organ specifications collected by Praetorius in *De Organographia*, the Gröningen Castle church organ was the largest, exceeding the size of
the monumental instruments in Hamburg's St. Jacobi and Danzig's St. Mary's
by several stops.[9] But this organ's remarkable nature had as much to do with its
scope as with the kaleidoscopic timbral potential immediately apparent from the
unprecedented specification (see specification 7-1).[10]

7. Johann Mattheson, *Grundlage einer Ehren-Pforte* (1740; reprint, ed. Max Schneider, Berlin: Leo
Liepmannssohn, 1910), 195.

8. For a list of the sources that include the Gröningen Castle church organ, see Hobohm, "Zur
Geschichte," 68. These sources include Friedrich Erhard Niedt, *Musicalische Handleitung*, 2nd ed.,
ed. Johann Mattheson (Hamburg: Benjamin Schiller's widow, 1721), translated into English as
The Musical Guide, trans. Pamela L. Poulin and Irmgard C. Taylor (Oxford: Clarendon, 1989), 106–
7.

9. In fact this list of specifications begins with an organ in Costnitz for which Praetorius had not,
in spite of his concerted efforts, acquired a stop list. Instead, he merely asserts that the instrument
has 70 stops. Praetorius, *Syntagma musicum*, 2:162–63.

10. Specification (with some corrections) and spelling as in Andreas Werckmeister, *Organum Gruningense redivivum* (Quedlinburg and Aschersleben: Struntz, 1705), paragraph 11; see also, Hobohm,
"Zur Geschichte," 54.

SPECIFICATION 7-1.
Gröningen Castle Church, David Beck, 1592–96

Oberwerk	Rück-Positiv	Pedal
Quintathön 16'	Quintathön 8'	Quintathön 16'
Principal 8'	Principal 4'	Principal-Bass 16'
Rohrflöt oder Gedackt 8'	Gedackt oder Rohrflöt 4'	Sub-Bass 16'
Groß-Qüer-Flöt 8'	Gems Horn 4'	Groß-Gemß-Horn 16'
Gems-Horn 8'	Octava 2'	Octav-Bass 8'
Octava 4'	Spitzflöt 2'	Klein-Gemßhorn 8'
Kleine Querflöte 4'	Quinta 1½'	Super Octav 4'
Nacht-Horn 4'	Sifflöt 1'	Klein Quintathön 8'
Quinta 3'	Mixtur IV	Grosse Quer-flöt 8'
Hohlflöth 2'	Zimbel III	Klein-Gemßhorn 8'
Mixtur VI–VIII	Sordunen 16'	Super Octav 4'
Cymbel II	Trompet 8'	Gedackt 4'
Kleine Brust zum	Krum-Horn 8'	Hohlflöt-Baß 4'
Ober-Manual-Clavier	Singend Regal 4'	Nachthorn 4'
Klein Gedact 2'		Quint-Bass 3'
Super Octav 1'		Gedackt Quint 3'
Zimbel II		Hohl-Quint 3'
Mixtur III		Gedackt Quint 1½'
Repetirend		Bauerflöt 1'
Zimbel-Regal 8'		Posaunen-Bass 16'
Groß Regal 8'		Sordun-Baß 16'
Rancket 8'		Trompeten Baß 8'
		Krumhorn 8'
		Rancket 8'
		Schallmeyen-Baß 4'
		Klein Regal-Baß 2'

The organ's emphasis on diversity is reflected in the four 8' flues on the Oberwerk, the three 8' flues on the Brustwerk, and the plentiful assortment of manual reeds (seven in total, all distributed between the Brustwerk or Rückpositiv). But the most striking manifestation of these nearly endless color possibilities is the behemoth pedal—quite simply the largest of any organ ever built in the sixteenth, seventeenth, or eighteenth century. The Gröningen pedal contained 26 stops, nearly half of the organ's total, and was divided between side towers, a chest inside the main part of the case, and compartments placed on either side of the keyboard. Here, too, reeds were abundant: seven in total, offering three distinct options at eight-foot pitch. But the extreme value accorded to variety of sound and the technological capacity to achieve such refinements can perhaps best be gauged by the seemingly esoteric inclusion of no fewer than three 3' flue stops in the pedal alone.

The conception of the Gröningen instrument might be seen as an extreme manifestation, even a fetishization, of the pride German musical culture derived from what it saw as its unique contribution to organ design and playing—the pedal. As far back as the *Spiegel der Orgelmacher und Organisten* (Mainz, 1511) of Arnolt Schlick, German writers were claiming superiority for their organs and organists because of the role of the pedal, which was capable of bringing off complex polyphony and executing stunning scalar passage work; Schlick suggested that other nations were beginning to study the pedals in emulation of the Germans.[11] A century later, Praetorius asserted that not only had the Germans invented the pedal, but they had repeatedly done the missionary work of introducing it to other countries; in spite of such efforts, however, its cultivation had withered, and in Italy and England, for example, it was rarely employed.[12] Germans of Praetorius's time cherished high-pitched pedal stops such as the characteristic Bauerflöt 1′ (as in Gröningen), particularly in delivering a cantus firmus; but according to Praetorius, Italians looked on such stops with disdain, an attitude that, again according to Praetorius, only served to verify their backwardness.[13] This Germanocentric view of the organ runs through to Mattheson, who, in the *Vollkommener Capellmeister* of 1739, took a rather condescending view of the pull-down pedals of Italy.[14] For several generations of German organists, the Gröningen instrument would have represented the very antithesis of this perceived deficiency.

When Praetorius wrote that the "organ excels and contains in itself nearly all other instruments" and is therefore the "instrument of instruments," he was articulating a pervasive conception of instrumental hierarchies.[15] For Germans, the proudly independent pedal was an essential feature in the most famous exemplars of their universal musical tool, and a more complete pedal than that at Gröningen could hardly be imagined. Indeed, the Gröningen instrument can be seen as a gesture toward a kind of ideal pedal: the most complete realization of the most characteristic feature of German organ playing and building. Consider again the presence of 3 pedal stops at 3′; these present 3 of the 4 possible 3′ registers listed by Praetorius in his Universal Table, a taxonomy of all the stops then being built.[16] It was not only for geographic and linguistic reasons that all the partici-

11. Arnolt Schlick, *Spiegel der Orgelmacher und Organisten* (1511; facsimile reprint, with translation and notes by Elizabeth Berry Barber, Buren: Frits Knuf, 1980), 28–29.

12. Praetorius, *Syntagma musicum*, 2:96.

13. Praetorius, *Syntagma musicum*, 2:140.

14. Johann Mattheson, *Der vollkommene Capellmeister* (Hamburg: Christian Herold, 1739; facsimile reprint, Kassel: Bärenreiter, 1954), 466.

15. Praetorius, *Syntagma musicum*, 2:11; English trans. in *De Organographia Parts I and II*, trans. and ed. David Z. Crookes (Oxford: Clarendon, 1986), 27.

16. Praetorius, *Syntagma musicum*, 2: between 126 and 127.

pants called to Gröningen in 1596 were Germans. Only they would begin to know what to do with such outlandish pedal riches.

The Organists' Banquet

An account of the 1596 meeting at Gröningen is to be found in a small treatise entitled *Organum Gruningense redivivum*, written in 1705 by the organ expert and prolific theorist Andreas Werckmeister. He was an organist in nearby Halberstadt, where he played an instrument originally built by the same David Beck.[17] Werckmeister was probably one of the driving forces behind the rebuilding of the Gröningen Castle church instrument, which by the first years of the eighteenth century had fallen into such disrepair that it was for the most part unplayable; as the leading organ expert in the region and the author of the influential *Orgel-Probe*, Werckmeister had been the obvious choice to serve as the chief consultant for the project.[18] Like the *Orgel-Probe*, the purpose of *Organum Gruningense redivivum*, which contained several passages lifted directly from the earlier treatise, was partly didactic, intended to instruct organists in the inspection of newly completed organs and to help congregations protect themselves from dishonest and inept organ builders. But it was also an account of the scope and effectiveness of the actual work done, an exemplary synopsis of a consultant's report, highly detailed, practically minded, and historically informed.[19]

Although Werckmeister held strong opinions on the proper direction of organ design—particularly in favoring the abandonment of the short octave and meantone tuning, which he saw as antiquated—he was acutely aware of the instrument's past. Well read in texts ranging from antiquity through his own century, he was a collector of theoretical writings, musical manuscripts, printed editions, and various miscellaneous works by important figures such as Praetorius and Buxtehude. *Organum Gruningense redivivum* was Werckmeister's last publication to appear before his death the following year, and as he stated on the title page (see figure 7-1), his purpose in writing the treatise was primarily to provide a context for his own decisions as consultant by describing the state of the "famous organ" (*berühmtes Orgel-Werck*) at the time of its dedication and the dilapidated condition in which he had found it more than a century later; the tract is an attempt to document and defend the ways in which the instrument had been

17. For a specification of this instrument see Praetorius, *Syntagma musicum*, 2:181–82.
18. Werckmeister, *Organum Gruningense redivivum*, introductory paragraph (unnumbered). (The treatise is unpaginated, but is provided with paragraph numbers, which I cite below.)
19. In fact Werckmeister mentions (para. 29) his full and detailed organ report sent to the Prussian administration, which paid for the renovation; Werckmeister does not include all of his findings in the pages of the *Organum Gruningense redivivum* for reasons of brevity and clarity.

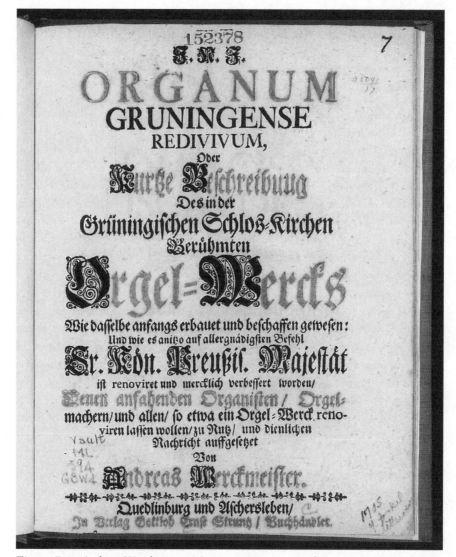

Figure 7-1. Andreas Werckmeister, *Organum Grunigense redivivum* (1705), title page. Courtesy of the Sibley Music Library, Eastman School of Music, University of Rochester, Rochester, New York.

"renovated" (*renoviret*) and "considerably improved" (*mercklich verbessert*) over the course of the previous year, 1704–5.

In nearby Quedlinburg, where he had once served as organist, Werckmeister had come upon a first-hand account of the Gröningen congress written by one of his predecessors, Hermannus Kauffmann. As reprinted by Werckmeister in *Organum Gruningense redivivum*, Kauffmann's short document relates that it had taken Beck and nine employees—not including the local artisans who, in accordance with guild regulations, would have discharged various ancillary tasks—four years to finish the instrument, at a cost to Heinrich Julius of ten thousand reichsthaler, "without food and drink" (*ohne Essen und Trincken*), that is, not including the considerable sum the duke had paid for the board of the organ builders. Kauffmann writes that it had cost the Duke another three thousand thaler—almost a third as much as the total construction costs—to assemble the impressive roster of players for the instrument's dedication.[20] Such an event could only have been sponsored by a single wealthy patron, and so it took place not in one of the famed Hanseatic organ cities, but at a ducal retreat. (This penchant for grand disbursement would leave the Duchy of Braunschweig-Lüneburg in dire financial straits after Heinrich Julius's death in 1613.) A sometimes careful historian, Werckmeister writes that a Halberstadt chronicle he had consulted confirmed the information given by Kauffmann.

Kauffmann reports that the participants "played and tested the organ one after the other according to their age."[21] Thus the list of players begins with one Ulrich Greißtopf from Magdeburg, "the first and oldest" (*der 1. und Älteste*), and continues on to the youngest, a similarly forgotten musician named Severus Grosse, from Hildesheim. Scanning the list, other interesting names appear, such as that of Antonius Schild (i.e., Schildt), whose son Melchior was a student of Sweelinck and one of the great organists of the first half of the seventeenth century.[22]

But it is a cluster of organists coming toward the bottom of the list, and therefore representing the younger members of the congress, that catches the eye: number 40, Johann Leo Haßler (i.e., Hans Leo Hassler) from Augsburg; number 42, Johanne Stephanus (i.e., Johann Steffens) from Lüneburg; number 43, Hieronymus Praetorius from Hamburg; and number 48, Michael Praetorius from Wolfenbüttel. These names stand out for a simple reason: aside from two pieces by the Nuremburg organist Hans Kaspar Hassler (Hans Leo's brother) and Cajus Schmiedlein from Danzig, they are the only Gröningen participants from whom any substantial quantity of music survives. Their birth dates suggest that the order of the list only roughly reflects the relative age of the players: in fact, Hassler (b. 1562) was two years younger than Steffens and Hieronymus Praetorius (both born in 1560), yet he played before them at the congress; Michael Praetorius (born in 1571) followed somewhat later. Kauffmann's list has Kaspar Hassler playing fifth, that is, near the beginning of the festivities, even though he was Hans Leo Hassler's twin. While Michael Praetorius was only

20. Werckmeister, *Organum Gruningense redivivum*, para. 11.
21. Werckmeister, *Organum Gruningense redivivum*, para. 11.
22. It is this same list of fifty-three organists that must be the one added to a copy of the third part of Niedt and Mattheson's *Musicalische Handleitung* now in the Cambridge University library. Presumably the owner (possibly Mattheson himself) had read Werckmeister's treatise on the Gröningen organ. See F. E. Niedt, *The Musical Guide*, trans. Poulin and Taylor, 179.

twenty-five years old in 1596, Steffens, Hans Leo Hassler,[23] and Hieronymus Praetorius were well into their thirties and came near the bottom of the list: given that these organists played toward the end, the congress was clearly made up of august, learned, and proven figures in the profession. In a word—and it is the one Werckmeister used, perusing the document more than one hundred years after the event—these were "famous" (berühmt) men, many still so after more than a century. According to Kauffmann's list, Carl Lauff was organist at the Gröningen Castle church, but receipts from the Wolfenbüttel treasury show that after the congress Michael Praetorius was awarded the post and entrusted with the care of the valuable organ.[24]

The music played on the new organ must remain for the most part a mystery; because of gaps in the historical record we have only the most fragmentary idea of the repertoire heard at the event, and indeed of organ playing more generally across Germany at the end of the sixteenth century. From these ruins it is hard to accumulate enough to construct anything as impressive as a golden age. Would Hieronymus Praetorius be considered a great figure of the organ tradition of the late sixteenth and early seventeenth centuries if not for the survival of a single manuscript, the so-called Visby tablature now on the Baltic island of Gotland? Had this book disappeared, he would hardly, if ever, be mentioned as an organist. Steffens is identified with two fantasias in the Celle tablature book of 1601. And we have a much better idea of Hassler's organ music largely because of the survival of a single multivolume manuscript, now in the Biblioteca Nazionale in Turin. The only surviving printed edition associated with a participant at Gröningen is the Musae Sioniae (part seven, 1609) and the Hymnodia Sionia (1611) of Michael Praetorius, which included several chorale preludes among its vocal works. Of course, the largest part of a contemporary organist's "repertoire" is not recoverable in any strict sense since it would have been improvised, as was certainly the case at Gröningen. Still, considering the stature of these men and the important positions they held at key musical centers across Germany, we can begin to see just how little remains, particularly by comparison with the fragmentary but still far more completely documented later half of the seventeenth century.

The congress would have provided a lively forum for the exchange of ideas on organ design and aesthetics. Indeed, it seems likely that Praetorius collected many of the far-flung specifications he assembled in De Organographia through contacts he made at the Gröningen meeting. The congress must also have fos-

---

23. Hassler dedicated his Neuen teutschen Gesang nach Art der welschen Madrigalien und Canzonetten to Duke Heinrich Julius. The volume was published in Augsburg the same year as the Gröningen congress.

24. Martin Ruhnke, Beiträge zu einer Geschichte der deutschen Hofmusikkollegien im 16. Jahrhundert (Berlin: Merseburger, 1963), 82–84.

tered a lively exchange between younger and older organists from north and south, although there was already, in the sixteenth century, a certain amount of mobility in the profession. Hieronymus Praetorius, member of a Hamburg dynasty of organists, had himself worked in central Germany, serving as organist in Erfurt's Preachers' Church (Predigerkirche) from 1580 to 1582, before he returned to take up his father's post at St. Jacobi in Hamburg. During his two years in Erfurt, Praetorius had played an organ completed in 1579 by Heinrich Compenius, who was also an organist and a participant in the Gröningen dedication (number nineteen on the list). (Could Heinrich Compenius have brought along his son Esaias, who would later become court organ builder to Duke Heinrich Julius and make repairs to the Gröningen organ?) While the dating of Hieronymus Praetorius's organ works is uncertain, his triumphant Magnificat cycle—its grandiose opening verses would have taken glorious advantage of the Gröningen organ's pedal—was probably written in the first decade of the seventeenth century.[25] It would not be at all far-fetched to think that Praetorius's meeting with a representative of the Gabrieli tradition as gifted as Hassler could have influenced his subsequent development, and it is entirely plausible that while no "Venetian" toccatas survive from Hieronymus Praetorius's hand, he could well have played such pieces in St. Jacobi before his sons, having completed their studies with Sweelinck, brought this style back from Amsterdam. In spite of the fact that only wisps of evidence have lingered in our own time, it is undeniable that by the last years of the sixteenth century and the crossroads at Gröningen, the organist's profession had reached a level of sophistication equal to that attained by builders such as Beck. At least some of the organists present at the 1596 congress were ready to push the Gröningen organ to its expressive limits.

The Gröningen Organ Seen from Either Side of the Seventeenth Century

The organists had not been invited to Gröningen by the duke simply to perform and to celebrate; as Werckmeister stresses, they had been charged with examining the organ, making sure it had fulfilled the contract and had been executed according to the precepts of good building. Werckmeister writes that the congress was devoted to the testing (*Probe*) and delivery (*Lieferung*) of the instrument—that is, the transfer of the organ to the owner's responsibility (terms that he also uses on the title-page of the *Orgel-Probe*). The crucial decision on whether the contract had been fulfilled required the advice and approval of real experts. This

25. Jeffrey T. Kite-Powell, *The Visby (Petri) Organ Tablature: Investigation and Critical Edition*, vol. 1 (Wilhelmshaven: Heinrichshofen, 1979), 29.

point proved to be of the utmost importance to Werckmeister, as he assessed the condition of the organ some one hundred years later, just having overseen significant repairs and renovations. It is here that the dissonant voices within his history of the organ begin to be heard, for Werckmeister went so far as to blame the organists for the organ's premature state of disrepair (*Decadenz*).

Although there are fifty-three numbered organists in the list of participants reprinted by Werckmeister, fifty-four were initially present. At about the halfway point in the list there appears an organist named only as Johannes N. von Wettin. Whether he played is not reported, but Kauffmann claims that the man "saw himself as the most beautiful and was excellently and richly dressed, but received not a penny because he was a slanderer of the organ and the organists."[26] The fellow is not granted a number, and only a final initial "N.," as if withholding the surname was a way of shaming the man. This is the only discordant note recorded, but it is a hard one to ignore, and while Kauffmann tries to discredit Johannes N. as a dandy and a malcontent, this mysterious figure plays an important role in Werckmeister's interpretation of events. Indeed, Werckmeister attempts to rehabilitate Johannes N. by suggesting that he may have had to suffer unjustly because he alone was brave and honest enough to voice objections to the numerous faults he saw in the organ.

In fact, Werckmeister makes the breathtaking claim that the Gröningen banqueters were simply unqualified for the vital job of inspecting the instrument: "And though to be sure the organists there as examiners understood the art of music and organ playing and were, some of them, famous at the time, as well as being well-trained composers, it appears nonetheless that they may have had little knowledge of the art of organ building."[27] Later, after enumerating a number of the instrument's defects, Werckmeister allows for the vague possibility that the examiners may have pointed out some of these problems, but the organ builder had failed to remedy them once the congress had disbanded. Aside from this and other conciliatory gestures, Werckmeister places the blame squarely on the participants of the Gröningen celebration.[28]

Werckmeister's attack on the technological know-how of the Gröningen examiners is not only historically inaccurate but arguably crosses the threshold into self-serving distortion. Let us return to the group of the four younger organists discussed earlier, Hieronymus Praetorius, Michael Praetorius, Hans Leo Hassler, and Johann Steffens. Each is known to have been not only a great organist, but a recognized organ expert as well. The organist in Hamburg's St. Jacobi Church

---

26. Werckmeister, *Organum Gruningense redivivum*, para. 11.

27. Werckmeister, *Organum Gruningense redivivum*, para. 13.

28. Werckmeister also suggests that some of the shoddy work might have been done by Beck's apprentices while the master was away. Werckmeister, *Organum Gruningense redivivum*, para. 12.

at the time of the Gröningen congress, Hieronymus Praetorius had recently overseen the expansion and repair of the organ by the local builder Hans Scherer
the Elder. Hans Leo Hassler was an expert in the construction of mechanical
musical instruments and must also have had a keen understanding of organs.
Prior to the Gröningen convention and his appointment that same year as organist of St. Johannis in Lüneburg, Steffens had apparently studied organ building with the same Hans Scherer.[29] Finally, there is Michael Praetorius, who later
not only gave extensive space in *De Organographia* to the history of the organ
and to the description and classification of pipes, but also collaborated with
Esaias Compenius on a short, unpublished treatise concerning the delivery and
examination of organs. Vincent Panetta has shown that Werckmeister possessed
a manuscript copy of this work and drew heavily on it—indeed, sometimes pla-
giarized from it—for his own *Orgel-Probe*.[30] From one perspective, it can hardly
be denied that these accusations regarding Michael Praetorius's incompetence
reflect poorly on Werckmeister's own integrity as a historian, if only because he
was directly indebted to Praetorius's work on organ design and inspection.

In *De Organographia*, Praetorius in fact stressed the responsibilities of examiners and reprimanded those who did not demand correction of all the faults
in an instrument; he ascribed these failures to lack of knowledge (*Unverstand*),
to the desire to appease the maker, or to a lack of conscientiousness and honesty.
The churches, he pointed out, suffered as a result.[31] Praetorius's writings show
him to have been a committed proponent of openness and the exchange of
information, and in the introduction to *De Organographia*, a work expressly written in German rather than obscurantist Latin, he made an eloquent plea for the
dissemination of useful knowledge. Even though he was only at the beginning
of his career as an organist and organ expert, could Praetorius really have been
as negligent as Werckmeister suggests? Could all the examiners, with the exception of the disgraced Johannes N., have shirked their duty simply to avoid de-
flating the festive spirit of the inauguration?

Once the builder Beck had stopped working, either because of poor health
or death, the contract to renovate and then to maintain the instrument went to
Esaias Compenius. Praetorius, too, continued to play the Gröningen organ; even
after his appointment as the duke's Kapellmeister, some ten years after the congress, he remained court organist. This rare combination of posts indicates the
importance of the instrument in the court's musical life. As organist, Praetorius
presumably helped to advise Compenius on the necessary upkeep, and over the

29. Fock, *Hamburg's Role*, 67–85.

30. Vincent J. Panetta Jr., "Praetorius, Compenius, and Werckmeister: A Tale of Two Treatises," in
Church, Stage, and Studio: Music and Its Contexts in Seventeenth-Century Germany, ed. Paul Walker
(Ann Arbor, Mich.: UMI, 1990), 67–85.

31. Praetorius, *Syntagma musicum* 2:108–9.

first two decades of its existence the instrument received the most expert care then available. However, given the sad state of the instrument by 1704, the result, at least in part, of the ravages of the Thirty Years' War, during which soldiers were quartered in the castle church, it is easy to understand Werckmeister's distemper.

Werckmeister was a renowned author of the definitive manual for testing organs and had been called as an examiner thirty times before serving as the consultant at the Gröningen rebuild. But although his standards were high and his eyes and ears sharp, he was by no means a dogmatic perfectionist; as he writes in both the *Orgel-Probe* and at the end of *Organum Gruningense redivivum*, flaws, albeit relatively inconsequential ones, sometimes had to be lived with.[32] But in a few important respects he believed that the Gröningen organ had not met even this minimum, universal standard, and Werckmeister often seems genuinely disappointed at the original examiners' lack of rigor. Among its most glaring oversights was the absence of hooks to hold up the bigger pipes, which, by Werckmeister's day, lay collapsed on top of each other, the poorly soldered pipe feet burst open. Werckmeister was even more outraged by the fact that the windchests had been so carelessly screwed together that many of the screws had connected the top board and table but then missed the frame and gone directly into the channels, so that when the glue gave way, as it had by the time Werckmeister was called in as consultant, the instrument was plagued by leaking wind that caused pipes to murmur and complain out of turn. Of course, it is difficult to know quite how the original examiners would have caught this defect while the glue was still fresh and secure. In the *Orgel-Probe* Werckmeister sensibly recommends that when contracting for an organ it is best to seek out a dependable builder with a solid reputation; David Beck certainly had a local record, having made the 39-stop instrument in St. Martini, Halberstadt, probably in the 1570s or early 1580s. Werckmeister was in fact serving this church as organist;[33] so in light of Beck's work in the region, his critique of the examiners appears exaggerated.

While Werckmeister criticizes the Gröningen organ's durability and the complicity of the examiners in failing to point out its defects, he is by and large enthusiastic about the original concept of the instrument and comes across as extremely protective of its historic qualities. He heaps praise on the "precious reeds" (*die kostbahren Schnarr-oder Rohr-Wercke*), particularly since many of these types of stops, such as the Krummhorns, were rarely encountered by the early eighteenth century; Werckmeister singles out the 16′ Sordun in the Rückpositiv for the "sweetness of sound of such a reed stop one will rarely find in

---

32. Werckmeister, *Orgel-Probe* (1698), 71; see also *Organum Gruningense redivivum*, para. 76.
33. Hobohm, "Zur Geschichte," 53.

any new organ,"[34] lauding it as a masterpiece (*Meister-Stück*) of the old master Beck. Throughout the treatise Werckmeister's recognition of the historical importance of the organ is evident, and he takes pleasure in the fact that, in spite of its generally disastrous condition, nothing had been changed since 1596.

What is so remarkable, given seventeenth-century organ culture's commitment to progress, is the care with which Werckmeister in his role as consultant safeguarded—or thought he was safeguarding—the rare treasure that was the Gröningen organ. This is all the more striking when one compares the apparently minimal interventions he recommended at Gröningen with the almost constant tinkering and wholesale alterations done to the large instruments in Hamburg. Although the builder Christoph Contius, whose instrument in Halle's Liebfrauenkirche J. S. Bach would later examine and approve, had re-formed many of the damaged pipes, he had resisted changing the cut-ups, thus allowing them to speak "according to their old fashion" (*nach ihrer alten Arth*).[35] In spite of the very different styles in organ playing between Werckmeister's period and that of the Gröningen congress, the sprawling pedal was left completely intact—perhaps as a monument to an earlier tradition. As for the four changes to the stop list of the Gröningen organ, at first glance they appear quite minor: the original 4' Rohrflöte on the Rückpositiv was replaced by a Gedackt 8' for playing continuo in concerted music, an alteration that marks the emergence of thoroughbass in the practice of organ playing. In addition, three flutes, on the Oberwerk and Rückpositiv, were replaced with mutations, making separable sesquialteras available on two manuals. Werckmeister remarked explicitly on the importance of $2\frac{2}{3}'$ and $1\frac{3}{5}'$ mutations (a $5\frac{1}{3}'$ register was also placed on the Oberwerk) in the *Orgel-Probe*, considering these stops essential not only for solo combinations but as constituents of the full organ (*volles Werck*).[36]

In order to deploy these new stops, as well as the reeds "im vollen Werck," Werckmeister stressed the necessity of getting more wind to the pipes, and it is in this regard that Werckmeister recommended the most thoroughgoing changes to the Gröningen organ. Indeed, the greater part of his critique, and recommendation for change, focused on the inadequacy of the wind: the constricting wind trunks, the use of narrow channels on broad chests, the too-small pallets. For it was only with the increase of wind pressure by about 20 percent and the construction of new, less crowded chests that the full organ could be powerfully sustained and the reeds made more vibrant, allowing them to be successfully drawn with numerous other stops. In addition, Werckmeister claimed that after

---

34. Werckmeister, *Organum Gruningense redivivum*, para. 45.

35. Werckmeister, *Organum Gruningense redivivum*, para. 35.

36. Werckmeister praises the Sesquialtera (particularly if separable) in the *Orgel-Probe* (1698), 73–74.

Example 7-1. Hans Leo Hassler, Canzon, mm. 105–11

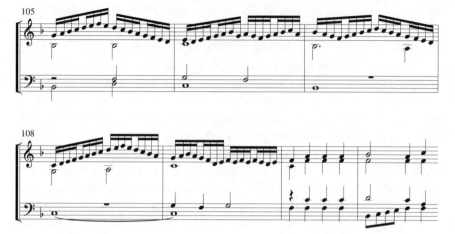

this fundamental improvement the Principals were able to achieve both the requisite gravity (*Gravität*) and a penetrating (*penetrant*), sharp (*scharff*) quality.[37] Because of the increased wind pressure, writes Werckmeister, the organ "sounds as good and lively now, as it sounded dead and mute in the previous one hundred years."[38] The musical and registrational implications of this transformation in the wind system can be seen clearly in a comparison of two canzonas, the first by Hans Leo Hassler[39] (example 7-1), the second by Werckmeister himself (example 7-2).[40] The Hassler piece is rather transparent, with an overlay of brilliant passagework, and it reflects the consort ideal of the late sixteenth and early seventeenth centuries; Werckmeister's, on the other hand, has the look of a plenum piece of his generation, with thick textures and a rollicking, wind-shaking pedal that would have been impossible on the Gröningen organ in its original state.

It is striking that throughout *Organum Gruningense redivivum*, Werckmeister presents these changes not as matters of taste but as remedies of intrinsic conceptual flaws. Nowhere is this subtle but essential difference in aesthetic orientation more evident than in the stops Werckmeister had recommended be removed from the organ, with, he is quick to point out, the concurrence of other organists. Out came the 8′ Querflöte on the Oberwerk, which Werckmeister described as an utterly "bungled stop" (*verhunste Stimme*) and also the 4′ Quer-

37. Werckmeister, *Organum Gruningense redivivum*, para. 42.

38. Werckmeister, *Organum Gruningense redivivum*, para. 47.

39. The Hassler canzona comes from Foà 3, no. 54, Turin, Biblioteca Nazionale Universitaria; for a modern edition see Hans Leo Hassler, *Canzonen für Orgel oder andere Tasteninstrumente*, ed. Alfred Reichling (Berlin: Merseburger, 1975), 6–9.

40. The Werckmeister canzona is found in Musikbibliothek der Stadt Leipzig, Ms. II 2. 51; modern edition in *Freie Orgelwerke des norddeutschen Barocks*, ed. Klaus Beckmann (Wiesbaden: Breitkopf & Härtel, 1984), 32–39.

Example 7-2. Andreas Werckmeister, Canzona, mm. 19–22

flöte. Yet these are just the precious stops, exciting new inventions at the time of the Gröningen congress, that are described with such fresh affection by Praetorius in *De Organographia*. Indeed, Praetorius singled out these flutes as being particularly beautiful on both the "glorious large organ in Gröningen" (*herrliche grosse Orgel zu Gröningen*) and its wooden counterpart built for Hessen Castle, the Compenius instrument now in Frederiksborg Castle[41] (see chapter 4).

Finally, there was the matter of the tuning. In *Organum Gruningense redivivum* Werckmeister predictably makes no secret of his views on what he calls the Praetorian tuning—meantone. In a typically rhetorical gesture he allows all people their taste, before going on to argue that noncirculating temperaments defy common sense and the demands of modern music making. Arguing his point with a particularly vivid metaphor, Werckmeister likens the combination of pure and impure intervals (and by extension pure and impure keys) to a party in which the guests are first treated to several glasses of fine wine but must then suffer a rather less palatable vintage filled with bile and vinegar. He compares his own more regularized temperament to the distribution of a spoonful of water into each glass of wine, a dilution that goes completely unnoticed. Interestingly, however, Werckmeister did not have the entire Gröningen instrument retuned immediately, but instead left the Rückpositiv in meantone for at least several months. One wonders if Johann Mattheson, visiting the instrument soon after the renovation, was one of the many visiting organists whom Werckmeister

41. Praetorius, *Syntagma musicum* 2:138–39.

showed around the instrument, watching and listening as they compared the competing tuning systems.[42] Werckmeister's decisions on the tuning—a common modernization made in the decades around 1700—encapsulate his concerted push to modernize on both utilitarian and aesthetic grounds.

In his excellent essay on the history of the Gröningen organ, Wolf Hobohm suggests that Werckmeister's critique of the original examiners resulted from the dilemma in which he found himself: on the one hand, having to praise the instrument as being worthy of costly repairs, while on the other, feeling obliged to cite the initial errors in construction that made these repairs necessary.[43] Accordingly, Werckmeister's polemical tactic was to shift blame chiefly onto the participants in the Gröningen congress. Though certainly important in accounting for Werckmeister's penchant for maligning Praetorius and company, Hobohm's explanation does not adequately note the extent to which Werckmeister appeals to universal standards—which, of course, with the even greater historical distance afforded by another three centuries, can quickly be seen not to be universal at all.

Werckmeister's entire report on the Gröningen organ is predicated on the distinction between those faults that existed from the outset, and therefore should have been detected at the dedication, and those that arose over time. However, Werckmeister treats this important distinction haphazardly, and the result is a curious mixture of historical sensitivity and blind self-assurance. The poorly screwed chests can certainly be judged by universal standards, but on the other hand Werckmeister characterizes the lack of manual mutations as a "fault" in the initial design rather than ascribing it to a change in tastes. Similarly tendentious is his interpretation of the original meantone tuning, which is attributed not to a positive decision to retain pure thirds, but to the backward nature of "Musica Mathematica" during Praetorius's time. Werckmeister believed that it was only after the rebuilding that the organ had achieved its true potential, that once freed, the historical legacy imprisoned in the previously dilapidated instrument could speak with its true voice. Just as the increased wind supply had added heft and power to the plenum throughout the instrument,[44] the subtle, more refined reed sound reflective of an earlier consort ideal had been effaced. Trans-historical recriminations such as those leveled by Werckmeister at Praetorius and his colleagues at the Gröningen congress epitomize the fluidity of organ aesthetics and the chimerical nature of golden ages and their promises of perfection. Organs may endure for decades, even centuries, but the ideologies which surround their initial construction do not.

---

42. Werckmeister, *Organum Gruningense redivivum*, para. 51.
43. Hobohm, "Zur Geschichte," 57–58.
44. Werckmeister, *Organum Gruningense redivivum*, para. 44.

Conceived as a universal German organ and approved by an impressive collection of organists, in its 1705 rebuild the Gröningen organ had in some respects
been converted into an eighteenth-century instrument, capable of playing the
organo pleno works of Werckmeister and his successors, most notably J. S. Bach.
But considered more broadly and in the context of the times, the minimal but
nonetheless important changes in the stop list show a resistance to making such
a conversion complete. All in all, the instrument looked, and probably sounded,
remarkably like it did in 1596. Werckmeister's Gröningen consultancy is thus
marked by an acute sense of curatorial responsibility inflected and sometimes
distorted by the aesthetic imperatives of his own time. It is an attitude born of
the dialectic of golden ages, whose agents acknowledge their debt to the past
even while they abnegate it.

Renovation and Restoration

Thus Werckmeister's engagement with the Gröningen organ was both retrospec-
tive and progressive, both proud of salvaging an important historical artifact and
unapologetic for having brought it back to life in a new guise which might gal-
vanize future musicians and enthusiasts to safeguard the instrument's legacy.[45]
It is a strange irony of history that the organ in Gröningen that Werckmeister
had been so instrumental in helping to rehabilitate was purchased in 1769 by
the congregation of St. Martini in Halberstadt. After some legal wrangling and
petitions on the part of Gröningen officials to keep their famous organ, royal
permission from Berlin (the area was then under Prussian control) was granted,
and the following year the organ was removed from the Gröningen Castle church
and installed in Halberstadt, where it took the place of the David Beck organ
on which Werckmeister had played each Sunday for the final decade of his life.[46]
Significantly, in describing the work done to the Gröningen organ under his
guidance, Werckmeister used the verb "to renovate" (*renoviren*) rather than "to
restore," and claimed that the renewal he had overseen had attained an ideal
residing within the original organ but never before realized. Werckmeister's self-
assurance is in many ways attractive, for his belief in renovation as renewal shines
with the optimism of a golden age, both brightening and obscuring the past (of
1596); his is an approach to the repair of usable historical artifacts that places
a laudable faith in the efficacy of contemporary knowledge and its attendant
aesthetic inclinations. The modern term "restoration," with its implied hopes for
the reclamation of an ideal—and unattainable—past, is epistemologically more
problematic and less confident than Werckmeister's "renovation." The disparity

45. Werckmeister, *Organum Gruningense redivivum*, para. 76.
46. Hobohm, "Zur Geschichte," 60–62.

between these terms raises a fundamental question: if the Gröningen organ as left by Werckmeister had come down to us with few intervening alterations, would we seek to recapture a "true" past of Beck, Praetorius, and Compenius or the instrument as "improved" by Werckmeister and Contius? Whatever choice we would make, our decisions would be as firmly a product of our own interaction with the past as were Werckmeister's. One hopes only that unlike Werckmeister, his modern-day counterparts would recognize not just the rewards but also the risks inherent in the quest for renewal, restoration, and kindred forms of nostalgia for a mythic golden age.

A LARGE EUROPEAN ORGAN IN A

SMALL FACTORY TOWN

8

EXORDIUM: THE CAHMAN ORGAN AT LEUFSTA BRUK

(1728)

LEUFSTA BRUK TODAY IS A PICTURESQUE MUSEUM VILLAGE, LOCATED 130 KILOME-
ters north of Stockholm. In the eighteenth century, however, it was a bustling
factory town, one of the leading producers of bar iron in all of Europe. The entire
estate, consisting of foundry, administration buildings, manor house, church,
housing for the workers, and the surrounding land, belonged to the Baron
Charles De Geer. In this unlikely setting, he commissioned the building of an
organ by Johan Niclas Cahman that stands today as one of the largest and best
preserved baroque organs in all of Scandinavia (figure 8-1).

Göran Söderström introduces us to the De Geer family and its Leufsta Bruk
estate in chapter 9. We learn about the Cahman organ and its historical context
from Axel Unnerbäck in chapter 10. Since we know so little about what music
was actually played on the Leufsta Bruk organ in its own time, in chapter 11
Eva Helenius-Öberg and Pamela Ruiter-Feenstra fill in the picture with new
information from archival sources on organs and organ playing elsewhere in Sweden during the eighteenth century. Finally, in chapter 12 Göran Blomberg relates
the story of the organ's decline and restoration during the twentieth century.

Johan Niclas Cahman (1680–1737) was the grandson of the Hamburg organ
builder Hans Christoph Fritzsche. His father, Hans Henrich Cahman, had ap-
prenticed with Fritzsche and immigrated to Sweden to establish a school of organ
building that would flourish until about 1820. When Johan Niclas built this
instrument, he was the leading organ builder in Sweden, having already completed organs for the cathedrals of Västerås and Mariestad. The Leufsta Bruk
organ suffered little change during the nineteenth century, but early in the twentieth its Ryggpositiv was removed and a harmonium installed behind its façade.
The Ryggpositiv was restored to its rightful place by John Vesterlund in 1933,
and the organ subsequently became an important locus for the performance of
baroque music in Sweden. It was most recently restored by Marcussen & Søn
in 1963–64.

Figure 8-1. The Johan Niclas Cahman organ (1728) in Leufsta Bruk Church. Photograph by Axel Unnerbäck, 1964. Printed with permission of Antikvarisk-topografiska arkivet, ATA, Stockholm.

SPECIFICATION 8-1.
Leufsta Bruk Church, Johan Niclas Cahman, 1728

Manual (Manual II)	Ryggpositiv (Manual I)	Pedal
C–c'''	C–c'''	C–d'
Qvintadena 16' Bass/Discant	Gedackt 8'	Offen Sub Bass 16'
Principal 8' Bass/Discant	Qvintadena 8'	Principal 8'
Rohrflöte 8'	Principal 4'	Gedackt 8'
Qvintadena 8'	Fleut 4'	Qvinta 6'
Octava 4' Bass/Discant	Qvinta 3'	Octava 4'
Spitzflöte 4'	Octava 2'	Rauschqvint II
Qvinta 3'	Mixtur IV (1728/1963)	Mixtur IV
Super Octava 2'	Voxhumana 8'	Bassun 16'
Mixtur V Bass/Discant		Trompet 8'
Trompet 8' Bass/Discant		Trompet 4'

All mixtures contain a third rank.
Coupler: Ryggpositiv-Manual
Mechanical action with slider chests
Temperament: equal
Pitch: Chorton

Recording

CD tracks 8–10: Alf Linder playing Johann Sebastian Bach, Trio Sonata in E-flat Major (BWV 525; recorded in 1971)

Registration

Unknown, but see chapter 22.

Selected Literature

Erici, Einar, and R. Axel Unnerbäck. *Orgelinventarium: Bevarade klassiska kyrkorglar i Sverige.* [New, rev. ed.] Stockholm: Proprius, 1988.
[Lewenhaupt, Carl-Gustaf]. *Dokumentation av Cahmanorgeln i Leufsta bruks kyrka.* Uppsala: Länsstyrelsens meddelandeserie, 1998.

9

AN ARCHITECTURAL TOUR OF LEUFSTA BRUK

GÖRAN SÖDERSTRÖM

THE *BRUK* COMMUNITIES (FACTORY TOWNS) WERE AMONG THE MOST SPECIALIZED villages in eighteenth-century Sweden. The most famous of them, Leufsta Bruk, once supplied much of the bar iron for Europe. Leufsta Bruk lies sixty-five kilometers northeast of the ancient university city of Uppsala and twice as far due north from Stockholm. Now it seems as though the town is truly in the middle of nowhere, but *bruk* locations were determined by several important factors. Naturally, they needed access to ore, especially iron ore, but even more importantly, in order for the ore to be processed, the *bruk* workers needed huge tracts of forest in order to have access to enough firewood to run the smelting furnaces, as well as access to water power to operate the hammering machines. For these reasons a *bruk*, like Leufsta, is often isolated in a large remote forest area near a source of water power, but also close to the sea for shipping. Leufsta Bruk is only about ten kilometers from the Baltic Sea. Because these villages were so isolated they needed to be completely self-sustaining, so the *bruk* operation usually included a large farm nearby. In the self-contained world of the *bruk*, social classes were strictly stratified. The manor house of the owner, complete with farm, lies near the center of the *bruk*. Along the street, the smithies' and upper-level workers' homes are positioned according to rank, with the master smithies' homes nearest the manor house, the next level of workers' barracks farther from the center, and so on. The church often occupies a central place opposite the manor house: the sacred power facing the secular. Sometimes, as in the Forsmark Bruk in Uppland, where the church lies in an eye-catching position at one end of the street, it functions as an architectural counterbalance to the grand manor house at the other end.

The location of Leufsta Bruk, which is almost completely preserved in its eighteenth-century state, is typical: the barren northern Uppland forest landscape, in what is still called Oland (Wilderness) County. At its height, the number of employed *bruk* personnel rose to 1,900 people, the size of a rather large city at that time. The story of this particular *bruk* dates back to the 1570s, when some farmers devised a machine for hammering rod iron near Risforsån. Early in 1596, the first true *bruk* village collaborated to build a hammering machine (a simple heavy iron weight lifted and dropped repeatedly onto an anvil by waterpower), and the place gradually evolved into a village of permanent *bruk* workers. Early on, it became clear that the *brukfolk* would need their own church: Leufsta Bruk lies in the parish of Österlövsta, and the entire parish was served by only one church, in a village ten kilometers away. The roads were never in good condition, and during muddy weather in spring and autumn, the *bruk* was almost totally isolated. The parish church in Österlövsta dates from the Middle Ages, and since that time it had been common to build chapels, especially in connection with castles, manor houses, and factories. Sometimes they are in the castle building itself, and sometimes they are free-standing, as in Leufsta Bruk.

The first simple wood chapel in Leufsta Bruk was built in 1615. The parish priest Magnus Ivari Leufstadius records that Queen Christina the elder, to whom the *bruk* was then pledged, had a small chapel built for the *bruk* workers and their families and also arranged "some help for the maintenance of the services." After her death in 1625, "the *bruk* was leased by the crown to foreigners, who . . . allowed the chapel to become derelict."[1] These foreigners were Wellem De Besche and the De Geer family of the Netherlands.

The De Geer Family at Leufsta Bruk

At that time Louis De Geer, who was living in Amsterdam, was one of Europe's most prominent arms dealers and was keenly aware of the political situation in Europe leading up to the beginning of the Thirty Years' War. He also knew that prices for raw materials to make weapons would soon skyrocket. De Geer foresaw that the common brass cannons then in use would be replaced by iron cannons, and that Sweden, with its iron ore mines, rich forests, and abundant water power, would be the best place for their production. Much of the Swedish ore currently was exported to be processed in Germany, where it was sold at twice the price; that fact also had not escaped King Gustav Adolf II, who wanted more control of the resource. In 1619 De Geer loaned 80,000 riksdaler to the Swedish crown for the war effort, and Sweden was to pay the interest in copper production. However, Sweden had 750,000 riksdaler in total debt, and it was not long before the revenues from the production of copper were unable to keep pace with the interest and insurance payments, many of which De Geer and his business part-

---

1. Magnus Ivari Leufstadius in a letter to the archbishop from 1666; ULA: Uppsala domkapitels arkiv.

TABLE 9-1.
The De Geer Family at Leufsta Bruk

Louis De Geer	1587–1652	
Emanuel	1624–1692	son
Charles	1660–1730	nephew
Charles	1720–1778	nephew
Charles	1747–1805	son
Carl	1781–1861	son
Emanuel	1817–1877	cousin's son
Louis	1824–1887	brother
Carl	1859–1914	son
Louis	1866–1925	brother
Louis	1887–1953	relative
Carl	1918–1978	son
Louis	1944–	son

ners had consolidated so that they were the sole recipients of the copper. De Geer took advantage of the situation to establish himself in Sweden in order to reap maximum benefit from the war, and although there was strong opposition from the landed gentry, De Geer arranged his immigration directly through King Gustav Adolf II and his chancellor Axel Oxenstierna. The crown was so deeply in debt to De Geer and his business partners that the choice had come down to allowing De Geer into Sweden or bankrupting the state.[2]

To expand production at Leufsta Bruk, De Geer recruited some skilled workers from France and the Netherlands, mainly Walloons (188 of them by 1694) from what are now Belgium, Luxembourg, and bordering France. They were smithies, handworkers, coal miners, and operators of the huge ovens. In 1643, the *bruk* was transferred directly to Louis De Geer's estate, and it remained in the possession of the family until 1917 (see table 9-1).[3] At the end of the seventeenth century, Leufsta was the leading iron *bruk* in Sweden and one of the foremost in Europe.

Louis De Geer died in 1652 without ever having visited Leufsta Bruk. His son Emanuel, on the other hand, maintained a home at Leufsta Bruk. He stayed there often and engaged himself fully in the *bruk*'s development; it was also he who built Leufsta Bruk from the beginning as an up-to-date model city with its still-preserved city plan and building structures. The manor house with its large garden (figure 9-1) sat on one side of Main Street; on the other side, and on North and South Streets, lay the hammersmiths' cabins.

2. Bernt Douhan, "Louis De Geer," in *Vallonerna* (Uppsala: Stiftelsen Leufstabruk, 1996), 38–39.
3. Douhan, "Louis De Geer," 45; the names also appear on a plaque in the church.

Figure 9-1. Leufsta Bruk manor house and gardens before the fire of 1719; detail from an anonymous painting. Photograph by Axel Unnerbäck.

Rather than rebuilding the derelict chapel, Emanuel De Geer had the children's French teacher "read on Sundays for the people," a practice that continued for nearly twenty-four years. Some of the *bruk* folk were Calvinists, some were "Papists," and some "know scarcely a thing about any religion," lamented Leufstadius. This dire report from the parish priest led the diocesan chapter to write a stern letter to Emanuel De Geer on 21 August 1666, arguing that the population of Leufsta Bruk had risen and that many inhabitants were unable to attend the parish church regularly because of the long distance "and their weariness." It was therefore necessary to build a chapel, as there had been before, and the chapter demanded that De Geer assume responsibility for building it. Such a chapel would also "adorn the other beautiful and plentiful houses, which the well-born Herr De Geer has built and organized like a little city."[4] But De Geer answered arrogantly and in the negative: in addition to developing the *bruk*, "should it be demanded of me to build a chapel, I cannot see how my income could suffer or endure such a thing."[5] He sent a gift of money for reparations to the parish church instead.[6] Emanuel never married and was criticized by the church leader not only for his Calvinism but also because he was carrying on "a

4. Letter from diocesan chapter to Emanuel De Geer, 21 August 1666; ULA, Uppsala domkapitels arkiv BI:2.
5. Letter from Emanuel De Geer to diocesan chapter, 7 September 1666; ULA, Uppsala domkapitels arkiv EV 88:1.
6. Letter from Magnus Leufstadius, 1 Nov. 1696; ULA: Uppsala domkapitels arkiv.

strangely unclean and scandalous household affair with that woman he is clandestinely seeing on the side."[7]

Upon Emanuel's death in 1692, his estate was willed to Charles De Geer, the son of Emanuel's brother Louis, who had inherited Finspongs Bruk in Östergötland. Charles was at that time an officer in the Dutch military, but he moved to Sweden after his inheritance and later received the title of county governor for his many contributions to the community.[8] It was Charles De Geer the elder who finally built a chapel at Leufsta Bruk for Lutheran services, thus breaking his family's Calvinist tradition. In a long correspondence with the diocesan chapter, he argued that the *bruk* ought to have its own priest. In 1696 he reported to the chapter his decision that at his own cost he would install a *bruk* preacher; and shortly thereafter he hired the preacher Johan Novelius.[9] Then a new chapel was built. Completed by 1703, it was situated very close to the current church. It was built of wood, had eight large windows, and was richly decorated, judging from one written description, in a style similar to that of the current church, with an altar, a pulpit, and a balcony. The church had no organ, probably for economic reasons, because Charles De Geer had just carried out large and costly building projects in the *bruk* and at the manor house. Although this church building and the one that followed it were owned by the De Geer family as part of the estate, the church was consecrated by the Swedish Church as a part of the Österlövsta congregation.[10]

The new church would not survive the summer of 1719, however. The Russians burned it to the ground along with all of the old *bruk* buildings, including fifty smithies' residences and the manor house. The attack came on 25 July in a campaign at the very end of the Great Northern War. After some initial doubts, Charles De Geer decided to rebuild the *bruk* completely. His intensive efforts toward that end lasted throughout most of the 1720s. The workshops and workers' living quarters were rebuilt first, followed by the manor house, and finally the church. Part of his ambition was to reestablish the work activity quickly and to give the workers roofs over their heads. In 1722 Charles received the *jus patronatus* through a royal decree, which, among other things, gave him the right to appoint a priest to the congregation.

By 1723 the workers' quarters were finished, and the work on a new manor

7. Leufstadius to the archbishop, 1666.

8. Marianne Sandström-Hanngren, "Brukets historia," *Brukseminariet: Kompendium* 5 (Uppsala: Uppsala University, [1981]: 6.

9. Axel Unnerbäck, *Leufsta bruks kyrka*, 3d rev. ed., Upplands kyrkor, vol. 141 (Uppsala: Ärkestiftets stiftsråd, 1977).

10. Since the sale of the *bruk* (excluding the manor house) to Gimo-Österbybruks AB in 1917, the church building has belonged to Österlövsta's congregation (Österlövsta kyrkoarkiv, kyrkorådsprotokoll 1927).

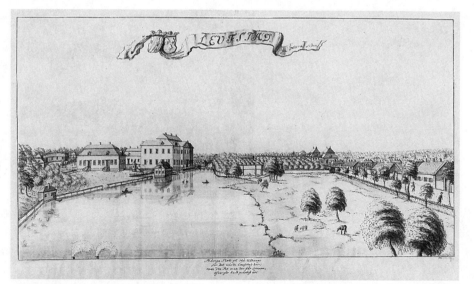

Figure 9-2. Leufsta Bruk, painting by Elias Martin, c. 1790. Printed with permission of Nordiska Museets arkiv.

house began. By 1725 production was again underway at the *bruk*. One year later, they had come so far as to break ground for the new *bruk* church that would be inaugurated in August 1727. The church's most significant possession, the large Cahman organ (figure 8-1), was not finished until one year later. The inscription "1728" found on the right pedal tower of the organ refers to the year marking the end of this enormous building project. Charles the elder died in 1730, and his nephew, Charles De Geer Jr., inherited the *bruk* at the age of ten. The De Geer family continued to maintain its Dutch connections: Charles the younger, although born in Sweden, grew up in Utrecht and returned to Sweden only in 1738 (see chapter 1).

The City Plan

The new architectural incarnation of the *bruk* is still preserved and serves as a rare extant example of an early-eighteenth-century European factory community. The *bruk* is built in strict accordance with the continental city plan ideal of that time. Along Main Street stand the splendid master smiths' houses, their long sides parallel to the street, each house divided into two spacious residences (figure 9-2, right). The houses were originally finished with red-colored timber but were plastered and painted golden yellow in the 1750s, matching the color of the manor house. The somewhat simpler *bruk* residences, still red to this day, are situated on the cross streets At both ends of the Main Street. Two other

Figure 9-3. Leufsta Bruk Church, exterior. Photograph by Axel Unnerbäck.

crossroads run at right angles from the middle of Main Street: one leaves the central axis of the manor house (figure 9-2, left) and runs between two warehouses. The other and more important Priest's Street lies to the south and is flanked by the *bruk* community's two most prominent buildings next to the manor house: the *bruk* church (figure 9-3) and the inspector's residence with the *bruk* office. These two large buildings are nearly identical from the exterior; the only primary differences are the large windows and decorative urns on the church compared to the chimneys on the inspector's house. The church has no steeple or bell tower. The current and the previous free-standing bell towers on the manor grounds across the street served not only the church but also the *bruk*. In this typical mercantile community, the city is dominated neither by the manor house nor by the church, except that both the secular and sacred powers are equally displayed in the *bruk*'s foremost administrative buildings, all presented in a restrained, sober architecture.

We do not know for certain which prominent architect was retained for the manor house, church, and *bruk* buildings. One likely candidate is Joseph Gabriel Destain, who created an architecture stylistically similar to that of Leufsta Bruk's manor house in the manor house of Björksund in Södermanland. Destain, who died in 1740, came to Sweden from France in 1716 and was first engaged to improve defense fortifications. He became active as an architect in the 1720s, after the Great Northern War. Among his known works are the manor houses of Tullgarn, Bergshammar, and Björksund in Södermanland.

Church and Organ

Although the church is Lutheran, its architecture reflects the Dutch Reformed tradition of Charles's family, with undecorated whitewashed walls and pews of unpainted sculpted fir. The floor and ceiling are covered with burnt gold tiles with herringbone patterns. The sole adornments are three domineering, similarly

Figure 9-4. Leufsta Bruk Church, pulpit and altar. Photograph by Axel Unnerbäck. Printed with permission of Antikvarisk-topografiska arkivet, ATA, Stockholm.

conceived, and equally valuable items: the altar, the pulpit (figure 9-4), and the organ. The heightened value of the pulpit and organ in Leufsta Bruk compared to other Swedish churches from the same time—in which the altar normally dominated—is another sign of the Reformed tradition. We also do not know who made the drawings or sketches of these fine items. The sculpture was probably done by the woodcutter Herman Buck, who in the early 1700s made the stylistically similar decorations on the south side gallery in the Stockholm's Great Church (Storkyrkan, now the Stockholm Cathedral). Very little is known about Buck. At the beginning of the 1700s he worked together with a famous woodcarver Burchard Precht in the Great Church in Stockholm in a style that is very close to both Precht's brilliant baroque and Leufsta Bruk's sculptures. He made, among other things, the four hymn boards, the ornamentation on the south balcony, and the ornamentation on the outside of the main altar, the so-called silver altar. Some scholars have wondered whether the sculptures in Leufsta Bruk (and Österlövsta) could have been made in Precht's studio.

The manor lord's seating section on the right side of the choir is no different

Figure 9-5. The Johan Niclas Cahman organ (1709–10) in Karlshamns Church. Printed with permission of Antikvarisk-topografiska arkivet, ATA, Stockholm.

from the seating section for the master-smithies on the left. The lords of the manor reveal themselves instead through their coats-of-arms, which discreetly but clearly adorn the altar and the pulpit. It was a Reformed virtue that even if one personally came from a wealthy environment, one would blend in with the bourgeois collective.

The building of such a large and richly ornamented organ simply for the enjoyment of the *bruk* is a completely singular stroke of cultural ambition. Such foresight and ambition must not have been solely to support the congregational singing. There is little doubt that Johan Niclas Cahman himself was responsible for the design of the organ and its placement and decoration, considering how closely the organ resembles the composition found in his earlier work, such as the organ in Karlshamn's Church (figure 9-5), which was built in 1709–10. The organ in Karlshamn had 24 stops, 10 on the main manual, 6 in the Rückpositiv, and 8 in the pedal. It was demolished in 1880 to make room for a romantic organ.

In the Leufsta Bruk organ (figure 8-1), it is not the North German tradition's typical verticality that prevails. What gives the organ its overwhelming monumentality is instead its strong horizontal emphasis and its breadth, not its height. In a skilled and clever way, Cahman not only worked around the problem of the ceiling height—far too low for such a large organ—he also succeeded in creating an architectural masterpiece. It was not possible to balance the width of the large organ cases within the height available. The middle tower actually touches the ceiling. Instead, Cahman created a clever illusion by using two marble-decorated columns under the balcony, which, as part of the total architectural composition, visually attach the organ to the floor and at the same time seem to lift the Rückpositv and the Hauptwerk. The four distinctly divided cases of the organ create a functional architecture that tells you visually how it is constructed and how it will sound. The upward diagonals created by the pedal towers and continuing along the top of the Hauptwerk case, and the downward diagonals created by the symmetrically placed balcony stairs—with railings of the highest quality Leufsta ironsmith work—further create the illusion that the organ begins at the floor and not the balcony railing, a powerful architectural motif that bears witness to a consciousness on the part of both the organ builders and the architect that the organ and the balcony should create a single coherent impression.

In spite of the richness of the baroque ornaments and the overwhelming impression of its grandiose architecture, and despite the fact that the organ does not have an actual point of connection to the *bruk*'s architecture, in its very distinctive functional shape the organ could be said to mirror not only the wealth of the owner and the importance of the *bruk*, but also something of the restrictive and cultivated "baroque functionalism" that characterizes the architecture of the village as a whole.

10

THE CAHMAN TRADITION AND ITS GERMAN ROOTS

AXEL UNNERBÄCK

WHEN BARON CHARLES DE GEER SET OUT TO REBUILD LEUFSTA BRUK AFTER THE devastating fire of 1719, his aim was to create a new setting representative of its time that could serve as a witness to the *bruk*'s solidity and build a functional living environment both for the workers and for the lords of the manor. The organ was the crowning achievement of the new Leufsta Bruk. For Charles De Geer, the choice of organ builder for the new church's organ ought to have been obvious. At that time, Johan Niclas Cahman in Stockholm was the nation's leading organ builder, having just completed a large instrument of 32 stops for the Cathedral of Åbo in Finland. In fact, the construction of the Leufsta Bruk organ falls in the middle of Cahman's most intensive working period. In the scant fourteen years between 1724 and 1737, he built no fewer than twenty-seven organs, five of them cathedral instruments and many with two manuals.

The Leufsta Bruk Organ

From the contract, it appeared that Leufsta Bruk's organ would be considerably larger than a parish church organ, and equipped with a powerful pedal division. The contract between Charles De Geer and Johan Niclas Cahman was signed in Stockholm on 20 December 1726.[1] It describes only the Hauptwerk and pedal divisions but in all other respects concurs completely with the organ as it stands today, describing the same disposition, the divided registers of the Hauptwerk, the compass, the keyboards, and the bellows system.

Cahman stayed in Leufsta several weeks in 1727. The account books say that this was for work on the organ in the parish church, but perhaps this is a mistake, because the work just then should have been on the organ in the *bruk* church. The organ could have been ready to deliver in Stockholm in the middle of August

1. There is a copy in the Härnösand cathedral archives, now in the Härnösands landsarkiv.

1727, and the contract promises payment for Cahman's journeyman during the installation of the organ in the church. At the inauguration of the church 22 October 1727 the organ was mentioned, but the inscription "Anno 1728" at the top of the right pedal tower indicates that it was not finished until then. That the work on the organ in Leufsta Bruk went on even to the end of 1728 seems likely, because in September of 1728 two jugs of schnapps were bought for Cahman's journeyman Erich Dahlberg; he died the following December in Löten, near Leufsta Bruk.

At its final stage of completion, the organ even had a Rückpositiv, which is not mentioned in the contract. A similar pattern is found in Cahman's organ for Härnösand Cathedral, which, according to the first contract in 1730, should have had only Hauptwerk and Pedal, but got a Rückpositiv on the advice of the organist at Stockholm's Great Church (Storkyrka), Ferdinand Zellbell, who was a close friend of Cahman's.[2] According to Carl-Gustaf Lewenhaupt, it is most likely that the Rückpositiv at Leufsta Bruk was added by Daniel Stråhle, who was Cahman's journeyman at the time.[3] He died in Leufsta Bruk in 1746.

With the addition of the Rückpositiv, the Leufsta Bruk organ (figure 8-1) became an instrument of a size and strength fully comparable to the larger city churches in the land. Perhaps the organ was an expression of the importance that Charles De Geer established for Leufsta Bruk as an industrial community. At the same time, it certainly was an expression of a genuine cultural and musical interest on the part of the De Geers.

Today, more than 270 years later, the Cahman organ is still fully functional. Long after the bruk's activity has faded and the hammering from the smithies has been silenced, the organ rings out in church services and concerts. With its brilliant architecture, its sculptured ornaments, and its masterful construction and handicraft, and not least through its magnificent and beautiful sound, the organ preserves an image of a time of prosperity, efficiency, and beauty united with an optimism for the future, anchored in the seventeenth century, when Sweden was a European superpower, but at the same time modern and forward-looking.

The organ in Leufsta Bruk is the most important source of knowledge about Johan Niclas Cahman's organ building. The instrument was built at a time when he had left the strict seventeenth-century North German tradition behind him and had already laid the foundation for the national organ tradition that dominated Swedish organ building during an eighteenth-century golden age. Johan Niclas Cahman had his roots in the North German organ tradition, having been born in Flensburg about 1680, but he was only a few years old when he came

2. Härnösands landsarkiv, Härnösands domkyrkans arkiv O 53 and 54.
3. *Dokumentation av Cahmanorgeln i Lövstabruks kyrka* (Uppsala: Länsstyrelsens meddelandeserie, 1998), 7.

to Sweden. He was a son of the organ builder Hans Henrich Cahman and Anna Christina Fritzsche, daughter of the famous Hamburg organ builder Hans Christoph Fritzsche, his father's teacher. Via Hans Christoph and his father, Gottfried Fritzsche, there was also a family connection to the famous organ builder Friedrich Stellwagen, who was married to Hans Christoph Fritzsche's sister, Theodora. Johan Niclas Cahman established himself as an organ builder in the end of the 1690s and was active until his death in 1737. By then he had built more than thirty-five organs, large and small.

The Swedish Organ Tradition

It is no coincidence that the Swedish organ tradition grew out of that of North Germany. As early as the Middle Ages, Sweden and North Germany had close political and cultural connections that also applied to sacred art and organ culture. In 1374 Master Werner, born in Brandenburg, signed an organ for Sundre Church in Sweden. Fragments of this organ are still extant at the State Historical Museum in Stockholm and provide an extremely important source of knowledge about the medieval Blockwerk organ. It is probable that many of the organs that existed in Swedish medieval churches had German origins or were built by German immigrant organ builders. As a member of the Hanseatic League, Stockholm belonged to a cultural partnership whose stronghold was in North Germany and the countries around the Baltic Sea. This collaboration between German and Swedish culture continued during the Renaissance, not least in the art of architecture. Despite Sweden's importance to seventeenth-century Europe, North German influence strongly dominated Swedish cultural life, including music in general and the organ in particular. With the Thirty Years' War, Sweden took over important North German centers, among them Stralsund, which belonged to Sweden until 1815. Certain areas between Bremen and Stade were also part of Swedish territory for a long time.

In the seventeenth century the art of organ building blossomed for the first time in Sweden. With the organ builders George Herman and Philip Eisenmenger, who moved from Rostock in the 1620s, an important organ workshop was formed in the Stockholm area. Their most important contracts were the large organs in Stockholm's Great Church (Storkyrkan), the Rückpositiv of which is preserved in Bälinge Church, and the German Church (Tyska kyrkan), still preserved in Övertorneå Church (Hauptwerk and Oberwerk; see chapter 25). These splendid instruments were completely in keeping with North German standards of organ building at that time.[4] After Herman's death in 1655, their previous

4. For more information on the organs in the Great Church, see Einar Erici and R. Axel Unnerbäck, *Orgelinventarium: Bevarade klassiska kyrkorglar i Sverige*, [new, rev. ed.] (Stockholm: Proprius, 1988);

coworker, the Swedish-born organ builder Frantz Boll, further forged the tradition. His last large contract, a new organ in Uppsala Cathedral, was a project Boll could not finish. His death in 1674 marked the end of the Rostock tradition begun in the 1620s. About ten years later Hans Henrich Cahman established himself as an organ builder, thus founding a new and living organ tradition that continued to flourish and develop nearly uninterrupted throughout the entire eighteenth century and up to around 1820.

Sweden's first contact with the Fritzsche tradition had already been established much earlier, when Cahman's master and father-in-law, Hans Christoph Fritzsche, performed a thorough rebuilding of the late medieval organ in St. Petri Church in Malmö and renovated the organ at St. Mary's in Helsingborg, both in 1662; he also built a new organ in the Halmstad Church in the later 1660s. In all three cases, Fritzsche was working in old Danish cities that had belonged to Sweden only since 1658. The Helsingborg organ was inspected by Dieterich Buxtehude, who had served as organist there until 1660; it was moved to Torrlösa in 1849.[5] The organ in Malmö is preserved in the Malmö museum. It is not impossible that Hans Henrich Cahman, at age twenty, could have helped in the building of these organs. The St. Petri organ can then be seen as an important source of knowledge in the study of the Cahman tradition and its North German roots.

Hans Henrich Cahman

Hans Henrich Cahman's first independent project after Fritzsche's death in 1674 was to complete the Fritzsche organ in Hamburg-Neuenfelde.[6] Exactly when he established himself in Sweden is unknown. In 1685 he worked on the organ in Landskrona, from 1688 to 1692 he built a new large organ in Växjö Cathedral,[7] and in the 1690s he built an organ in the Stockholm Royal Castle Church. Cahman's largest work, a new 50-stop organ with a 32' façade in Uppsala Cathedral was finished in 1698; he died one year later. The organ he began in the

and Göran Blomberg and Mads Kjersgaard, "Bälingeorgelns restaureringsfråga" (unpublished report [1990], in Antikvarisk Topografiska Arkivet, Stockholm). On the organ in the German Church, see Erici and Unnerbäck, *Orgelinventarium;* and Lena Weman Ericsson, ed., *Övertorneåprojektet: Om dokumentationen av orgeln i Övertorneå och rekonstruktionen av 1684 års orgel i Tyska kyrkan* (Piteå: Musikhögskolan, 1997), and *Övertorneåprojektet: Om restaureringen av orgeln i Övertorneå* (Piteå: Musikhögskolan, 1999).

5. Kerala J. Snyder, *Dieterich Buxtehude: Organist in Lübeck* (New York: Schirmer, 1987), 33.

6. Gustav Fock, *Hamburg's Role in North European Organ Building,* edited and translated by Lynn Edwards and Edward Pepe (Easthampton: Westfield Center, 1997), 72.

7. Bengt Kyhlberg, "Kring Hans Heinrich Cahmans orgelbygge i Växjö domkyrka 1688–1691," in *Kronobergsboken: Hyltén-Cavalliusföreningens årsbok* (Växjö: Kronobergs läns hembygdsförbund, 1964), 54.

Figure 10-1. The Hans Henrich Cahman organ (1690) in Virestad Church. Photograph by Axel Unner-bäck.

Skara Cathedral was completed by the organ builder Johan Åhrman, while the organ project in the Riddarholms Church in Stockholm was completed by his son Johan Niclas Cahman, who from that point on took over his father's work-shop.

At the time of his death, Hans Henrich Cahman, who had moved from place to place, had his workshop in Stockholm. His large organs have all disappeared: the organ in the Stockholm Castle Church was lost in the castle fire of 1697, and the Uppsala organ during the cathedral fire in 1702. The organ in Växjö met the same fate. At the same time he was building his large instruments, he also built positive organs and other keyboard instruments. Three positive organs from his time in Växjö are known, and one of them, which was transported to the Virestad Church in Småland in 1690, is preserved (figure 10-1). This instrument is in the Smålands Museum in Växjö and paints a picture of an extremely skilled organ builder. Both material and handicraft are of the highest quality, the metal pipes are extremely well made, and the sound of the more than 300-year-old instrument has the freshness and vitality of youth. Because the pipes have been preserved undisturbed and unchanged, they can provide a picture of the strong, almost strident sound ideal that Cahman brought to Sweden from the North German organ tradition. The bellows are nearly unique in that they still have their original bellows weights in the form of metal ingots nailed fast to the bellows board, revealing the original wind pressure of 53 millimeters. That wind pressure plays a large role in the authenticity of the organ's sound is obvious, and in the ongoing discussions about wind pressure in high baroque organs, the

Virestad organ provides an important contribution to an area in which many uncertainties remain.

The Virestad organ is a small instrument of only 8 stops based on a Principal 4' which dominates the sound, strengthened by a Qvinta 3', an Octava 2', a Ters, a Mixture, and a Scharf with thirds. It has only one flute stop—Gedackt 8'—and one reed, Trumpet 8'.[8] It is obvious that Cahman continued the North German tradition of Fritzsche and Scherer, strengthening it somewhat in the dispositions of his larger organs.

Johan Niclas Cahman

When Hans Henrich Cahman died in 1699, his son Johan Niclas, then about nineteen years old, was left in charge of the work for the large organ in Riddar-holms Church, the site of the royal tombs in the middle of Stockholm. The assignment was both prestigious and complex, reflecting the fact that his father had without a doubt been the leading organ builder in the country. Hans Henrich Cahman's plan for an organ of 28 stops was a technically complicated construc-tion, with the Hauptwerk and pedal each divided into two halves, "and between them a completely free-standing low section containing the Oberwerk next to where the keydesk and Pedal is situated."[9] This special design, reminiscent of Frantz Boll's organ built in Uppsala Cathedral in the 1670s, was necessary to provide enough space for a large orchestra for royal funerals. Johan Niclas Cah-man ought to have been well prepared for this challenge. A thorough education from his father and his coworkers during the organ-building project in Uppsala Cathedral should have meant that he was used to large and difficult projects. He certainly must have also been in on the work of building the Riddarholms Church organ from the beginning.

When the work in the Riddarholms Church was finished in 1700, Johan Niclas Cahman moved to Västerås, where he built a new 32-stop organ in the cathedral there. Cahman married Elisabeth Jernstedt, the daughter of the factory owner and alderman Johan Jernstedt, giving him a higher social position than he would have had as a craftsman. Some part of the economic security he enjoyed was due to an inheritance from his father-in-law.

His primary occupation, however, was organ building. Many organs were born in his workshop in Västerås, including a 22-stop organ for Mariestad Cathedral in 1705, which is still preserved, although extensively rebuilt, in Kölingared

---

8. See Abrah. Abrah:s Son Hülphers, *Historisk Afhandling om Musik och Instrumenter* (1773; fac-simile reprint with an English introduction by Thorild Lindgren and a note on the organs by Peter Williams, Amsterdam: Frits Knuf, 1971), 287; and Erici and Unnerbäck, *Orgelinventarium*, 466–67. A complete documentation of the organ by Niclas Fredriksson is forthcoming (Göteborg: GOArt).

9. Hülphers, *Historisk Afhandling*, 203.

Church. The organ-building collaborations were less intensive during the latter part of the decade, perhaps because of the weaker economic situation in Sweden during the Great Northern War of 1700–21. In 1711 the Cahman family moved from Västerås to Stockholm, where Johan Niclas Cahman earned his income for nearly a decade as a tax collector for Södermalm in Stockholm. To improve their financial situation, he and his wife started a linen shop near Slussen in central Stockholm. The shop succeeded, and now Cahman could also add the title of merchant to his accomplishments. He continued his organ-building shop side by side with his work as civil servant and merchant, but on a smaller scale. Apart from the building of a few minor new small organs, he held exclusive organ maintenance and repair contracts with many congregations.

In 1721 Cahman gave up his position as a tax collector. With that, a period of intense creativity and increased prosperity began. In 1723 he purchased land in the Maria Magdalena parish, where he also established his new workshop, since his old workshop near St. Catharine's Church had recently been destroyed in a city fire. His residence near the street had four rooms and a kitchen, beautiful furniture, carpeting in three rooms, paintings, rich silver in the cupboards, and linen in the wardrobes. In the workshop, smithies and various organ-building apprentices pursued their craft. The obviously very well organized organ-building shop had now reached a high point, the ultimate expression of which was the famous organ in Uppsala Cathedral, completed in 1731 (figure 10-2). The organ had 40 registers on Hauptwerk, Oberwerk, and Pedal and was considered a very large step forward in Cahman's output. The official inspection of the organ declared that comparing Cahman's earlier organs in the Västerås Cathedral and the Riddarholms Church with the new organ in Uppsala was like "comparing water to wine."[10]

From that moment on, we can observe how Cahman worked consistently to establish himself as the leading Swedish organ builder. The times were favorable. Very few organ builders were working in Sweden in the 1720s, the economy there had gradually improved, and the authorities viewed efforts in entrepreneurship, national industry, and technical evolution positively.

Cahman took advantage of the new climate of entrepreneurship to strengthen his position against that of his competitors. In 1724 he lobbied the government to restrict organ building and repair contracts only to builders that had passed an examination, a plan the government chose to follow. Four years later Cahman wanted the government to decide that he alone, in the cooperation with the Royal Chapel-master, should give the examination, but he was not allowed to develop a monopoly. Yet, after 1728 he is often referred to as director, or director

10. Hülphers, *Historisk Afhandling*, 184 n. 23. See also N. J. Söderberg, "Studier till Uppsala domkyrkas historia, II: Orgverk i domkyrkan," *Kyrkohistorisk årsskrift* 135 (1935), 47–145.

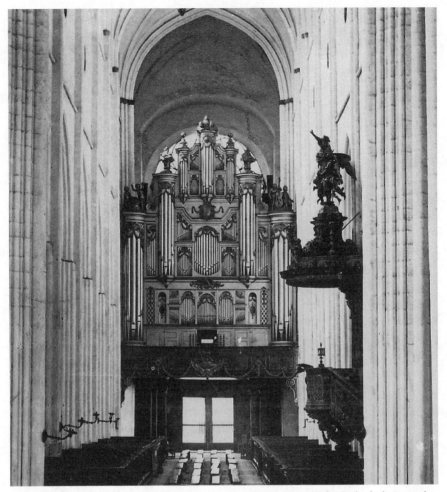

Figure 10-2. The Johan Niclas Cahman organ (1698) in Uppsala Cathedral. Printed with permission of Antikvarisk-topografiska arkivet, ATA, Stockholm.

of the organ building shops, which indicates that in reality he was looked upon as a sort of supervisor for the entire organ-building profession.

For the rest of his life Cahman continued to be successful as an organ builder. He produced more large organs like the Uppsala Cathedral organ, small single-manual organs for parish churches, and small positives like the 6-stop positive in the church of the Drottningholm Royal Castle. [11]

It was during this period that he built the famous organ in Leufsta Bruk.

11. See Erici and Unnerbäck, *Orgelinventarium*. The Drottningholm positive was recently restored by the Swedish organ builder Mats Arvidsson, who among other things reconstructed the original bellows system. Its four-foot façade is partially hidden by a balcony in the Drottningholm Castle Chapel.

Because the organ is well preserved, we have a good picture of Cahman's excellent craftsmanship, intelligent construction, fine pipe making, and art of voicing. As a whole, the Leufsta Bruk organ seems to represent a personal style, based on the North German tradition but at the same time something different, an innovation improved by a skillful craftsman and artist. There are indications that Cahman was well aware of developments in other countries. In his proposal of 1732 for a new organ in Linköping Cathedral, he names newly invented stops such as the Vox humana, of a type that was developed by Johann Josua Mosengel in Königsberg, and the Viola di Gamba, invented by Silbermann in Saxony.[12]

In looking at the technical parts and pipe construction of Cahman's instruments, we can see many aspects in common with his father's organ-building practice, as found in the Virestad organ. The principles that Johan Niclas Cahman followed in his early organs seem to remain the same until around 1730: uniform and rather narrow scaling, high cut-ups in the flutes, and oak windchests with narrow channels. Hülphers reported that Cahman's wind channels were criticized as too narrow, causing the organs to sound softer than they ought according to their size and specification.[13]

In the disposition of his organs, however, he departs from his father's practice. The richness of mixtures and mutations of the North German baroque tradition was often restricted to a Qvinta 2⅔' and one single mixture (with a third-sounding rank) in the manuals. The reeds included were Trumpets and a Basun 16', as well as a Vox Humana in the Rückpositiv or Oberwerk. As in Leufsta Bruk, all of his organs from that period have a full octave in the bass. According to his letter to the bishop of Linköping in 1732, he preferred a temperament that allowed playing the instrument in all of the keys: "From my own perspective, I would like to say that I think one has come far enough when all 12 steps within the octave could be so tempered and equaled that all the fifths beat a little bit, so that all the thirds have been helped somewhat, so that with tolerable satisfaction one can play in all keys—as well in C♯, F♯, and G♯ major as in C, D, and F major, and then also in B major, the thirds that used to be too high and too horrible become as tolerable as some of the others."[14]

As can be seen in Leufsta Bruk, Cahman still built his larger organs in the tradition of the North German organ architecture, but transformed them into

12. Axel Unnerbäck, "Domkyrkans orglar från Cahman till Setterquist," in *Linköpings domkyrka III*, Sveriges kyrkor, 225 (Stockholm: Riksantikvarieämbedet, 2001): 295–309.

13. Axel Unnerbäck, "Orgelbyggare, tjänsteman och köpman: Ett bidrag till Johan N. Cahmans biografi," parts 1 and 2, *Orgelforum* 6, no. 2 (1984): 17; 7, no. 1 (1985): 14.

14. From a letter of 15 April 1732 to the bishop of Linköping about the scientist Christopher Polhem's suggestion for an equal-beating temperament. Linköpings stiftsbibliotek, handskriftssamlingen, N 12. (See also chapter 1.)

what we can call a Swedish late-baroque style, with very fine proportions, excellent pipe construction, and not too many ornaments.

In building the new 40-stop organ in the Uppsala Cathedral around 1730, Cahman introduced new organ architecture and a new sound aesthetic. From that point on, with only a few exceptions, the Rückpositiv disappeared from Swedish-built organs, replaced by an Oberwerk. The pedals were no longer placed in independent cases, but connected to the Hauptwerk, creating a high, pyramidlike architecture based on a very broad console and crowned by the three turrets in the Oberwerk, with the highest in the middle. In January 1733, when the Göteborg Cathedral parish signed a contract for a new Cahman organ, the parish requested a façade the same shape as the one he had built in Uppsala. Cahman's successors applied this same design to large instruments as well as to one-manual organs. Even the organ builder Wahlberg in Linköping used Cahman's façade design as a prototype, in spite of the fact that he had been educated in the tradition of Casparini and Mosengel, which had been brought to Sweden in the 1740s by Wahlberg's master Jonas Wistenius.

From the Uppsala instrument we can observe that Cahman abandoned his previous scaling practices and used a wider scaling for the stops. In the contract he commented that most of the stops needed to be "wider," "much wider," "a wide scaling," and so on.[15] Evidently he recognized that a large cathedral approximately a hundred meters long and thirty meters high with a problematic acoustic needed a different, more voluminous sound.

Cahman's Successors

The North German organ introduced by Hans Henrich Cahman and developed by his son Johan Niclas into a Swedish late-baroque organ style was continued by his successors, but not unchanged. Olof Hedlund, the journeyman who took over his workshop, seems to have adhered closely to his master's tradition. But another journeyman, Daniel Stråhle, after pursuing a theoretical-technical education under the famous scientist and inventor Christopher Polhem, had an ambition to develop organ building on scientific grounds, even if, in practice, he still worked within the framework of the Cahman tradition. Stråhle's successors, Jonas Gren and Petter Stråhle, leading Stockholm organ builders from 1750 to 1765, frequently referred to their collaboration with the Swedish Academy of Sciences, a reflection of a time when the sciences had gained an important position in society and administration. However, very few of their organs are preserved, and it has not yet been determined whether they actually applied scientific methods in the construction and scaling of their organs. Cahman's level

---

15. The contract is reproduced in Söderberg, "Studier till Uppsala domkyrkans historia, II."

of quality in the hand crafting, especially the pipe making, is still recognizable, but the wind supply systems and scaling of the stops reveal that Cahman's late-baroque aesthetic had been replaced by another musical ideal. The last important organ builder in the chain was Olof Schwan, successor to Gren and Stråhle. Schwan was highly respected as an organ builder, and his close connection to some leading architects, authors, and musicians made him, to a certain degree, a part of the cultural establishment of the Gustavian era. With his death in 1812, the baroque tradition of Johan Niclas Cahman reached its end as a living, creative organ-building tradition. The baroque organ was considered passé; elements of the early romantic style had already been introduced in the large organs of Schwan; and some years later the early romantic organ, in the tradition of J. G. Mende, was introduced into Sweden.

Mercantilism, the dominating political movement of the first half of the eighteenth century, formed the frame within which Johan Cahman lived and worked. He was also a product of his time: enterprising, multifaceted, technically gifted, and a clever businessman. He was musically talented and had a persuasive way of communicating with people. Likewise, the Leufsta Bruk organ was a reflection of its time: displaying a level of technical and handicraft skill as genuine as that of the famous ironsmiths from Leufsta Bruk, along with clarity of construction, an economical disposition, and a sound that is overpowering, both intellectually and musically. The instrument is an integral part of the highly valuable industrial, intellectual, and artistic environment of Leufsta Bruk, but also stands alone as an extraordinary work of art.

II

FROM CATHEDRAL TO RURAL PARISH: ORGANS AND ORGANISTS IN EIGHTEENTH-CENTURY SWEDEN

EVA HELENIUS-ÖBERG AND PAMELA RUITER-FEENSTRA

THE GREAT NORTHERN WAR OF 1700–1721 TOUCHED EVERY ASPECT OF LIFE IN Sweden and also played a role in the story of the Cahman organ in Leufsta Bruk. The war began in part because when King Charles XI died in 1697 after a prolonged illness, he left an heir who was just fourteen years old. Denmark could not resist the opportunity to try to wrest land from the giant that Sweden had become during the seventeenth century and began a campaign to organize a great coalition of powers against Sweden that would include Russia, Poland, and even England. The young King Charles XII spent his short life on the battlefield, returning home to Sweden only briefly in 1715 to plan his campaign against Norway. Although the war would end in defeat for Sweden and an heirless death on the battlefield for her young king, the first great battle of the war ended in a decisive victory over the Russians at Narva, outside of St. Petersburg on the Gulf of Finland. This victory was celebrated in grand style with festive music at Uppsala Cathedral in 1701:

> At the beginning of the High Mass, all of the musicians assembled at the large new organ, among them were the Old Rudbeck, Professors Vallerius, Reftelius, and Bellman with a large number of students. The procession began with beautiful instrumental music. Then the musicians separated themselves into groups: one part went behind the altar onto a specially built podium, so that they could be seen over the altar. Under Prof. Reftelius' direction, they answered the group at the new organ *in alternatim* with beautiful choral music in place of the Gradual psalm. . . . They performed again from three stations: Prof. Reftelius directed from the old organ and Prof. Vallerius from above the altar, but Prof. Rudbeck was the only one left at the new organ; the musicians were absolutely heavenly.
>
> After the sermon, the musicians divided themselves into four stations, in which the fourth group was placed at the coronation altar at the south door,

and consequently opposite one another. Each group was provided with singers and instruments. . . . Rudbeck began on the new organ with "O God, We Praise Thee," of which he and his group sang the first verse; then the group at the old organ sang the second verse, and so on back and forth, all choirs sang one verse alternating from one to another until the end of the hymn; during the singing of this hymn, twenty-four guns were fired twice from the church court-yard and six guns were fired twice from the castle. For the recessional, Zellinger played the timpani, and then all of the musicians gathered at the new organ, and each participated with gusto. At the end, during the evening prayer, Prof. Bellman played superbly, and to conclude, we sang: "My soul doth magnify the Lord."[1]

Three of the organists mentioned in this description were also key players in the production of the hymnal used in Sweden throughout the eighteenth century, and they provide a fascinating view of the breadth of learning present in Sweden's intelligentsia. Olof Rudbeck (1630–1702) was a professor of architecture and medicine who codiscovered the lymphatic system. He was also a composer and a specialist in linguistics, antiquities, botanical garden architecture, organ build-ing, botany, chemistry, mathematics, physics, music, astronomy, and technology. Harald Vallerius (1646–1716) was Rector Cantus at Uppsala Cathedral and Uni-versity, as well as a mathematician, professor, and prolific author, composer, and organist. He also played the violin, dulcian, bassoon, and flute, and performed thoroughbass on keyboard instruments.[2] Johan Arendt Bellman (1664–1709) was a professor of elocution and a musician who was the grandfather of the well-known art song composer, Carl Mikael Bellman (1740–95).

The "new organ" mentioned above had been completed in 1698 by Hans Henrich Cahman (see chapter 10), the father of Johan Niclas, who built the Leufsta Bruk organ. It contained 4,000 pipes, including a 32′ Principal in the pedal, but was destroyed in a fire in 1702.[3] It was in this parish, at about this time, that the brothers who would grow up to be the first two organists of Johan Niclas Cahman's organ in Leufsta Bruk were baptized: Lorentz Bäck, on 6 May 1700, and Henric Bäck, on 25 November 1701.

The First Organists at Leufsta Bruk

Lorents Bäck, the father of Henric and Lorentz, was a master carpenter in Upp-sala and a member of the cathedral parish. Although little is known about the

1. Letter from Professor Mikael Eneman to the mayor of Enköping, 1701; cited in Harald Göransson, "Koralpsalmboken 1697: Studier i svensk koralhistoria" (Ph.D. diss., Uppsala University, 1992), 171.

2. See Göransson, "Koralpsalmboken 1697," 44.

3. Abrah. Abrah:s Son Hülphers, *Historisk Afhandling om Musik och Instrumenter* (Westerås, 1773; facs. ed. with an English introduction by Thorild Lindgren and a note on the organs by Peter Wil-liams, Amsterdam: Frits Knuf, 1971), 213. Its specification is given in Olaus Olai Bergroth, "Instru-menta Musica" (Ph.D. diss., Uppsala University, 1717), 19–20.

family, the godparents listed in the baptismal records of Lorents Bäck's five children[4] reveal that Lorents had connections in higher social classes than were usual for a common carpenter. The fact that professors' wives and cathedral employees were named as godparents suggests that Lorents Bäck might have been employed by the university. Among the godparents of the Bäck children were Sara Swedberg, wife of the theology professor and hymn poet Jesper Swedberg, who had preached the sermon at that festival service. Their son Emanuel Swedenborg (1688–1772), the natural scientist, philosopher, and theologian, was one of the intellectual giants of eighteenth-century Sweden; his teachings later inspired the Swedenborgian church. Godparents formed the social security system of the age, and it is likely that they made it possible economically for the intellectually gifted Bäck brothers to study. Both brothers had professions that demanded an academic education: Lorentz and Henric were bookkeepers, and Henric was also a regiment enrollment scribe and eventually a *bruk* inspector. Acquiring these positions would not have been possible without early training at school, probably at what is still called the Uppsala Cathedral School.

The Great Northern War dragged on. At the age of seventeen, the young Henric Bäck (1701–73) was enrolled in the army as a military musician at a time when Charles XII was suing for peace in order to buy time to build up his army secretly for a new campaign against the Danes. Why Bäck belonged to the Västmanland (and not the Uppland) regiment is not clear, but we know that he was at the siege of Fredrikshald, Norway on 30 November 1718 when the king was killed in action, effectively ending the war.[5] In 1719, the year a division of the Russian navy burned the entire estate of Leufsta Bruk to the ground, Henric stayed in his regiment, where he became an enrollment scribe. However, after the Nystad Peace agreement of 1721, all of the army "oboists" were dismissed owing to a lack of funds.[6] ("Oboist" in this context seems to have been a military term designating a professional musician, not necessarily an oboe player.) At that time a number of the newly unemployed oboists turned toward the largest employer of musicians: the Swedish Church. Thus came the metamorphosis from oboist to organist.

In 1721 Henric went to Västerås to learn to play the organ, probably to study with the cathedral organist Ernst Ferdinand Pape (1680–1743), who played the organ built in 1702 by Johan Niclas Cahman, with 32 stops on two manuals and pedal.[7] Pape had an excellent reputation as an organist, was highly esteemed as

4. Uppsala Landsarkivet [ULA], Uppsala Cathedral Archive C a:1 (Birth and Baptismal Book, 1693–1706).

5. A brief biography of Henric Bäck with information about his death is found in ULA, Österlövsta Church Archive F I:1 (Death and Burial Book, 1769–1812).

6. According to a decree of 27 June 1720, § 17, in *Modée, Utdrag Utur alle ifrån den 7. Decemb. 1817. utkomne Publique Handlingar, Placater, Förordningar, Resolutioner Ock Publikationer &c.* Vol. 1 till 1730. Stockholm 1742, 238–43.

7. Hülphers, *Historisk Afhandling*, 225.

an organ teacher, and had many pupils. Henric Bäck most likely studied with Pape for four years before he became organist in the Österlövsta parish in 1725, following the completion of a new one-manual organ by Cahman with 9 stops.

As organist in the Österlövsta Church, Henric Bäck was employed by the county governor, Charles De Geer (1660–1730), owner of Leufsta Bruk, Österby Bruk, Hargs Bruk, and the Väsby, Tobo, and Örbyhus manors. The primary source documenting the lives of the people working at Leufsta is the *bruk* archive.[8] The so-called *bruk* books contain accounts concerning every person employed by or involved with the *bruk*. With exceptional accuracy, all of the expenses, such as medicine, visits to the surgeon, and purchases from the street shop (including tobacco, food, clothes, reading primers, and hymnals) are listed and deducted from the yearly salaries. Thus, when we first meet Henric Bäck in the archives, he is called "organist" (1725–31) and "monsieur" (1732–33). In the period 1730–32, he is paid as organist both at the Österlövsta parish church and at the Leufsta Bruk church, where the new Cahman organ was completed in 1728, the crowning achievement of years of rebuilding from the destruction of the war.[9] In addition to the annual salary for the two organist positions at the parish and at the *bruk*, Bäck had other responsibilities at Leufsta that are reflected in the account books on his credit side. Included among these tasks were posts at the general store and at the iron-loading dock at the harbor from 1730 to 1731.[10] These other engagements soon took all his time. In 1740 he returned to Leufsta Bruk as inspector, a position he retained until his death on 23 July 1773. As inspector, Henric was an important person at Leufsta, responsible directly to Baron Charles De Geer for all of the *bruk*'s activity.

Henric Bäck was succeeded as organist in Leufsta Bruk by his slightly elder brother Lorentz (1700–1780) and in Österlövsta by his brother-in-law, Bengt Norin, who was married to Anna Margareta Bäck. It is not known where Lorentz received his organ education. Because blood relatives maintained strong relationships and the family formed a social network, it seems likely that Lorentz may also have studied with Pape in Västerås. Lorentz, like Henric, had other duties at Leufsta Bruk. But unlike his brother, Lorentz never left Leufsta and its organ: his name is recorded in the account books for forty-five years, from 1735 until his death in June 1780. His first salary confirms his double task as organist and bookkeeper at the *bruk* office. Lorentz Bäck was also paid for "tuning and maintenance of the harpsichord in the manor" in 1753.[11] The instrument referred to

8. Now held in the Korsnäs Archive, kept in the Inspector's House in Leufsta Bruk. The Leufsta Archive at the National Archives in Stockholm also contains valuable information on the De Geer family and its estates and patronage churches.

9. Korsnäs Archive, Leufsta Bruk Archive vol. 86 (Account Book, 1723–35), 292, 498.

10. Korsnäs Archive, Leufsta Bruk Archive, vol. 86, 292.

11. Korsnäs Archive, Leufsta Bruk Archive, vol. 282, 368.

could be the harpsichord built by the famous Hieronymus Albrecht Hass in Hamburg,[12] which is still in the manor house. The fact that Lorentz Bäck was entrusted with the maintenance of the manor harpsichord gives us a clue that there could be more connections between the private music making in the manor and the more public presentations of music in the *bruk* church.

Lorentz Bäck also served as a music teacher at Leufsta in some official capacity. From 1738 to 1746, Lorentz was paid room and board for one of his music pupils, Carl Boivie.[13] A statement showing that Lorentz also was paid for violin strings that were bought for him and his pupils reveals that in addition to organ students, he also taught string students,[14] including his son Hinric, who became cathedral organist in Göteborg in 1770. These music students probably took part in a *bruk* ensemble. When the new organ in the Västland Church was inaugurated in 1747, the word *capell* is used in the accounts, which record a sum paid "to the organist in Leufsta, Bäck, who made music with his ensemble and who approved the organ."[15] This *brukscapell* could have had woodwind instruments too, because in 1738 "a bassoon with an oboe reed" was bought for Baron Charles De Geer.[16] A substantial amount of chamber music is preserved in the Leufsta music collection[17] and may have been used by the *brukscapell*, which consisted of people with whom the baron enjoyed playing (his children, the Bäck brothers, and Lorentz's pupils). Additionally, when ordered by De Geer, this *capell* sometimes may have played outside Leufsta, especially in the many patronage churches belonging to his estate.

The Hülphers Catalog of Eighteenth-Century Swedish Organs

Through the marriage of Henric Bäck's son, Carl Henrich (1742–1814), to Elsa Johanna Hülphers (1765–1843) in 1785,[18] the Leufsta organists knew Elsa's father, Abraham Abrahamson Hülphers (1734–98; figure 11-1), the most impor-

12. Donald H. Boalch, *Makers of the Harpsichord and Clavichord, 1440–1840*, 3d ed. (Oxford: Oxford University Press, 1995), 366.

13. Korsnäs Archive, Leufsta Bruk Archive, vol. 128, 177 (1738); vol. 134, 193 (1739); vol. 139, 185 (1740); vol. 145, 211 (1741); vol. 150, 217 (1742); vol. 155, 217 (1743); vol. 161, 221 (1744); vol. 165, 217 (1745); and vol. 169, 217 (1746).

14. Korsnäs Archive, Leufsta Bruk Archive, vol. 128, 177 (Bruk accounts 1738).

15. ULA, Västland Church Archive K I:1 f. 10. See also Birger Olsson, *Olof Hedlund Orgelbyggare. Levnad, verksamhet, orgelverkens öden*, Skrifter från Institutionen för Musikvetenskap, no. 55 (Göteborg: Göteborg University, 1998), 140.

16. Korsnäs Archive, Leufsta Bruk Archive, vol. 115 (office accounts, 1734–42).

17. Now in the Uppsala University Library; see Albert Dunning, "Die De Geer'schen Musikalien in Leufsta: Musikalische schwedisch-niederländische Beziehungen im 18. Jh.," *Svensk tidskrift för musikforskning* 48 (1966): 187–210.

18. Viktor Ekstrand, *Svenska landtmätare 1628–1900: Biografisk förteckning* (Stockholm: Sveriges lantmätareförening, 1896–1903), 68.

Figure 11-1. Abraham Abrahamsson Hülphers, portrait by Branting Nilsson (?). Printed with permission of the National Swedish Art Museums, Stockholm.

tant figure in the history of the organ in eighteenth-century Sweden. In *Historisk Afhandling om Musik och Instrumenter* (An Historical Dissertation on Music and Instruments), Hülphers collected the specifications of almost every extant organ in Sweden. His preserved correspondence in two comprehensive volumes contains letters from many Swedish musicians as well as instrument makers of the day.

Abraham Hülphers was a tradesman, born in Västerås to a wealthy merchant who gave his son a good education. In 1761 he entered into partnership in the family company, then called Abraham Hülphers & Son, and in the same year married Anna Christina Grave, the daughter of another *bruk* owner, Sebastian Grave. Thus, in 1775, after the death of his father-in-law, he was appointed managing director of the Fredriksberg and Annefors Bruk. Additionally, he assumed the responsibility of the Ulriceberg blast furnace. However, Hülphers, who had a passion for research and writing, always devoted time and energy to his writing, despite his numerous professional activities. An avid traveler, he also kept prolific travel journals, undertook genealogical studies, and maintained a sumptuous appetite for music, witnessed by his collection of keyboard instruments and organs and by his library, which included Praetorius's *Syntagma Musicum*.[19] He never became a fellow of the Royal Swedish Academy of Music, but he belonged to several other learned societies.

Hülphers's *Historisk Afhandling*, begun during the 1760s, is divided into a first

---

19. Thorild Lindgren, introduction to the 1965 facsimile edition, 19. For Hülphers, see also Torbjörn Norman, *Abraham Hülphers och Dalaresan 1757*, Introduction to the facsimile edition of the Dalacarlia journey; Olle Franzén, art. Hülphers, *Svenskt biografiskt lexikon*, 19: 539–43.

section on music and musical instruments, a second section on church music, and a third section describing the organs in Sweden around 1770. Hülphers worked tirelessly, sending questionnaires asking for information about organs in every Swedish parish and cathedral chapter. He carried out his research in a methodologically modern way, even though he had to depend on the accuracy of his informants and the sources available to them. Consequently, each of his informants as well as their intentions must be taken into account when using his collection. Many facts about organ building, for example, came from the Linköping cathedral organist Johan Miklin (1726–87), whose information often came from the organ builder Jonas Wistenius (1700–1777). Hülphers's editorial work and the way in which he handled source material can still be judged by examining the existing collection of manuscripts and tender documents used in preparation for printing. The Hülphers material in total is easily the most important individual source regarding organs and musical life in eighteenth-century Sweden.

Forty-three Swedish town churches lacked organs, for various reasons. Many churches on the Finnish west coast and Swedish east coast were damaged by the Russians at the end of the Great Northern War. Other organs were destroyed by numerous fires that reduced whole communities to ashes. Some parishes had an organ earlier, either a sixteenth- or a seventeenth-century positive organ or even an instrument from the Middle Ages that was no longer usable. Some had never had an organ in the church.

Of the thirteen cathedral cities, eleven boasted instruments of two manuals. The two exceptions, Växjö in Sweden and Borgå in Finland, lost their organs to fires. Of the eleven two-manual instruments, six were built by the Leufsta Bruk master Johan Niclas Cahman. Among the cities with foreign trade privileges (*stapelstäder*), Stockholm dominated the organ landscape. The Great Church (Storkyrka, now Stockholm Cathedral) housed the largest organ in Sweden, with three manuals and 45 stops, built in the 1690s by George Woijtzig. Hülphers lists only three other organs with three manuals in Sweden: the German Church (Tyska Kyrka) in Stockholm and the Linköping and Visby cathedrals. In the larger *uppstäder* (those with only domestic business privileges) and richer country parishes, two-manual organs were most typical. Smaller towns or country parishes had mostly one-manual organs, the larger ones often with a pull-down pedal.

Hülphers's work makes it possible to compare the Swedish organ landscape to conditions abroad. Johann Mattheson (1681–1764) lists eighty-seven city organs.[20] Only four of them had four manuals. The largest of these was in Prague, while the other three were all in Hamburg churches. Thirty-two churches had

20. In his *Anhang von mehr als 60 Orgel-Werken* printed in Friedrich Erhardt Niedt's (1674–1708) *Musicalische Handleitung* (2d ed. vol. 2, 1721).

TABLE 11-1.

A Comparison of Organs in German and Swedish Listings

Manuals	Mattheson, 1721, and Adlung, 1768	Hülphers, 1773
4	8 organs with 52–75 stops	no organs
3	59 organs with 27–65 stops	4 organs with 33–45 stops
2	77 organs with 14–38 stops	40 organs with 11–40 stops
1	2 organs with 10 and 14 stops	54 organs with 5–22 stops

three-manual organs, and twenty-five churches had two-manual organs. Mattheson lists only one organ with a single manual, a positive in Königsberg. Of these eighty-seven organs, only eight were found in cities that did not belong to the Hanseatic League.

In 1768, half a century later and contemporary with Hülphers's book, Jacob Adlung published a supplement to Mattheson's list in his *Musica Mechanica Organoedi*.[21] Of the eighty-three additional city organs Adlung mentions, only three are four-manual organs: Merseburg, Halberstadt and Eisenach. Twenty-seven are three-manual organs. The fifty-two two-manual instruments dominate the Adlung list, whereas he also only mentions one instrument with a single manual. The organ landscapes from these three important eighteenth-century sources are summarized in table 11-1.

Clearly, in Sweden, in stark contrast to the continent, single-manual organs were most common. One such typical Swedish single-manual organ from Torstuna in 1737 had 10 stops on one manual with a full bass octave. The church archives include an 8 August 1737 contract with Olof Hedlund about the organ to be built for Torstuna Church: "[This is] a strong and large congregation. The organ will consist of 10 stops on one manual with a full bass octave. The stops and spellings will be modeled after Cahman's project of May 25, 1731."[22] The German stop list (see specification 11-1) includes the following stipulations: "that the Principal 8′ is of fine English tin, and that the other stops are a metal alloy of 16 parts (marker) lead and 4 parts tin. The aforementioned stops in the organ division [are] so deep and manly that one can use them all simultaneously. . . . Of these 10 stops, four will be half [divided] stops, so that the organist can play stanzas of hymns as if on two manuals."[23]

21. Jacob Adlung, *Musica mechanica Organoedi* (1768; facsimile reprint, ed. Christhard Mahrenholz, Kassel: Bärenreiter, 1961).

22. ULA, Torstuna Church Archive O I a:2 (documents on church and vicarage, 1754–1851, including a contract with Olof Hedlund on organ building, 8 August 1737).

23. ULA, Torstuna Church Archive contract with Olof Hedlund.

SPECIFICATION 11-1.

Torstuna Church, One-Manual Organ, Olof Hedlund contract, 1737

Qvintadena 16'
Principal 8'
Spits Flöte 8'
Qvinta 6'
Octava 4'
Rohr Flöte 4'
Qvinta 3'
Super octava 2'
Mixtur IV
Trompet 8'
Tremulant [listed in examination report; not in contract]

The indication "as if on two manuals" could imply that the two-manual organ was the liturgical ideal. Divided stops were found on many one-manual organs in Sweden. The presence of divided stops certainly allows for greater versatility in registration as well as the repertoire, hymns, and improvisations performed on the instruments. Leufsta Bruk also had divided stops in the manual, and from its disposition, one could guess that the 4 divided stops in Torstuna were four of the five found in Leufsta: Principal 8', Qvintadena 16', Octava 4', Trompet 8', or Mixtur IV. The original Cahman contract for the Leufsta organ did not include the specification for the Ryggpositiv; perhaps the manual stops of the Leufsta organ were divided because it was originally conceived as a one-manual instrument.

Registrations for a Two-Manual Organ

Compared to continental European standards, most Swedish churches were smaller in every dimension, particularly in height—a help in the long, cold winters, but a factor that greatly affected organ building and design. A 32' stop was highly unusual, and even full-length 16' stops were included only according to the available space. Thus, the typical church organs found in the southern third of Sweden were either one- or two-manual organs. Two-manual instruments with Rygg-Positiv divisions, such as that at Leufsta Bruk, needed less height and were ideal in the medium-sized Swedish church.

Johan Niclas Cahman's organ for Västerås Cathedral (1702) also contained two-manuals, with its 32 stops divided among three divisions: Manual, Rygg-Postiv, and pedal. When Jonas Gren and Petter Stråhle renovated it in 1757–58, they retained all of the original stops and added a Principal 16' stop to the pedal.[24] In a letter of 1763 to Hülphers, Petter Stråhle drew up a representative two-manual organ with a fully developed pedal. His hypothetical specification[25] (see specification 11-2) is nearly identical to Cahman's specification for Västerås. The only differences between the two specifications are that Västerås included a tremulant on the manual, whereas Stråhle did not, and Stråhle's specification included a Principal 16' in the pedal, a stop that Cahman did not originally install in Västerås, but the one stop that Gren & Stråhle added to the instrument in 1758.

The Leufsta Bruk Cahman organ also boasted two manuals and a well-developed pedal. The Leufsta Bruk organ has fewer stops—28 total, 5 of them divided. The Leufsta organ has fewer reed stops but more mixtures, including third-sounding pitches[26]: the Leufsta Ryggpositiv lacks a 2' flute found on the other two specifications, as well as a Cornetin 2' in the pedal.

These similar organ specifications from 1702 to 1763 reveal an organ builder's perspective on what is appropriate for liturgical use in eighteenth-century Sweden as well as Stråhle's respect for Cahman's design.

SPECIFICATION 11-2.
Stråhle's Specification for a Two-Manual Organ (c. 1763)

Manual	Rygg-Positiv	Pedal
Qvintadena 16'	Quintadena 8'	Principal 16'
Principal 8'	Gedact 8'	Subbas 16'
Flaggfleut 8'	Principal 4'	Octava 8'
Kortfleut 8'	Spetzfleut 4'	Gedact 8'
Fleutraversier	Quinta 3'	Octava 4'
Octava 4'	Octava 2'	Scharf 3. Chor
Fleut 4'	Scharf 3. Chor	Basun 16'
Qvinta 3'	Trompet 8'	Trompet 8'
Octava 2'	BårFleut 2'	Trompet 4'
Scharf 3. Chor	Spärrventil	Cornetin 2'
Trompet 16'		Spärrventil
Trompet 8'		
Trompet 4'		
Vox virginea		
Spärrventil		

24. Hülphers, *Historisk Afhandling*, 174.

25. Letter from Petter Stråhle to Hülphers, Västerås, 1763?, in VSB, Coll. Hülphers C b 2, fol. 426v–427r. Petter Stråhle (1720–65) was the nephew of Daniel Stråhle, Cahman's journeyman (see chapter 10).

26. Einar Erici and Axel Unnerbäck, *Orgelinventarium*, [new, rev. ed.] (Stockholm: Proprius, 1988), 188.

For his theoretical organ, Stråhle gave a detailed discussion of registration, valuable organ-building information, and instructions for liturgical organ playing: hymn introductions, preludes, and improvisations. Stråhle lists specific functions of the organ in the liturgical setting. Given the similarity of the Cahman Västerås organ and the Leufsta Bruk organ, Stråhle's registration indications could be applied and adapted to all three instruments. This document is translated in full here because its information is pertinent to eighteenth-century organ registration practice in general.

When one wishes to intone a hymn with the vox virginea, one should use the following stops: In the Manual, which plays on the lower keyboard, take the Flaggfleut 8' and vox virginea. In the RyggPositiv, which is the upper keyboard, take the Gedact 8' as the bass. In the pedal, draw only the Subbas 16'.

If one wants to intone with the Trompet 8' in the Manual, one should draw the following stops: in the Manual, take the Flaggfleut, or Korttfleut and Trompet. For variation, you may include the Fleut 4'; it cannot hurt. In the Ryggpositiv, take the Gedact 8'. If you want to draw the Spetzfleut with it, that would work, and if you would like to play a running bass on the Ryggpositiv, you may take the Gedact 8' and Bårfleut 2'. In the pedal, draw the Subbas and Gedact 8'. If you want a stronger pedal, draw the Principal 16' and Gedact 8'.

If one wants to intone using the Trompet 8' in the Ryggpositiv, one should draw the following stops. In the Manual, choose as the bass Flaggfleut alone, or Flaggfleut and Fleutraversier, or Flaggfleut and Fleut 4', or Korttfleut and Fleut 4', or Fleutravers and Korttfleut. If one also wants to play a running bass line, one may use the Fleutravers alone. (NB: The Fleutravers sounds most natural in the unmarked octave [tenor c to b] and can play passages in the c'-b' octave, but use the c"-b" octave sparingly, because there the stop can be thinner and screaming and works less well. Ditto NB: In the great octave [C-B], the Fleutravers stop and Gedact correspond, which should not be used when one wants to play imitation, or play the stop in the manner of the transverse flute.) In the pedal, use the same stops as to accompany the Trompet playing in the Manual.

P. S. Ditto. An alternative: in the Manual, take the Qvintadena 16' and in the RyggPositiv, Bårfleut 2', pull the coupler, and play on the lower keyboard. This sounds very nice together. In the pedal, one may take the Subbas with or without the Gedact according to personal preference. If one wants to choose the Subbas and Cornetin together, it is agreeable and sounds quite curious.

For these Preludes or intonations, use the stops annotated on the other page without including the vox virginea or any of the Trompets.

If one wants to couple the manuals, then one can take the Flaggfleut in the Manual and Spetzfleut in the RyggPositiv (NB: then one plays on the Manual or the lower keyboard) or also Flaggfleut and Bårfleut, or Korttfleut and Spetzfleut, or Gedact 8' in the Ryggpositiv and Fleut 4' in the Manual, or the Korttfleut and Bårfleut together. (NB: However, if one wants something in between, play the running passage on the upper or lower manual, as you wish. In this way, one can vary the playing considerably.) But in the pedal, use the Subbas alone, or with the Gedact 8,' or Principal and Gedact if one wants a stronger bass.

If one wants to accompany concerted music, then one can draw the Principal 8' and Quintadena 16' in the Manual. If one wants something stronger, one can add the Fleut 4'. In the pedal, draw the Principal 16' and Gedact 8'. If a stronger registration is needed, add the Octava 4' also.

For intonations and preludes, choose according to your preference in the Manual and RyggPositiv from the aforementioned stops; then you can take in the pedal the Subbas 16' and Cornetin, or Gedact 8' and Cornetin, or all three stops at once. (Whenever you add stops in the Manual or the Ryggpositiv, make the pedal stronger as well.)

All stops that are flutes* and Subbas should not be used with mixture stops on the organ, nor the Gedacts and Fleuts, because they are also flutes (NB: Gedact 8' is the same as Fleut 8', but is called Gedact because it is 8' deep [=sounding 8']. But when it is 4', it is called Fleut. Subbas 16' is the same as Gedact 16'; in German it is called Untersatz 16'. NB: Flaggfleut and Spetzfleut are similarly constructed; the difference consists in that one is 8' and the other 4'.)

Forgive the haste in which this was poorly written.

*By this is meant all stops that have the word Fleut in their names, with prefixes such as Flagg, Spetz, or Kortt, combined with Fleut. (NB: otherwise all of the stops that do not have shallots and tongues are part of the flute family, and the others are reeds.)[27]

Several observations can be made from Stråhle's registration advice. First, the main manual was clearly built as the lower manual, and the Ryggpositiv was the upper manual, as is the case in Leufsta Bruk. Reed stops were commonly used to play the chorale melody for hymn introductions. Although Stråhle cautions against combining flutes at the same pitch level, he makes exceptions when combining the Fleutraversier with another 8' flute stop. Stråhle also mentions a 16' and 2' combination twice: one achieved by coupling the Bårfleut 2' to the Qvintadena 16' on the manual, and the other by combining Subbas 16' with Cornetin 2' in the pedal. As this is added in a postscript and described as curious, it may reveal an experimental side of Stråhle. Each of the flutes appears to be scaled to function well with any other flute at a different pitch level in both manual divisions. The "ornamented running passages" listed more than once by Stråhle could well be improvised material. Also it is important to note the use of the 16' in both manual and pedal for accompanying instrumental music. A number of Hass harpsichords were built with 16' strings around the same

27. Västerås, Coll. Hülphers C B 2, fol. 426r–427v.

time period and were likely also used in ensemble music. Finally, Stråhle offers the valuable suggestion regarding playing technique (do not use "sharp playing" with flutes), demonstrating a keen awareness of the close relationship between organ design and playing technique.

As well as accompanying hymns, the organ often played with instruments in Sweden, particularly in cathedrals on feast days. Lund Cathedral's organist Christian Wenster (1735–1823) "asserted that when stronger musical instruments (like kettledrums and trumpets) are used in a concert, for certain solemn occasions, or during high feast days, the organ must be able to sound louder than all of them combined, and thus must be rich in stops, consisting of no fewer than 29 stops."[28]

Larger works were occasionally performed in the church at Leufsta Bruk, because among the music preserved from the Manor House is an Easter cantata by Hinrich Philip Johnsen (1717–79) that was performed in the Leufsta Bruk Church on Easter Day, 1757.[29] Johnsen was born in Germany, began working as a court musician at the Royal Chapel in Sweden in 1743, and then became organist and later Capellmaster at the St. Klara Church in Stockholm. He published a song collection and taught more than thirty Swedish organists.[30] We also know from Johnsen that the Leufsta Bruk organ's higher "Chorton" pitch was normal for eighteenth-century Sweden:

> The organ should be tuned to Chorton, in part for better and livelier strength, and in part because in the whole world, chorale books are established for Chorton. If the organ were tuned in Kammerton instead, all of the chorales would have to be transposed up one tone higher. . . . Furthermore, if the temperament is not all correct, much dissonance will exist in certain chords, which would not tolerate certain transpositions. Such a tuning on an organ would force the congregation to sing very low and soft, which would be antithetical to our greatest purpose of giving thanks and praise to God in our hymns.[31]

Often a Gedackt 8' rank would be tuned to Kammerton, or low pitch, especially in the city churches, so that the organist could accompany instrumentalists without having to transpose into keys that might not work with the organ's tuning.

28. Lund, Landsarkivet, Karlskrona town parish K III a:2 (Parish and Church Council meeting minutes 1755–64), 1622–32, 25 October 1759.

29. Score, transverse flute 1–2, violin 1–2, basso continuo, canto. Cf. Albert Dunning, "Die De Geer'schen Musikalien in Leufsta: Musikalische Schwedisch-Niederländische Beziehungen im 18. Jh." *Svensk tidskrift för musikforskning* 48 (1966): 208.

30. Hülphers, *Historisk Afhandling*, 109. The title of his song collection is *24 Oder af våra bäste poëters arbeten* (Stockholm, 1754).

31. Cited in Hülphers, *Historisk Afhandling*, 318–20. Incidentally, Hülphers cites Miklin's discussion of temperament, in which he mentions equal temperament as a theoretical but not an artistic temperament, and he lists Neidhardt as a possible unequal temperament for the organ.

The Strängnäs Cathedral archives from 1720 describe the repairs and additions that Johan Niclas Cahman made to the cathedral organ, including a description of Kammerton and Chorton found on the same organ: "The Werk and Ryck Positiw should also be improved, voiced, and tuned, and in the Oberwerk, a Gedackt 8' stop and the pedal Untersats 16' tuned for instrumental music shall be put into French pitch."[32]

Although no record of how the hymns were performed in Leufsta Bruk exists, a telling document from the Linköping Diocese in 1795 sets different require-ments for city and country church organists. The city organist must be fully conversant with the theory of hymns executed in three manners: with an ordinary thoroughbass accompaniment, with chords in the left hand and the melody in the right hand, and with chords in both hands.

Organists in large rural parishes must be capable of meeting the first two requirements, while those in small rural parishes are only expected to "play the hymns with chords in the right hand."[33] In the eighteenth century, at least, the baron probably held the organists at Leufsta Bruk to the standard of a city or-ganist.

The 1697 Swedish Hymnal as a Foundation for Organ Playing

The triumvirate of organists that participated in the festival service in Uppsala in 1701 was also responsible for creating the hymnal that would have been used in Leufsta Bruk. Its birth was a troubled one. During the last years of Charles XI's reign, Jesper Swedberg began preparing a new royal *Psalmbok*. But it had only just appeared in 1694 when he was unfairly accused of unorthodoxy. The new hymnal was withdrawn and a modified version, *Then Swenska Psalmboken 1695*, partly based on Swedberg's work, was published in 1697. Olof Rudbeck and Harald Vallerius were also commissioned by the King to provide melodies for the new hymnal,[34] and eventually the offical version became known as *Den Svenska Koralpsalmboken 1697*. Although Swedberg, Rudbeck, and Vallerius must have been embroiled in theological and political intrigue, the defeat of the Russians seems to have brought them together in 1701 to perform the Te Deum and Magnificat from their new hymnal.

The *Koralpsalmbok 1697* contains 413 texts and 250 melodies, primarily in unequal rather than equal note values. Many of the tunes were reused for various texts, sometimes successfully, but often familiar tunes took precedence over the most appropriate one for the text. Nearly half of the tunes came from German

32. ULA, Strängnäs Cathedral Archive A I:1 (Minutes 1717–1824), 22 Apr. 1720.

33. Cited in Gösta Morin, "Bidrag till sjuttonhundratalets svenska koralhistoria," *Svensk tidskrift för musikforskning* 26 (1944): 147.

34. Göransson, "Koralpsalmboken 1697," 196.

Figure 11-2. *Den Svenska Koralpsalmboken* (1697), chorale 173, "Jesu! tu tigh sielf upwäckte."

melodies, and one-tenth were Latin or Gregorian.[35] Vallerius, known as a skillful continuo player, chose to include figured bass settings for most of the 250 tunes in the *Korapsalmbok 1697*. The tunes lacking a figured bass are Gregorian-style melodies. This turn-of-the-century hymnal straddles the fence between Renaissance and baroque harmonies as well as between modality and tonality. Some of the hymns are treated in Renaissance style, with mostly root-position chords. Many other hymns include first-inversion chords, some seventh chords, and cadential 4–3 suspensions.

A brief survey of the same chorale as it appears in the *Koralpsalmbok 1697* and in four eighteenth-century arrangements illustrates some interesting regional differences in performance practice, varying degrees of musical taste, and experience. We will look at chorale number 173 from the *Koralpsalmbok 1697*, "Jesu! tu tigh sielf upwäckte" (figure 11-2). It is set similarly to all of the chorales found in this collection: the soprano and bass are given, the bass line in F-clef with figures, the soprano in C-clef; a meter is indicated; and the text of the first stanza is interlined.

Johan Everhardt was the director of music in Skara,[36] a cathedral city in southwest Sweden. The elegant engraving of Everhardt's name on the front page of his *Choral-Psalmbok, 1744*[37] (figure 11-3) suggests that the work was consid-

35. Göransson, *Koral och Andlig Visa i Sverige* (Stockholm: Norstedts, 1997), 56. The remaining melodies are Swedish, Dutch, Strassburgian, Genevan Psalms, Danish, Bohemian, Nordic, English, French, and Italian.

36. Hülphers, *Historisk Afhandling*, 116.

37. Johan Everhardt, *Choral-Psalmbok a Cant: & Bass.* (manuscript with engraved title page, Scara, 1744), housed in the Musikhistoriska Museet in Stockholm; below the engraving is written a date, 25 January 1789, and the place, Skara.

Figure 11-3. Johan Everhardt, *Choral-Psalmbok* (1744), title page. Printed with permission of Statens Musiksamlingar: Musikmuseet, Stockholm.

ered prestigious; a practical and honorable task undertaken by a learned musician. Everhardt also presented his chorales with soprano and figured bass, employing the more modern G-clef (figure 11-4). Although his harmony is similar, his bass line is more active, using quarter notes rather than the half notes of the *Koralpsalmbok 1697*.

Johan Björkman, organist and cantor in Hyby, produced a manuscript chorale book in 1763.[38] Hülphers cites Lars Schult from Rosaby, who stated that organists "must . . . have some knowledge of composition, which all can witness from good insight." Hülphers continues, citing Björkman from Kalmar as an example, "for he prepared a thoughtful collection on organists' duties and the proper use of the organ for solos as well as for hymn singing," and adds that Everhardt from Skara has also proven himself by authoring a manuscript about the structure of organs,[39] confirming the significance of this activity for organists and cantors,

38. "Gradual-Bok, eller Then Svenska PsalmBoken," called "Hybyboken 1763," on deposit at the Svensk Koralregistrant (SKR), Institute of Musicology at Lund University, by its owner, Elisabet Wentz-Janacek.

39. Hülphers, *Historisk Afhandling*, 197. Hülphers also named Zellbell Jr., Johnsen, and Miklin.

Figure 11-4. Johan Everhardt, *Choral-Psalmbok* (1744), chorale 173, "Jesu tu tigh sielf upwäckte." Printed with permission of Statens Musiksamlingar: Musikmuseet, Stockholm.

Figure 11-5. Johan Björkman, "Gradual-Bok, eller Then Svenska PsalmBoken," called "Hybyboken 1763," chorale 173, "Jesu tu tigh sielf upwäckte." On deposit at the Svensk Koralregistrant, SKR, Institute of Musicology, Lund University. Printed with permission of the owner, Elisabet Wentz-Janacek.

along with the composition of their own arrangements of the hymns, in order to prove their competence.

Two settings of chorale number 173 are included in Björkman's chorale book. The first (figure 11-5) is similar harmonically to the versions of *Koralpsalmbok 1697* and Everhardt. Björkman uses a C-clef in the treble, a bass with figures, and some chord tones with some eighth-note passing motion in the bass. He also adds small passing tones, neighboring tones, an appoggiatura, and three cadential trills to the soprano. The composed nonharmonic tones are written as grace notes. The second setting included in Björkman's collection is written in a different hand (figure 11-6). The treble clef is employed, and the right hand is given three voices, while the bass line has lost its figures. Notable are the composed interludes between phrases, ranging from seven to forty notes written primarily in stepwise motion as thirty-second notes but unmeasured. The harmony given in the ornamented version differs from that of the first setting. Only two such elaborate settings are found in the appendix of Björkman's hymnal.

Figure 11-6. Johan Björkman, "Gradual-Bok, eller Then Svenska PsalmBoken," called "Hybyboken 1763," alternate setting of "Jesu tu tigh sielf upwäckte." On deposit at the Svensk Koralregistrant, SKR, Institute of Musicology, Lund University. Printed with permission of the owner, Elisabet Wentz-Janacek.

Koralhandskrift A12 at the Music Library of Sweden features the chorales of *Koralpsalmbok 1697*, written out in four to seven voices (averaging six), with composed interludes and thoroughbass figures included (figure 11-7).[40] The interludes are not nearly as flamboyant as those found in the appendix to Björkman's hymnal. The density of the chords in A 12 is unusual for the organ, particularly if the instrument has flexible winding, because so many pitches in the bass would draw considerable wind. The A 12 settings could have been used on a one-manual organ with no pedals as a foundation for congregational singing. This extensive doubling could only be played on the organ at a rather stately tempo with clear articulation between each chord, suggesting clues for the performance practice of hymn singing and playing.

Anders Bonge, cantor at the Göteborg Gustavi Cathedral, features written-out four-part harmony in open score with ornamentation and figured bass throughout his manuscript "Koralbok," 1782[41] (example 11-1). Each voice has

40. Stockholm, Music Library of Sweden, Koralhandskrift A 12.
41. Anders Bonge, "Koralbok," GLA, Göteborgs Gustavi domkyrko församling, PIII:1.

Figure 11-7. Music Library of Sweden, "Koralhandskrift A12," chorale 173, "Jesu tu tigh sielf upwäckte." Printed with permission.

passing tones and neighboring tones, but the soprano is the most elaborately ornamented, with additional flourishes and smaller note values for the figuration. The alto and tenor voices either begin above the soprano or are intended to be played down one octave. If the tenor was transposed an octave lower, the fourth quarter note in the first measure would land below the bass line. Although compensation for this voice-crossing could be made by drawing a 16′ stop in the pedal, one could also play these settings on a two-manual organ, playing the ornamented soprano solo on a colorful combination including a reed stop in the Ryggpositiv (closer to the ears of the congregation), and playing the alto and tenor on the manual and the bass in the pedal.

The composed and written-out ornamentation in the previous three sources appears in small notes, both as if the decorations are subservient to the melody notes and also as if they are improvisation ideas lightly sketched into the score.

Following the three methods of playing hymns in the Linköping document from 1795, the hymns of the *Koralpsalmbok 1697,* as well as Everhardt's and Björkman's settings of them, could be treated "with an ordinary thoroughbass accompaniment." All sources except A 12 could function "with chords in the left hand and the melody in the right hand," and certainly A 12 requires playing "with chords in both hands," which would also work in the other four sources. One can imagine an introduction to hymn number 173 played on a two-manual

Example 11-1. Andres Bonge, Chorale 173, from his *Koralbok* (1782)

organ according to Stråhle's instructions, with the trumpet 8′ in the Ryggpositiv, accompanied by 8′ and 4′ flutes in the manual and 16′ Subbass (or 16′ Principal) and 8′ Gedackt in the pedal. The differences among these four arrangements are striking. Yet each reveals one facet of the prism of musical-liturgical practices in eighteenth-century Sweden.

12

BACH COMES LATE TO LEUFSTA BRUK: AN ORAL HISTORY

GÖRAN BLOMBERG

BY 1728, THE YEAR PROUDLY DISPLAYED ON THE PEDAL TOWER OF THE LEUFSTA Bruk organ, Johann Sebastian Bach had already composed most of his best-known organ works, and this instrument is wonderfully suited to their performance. And yet there is no certain evidence that any of them were played here before the twentieth century. The De Geer family music collection,[1] now at the Uppsala University Library, contains music by Antonio Vivaldi, George Frideric Handel, and Georg Philipp Telemann, but none by Johann Sebastian Bach, nor even his sons. During the nineteenth century, Carl Johan Moberger (1763–1844) achieved fame in Sweden for his brilliant performances of Bach's music. He served as organist at Gävle, a town about sixty kilometers from Leufsta, and performed also in Uppsala. But we do not know whether he ever played the Cahman organ at Leufsta Bruk; all his papers were destroyed in the Gävle fire of 1868.

At the dawn of the twenty-first century, the Leufsta Bruk organ is recognized as the most outstanding eighteenth-century organ in Sweden, and Bach's music is performed frequently during organ academies, music festivals, and summer concerts for tourists. But before this came to pass, the organ suffered decline, neglect, and partial destruction. The story of its degradation and subsequent restoration during the twentieth century is recorded mainly in the memories of the people of Leufsta Bruk, and their stories form the most important source material for this account.[2]

---

1. Albert Dunning, "Die De Geer'schen Musikalien in Leufsta: Musikalische Schwedisch-Niederländische Beziehungen im 18. Jh.," *Svensk tidskrift för musikforskning* 48 (1966): 187–210.
2. The following people (listed in alphabetical order) have provided information:

> Erik Berggren, 1907–92, born in Leufsta Bruk, the son of a decorator at the manor; among other things, he made a cover for the harmonium (letter to the author, 18 Aug. 1975; personal contacts 1975–81).
> Yngve Karlsson, born 1936 (information provided at Leufsta Bruk, July 2000; additional information from telephone call 16 Aug. 2000).

Organ culture in Sweden during the late nineteenth century came under the influence of French romanticism, both in organ building and in playing. With the exception of Gustaf Mankell (1812–80), the organist of St. Jacob's in Stockholm and also the professor of organ at the Royal Academy for Music, Bach was quite out of fashion. Mankell's veneration of Bach gave him a reputation as a pedant. He is the model for the organ professor in August Strindberg's short story "Den romantiske klockaren på Rånö," who forced his students to play Bach's fugues. But because romantic music was then in style, many older organs, including those of Cahman, were exchanged for modern instruments. There is however just one casualty on the Leufsta organ of the wish to be up to date: in 1858 the Quintadena 16′ was revoiced and made into a Borduna 16′, which was more in accordance with the taste of the time.

Apparently there was no wish to be "modern" to the extent that the people wanted a new instrument at Leufsta. It is also possible that lack of money had its influence: the Englishman Sir Henry Bessemer patented a new smelting process in 1855, pumping air into molten metal to remove more carbon, and it made older techniques of iron production less economically competitive.

Decline

Very little happened to the organ during its first 190 years. The first sixty-four years of the twentieth century brought many more changes than that first period. The written sources provide a great deal more information about the organ's third century than its first two, but there are still important gaps. These gaps will be addressed here with the oral history surrounding the organ from around 1910 onward.

At the beginning of the twentieth century a disaster befell the organ: the Rückpositiv was taken out, and a harmonium was placed behind the old prospect. It has been stated that the organ was unplayable at the beginning of the twentieth century, but this is not correct; the organ was first taken out of use, then deliberately rendered unplayable.

The organ was played at least up to the years around 1910, but in 1912 it was said to be unplayable. The organist Carl Sjöholm was in service up to 1908. He is reported to have nearly lifted the roof off with his performances of the Easter hymns. There was a cantor at Uppsala Cathedral, Harald Colleen (1879–

Ellen Kåverud, born 1922 at Leufsta Bruk (several contacts with the author since 1975; telephone interview, 12 Feb. 2000).
Harry Moberg, 1915–92, and Valter Moberg, born 1915, brothers and organ builders (several personal contacts since 1975).
Vilhelm Monié, 1900–1993 (several contacts 1981–91).
Sten Westergren, born 1922 at Leufsta Bruk (interview, September 2000).

1949), who is said to have played the organ on festive occasions. Vilhelm Monié mentions that an organist from Stockholm or Uppsala used to come to play the organ at the Christmas morning service. On those occasions, the bellows treader was not able to supply the wind by himself, but had to ask for an assistant to pump the second set of bellows (see chapter 19).

August Strindberg's brother Olof was the baron's gardener. He changed the baroque garden into a nineteenth-century park. August was very interested in exotic plants, and he prompted Olof to buy seeds for tea and coffee plants. August himself also sent seeds to his brother and followed their development very closely. In a letter of 14 February 1912,[3] Olof mentions that there had been some busy weeks decorating the church for "a patriotic feast and inauguration of a new organ." Of course, there was no mention of Bach, because it was the harmonium that was being inaugurated.

The harmonium was purchased in 1912. At first, it was placed beside the old organ, and no harm was done to the Cahman instrument. We know that the harmonium was still in its original location in 1914 for the funeral of Baron Carl. He would not have permitted any changes to the old organ during his lifetime.

During the reign of his successor, Baron Louis, sometime between 1914 and 1916, the Rückpositiv pipework was taken out, and the harmonium was installed behind the old prospect. In 1916 there was a wedding in the De Geer family. The archbishop Nathan Söderblom, a great name in more recent Swedish church history, officiated, and Patrik Vretblad played the organ. Vretblad had a profound interest in historical music; his first important work on Johan Helmich Roman was published in 1914. Vretblad also published organ arrangements of Roman's music. The "Drottningholms Musiken" has recently become much appreciated as wedding music, but for this wedding he played excerpts from Richard Wagner's *Lohengrin* and Giacomo Meyerbeer's *Le prophète* on the harmonium.

Why, then, if it is clear that the old organ was still in working order at least in 1908, was it taken out of use and eventually damaged, almost fatally? It was not because the organ was out of fashion. In 1908 a new cantor came to Leufsta Bruk named John Johansson. In nineteenth- and early-twentieth-century Sweden, local schoolteachers held the title of "cantor" and were also expected to play the organ in the church. Many of them did both jobs very well; some of them, however, could not play the organ at all, or just barely. Johansson belonged to the latter category. Nevertheless, he was a friend of Baron Louis. They played cards together and were on a first-name basis, something almost unheard of between a simple schoolteacher and a member of the high nobility. According to tradition, when Baron Louis asked him to come to Leufsta, Johansson answered that he could not play the organ, and the baron answered, "It does not

3. Kungliga Biblioteket, Stockholm.

matter." I talked to only one person who could muster any sympathy for Cantor Johansson, and none of the main sources for this history painted a favorable picture of the man. Cantor Johansson wanted the harmonium simply because he could not play the old organ. Several people I talked to doubted that he could play at all; he certainly could not play the pedals.

Vilhelm Monié (1900–1993) was particularly critical of Johansson. In a chapter on the organ, which he intended to be included in his memoirs, he describes what happened in detail,[4] recalling his genuine anger when part of the organ was dismantled in order to put the harmonium inside it. It seems clear that people did not like the idea of damaging the old organ. Monié was not the only source to report that Cantor Johansson told the schoolchildren to go home and tell their parents that it was not possible to repair the old organ and that the pipes in the façade did not play anyway. John Johansson played the harmonium from the beginning of his tenure. At first he used the school's harmonium. Vilhelm Monié himself was among the schoolchildren who helped to carry the harmonium from the school for Sunday service and back again on Monday. At this time he was tempted, like all the other young boys, to take one of the small pipes as a toy, but he proudly reports that he resisted the urge. He continues:

> The old organ had been sounding for a couple of hundred years. Generations of tired blacksmiths and other workers, together with wives and children, had taken their place in the church to listen to the clergyman's everlasting appeal for confession of sins, and threats of eternal damnation for those who persisted in sin. I believe, however, that many people, probably most of them, did not care for the warnings of the priest. They had come to the church to rest for a couple of hours from their hard work and to listen to the roar of the organ. The people of Leufsta loved their organ. It somehow was part of the *bruk* itself. But a new era was coming. What would become of the organ?[5]

Cantor Johansson, however, was not content with just having a harmonium. According to Monié:

> Very soon the schoolteacher began to complain. The harmonium could not stand at the right side of the organ loft. The organist had to be able to see and to hear the parson. No, the harmonium had to stand in the middle. But there stood the old organ. It could not be moved, it was just in the way. There is not much to stop a pair of sharp-edged axes. It did not take long to hew the middle section to pieces; the pipes were thrown in a heap on the floor. Indeed, a deplorable sight! I was standing up there among all the junk, I put out my

---

4. Vilhelm Monié, *Minnen från Leufsta bruk 1900–1927*, ed. Karin Monié (Stockholm: K. Monié, 2000). The chapter on the organ, "En orgelinvigning och sedan," was omitted from the book by accident, according to Karin Monié, who kindly put it at my disposal. I also refer to several talks with Vilhelm Monié during the 1980s. Quotations by kind permission of Karin Monié.

5. Monié, "En orgelinvigning," 1.

fingers into the square wind channels, now cut off, and I felt a vehement anger against those who had committed this disgraceful act. They ought to be punished, those who were guilty of this disgraceful act, the schoolteacher, the organist, the *bruk* manager, maybe the baron himself. No, Johansson ought to be happy. The old organ, deprived of its front section, would not annoy bad organists any more.[6]

Even during this period of decline the organ was still held in high esteem. Also, people have told me that there was a custom of bringing visitors to the church, above all to have a look at the famous organ, even during the days of decline. Children also sometimes stole up to the organ balcony, worked the bellows, and pulled some trackers at the back of the Hauptwerk to hear the sound. That was, of course, strictly forbidden. Sten Westergren mentions that his sister was punished for playing just a couple of notes on the harmonium in the schoolroom. "Today, she would have got training at the music school." There was absolutely no thought of giving talented children the chance of learning to play the Cahman organ.

Olof Strindberg mentions "a patriotic celebration" to inaugurate the harmonium. The event left a very bad impression on Monié and others, because they got what they considered bad music, in comparison with the old organ, intertwined with political propaganda. Sven Hedin was the speaker for the evening, and his patriotic ideas represented the extreme right at that time. The actual inauguration of the harmonium was in fact devoted to a political speech. Political pamphlets were distributed by young men wearing blue armbands.

> It may be that we did not understand the music, but we were used to the powerful tones of the old organ, so we felt relieved when the harmonium twittering came to an end. Now the solemn speech for the harmonium would begin. But were we ever swindled! He certainly could yell and carry on, this "famous" speaker from Uppsala, but he did not even mention the harmonium. No, the speech dealt with the defense question, and the threat from Russia. While the orator worked himself into a rage, not unlike the dictators of later times, the church emptied. The listeners were met at the door by the young men in blue, distributing *A Word of Warning* by Sven Hedin.[7]

The First Restoration

In the 1930s the organ reform movement came from Germany, where it had originated, to Sweden. With that movement and its interest in historical organ

---

6. Monié, "En orgelinvigning," 4.

7. Sven Hedin published the pamphlet *Ett varningsord* [A Word of Warning] in 1912 (Stockholm: Bonnier; 1 million copies); and in 1914, *Andra varningen* [The Second Warning] (Stockholm: Kungl. boktryckeriet).

building also came the resurrection of the Leufsta organ. Bertil Wester, who was a scholar and an early pioneer in this field, stood behind a program for the restoration of the organ, which was carried out by John Vesterlund, a local organ builder; in 1933 Vesterlund was one of the smaller organ builders who associated themselves with the ideas of the organ reform movement. The major organ builders in Sweden at that time clung to the contemporary, romantic organ tradition, which they themselves had developed.

The restoration has been heavily criticized, but not all of the criticism is justified. It is true that during the restoration, pneumatic stop action was installed for the Rückpositiv, but that was the only major, intrusive change to the instrument. The organ builders who carried out the restoration did not know much, but then fortunately they did not do much either. The organ as a whole was left more or less intact, apart from the stop action of the Rückpositiv. At that time, the organ reform movement expressed the thought that old organs should be respected as they were and preserved without changes. In practice, though, they rebuilt and changed most old organs extensively in order to correspond to what they saw as the needs of modern liturgical practice.

This was a point when we might expect that Bach would have come to Leufsta Bruk. It is rather likely that he did, soon after the restoration. However, he was not included in the concert program for the reinauguration of the organ in October 1933. There we find three significant names: Johann Pachelbel, Handel, and Dieterich Buxtehude. Gunhild Schedin, an organist, musicologist, and pioneer for the ideas of the organ reform movement during the late 1930s, played the organ.

The reinauguration of the organ prompted a great celebration. Dignitaries came from far and wide for the event, and the young boys of Leufsta were given the task of meeting them at the bus and bringing them to their respective lodgings. Sten Westergren was then a boy of eleven, and it fell to him to escort Folke Henschen, a well-known surgeon, to the pharmacy, where he was to stay. Sten did as he had been taught: he went to the kitchen entrance. For this he received a heavy scolding: he should have known better than to lead an honored guest through the back entrance! The great surgeon felt such pity for him that he gave him a whole Swedish crown.

The Moberg twin brothers Harry and Valter, who later became pioneers in historical organ restorations in Sweden, worked for John Vesterlund while he was restoring the organ in Leufsta and recall the magic of discovering it. Valter also recalls a Christmas service shortly after the restoration, probably in 1934. All cars were banned, and only horses and sleighs rode through the village. Cantor Johansson, who continued to serve until 1938, played the service with one finger. That was his method: one finger, strong registration, forceful singing. Valter Moberg also remembers, however, that the organ was not greeted with universal acceptance at the reinauguration. It was called a *skrikorgel* (screaming organ), because it was so different from the stylistic ideal at that time, "some kind of strange half-romanticism." It was mainly the professionals who had objections; they followed the trends and heard what they were taught to hear. The lay people listened for themselves, and they liked it, according to all those interviewed. For instance, Ellen Kåverud does not remember any negative opinions from the village itself. There was only pride in the organ and in its rebirth. In fact, part of being proud of coming from Leufsta Bruk meant being proud of the organ.

Socialism came rather late to Leufsta Bruk. The workers had been content with the patriarchal social order of the *bruk*, which had always had a progressive system of social welfare. Leufsta Bruk gave its inhabitants a basic social security long before such things became common in Sweden: free medical care, free schooling, and a kind of basic pension system from the eighteenth century onward. Also, the blacksmiths and their craft were held in high esteem. But when socialism came to Leufsta Bruk, it came full strength. The conflicts, however, did not become really acute as long as the *bruk*—meaning the industrial and economic institution—still belonged to the barons. In 1917 the ironworks were sold to Gimo Bruk AB. That was when the social tensions really became manifest.

Into this tense political atmosphere came both the near-destruction and the restoration of the Cahman organ. The old organ was built in the first place to function both as a symbol of power and as an expression of genuine musical interest. Now it was a symbol of pride for the people of the village and a source of consolation. It was perceived that some authority had destroyed the old organ in favor of an inferior instrument. Even though the Rückpositiv had been destroyed merely to cover up for the incompetence of a single cantor, that cantor both assumed the trappings of power and was widely regarded as a representative of that power. Furthermore, because the harmonium behind the old prospect had been used in conjunction with the dissemination of right-wing propaganda, the restoration of the old organ had political meaning as well.

At Last: Bach at Leufsta Bruk

We can say for certain that in 1938 Bach came to Leufsta Bruk. A church music conference, "Leufsta Bruk Days for Church Music and Church Art," was arranged at Leufsta. Its scope was broad: new ideas about liturgy, organs, organ restoration, and repertoire. The festival concert on that occasion was dedicated to Bach and followed by compline (figure 12-1). Henry Weman, organist of Uppsala Cathedral and one of the leading ideologists of the early organ reform movement, played the organ. The festival was inspired and to a large extent arranged by Einar Erici. He was a medical man, but he did what neither the

Leufstabruksdagarna

för

Kyrkomusik och Kyrkokonst

Fredagen den 30 september 1938 kl. 8 em.

BACH-KONSERT

i Brukskyrkan

Program

1. Toccata och adagio, C-dur.
   (Orgel: *Domkyrkoorganist H. Weman*).

2. Adagio ur konsert E-dur.
   (Violin: *Fru Greta Roos*).

3. Två koralförspel:
   a) När vi i högsta nöden stå.
   b) Till dig jag ropar, Herre Christ.

4. Tre andliga sånger:
   a) Jesus, min Herre, till dig jag längtar.
   b) O mänskohjärta, vänd dig stilla.
   c) Jesu, du är min.
   (Solosång: *Fru Ingeborg Eklöf*).

5. Fuga, Ess-dur.
   (Orgel).

Completorium

Figure 12-1. Concert program from the 1938 Leufsta Bruk conference on church music.

National Antiquities Board, the church musicians organization, or musicologists had managed to do: he documented the historical organs in Sweden, and he took the original program of the organ reform movement seriously—to restore and preserve but not change historical organs (see chapter 24).

The same year, Torsten Lind (1900–1995) was appointed vicar of Österlövsta, which also included the responsibility for Leufsta Bruk. With him, Bach certainly came to Leufsta. Lind was himself a good organ player. He did not perform in formal concerts, but he frequently played the organ on more informal occasions.

Above all, Lind took a deciding part in the restoration of the organ in 1964. Without his untiring efforts the funds for the work would not have been raised.

Yngve Karlsson recalls his four years as deputy organist, beginning at age sixteen in 1952. Torsten Lind was having an argument with the cantor—not an unusual occurrence—and had encouraged Yngve to begin playing for services. Lind instructed the young organist on which stops could be used and which could not. At that time, the pneumatic stop action of the Rückpositiv was in bad condition, and only 3 stops could be used. Lind also told him which ones he should use for different hymns and for different parts of the liturgy. Torsten Lind always came up to the organ balcony after the service. If he climbed the stairs calmly, Yngve knew that everything had gone well. If he came running up the stairs, something had gone less well, and then Lind told him how it should be next time. On more demanding occasions, when the organ was demonstrated for groups, Lind played the organ himself. Karlsson remembers playing baroque and romantic repertoire out of August Lagergren's *Orgel-Skola* and the repertoire of the organ reform movement from Henry Weman's *Orgelskola*, as well as music out of *Ved Orglet,* versetti by Domenico Zipoli, and chorale preludes edited by Henry Weman and Oskar Lindberg. Yngve Karlsson thinks that he probably dared to play for services at Leufsta because he was young and did not know how many players were afraid of the foreign and antique Leufsta organ; many, also, were frankly afraid of Pastor Lind.

Augustin Mannerheim (born 1915) describes his first encounter with the Leufsta Bruk organ as an "organ shock":

> It was in January 1940. A soldier was standing in the pulpit of Leufsta Bruk. He talked about joining the Swedish volunteer corps in Finland. His fellow speaker, who was to climb into the pulpit and give an overview about the situation in Finland, was [the member of parliament] Levi Jern. When the assembled people had left, I—that soldier—sat on the organ bench and tried the Cahman organ; according to all reports it was in bad condition. Up until then, I had only "crescendo-diminuendo noodled" on pneumatic instruments with string stops. I pulled a stop which must have been the Principal 8'. I had the first organ-shock of my life. There came forth, a little slowly, a sound of amber, like the cloudiness of an old eye, with descending formations, all filled with light. I suppose that the unevenness of the bellows with a pumper added to the sensation of something living.[8]

According to his story, he more or less had to be carried away from the organ by force, while the MP reminded him that the reason they were there was not to play the organ, but to save Finland.

8. Augustin Mannerheim, "Min hemorgel—Bruno Christensens mästarprov," *Orgelforum* 4, no. 2 (1982): 37.

Augustin Mannerheim's family belongs to the Swedish and Finnish nobility; his uncle was Gustaf Mannerheim, the marshal of Finland. The sound of the Leufsta Bruk organ made a deep impression on Augustin and influenced his thinking in that area for the future. It should be mentioned that no one had told him that he was going to meet a remarkable instrument; almost nobody thought so at that time, and his references were the late romantic organ. Augustin later participated in the discussions of new paths for organ building during the organ reform movement, and he had a house organ built for his estate, Grensholm, in Östergötland. Family tradition did not permit Augustin to study humanities or enter an artistic field; he trained as a forester and took over the family estate. He is a humanist, however, and developed a theory on metrics in music that led to an honorary doctorate; he is also a poet and an excellent organist.

The Postwar Period and the 1964 Restoration

The postwar years saw new influences on the organ reform movement. From then on, there were three main lines of development: the organ reform movement in its original form from the 1930s, new currents, and the old, so-called romantic tradition. The Leufsta Bruk organ found itself in the center of these discussions; in fact, it became a lightning rod for strong opinions from all sides. Henry Weman, who had played for the reinauguration, later wrote: "The fascination for us lies, maybe, more in the looks of this organ, maybe the most magnificent among Swedish organs, but we are not immediately prepared to accept its strange (singular) world of sound, which is so different from what we choose to recognize today." Torsten Nilsson compared the Cahman organ with a new organ belonging to the current "romantic" tradition: "What musicality from this creation! Quite as much alive as the organ at Särna Church from 1950 is dead, the organ from 1725 [sic] at Leufsta Bruk means life." But Gösta Westblad took a polemical position against Nilsson, actually calling the Cahman organ a "monster" and contrasting it with what he regarded as the architectonic beauty of a Silbermann organ: "One might ask whether it is the organ or the altar which is the center of the [Leufsta Bruk] church."[9]

By this time, Bach had definitively settled down at Leufsta Bruk. Important organists, notably Alf Linder (see chapter 22), made recordings for the Swedish radio from the early 1950s onward (CD tracks 8–10). The fame of the Leufsta organ can be said to begin with this time. One of Alf Linder's programs from 1957 may be considered representative: Johannes Speth, Johann Ulrich Steigleder, Pachelbel, Paul Kickstat, and J. S. Bach.

9. See Göran Blomberg, "Liten och gammal—duger ingenting till": Studier kring svensk orgelrörelse och det äldre svenska orgelbeståndet ca 1930–1980/83 (Uppsala: Swedish Science Press, 1986), 297; quotation from Henry Weman, "Den nya orgeltonen: En klangstudie," Musikvärlden 4 (1948).

The restoration of 1933 had been technically problematic, especially in connection with the pneumatic stop action for the Rückpositiv. Repairs had been carried out on different occasions during the 1940s and 1950s. A new restoration was due and was completed in 1964, although it took a long time to plan and negotiate. In the original restoration proposal papers from 1955, rather substantial changes were suggested, including lowering of the cut-ups and the installation of pedal couplers, which would have necessitated the installation of a new action and new keyboards.[10] Both were standard practice within the ideology of the organ reform movement, with its goal of amending the old masters. John Vesterlund, whose reputation was no longer what it had been, had long since left Leufsta Bruk, and although the Moberg brothers had been specializing in organ restorations in Sweden, their relationship to Vesterlund as apprentices made it difficult for them to get the contract.

Marcussen & Søn got the commission to do the restoration in 1964. They were the leading firm in a Danish tradition that was internationally regarded at the time (see chapter 24). Henry Weman was by then firmly in the second stream of the organ reform movement, having adopted many of the new ideas; he had thrown his weight in favor of Marcussen. It was announced that the restoration's aim would be to restore the Cahman instrument, guided strictly by preservationist methods. Even so, Weman stressed the fact that there was a dual scope for the restoration: to "preserve the Cahman sound" and to "achieve a living sound."[11] Today, we see no conflict between these two poles; we experience the Cahman sound as very much alive. The organ was reinaugurated in May 1964 with a concert by Henry Weman; the archbishop Gunnar Hultgren was the celebrant. In the afternoon, there was a performance of the Easter cantata by Hinrich Philip Johnsen, which had its first performance there in 1757 (see chapter 11).

Following the restoration, the organ was used for several public concerts. Along with a repertoire of North German literature and Bach, a good deal of French baroque music was played, even if the instrument is not ideally suited for it. This new interest in the French baroque was a reaction against the single-minded focus on the North German baroque, Bach, and neo-baroque organ literature in the 1950s and early 1960s.

I remember my own first visit to Leufsta Bruk quite well. It was at the beginning of 1965, and I had come to Uppsala to study musicology. The department there arranged an excursion to historical organs in the Uppland region. Pastor Torsten Lind, who had been pivotal in getting the organ restored, met us in Leufsta Bruk and through his contacts with the De Geer family made it possible

10. Österlövsta församling, Kyrkoarkivet: Plan for the restoration, 9 July 1955. After the intervention of R. Axel Unnerbäck, these changes, among others, were not carried out; see chapter 24.
11. Österlövsta församling, Kyrkoarkivet: Writ from Henry Weman to Riksantikvarieämbet, 2 June 1962.

for us to visit the library in the manor house, full of light from the May sun on the water of the lake outside. My first meeting with the organ was a decisive moment for me, both wonderful and strange. I can empathize with Henry Weman's 1948 reactions to the sound, because with my own background in organ reform instruments, I too expected more brightness from the mixtures, as in the organs I knew well.

In 1973 the present cantor, Birgitta Olsson, came to Österlövsta and Leufsta Bruk in her first appointment as a church musician, because of her passion for the Leufsta Bruk instrument. This was by no means common at the time. The organ was already well known, but this was before historically informed playing techniques were widely discussed, and the instrument was not something that held any special attraction for most organists. She has since then been active in organizing programs around the organ.

Interest in the organ grew steadily in the 1970s, on the part of both international performers wanting to play there and people from outside Leufsta wanting to hear the instrument for themselves. Birgitta Olsson and I arranged informal concerts for visitors, and in 1981 we began an annual series of Cahman festivals centered on the organ, held in August. The North Uppland International Organ Academy has grown out of this activity and recently become a permanent institution. Since the 1987 double Cahman and Buxtehude celebration (250 years after Cahman's death, 350 after Buxtehude's birth), an international role for the Leufsta Bruk organ as a teaching, recording, and performance instrument has been firmly established, transforming it in a short time from an instrument for marginalized specialists in early music to one of the central instruments in the organ landscape of northern Europe.

13

THE MUSICAL CULTURES OF
EIGHTEENTH-CENTURY GERMANY

CELIA APPLEGATE

AT THE START OF THE EIGHTEENTH CENTURY, GERMAN EUROPE WAS NO LONGER characterized by a strong, diverse, and culturally confident urban culture, as it had been a century earlier, but was instead dominated by countless large and small courts. These courts, for better or for worse, held the key not only to the political future of Germany, but to its economic and cultural development as well.

The most marked alteration to the landscape of central Europe, and the one with the most significant cultural consequences, came not through rural development of one sort or another, but through the tremendous growth in the number and size of so-called residential cities. A residential city was an urban community whose entire raison d'être was provided by its princely court. As once-vital urban areas such as Nuremberg, Augsburg, Schwäbisch Hall, and Cologne languished, Munich, Vienna, Weimar, Stuttgart, Mannheim, Hannover, and Berlin grew. (The only exceptions to the rule that proved crucial to musical life were the still-vital trading cities of Hamburg, Bremen, Frankfurt, and Leipzig.) Berlin mushroomed in size from a town of 12,000 in 1648 to 150,000 in 1800. Other residential cities expanded less dramatically, but still showed impressive growth.

Residential Cities and a New Social Order

The residential cities of German-speaking Europe were peculiar places when viewed from the vantage point of European urban history as a whole. Foreign observers could hardly resist the use of words like "parasitic" and "artificial" to describe them, and indeed they represented a sad break with the traditional German association between "city air" and freedom. As many as half of a residential city's inhabitants might be on the prince's payroll—in Berlin, a full 20 percent were soldiers and their dependents—and the rest worked their various trades partially or wholly dependent on court building projects, luxury consumption, and other expenditures. These people were not citizens in the sense of self-governing members of the old corporate order of the German imperial town. They enjoyed employment rather than independence, often unprotected by the traditional umbrella of guild organization and hence vulnerable to the shifting fortunes of the princes, their wars, their whims, and their inconsistent, often ill-formed taste. Still, the allegedly free imperial cities themselves included large numbers of people outside any corporate guild and hence on the margins of urban life. Social inequality as such was not, then, the distinctive feature of residential cities; rather, the absence of a certain intertwining of social, political, economic, and moral responsibility—the hallmark of what historian Mack Walker called the "German hometown"—marked out these new cities as representatives of a different, possibly more modern, order of things.

Reflecting this, the residential cities became incubators of a new social group, which one calls middle class only at the cost of misconstruing its means of existence and relationship to public life. This group was interposed between the nobility and the lower classes and derived its social and economic identity not from commerce and industry but from state service. The unavoidable presence of secular authority in central Europe conditioned other developments. The *Beamtentum* or estate of civil servants reflected in its size the territorial complexity of the empire and in its sophistication the density of the territorial states' intervention in social and economic affairs. As states looked to expand their power, they underwent a historic transformation from personal rule to a bureaucratic system of law, regulation, and an increasing monopoly of powers and privileges that had previously been dispersed across the old corporate order. The expansion of state bureaucracies in turn affected religious, administrative, military, and educational institutions. In all these institutions, the nobility was still guaranteed positions of importance and incomparably greater ease of acceptance and promotion. But at the same time, members of nonnoble estates could increasingly rely on individual achievement, whether of wealth or educational accomplishment or administrative skill, to move slowly above their birth rank and acquire a limited influence in public affairs. By the last decades of the eighteenth century, whatever complicated boundaries among the social orders persisted, it was certainly the case that the majority of German states was ruled by a combination of aristocratic and educated elites, who together could be called the *Beamtentum*.

The gradual alteration in the social composition of ruling elites brought greater prominence to universities, which became the training ground for nobles and nonnobles who wished to serve the state. Thus, the *Beamtentum* drew further social definition by its close and mutually dependent relations with the universities. By the end of the eighteenth century there were nearly fifty universities, almost half of which had been founded since 1600. In this regard, at least, the German-speaking areas far outgrew other parts of Europe: in France, for instance, which for all its centralization still contained many regional centers of considerable vitality and importance, there were only twenty-two universities in 1800; in England, only two. At the same time, the status of universities as self-governing corporations in the old order gradually disappeared as newly ambitious states successfully exerted greater control over them as a means of monitoring the production of their officials. They pressed for educational reforms that would benefit the state itself and made a degree in law a requirement for state service. For men without a title, the university became the only route to a change in status and an escape from what Mack Walker has called "the static dull complexities of Germany's predominant hometown and country life."[1] Universities provided a common experience of "mixing and changing," even for the poor students who "arrived at the universities on foot, like vagabonds," and left hardly richer but more capable of participating in a changing public world, even from their poorly paid posts as tutors and rural pastors.[2]

This brief overview of economic and social life in a politically fragmented Germany suggests that the significant divisions within cultural life fell along lines not of class or estate (peasant versus bourgeois versus aristocratic) nor of place (rural versus urban), but of the peculiar intertwining of class, place, confession, size, and tradition. Understanding the position of music in eighteenth-century culture as a whole thus requires both an acknowledgment of complexity and a recognition of those crossings of sociocultural boundaries that did occur. Roughly speaking, three kinds of cultural networks coexisted, one courtly and cosmopolitan, one primarily oral and local, and one literary and embryonically national.[3] Music played a role in each, making the question of how it "mirrored" social and political contexts answerable only on multiple levels. By the end of the century, the density of interaction among these levels made a tripartite division of German culture no longer possible in musical life. At the same time, as we shall see, cultural unity of the sort desired by German nationalists remained more the subject of exhortation than the reality of lived experience.

1. Mack Walker, *German Home Towns: Community, State, and General Estate, 1648–1871* (Ithaca, N.Y.: Cornell University Press, 1971), 130.

2. Anthony La Vopa, *Grace, Talent, and Merit: Poor Students, Clerical Careers, and Professional Ideology in Eighteenth-Century Germany* (Cambridge: Cambridge University Press, 1988), 1–2; on university foundings and reforms in general, see Charles McClelland, *State, Society, and University in Germany, 1700–1914* (New York: Cambridge University Press, 1980).

3. For a fuller discussion of this tripartite division, see the chapter on eighteenth-century culture in James Sheehan, *German History, 1770–1866* (Oxford: Clarendon Press, 1989), 144–206.

Music in a New Social Construct

From 1650 to 1800, the most active and well-funded centers of musical life lay primarily in the princely courts and residential cities. We have already seen the extent to which these courts dominated political and economic recovery after the Thirty Years' War, so it comes as no surprise to find them setting the pace of aesthetic developments as well. National history writing in the nineteenth and early twentieth centuries blamed the multitude of small states for German "weakness"; later twentieth-century historians preferred to call it "backwardness" in comparison to the so-called Atlantic nations. Likewise, music historians saw court culture as largely responsible for an alleged neglect of German musicians and predominance of Italian and later French opera. Such judgments in turn precluded efforts to understand princely regimes and courts on their own terms and hence to appreciate the extent of their adaptability and creativity. Yet, as more recent research has shown, the German courts as a group were marked by a kind of cultural coherence that amounted to unity, even across confessional divides. The growth of a distinctive courtly "institutionalization of music" began at the larger, wealthier courts of the empire and spread to the smaller, necessarily imitative ones.[4] And although for hundreds of years this musical milieu defined itself through social exclusivity and an enforced separation from urban *bürgerlich* musical life, it nevertheless developed musical practices that ultimately and indirectly served later efforts to create a unified national musical culture.

By the late seventeenth century, the initial court preference for Dutch singers and Italian instrumentalists had shifted to the well-known prominence of Italians in both singing and instrumental performance that went hand in hand with the domination of theatrical over chamber and church music in the baroque court. Here, too, the reductionist view that Italian opera served merely as the ostentatious representation of power obscures, Erich Reimer has argued, the more complicated functioning of court music within the political economy of early modern states. Certainly the baroque opera, with its elaborate plots and theatrical realizations, did provide a wonderful demonstration of princely aspirations, and certainly the stately procession of new opera houses from the 1650s on directly reflected the extension of the German version of early modern absolutism even to ludicrously small principalities. But behind representation lay the transformation of the princely court, following the French model, into an instrument for stabilizing and domesticating the nobility through the rituals, etiquette, and entertainments (opera chief among them) of this new social construct. Whether as representation of power, ideological argument for princely authority, or diversion

---

4. Erich Reimer, *Die Hofmusik in Deutschland, 1500–1800: Wandlungen einer Institution* (Wilhelmshaven: Florian Noetzel Verlag, 1991), 16–17.

from political intrigue, court music altogether constituted an institutional system operating at a cosmopolitan level of European culture.

Attentive though they were to native economic development, the princes proved themselves consistently indifferent to anything like native cultural development. In contrast to Frederick the Great's oft-quoted contempt for the German language and its meager literary accomplishments, the princely preference for Italian or French musical culture did not reflect disdain for native German musical work as such. Rather, it reflected the specific function of art in connecting princes and nobility alike to their social and political equals across all of Europe—in asserting an aristocratic identity over a national or local one. Moreover, even if they did not set the dominant musical style or fill the most prestigious courtly positions, many German musicians found employment in the musically ostentatious courts and opportunities for modest social advancement within the court ensembles.

Neither music nor ritual nor festivities of any sort served a geographically expansive function for the vast majority of residents of German Europe in the seventeenth and eighteenth centuries. Far from connecting people beyond their local boundaries, popular culture reinforced the exclusivity and cohesion of traditional communities, whether they were villages, cities, or guilds. Music played a distinct role within these communities, an essential part of intertwining secular and sacred celebrations. Musicians, in contrast, had uncertain status, a legacy of the medieval period, in which they had had no strong association with a social class, caste, or station and had constituted a professional group connected by only the loosest ties.[5] By the end of the thirteenth century, some had joined together into corporations, establishing what would be an enduring division within German musical culture between the citizen-artist and the itinerant one. To be a member of an organization, whether it was a town piper association, a band, or a loosely constituted musicians' fraternity, was to trade away a certain kind of insecure autonomy and freedom to travel for the more predictable conditions of life within regulated institutions. Resident musicians within town piper associations, for instance, had the status of low-ranking civil servants, with corresponding rights and obligations within a community.

But pursuit of the guild strategy never entirely worked for musicians, in part because opportunities outside the hometown milieu always beckoned and in part because the controlling guilds in communities did not quite accept them as equals. Their status never brought the security of more conventionally productive trades, let alone the possibility of elevation into the urban patriciates. They were

5. Walter Salmen, "The Social Status of the Musician in the Middle Ages," in *The Social Status of the Professional Musician from the Middle Ages to the Nineteenth Century*, ed. Walter Salmen, trans. Herbert Kaufman and Barbara Reisner (New York: Pendragon Press, 1983), 7.

often the butt of attacks on their privileges from other guilds, a circumstance that in 1653 led to an unusual supralocal effort on the part of central German musicians to obtain imperial approval for uniform standards within communities. The Saxon Town Musician Articles, which the emperor himself confirmed, consisted of twenty-five specifications of musicians' guild privileges ranging from a monopoly over local performances to conditions for substitute musicians to payment and moral instruction of journeymen.[6] However, although over one hundred musicians from forty-three localities signed onto them, the articles did not represent a step toward gradual unification of musical employment across central Europe, but only a briefly successful attempt to strengthen the position of musicians in a handful of localities. In any case, the outlook for town musicians' futures was not bright. Heinrich Schwab has written about "the artistic stagnation of the town musician" in the course of the eighteenth century, a situation exacerbated by the shrinking ambitions of church music and musicians in the same period. By the start of the nineteenth century, most towns were simply abolishing the statutes that had long since ceased to secure guild monopoly over town musical performances.[7]

Moreover, although the prominence of guild musicians in church music and town secular entertainment persisted, albeit unevenly, throughout the eighteenth century, the capacity of the princes to undermine guild strength—something amply demonstrated in the residential cities—was particularly effective against musicians' organizations. A well-trained city musician could leave to serve a prince or pick up extra income through work outside the town walls. Life within the musical institutions of a town still offered more security than in a court ensemble, which might dissolve if a prince died or suffered financial reversals. The writer and composer Johann Beer noted that the hectic schedule of a court musician meant "there is no difference made between day and night," and "in comparison to this, things are a little calmer in the cities."[8] But town musicians had to engage in constant bickering with both the town leadership and outside authorities over the presence (only increasing in the eighteenth century) of publicly performing amateurs and traveling musicians, alone or in companies, who made their way from court to court, often stopping in the more prosperous cities on the way. Life as a guild musician also entailed constant policing of the un-

---

6. For a full discussion, see Martin Wolschke, *Von der Stadtpfeiferei zu Lehrlingskapelle und Sinfonieorchester* (Regensburg: Gustav Bosse Verlag, 1981), 33–36.

7. Heinrich W. Schwab, "The Social Status of the Town Musician," in *The Social Status of the Professional Musician from the Middle Ages to the Nineteenth Century*, ed. Walter Salmen, trans. Herbert Kaufman and Barbara Reisner (New York: Pendragon Press, 1983), 36–37, 51.

8. Cited in Richard Petzoldt, "The Economic Conditions of the Eighteenth-Century Musician," in *The Social Status of the Professional Musician from the Middle Ages to the Nineteenth Century*, ed. Walter Salmen, trans. Herbert Kaufman and Barbara Reisner (New York: Pendragon Press, 1983), 176–77.

certain boundaries between oneself and the "beer fiddlers" and vagabond players, musicians with no status who had neither place nor position and therefore lived on the margins both of hometown and court. Neither vigilance nor litigiousness could alter the fact that the weight of power over musical as well as economic and political matters had shifted away from independent towns to the courts and their dependent urban centers.

Music in Eighteenth-Century Leipzig: J. S. Bach

One might object that cities like Hamburg and Leipzig managed to sustain astonishingly rich musical cultures, before and especially after the Thirty Years' War and well into the era when urban culture declined and court culture flourished. Both Hamburg and Leipzig were indeed exceptional places, in different ways, even in an empire that seemed at times to be made up entirely of exceptions. Leipzig, although not an imperial free city like Hamburg or Frankfurt am Main, nevertheless managed slowly after 1648 to recoup its position as the most important trade center of central Europe, surpassing Frankfurt in annual volume of trade by 1710.[9] Its renewed prosperity allowed it to spend a certain amount of money, never lavish, on its cultural institutions. These operated under a variety of complicated charters, more or less independent of direct princely intervention. Thus, ever since the Reformation, the powerful city council of Leipzig, headed by its mayor, had direct control over the famous Thomasschule and more vexed control over the city churches, in concert with church authorities. The university, one of the finest in German-speaking Europe, was itself a proudly self-governing corporation, but came under increasing interventionist pressure from the Saxon court and engaged in frequent disputes with the city council over such issues as who had the right to control (and finance) the university's musical activities.

This plethora of alternately competing and cooperative authorities even among a very limited group of people characterized many a smaller German community as well. It ensured an equilibrium of balanced conflict, with an overarching authority—a reigning or neighboring prince and the emperor himself—available to step in and take one side or the other. Such balanced conflict did not necessarily foster artistic excellence, nor was it the purpose of these institutional arrangements to do so. Johann Sebastian Bach's frequent clashes with city, church, and university authorities demonstrated that musical greatness emerged often in spite of such conflict and not because of it. Nor was pursuit of musical greatness

9. See Gerald Lyman Soliday, *A Community in Conflict: Frankfurt Society in the Seventeenth and Early Eighteenth Centuries* (Hanover, N.H.: University Press of New England, 1974). Frankfurt, as Soliday has shown, was a "community in conflict" well into the eighteenth century, and the struggles between the urban aristocracy and the burgher-citizens certainly impeded the development of its cultural life until later in the century.

Bach's only argument in such disputes; more often he asserted his rightful priv-ileges within the corporate system in order to protect his legitimate sources of income. His career illustrated, moreover, the profound differences between the local and courtly musical cultures. Bach, like many practicing musicians by the start of the eighteenth century, moved back and forth between these two cultures in the course of his career, submitting at times to the contentious discipline of corporate town institutions and at other times to the humiliating servitude and insecure tenure of the court musician.[10] It is hard, nevertheless, to avoid the conclusion that court music, when all was said and done, provided more scope for creativity and more encouragement of artistic genius than did the "static dull complexities"[11] of town life. Bach, for his part, tried for the best of both worlds, for the pious seriousness and guild security of town culture accompanied by the artistic control and independence that could be achieved by the higher-ranked court musicians. Christoph Wolff, in his recent biography of Bach, clearly be-lieves that Bach achieved this squaring of the circle, becoming by the end of his life "practically invulnerable" to the institutional constraints of town life and therefore "to some extent ungovernable." But one should not expect the town authorities themselves to have been pleased with a state of affairs so at odds with the workings of hometown constitutionalism. And indeed, as the mayor of Leipzig infamously declared in the search for Bach's successor, the Thomas-schule now "needed a Cantor and not a Capellmeister."[12]

Music for a Literary Culture: Johann Mattheson

Bach's career, remarkable both for its provinciality and for its tantalizing moments of courtly fame, also reveals glimpses of yet a third emerging culture, which increasingly became the site of important musical developments in central Eu-rope. The first printed reference to Bach—Johann Mattheson's 1717 observation that he had "seen things by the famous organist of Weimar, Mr. Joh. Sebastian Bach, . . . that are certainly such as must make one esteem the man highly"— was a direct indication of this third culture's existence. So too was Mattheson's request to Bach in 1720 for biographical information for a planned dictionary of musicians (Bach never provided any, despite repeated queries). Likewise, when the mayor of Leipzig pressed for Bach's appointment because he was eager to

10. The best account of his struggles within town culture is Christoph Wolff, *Johann Sebastian Bach: The Learned Musician* (New York: W. W. Norton, 2000), passim; his immersion in the politics of the Dresden court is better portrayed in Ulrich Siegele, "Bach and the Domestic Politics of Electoral Saxony," in *The Cambridge Companion to Bach*, ed. John Butt (Cambridge: Cambridge University Press, 1997), 17–34.

11. Walker, *German Home Towns*, 130.

12. Mayor Christian Ludwig Stieglitz, quoted in Wolff, *The Learned Musician*, 253. The Capell-meister was the director of all musical affairs and the resident composer at a court.

appoint a "famous man" to the cantorate in order to "bolster the attractiveness and reputation of the city," we sense the presence of a new set of cultural assumptions at work.[13] These moments all concern Bach's reputation—a simple enough cultural concept, one might think, except that in early-eighteenth-century Germany it was anything but. The cultural milieu of locality and hometown, the one into which Bach was born and spent most of his life, understood reputation in terms of the quality of *Eigentum*, which meant property in some derivative sense but was primarily a social quality, a question of "social self and dignity" that came with membership in the community. Mack Walker has described it as "individuality within a community" or "identity as a silhouette projected on community" which can be "rendered and reflected only by community."[14] Divorced from this community, individual artistic achievement made no sense, and it certainly did not earn one a reputation in any desirable sense of the word. Reputation in court circles was by contrast a matter of virtuosity and display, the purpose of which was to cast not one's own shadow upon the aristocratic world at large, but rather that of the prince one served.

Mattheson was, however, deploying yet a third notion of reputation when he referred to the "esteem" in which Bach ought to be held, and later, in disappointment over Hamburg's venal failure to appoint Bach to the important post of organist at St. Jacobi, when he wrote of the "certain great virtuoso" who had performed brilliantly but in vain. This kind of reputation was earned by an individual through striving and merit. It marked one out for notice from a world considerably larger than a single community, and most important, it was a literary and not merely an oral tradition. It existed in the written and published documents that circulated among the educated inhabitants of independent towns and residential cities alike. The social core of the third culture to which this notion of reputation belonged consisted of an unprecedented melange of the merchants, patriciates, and pastors of the burgher order alongside the new bureaucratic elites that served the princes. These people established what James Sheehan has called a literary culture: "a culture of readers and writers for whom print had become the essential means of communication and printed matter the primary source and subject of cultural activity."[15] Although Germans had read printed matter for some three hundred years by Mattheson and Bach's time, the second and third decades of the eighteenth century marked what we might call the take-off point—a point at which the number of people regularly reading and writing was sufficient to constitute a "sustained, secular reading public." Numbers of books published in Germany and numbers of new periodicals both rose dramatically,

13. All three quotations from Wolff, *The Learned Musician*, 179, 2, 237–38.
14. Walker, *German Home Towns*, 2–3.
15. Sheehan, *German History*, 153.

decade by decade as the century progressed, each feeding off the other as both books and periodicals reviewed each other's writing.

This take-off phenomenon was not only new to central Europe, but as it coalesced, literary culture became the only truly national culture in the German-speaking lands. It constituted a social network of shared values and concerns that crossed over the geographical, social, and political barriers that divided one locality from another and the privileged aristocracy from all. In contrast to what I have described of the geographically bounded nature of hometown culture and the cosmopolitan, socially elite nature of court culture, literary culture alone expressed the nationality of Germans. This was a quality that grew ever more distinct in the contemplation of it and in the increasingly self-conscious contribution of works of art intended to express it. Establishing a national community through print became the crucial underlying project of participants in literary culture.

Historians have for the most part explored this as a project that consisted of writing literature and developing the expressive capacities of the German language, for, to be sure, language was the first and for decades the most important defining characteristic of what it meant to be German. The participation of music—or to be exact, of people writing about music—in the nationalizing project of literary culture is more obscure to us, even though the writings of musical scholars and aestheticians, extracted from this general context, have long drawn the attention of philosophers and musicologists. But musical matters were more central to the makers of this new nationalizing culture than we have acknowledged, and, vice versa, the makers of this national culture contributed substantially to new developments in musical life in ways that have been recognized, though not often in such terms.

To put it schematically, two major trends in musical life that took off in the early eighteenth century directly reflected the growth of literary culture and the diverse social groups that defined it. The first was a trend toward a modest yet functioning musical marketplace, separate from court institutions and free of guild restrictions, in which musicians could earn money—by playing for the growing numbers of amateur groups (*collegia musica, Musikkränzlein,* and the like), by performing in the new phenomenon of the public concert, and by participating as middlemen, copyists, publishers, sellers, and of course composers in the expanding commercial realm of musical publishing. Organists, for example, who lacked status among the town musicians and who, especially later in the century, suffered from a fashionable dislike of the organ's sound, often founded local *collegia musica* to supplement their income as well as to expand their musical horizons.[16] The instrumentalist Georg Christoph Grossheim of Kassel pro-

---

16. Arnfried Edler, "The Social Status of Organists in Lutheran Germany from the Sixteenth through the Eighteenth Century," in *The Social Status of the Professional Musician from the Middle Ages to*

vides a different perspective: he lost his position in the orchestra of Frederick the Great when the king died in 1785 and the orchestra was dissolved, so he began giving music lessons and founded a music trade, all the while looking to return to a regular court position.[17] Interestingly, as Erich Reimer has shown, the established institutions of court music did much to further the development of this musical marketplace, overcoming a crisis of court music in the latter decades of the eighteenth century by, for instance, opening up courtly perform-ances to a limited audience or supporting the development of national theaters.[18] The princely courts also stood, as we have seen, behind the development of the new social groups who became the "consumers" in the musical marketplace. The social core of literary culture—educated and culturally ambitious people, very often members of the bureaucratic elites—enjoyed music in new settings, such as in concerts or private homes. Their activities contributed to the gradual com-modification of music and established the beginnings of an organized public interest in the arts.

The second trend, no less important in shaping the cultural meaning of music in modern Europe, was a slow accumulation of writings about music: critical, scholarly, and imaginative, and all concerned ultimately with answering the ques-tion of how music fit within the humanistic project of enlightenment. No figure was more central to this second trend than Johann Mattheson of Hamburg, organist, composer, and founder of an entire tradition of musical writing in cen-tral Europe. In 1722 Mattheson's first major venture in musical criticism, which became the first musical periodical in Europe, modeled itself explicitly on the scholarly periodicals and moral weeklies of literary culture. He called it *Critica Musica* and gave it a suitably ponderous and verbose subtitle, laden down with claims to erudition—"searching critiques and assessments of the many opinions, arguments, and objections," designed "to eradicate . . . all vulgar error and to pro-mote a freer growth in the pure science of harmony."[19]

Nor did Mattheson confine his efforts to exchanging erudition with other scholarly types. In 1728 he began a second periodical aimed at a slightly broader audience of literate, educated people. He titled it *Der musicalische Patriot* to

the Nineteenth Century, ed. Walter Salmen, trans. Herbert Kaufman and Barbara Reisner (New York: Pendragon Press, 1983), 75, 89–90.

17. See Klaus Hortschansky, "The Musician as Music Dealer in the Second Half of the Eighteenth Century," in *The Social Status of the Professional Musician from the Middle Ages to the Nineteenth Century*, ed. Walter Salmen, trans. Herbert Kaufman and Barbara Reisner (New York: Pendragon Press, 1983), 205–6.

18. Reimer, *Hofmusik in Deutschland*, 125–41.

19. The full title of the journal, published in Hamburg between 1722 and 1725, read *Critica musica, D.i. grundrichtige Untersuch-und Beurtheilung vieler Theils vorgefassten Theils einfältigen meinungen Argumenten und Einwürffe so in alten und neuen gedruckten und ungedruckten musicalischen Schriff-ten zu finden; zur müglichsten Ausräutung aller groben Irrthümer und zur Beförderung eines bessern Wachsthums der reinen harmonischen Wissenschafft, in verschiedene Theile abgefasset und stück-weise heraus gegeben von Mattheson.*

signal its kinship with another periodical in his native Hamburg that was similarly aimed at the "German-speaking community" and called the *Patriot*. This use of the term "patriot" in turn provides us with an important clue in explaining his purposes. In Mattheson's day, the term carried several overlapping connotations, including devotion to one's native land, a unit with an identity as various as the innumerable territorial entities of central Europe, and a consciousness of being a citizen of the empire, which for all its shortcomings represented for the vast majority of its inhabitants the embodiment of *Deutschland*. The word "patriot" also evoked a discourse of "baroque language and cultural patriotism" dating back to seventeenth-century efforts to find the missing ground for the development of national consciousness.[20] To describe oneself as a patriot in this final sense was to appeal to an imaginary community, an "invisible intercourse of spirits and hearts," in Herder's words, the existence of which might somehow be secured through language. Mattheson's choice of *Patriot* for the journal's title reflected his belief in the idea of a common good, and a defensiveness about Italian opera and other influences from outside the various communities to which the patriot belonged. The historian Reinhart Koselleck has described this defensiveness as a "concrete fear of the cultural infiltration of foreigners [*Überfremdung*] and political powerlessness."[21] Literate people knew that German culture existed, but lacking the confident assertion of a deeply rooted existence that Herder would bring to the understanding of nationness half a century later, German culture seemed to them a vulnerable, elusive tenuity, too dependent on the fortunes of princes to seem secure. The baroque understanding of culture, after all, saw it neither anthropologically (as a way of life) nor liberally (as the creative work of individuals), but paradigmatically (as the expression of the power and glory of ruler and God).

Mattheson thus sat down to write about music in a discursive context fraught with cultural and even political significance. The particular aspect of his many writings that draws our attention is the self-consciously public way in which he made contributions to ongoing debates about the content of collective life. In the broadest sense, his mission became to secure a place for musical discourse within the emerging public world of literary culture. His success in this mission must be seen as long term. For much of the eighteenth century, musical journals like his came and went, as did periodicals of a more general sort. Their print run rarely exceeded four hundred copies, and efficient distribution was in any

---

20. On this meaning of "patriot," see the discussion of "Bürger," a term with an even more complicated historical development, in *Geschichtliche Grundbegriffe*, ed. Otto Brunner, Werner Conze, and Reinhart Koselleck, 8 vols. (Stuttgart: Klett-Cotta, 1987–92), 1:686.

21. Koselleck, "Volk, Nation, Nationalismus, Masse," in Brunner et al., *Geschichtliche Grundbegriffe*, 7: 305–6. On the patriot as one devoted to a community's well-being, see Mary Lindemann, *Patriots and Paupers: Hamburg, 1712–1830* (New York: Oxford University Press, 1990), 5.

case impossible given the multiplicity and geographical incoherence of state boundaries and the ludicrously difficult conditions of travel. By 1750 only about 15 percent of the German-speaking population was literate, and although that figure began to rise rapidly over the next hundred years, regular purchase and reading of periodicals remained an activity confined to a small segment of the population of towns and cities. Within this already limited context, musical writing and journalism, along the lines established by Mattheson, eked out a precarious existence, a tag-along poor cousin to the only slightly more stable publications of literary culture. On the one hand, one would seek in vain throughout the eighteenth century for sustained discussions of music in any but the musical journals themselves. With a few exceptions (Christian Schubart's *Deutsche Chronik*, for instance), writing about music was no way to secure recognition from a dispersed and barely recognizable set of readers and fellow writers. For several generations of eighteenth-century German humanists, music rated low among the arts, too distant from language to seem capable of expressing ideas and too integral a part of the ritualistic worlds of court and church to seem an elevating pursuit for the rational public.[22]

On the other hand, musical writers did establish their own journals way in advance of other fields of artistic knowledge. And although subject to constant closures and marked by tiny readerships, these journals together constituted a nearly continuous succession of musical reading matter into the nineteenth century, broken only from 1728 to 1736 and again from 1770 to 1778.[23] We are not accustomed to regarding this miscellaneous collection of short-lived journals as a whole, yet if we do, we see that there was by the end of the century a remarkable accumulation of musical knowledge. Embodied in such works as Ernst Ludwig Gerber's *Historical-Biographical Lexicon of Musical Artists* (1790–92) or J. N. Forkel's *General History of Music* (1788), musical knowledge was intended by its creators and compilers to make clear that music too formed a part of the educated person's *Bildung*, or humanistic development. Full participation in literary culture required a certain distancing from the traditional musical practices of court, church, and town. According to the spokesmen of this third musical culture, educated people—in other words, the concert-going public—should no longer regard music merely as the decoration of a frivolous court life, the accompaniment of moribund liturgies, or the entertainment of uneducated peasants and townsmen. Music, the equal of poetry and painting, provided "a means toward the perfection and the ennobling" of the human race; an understanding

---

22. On the intellectual dismissal of music, see Bernd Sponheuer, *Musik als Kunst und Nicht-Kunst: Untersuchungen zur Dichotomie von "hoher" und "niederer" Musik im musikästhetischen Denken zwischen Kant und Hanslick* (Kassel: Bärenreiter Verlag, 1987).

23. Based on the list of German musical periodicals in *The New Grove Dictionary of Music and Musicians*, ed. Stanley Sadie (London and New York: Macmillan, 2000), s.v. "Periodicals."

of music informed by knowledge and criticism led just as surely as did poetry "to the temple of perfection and freedom."[24]

Germany as a Land of Classical Masters

Within the discursive context of musical journalism, as it attempted to shape the aesthetic values of the new consumers of music, the idea of a distinctively German genius for music and a submerged, unrecognized unity of German music making began to emerge. This idea of Germany as the preeminent land of music kept the courts with their Italianate taste and Francocentric notions of culture at arm's length and suggested the possibility of a musical transcendence of the stifling provinciality of town life. The serious, ennobling musical experiences to which musical writers referred involved above all the works of "German com-posers," a national moniker that carried increasing cultural meaning as the cen-tury wore on. A national culture requires, historians have suggested, the creation of a "unity of judgment and taste" transcending "territorial boundaries," and by the end of the century, musical writers had their eyes firmly on that goal.[25] When in 1798 the successful novelist and literary critic Friedrich Rochlitz began a new and precedent-breaking, long-lived musical journal, the *Allgemeine Musikalische Zeitung*, he launched the first issue with a plea for a deepening of musical taste among the general public and pledged the journal to the enlightenment tasks of education and improvement.

At the same time, he pressed the case for greater recognition of the German musical past, a construct if there ever was one and yet a construct increasingly filled in through the writings of Rochlitz and his colleagues. Less than a quarter century earlier, Charles Burney had asserted in *The Present State of Music in Germany, the Netherlands, and the United Provinces* that although "a musical spirit" was "universally diffused throughout the [German] empire," the Germans for the most part lacked a "national music."[26] But in the ensuing decades, the gathering force of musical writing had insisted to the contrary that Germany was in fact a land of "classical masters," indeed a land of unrecognized musical ge-nius. Ernst Ludwig Gerber, for instance, in his massive compendium of musical biography (first published in 1790) wrote of the "remarkable era" of music making in which he and his fellow Germans lived and in which "the true and actual classical masters of our time and for eternity have worked." His list of these

24. Friedrich Rochlitz, "Die Verschiedenheit der Urtheile über Werke der Tonkunst," *Allgemeine Musikalische Zeitung* 1, no. 32 (9 May 1799): 497–505.

25. Hagen Schulze, *The Course of German Nationalism: From Frederick the Great to Bismarck, 1763–1867* (Cambridge: Cambridge University Press, 1991), 46.

26. Charles Burney, *The Present State of Music in Germany, the Netherlands, and the United Prov-inces*, 2 vols. (London: T. Beckett, 1775), 2:70, 340.

masters began with Johann Sebastian Bach and continued to "Benda, Gluck, Graun, Händel, Hasse, Haydn, Hiller, Kirnberger, Marpurg, and so on."[27] For Gerber, then, the problem was not the absence of a national music but the absence of a public sufficiently educated in musical history to appreciate the national music they already possessed.

Gerber's views reflected the gradual emergence of patterns in the identification and description of a distinctively German music—patterns that had taken shape over the past several decades of musical writing (Burney's included). The musicologists Arno Forchert and Bernd Sponheuer have identified two especially persistent ones. The first, "cosmopolitan-universalist" pattern credited German musicians with absorbing the best of Italian and French culture and creating something mixed. The second pattern, which Sponheuer calls "exclusive," identified traits specific to German music and held them up in diametric opposition to foreign music—thoroughness (versus thoughtlessness), profundity (versus superficiality), harmony (versus melody), and effort (versus mere showmanship or ease).[28] These ways of writing about Germanness both emerged easily out of Enlightenment Europe's comparative and empirical interest in national differences and characters of peoples, an interest that pervaded the writings of Montesquieu's many admirers. But by the end of the century, in Gerber's and Forkel's generation native German superiority in music was being asserted, on the grounds either that the German mixture was better than its constituent parts or that the traits of Germans were better than the traits of foreigners. Gerber's list, unprepossessing as it appears at first reading, reflected that development and, in the content of the lexicon's biographies, backed it up with accounts of native German accomplishment.

Finally, to call this list of German composers "classical masters" was also to invoke the decades of literary and cultural debate over the capacity of the German language to produce a "classical" literature. This debate reached a culmination of sorts with Goethe's 1795 essay "Literary Sans-Culottism," in which he defended German prose as not yet capable of classical grandeur but certainly full of promise: true classics, thought Goethe, could not be conjured out of thin air but rather developed out of the efforts, good and bad, of one's predecessors and contemporaries.[29] Gerber's use of the term would seem to suggest that music already had its classics, an assertion that Forkel's publication in 1802 of the first

27. Ernst Ludwig Gerber, *Historisch-Biographisches Lexikon der Tonkünstler*, ed. Othmar Wessely (1790–92; reprint, Graz: Akademische Druck- u. Verlagsanstalt, 1977), iv.

28. Bernd Sponheuer, "Reconstructing Ideal Types of the 'German' in Music," in *Music and German National Identity*, ed. Celia Applegate and Pamela Potter (Chicago: University of Chicago Press, 2002); and Arno Forchert, "Von Bach zu Mendelssohn: Vortrag bei den Bach-Tagen Berlin 1979," in *Bachtage Berlin: Vorträge 1970 bis 1981* (Neuhausen-Stuttgart, 1985), 211–23.

29. From "Literarischer Sanscullottism," cited in T. J. Reed, *The Classical Center: Goethe and Weimar, 1775–1832* (Totowa, N.J.: Barnes & Noble, 1980), 17–18.

biography of Bach made explicit. Forkel placed Bach at the center of an educational project that he explicitly compared to that of training in Greek and
Roman classics at gymnasium and university—in other words, the central educational experience of Germany's ruling elites. Bach himself, in Forkel's comparison, was the musical counterpart to the Greek and Roman authors; he "was
the first classic that ever was, or perhaps ever will be," at least in terms of the
higher musical education of a cultivated person.

Forkel, moreover, placed Bach among the classics by "playing the patriot card"
more artfully and deliberately than any musical writer so far, including Mattheson. The very title page of the biography dedicated it to "patriotic admirers of
true musical art." The foreword claimed that "this undertaking" concerned not
just art as such but also "the honor of the German name." Bach's works were
"an invaluable national patrimony, with which no other nation has anything to
be compared." Whoever undertook to save them from oblivion "performed a
service to the fatherland." And even more, whoever cared about the German
fatherland had a duty to "support such a patriotic undertaking, and so far as
possible to hasten its further acceptance." Forkel hoped, he wrote, to "remind
our public of this duty and to awaken in the heart of every German man
this exalted enthusiasm." It would not be enough, he insisted, to be read only
by the small circle of those learned in this art: "allow me to repeat myself once
again; this is not a concern of art alone, this is a *national concern* [*National-
Angelegenheit*]."[30]

The strenuousness with which Forkel made his case did not come out of
nowhere, nor did it reflect some suddenly rising tide of nationalism. His remarks
came, rather, at the end of a long century of discussion and debate, at times
intersecting, and other times dissociated, about what the place of music was in
hierarchies of aesthetic value, and about who the Germans were and what constituted their national culture. They came also after a century of slow transfor-
mations in the livelihoods of professional musicians, whose worlds of employment had become ever more precarious. They came, finally, as the culmination
of a lively yet little-known tradition of writing about music, in which Forkel, like
Mattheson before him, formed an important link between the small numbers of
people highly educated in musical things and the somewhat larger world of educated people in general. Under fragmented political and vulnerable economic
circumstances, musicians increasingly needed the interest of such people. They
sought to secure it not simply by playing beautiful music, but also by invoking
notions of music's classical status and patriotic importance. Nationalism entered
into this constellation of social and cultural changes as a strengthening and link-

30. J. N. Forkel, *Über Johann Sebastian Bachs Leben, Kunst, und Kunstwerke*, ed. Claudia Maria
Knispel (1802; Berlin: Henschel Verlag, 2000), 21–22.

ing agent, a means to connect musical life to social life as a whole and to larger problems of cultural meaning—a means, in short, of becoming important to the people who seemed to be shaping the world of German-speaking Europe as it changed. Inclusion in educated society promised some measure of security to professional musicians and some guarantee of progress in the face of what a number of musical spokesmen considered the imminent threat of decline.

From the long perspective that links the Bach of the early eighteenth century to the Bach of the late nineteenth century, no moment was more important in preserving his works and placing them at the center of a northern and largely Protestant European musical world than the decades at the turn to the nineteenth century. The recovery of Bach for a general musical public some fifty years after his death took place against a political and economic backdrop of fragmentation, stagnation, and yet at the same time a deeply rooted adaptability. More important, Bach's survival, if one wishes to call it that, owed little to the courts or the town musical institutions that sustained him in his lifetime. Though still viable in 1800, neither was capable of providing the kind of cultural meaning for Bach in particular and music in general that would make them compelling for precisely those people who were shaping the Europe of the future. Certainly one would not wish to argue that the music of Bach survived only because of its adoption by the patriotic-literary milieu that this essay has described. But in sorting out the complicated means by which culture changes and the equally complicated ways in which cultural products—such as Bach's music, a musical instrument, a building, or a painting—mirror the social worlds in which they are enjoyed, we need to acknowledge not only the universal beauty of some things but also the strange contingencies that account for their presence in our midst.

PART III

A FRENCH ORGAN IN COPENHAGEN

14

EXORDIUM: THE CAVAILLÉ-COLL ORGAN IN THE JESUS CHURCH, COPENHAGEN (1890)

ARISTIDE CAVAILLÉ-COLL (1811–99) WAS THE LEADING ORGAN BUILDER IN ALL OF Europe during the latter part of the nineteenth century, and his organ in the Jesus Church in Valby, a section of Copenhagen, is the only one he ever built in Scandinavia. By choosing this organ as the focus of part III, we gain the opportunity to look beyond northern Europe to France and even to Italy. The Jesus Church was constructed at the initiative of Carl Jacobsen, owner of the famous Carlsberg Brewery and the leading patron of the arts in Copenhagen; its striking architecture and decoration were inspired by his love of antique art and his travels in Italy and France. Sverker Jullander introduces us to Carl Jacobsen in chapter 15 and paints a sweeping picture of the church and its organ, dealing with the theological, artistic, economic, and musical issues that they raise. In chapter 16, Barbara Owen places Cavaillé-Coll's organs within the context of the numerous technological changes that marked nineteenth-century organ building. In chapter 17, Jesse Eschbach and Lawrence Archbold consider additional factors that made Cavaillé-Coll so successful in his own time and so widely admired today. And in chapter 18, Paul Peeters compares Cavaillé-Coll's career with that of his German contemporary Eberhard Friedrich Walcker.

With only 20 stops, the Jesus Church organ (figure 14-1) is one of Cavaillé-Coll's smaller instruments, but it nonetheless conveys the grandeur of the French symphonic style. It was installed soon after the completion of the church under the supervision of Félix Reinburg, second in command in the Cavaillé-Coll firm. The organ has suffered only one change during the past century: the removal of its original Voix céleste, which has since been replaced with a replica.

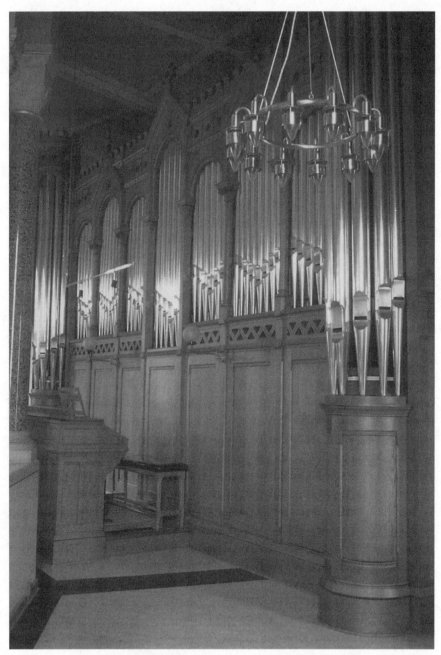

Figure 14-1. The Aristide Cavaillé-Coll organ (1890) in the Jesus Church, Copenhagen. Photograph by Annelise Olesen, 2000. Courtesy of Musikhistoriskmuseum, Copenhagen.

SPECIFICATION 14-1.

Jesus Church, Valby (Copenhagen), Aristide Cavaillé-Coll, 1890

Grand Orgue (Manual I)	Récit Expressif (Manual II)	Pédale
C-g'''	C-g'''	C-d'
Bourdon 16'	Flûte traversière 8'	Soubasse 16'
Montre 8'	Viole de gambe 8'	Bourdon 8'
Bourdon 8'	Voix céleste 8' (P. G.	Basse 8'
Flûte harmonique 8'	Andersen, 1963)	Bombarde 16'
Salicional 8'	Flûte octaviante 4'	
Prestant 4'	Octavin 2'	
Flûte douce 4'	Trompette harmonique 8'	
Plein-jeu IV	Basson-Hautbois 8'	
	Clairon 4'	

Couplers: Récit/Grand Orgue, Récit/Pédale, Grand Orgue/Pédale
Swell for Récit
Fixed combinations:
   Fournitures (Montre 8', Prestant 4', Plein-jeu IV)
   Anches (Trompette harmonique 8', Clairon 4')
Effets d'orage
Mechanical action with slider chests. Pneumatic levers for some of the façade pipes
and for all wooden manual pipes.

Recording

CD track 11: Sverker Jullander playing César Franck, *Pièce héroique*

Selected Literature

Hansen, Jørgen Haldor, and Ole Olesen, *Jesuskirkens orgler*. Copenhagen: Jesuskirkens Koncerter, 1993.

Den Danske Orgelregistrant, Copenhagen, Jesus Church: <http://www.musikhistorisk museum.dk/reg/kkbh_jesus_cavaille_oid_rammex.htm>

TABLE 14-1.

Sverker Jullander's Registration for César Franck, *Pièce héroïque*
Cavaillé-Coll Organ of the Jesus Church, Copenhagen

Time	Action
Initial registration	Récit (chords): all stops except Trompette harmonique 8′ and Clairon 4′ G.O. (melody): Bourdon 16′, all 8′ flue stops, Récit coupled Pedal: All stops except Bombarde 16′, manuals coupled
1:11	both hands on G.O.
1:15	+ Trompette. harmonique. 8′
1:48	− Trompette. harmonique 8′; Récit (arpeggi), G.O. (melody)
2:13	both hands on Récit
2:35	as in the beginning
2:48	both hands on Récit
2:54	− Octavin 2′
3:01	Pedal: − coupler Récit
3:04	G.O. (upper voices): Salicional 8′, Flute harmonique 8′, Bourdon 8′, no coupler Récit (lower voices): Flûte trav. 8′, Viole de gambe 8′, Flûte oct. 4′, Basson/Hautbois 8′
3:57	Récit (upper voice[s]), G.O. (lower voice[s])
4:25	Ped: + coupler Récit
4:28	Récit: + Octavin 2′
4:33	G.O.: Bourdon 16′, all 8′ flue stops, Récit coupled
5:00	both hands on G.O.
5:22	both hands on Récit
5:47	as in the beginning
6:10	both hands on G.O.
6:14	G.O.: Prestant 4′, Plein jeu Récit: + Trompette. harmonique 8′, Clairon 4′ Pedal: + Bombarde 16′

15

FROM BEER TO BRICKS TO ORGAN PIPES: CARL JACOBSEN AND THE JESUS CHURCH

SVERKER JULLANDER

IN THE SUMMER OF 1890, THE MASTER ORGAN BUILDER FÉLIX REINBURG AND HIS team from the Cavaillé-Coll firm of Paris found themselves in Denmark, entrusted with the task of setting up a church organ on the outskirts of the capital. Even Aristide Cavaillé-Coll himself, at the age of seventy-nine the world's most celebrated organ builder, is reported to have come to Copenhagen to supervise the work.[1] Every day his carriage drove from the fashionable Hôtel d'Angleterre, in the center of Copenhagen, out to Valby, a suburb with a dubious reputation. Here a church was being built, a church whose interior was to surpass all the large city churches in beauty.

Félix Reinburg and his men had never before been sent so far north, and they may have found the Scandinavian setting somewhat exotic, but otherwise this job was not very different from many others. The Cavaillé-Coll firm had received many previous commissions from abroad, including the North and South American continents. Moreover, the organ was not very large, and there was nothing unusual in its layout or specification to distinguish it from other organs of the firm.

From a Danish perspective, however, the installation of such an instrument was a unique event. Never before had a French organ builder—let alone one of such fame—built an instrument for a Scandinavian church. Moreover, the style and sound of the organ was completely foreign to the Danish tradition.

The story of this Cavaillé-Coll organ cannot be told only in musical terms, since it is intimately linked to that of the equally unique church where it stands. And since this church owes its existence and highly remarkable appearance to

---

1. Jørgen Haldor Hansen and Ole Olesen, *Jesuskirkens orgler* (Valby: Valby sogns menighedsråd, 1976), 18.

one man, Carl Jacobsen, the story must begin with him, the owner and leader of the Ny Carlsberg Brewery and Denmark's most important patron of the arts.

The Jacobsen Family

In 1801, twenty-eight-year-old Chresten Jacobsen began working in a Copenhagen brewery. Jacobsen came from Jutland, where he had worked on his father's farm until 1800. He seems to have done well in the capital, because in 1826 he acquired a brewery of his own. Chresten Jacobsen was influenced by the new philosophical and political ideas of his time, and he seems to have embraced the ideals of national romanticism while also taking a lively interest in the development of natural science.

On Chresten's death in 1835, his small brewery was taken over by his son, Jacob Christian Jacobsen (1811–87),[2] who shared his father's scientific interests and applied them to the production of beer, producing the first Bavarian-type beer in Copenhagen and securing the family fortune. The new product required new premises. Jacobsen investigated several possibilities but decided in the end to locate his new brewery in Valby, on the outskirts of the city, where a vein of fresh water had recently been found. The new brewery started in 1847. It was named Carlsberg, after the brewer's five-year-old son, Carl; the latter part of the name, "berg," referred to the Valby hill.

J. C. Jacobsen enjoyed a leading position among Copenhagen brewers. In fact, Jacobsen appears as a perfect representation of the nineteenth-century paterfamilias burgher and industrialist. He based his success on innovation and superior quality, not on price dumping or smart publicity. The continued success of the brewery was ensured by Jacobsen's passionate interest in constantly improving his products, as well as by his ability to develop the skills of his staff and to keep them in the firm by means of an ingenious system of rising wages, growing benefits, and a kind of social security. His political interest, like that of his father, was linked to patriotism and a belief in the necessity of political and economical reform, including free trade. He was a national liberal and served several terms as a member of parliament.

His many study and business travels in Europe had awakened in him a profound interest in visual arts and architecture. He frequently purchased sculptures and paintings, and his rapidly increasing wealth enabled him to become the country's foremost patron of the arts. He was also the driving force behind the restoration of Frederiksborg Castle and the founding of a Museum of National History in the building.

2. The brewery was formally owned by Chresten's widow until her death in 1844.

Figure 15-1. Carl Jacobsen, portrait by August Jernsdorff, 1893. Printed with permission of Det Nationalhistoriske Museum på Frederiksborg, Hillerød.

Carl Jacobsen (1842–1914; figure 15-1) was J. C. Jacobsen's only surviving son. Before Carl followed in the footsteps of his father in the brewer's profession, Jacob Christian wished his son to have the university education he himself had been denied. An extremely domineering father, he sought to control every aspect of his son's life until he was almost twenty-five. Jacob Christian forced his son to break his secret engagement to a cousin, considering Carl too immature to begin married life. In order to separate him from the young woman, he sent Carl abroad and absolutely prohibited him from visiting Denmark for four years. (A grand tour of the important breweries in Europe was part of the plans for his education anyway, but the undesired engagement hastened it and prevented Carl from completing his university studies.) Carl made good use of his years in exile, visiting many breweries, working in some of them, and learning a great deal about the latest developments in the profession.

When Carl returned to Denmark in 1870, he began running a new brewery on the premises of Carlsberg. Called the Annex or sometimes Ny Carlsberg (New Carlsberg), Carl leased the property from the "old" Carlsberg but left his father ultimately in control. The elder Jacobsen became increasingly discontented with the way Carl was running his factory—neglecting product development, spending far too much on art, and, above all, in order to increase production to meet rapidly growing demand, shortening storage periods. In the eyes of the old man, this was an unacceptable concession to commercialism that jeopardized the quality of the product.

In 1880 the conflict became acute, and Jacob Christian gave his son notice on the lease of the Annex. Carl founded an independent brewery immediately outside, and there were fierce lawsuits until 1882. They were reconciled four years later—seven months before the father's death—but twenty more years were to pass before, in 1906, the two breweries were finally united under the direction of Carl Jacobsen.[3]

Although himself the son of a brewer, J. C. Jacobsen can be regarded as a self-made man. Carlsberg was his creation, and its enormous expansion took place under his leadership. Carl, on the other hand, was able to enjoy the fruits of the success of the firm. The similarities between the two, as industrialists and as donors, are obvious. Both were competent and successful managers, conscious of the welfare of their workers, and also patrons of the arts on an unprecedented scale in Denmark. At the same time, there were important differences between them, which mainly concerned the relationship between industrial and art-related activities.

For the elder Jacobsen, the first priority was always to maintain and enhance the quality of the beer. This meant that investments considered necessary for product development—including research—were always given priority over art donations, so that planned donations sometimes had to wait.[4]

Carl, on the other hand, although certainly interested in and knowledgeable about brewing matters and the general development of his firm, had his heart elsewhere. As a young man he developed a passion for beauty that was to have a lifelong influence. He began to collect antique sculptures, a collection that quickly outgrew his own residence and eventually was housed, beginning in 1897, in the Ny Carlsberg Glyptotek, a sculpture museum designed by him near Tivoli Gardens in Copenhagen. Carl can be regarded as a professional in some aspects of art history; his catalog of the Glyptotek's sculptures was respected by scholars, and he even published an article in an international scholarly journal.[5] Toward the turn of the century, his donation activities took such heavy tolls on the financial resources of Ny Carlsberg that in 1901 the managing director felt compelled to warn him that he was endangering the future of the firm.[6] His passion for beauty seemed to grow to an obsession, and one of his legal advisors even

---

3. Kristof Glamann, *Carlsbergsfondet* ([Copenhagen:] Rhodos, 1976), 75.

4. Kristof Glamann, *Bryggeren J. C. Jacobsen på Carlsberg* ([Copenhagen:] Gyldendal, 1990), 199.

5. The article, published in *Revue archéologique* in 1903, dealt with portraits of the Roman emperor Caracalla as a child.

6. Like his father, Carl had a dislike for limited companies, so there was no clear demarcation between the firm's capital and his personal fortune.

considered obtaining a declaration of legal incapacity for him.[7] Although he always remained in control of his firm, he grew less and less interested in the firm's daily management tasks.

The difference in priorities between father and son can be clearly seen when comparing their two charitable foundations. Carl's Ny Carlsbergfondet was entirely devoted to the promotion of the arts, in particular the Glyptotek. By contrast, the arts were outside the scope of Jacob Christian's Carlsbergfondet, whose objective was to continue the development of the Carlsberg laboratory and to promote the natural sciences and some other disciplines, namely mathematics, philosophy, history, and linguistics. J. C. Jacobsen's art donations were always paid for personally.

Carl believed that works of art should be accessible to all, not only to museum goers; as he himself put it, "living art belongs to the living people."[8] It was not always important for him to acquire the original of a sculpture, since he believed that a faithful reproduction could produce the same aesthetic experience in the observer. His attitude was more that of a scholar than of a collector. As a brewer, Carl was, to a much greater extent than his father, a modern businessman, sensing the advantages of mass production and the importance of advertising. As an art collector, however, the notion of art as a financial investment seems to have been foreign to him. The creation of the Ny Carlsbergfondet separated these two spheres, to their mutual benefit.

The Building of the Jesus Church

Even for a donor of Carl Jacobsen's stature, the idea of building a church must have been regarded as eccentric. The motives behind the church project were religious as well as aesthetic, psychological, and social. First, the unusual name chosen for the church was no coincidence. Carl's faith, so different from his father's basically rationalist outlook, was centered around Jesus, whose human nature interested him more than his divine nature. He was concerned with "Jesus as *human being*, his example and his word."[9] Aesthetically, Carl was not an ordinary patron of the arts. If anything could be described as his life project, it was not the brewery but the promotion of beauty, mainly in the form of the visual arts. The Jesus Church, with its extremely rich artistic decoration—unprecedented in Lutheran Denmark—bears ample testimony to the importance

7. Kristof Glamann, Øl og marmor ([Copenhagen:] Gyldendal, 1995), 197.

8. Quoted in Torben Holck Colding, "Carl Jacobsen," in *Dansk Biografisk Lexikon*, 3d ed., vol. 7 (Copenhagen: Gyldendal, 1981), 170.

9. Carl Jacobsen's annotations on the creation of the Jesus Church, archive of the Carlsberg Foundation, quoted in Dorothea Zanker-v. Meyer, *Die Bauten von J. C. und Carl Jacobsen: Zur Bautätigkeit einer Industriellenfamilie in Dänemark* (Berlin: Deutscher Kunstverlag, 1982), 147.

he laid on the aesthetic side of religion. Psychologically, in later years, Carl's personality acquired traits of megalomania. Sometimes he acted more like royalty than a businessman. The idea of building a church can be seen in this context: the ostentatious presence of Carl and his wife, Ottilia, in several places in the Jesus Church has been called blasphemous.[10] One of the functions of the church is that of a family shrine; the crypt contains tombs for Carl, his wife, his parents, and four of his children. The four church bells were named after these children, who all died while the church was being built. Socially, Carl, like his father, was a true industrial paterfamilias, and Valby was a rapidly growing suburb with a real need for a parish church. From this perspective, the building of the Jesus Church can be seen as an act of public-spiritedness and of making beautiful art accessible to every one; a church is a less exclusive setting than an art museum.

In 1862, Carl Jacobsen first experienced the beauty of Ravenna, and he is reported to have said that if he were ever to build a church, it would be modeled on Ravenna's old basilicas.[11] Even while Carl was still running his brewery on lease from his father in 1879, he acquired a piece of ground with the intention of building a church.

In 1882, Carl received his inheritance, one million Danish crowns, prematurely as a result of the conflict with his father. Carl had no need for the money, and he did not intend to keep it for himself. He divided the sum into four parts of 250,000 crowns, each part constituting a donation for a specific purpose: the Workers' Donation, for the social welfare of the Carlsberg staff; the Museum Donation, for the purchase of objects for the future Danish Museum of Decorative Arts; the Art Donation, to endow the Ny Carlsberg Glyptotek; and the Church Donation, for the building of a church at Valby.[12] The last donation laid the financial basis for the building of the Jesus Church; however, the actual costs of the building turned out to be much higher: 600,000 crowns up to the year after the inauguration,[13] another 200,000 for decorations added later, and still another 500,000 for the bell tower, erected in 1894–95.[14] The necessary extra means was supplied by Carl himself, with the exception of funds for the bell tower, which were donated by his mother as a birthday present for her son.[15]

10. Sylvester Roepstorff, "Jesuskirkens teologi," in *Carl Jacobsens helligdomme*, ed. A. M. Nielsen (Copenhagen: Ny Carlsberg Glyptotek, 1998), 30.

11. Henry Ussing, *Min Livsgerning som jeg har forstaaet den*, vol. 1 (Copenhagen, 1939); quoted in Glamann, *Øl og marmor*, 145.

12. Flemming Friborg, "Carl Jacobsens helligdomme," in *Carl Jacobsens helligdomme*, ed. A. M. Nielsen (Copenhagen: Ny Carlsberg Glyptotek, 1998), 53f.

13. Erik Schiødte, "Jesuskirken i Valby," *Tidsskrift for Kunstindustri* 8 (1892): 1–14; reprinted as *Jesuskirken i Valby: Festskrift på 100 års dagen 15. november 1991* (Copenhagen: Valby Sogns Menighedsråd, 1991), 14.

14. Colding, "Carl Jacobsen," 168.

15. Glamann, *Øl og marmor*, 142; A. Bliddal, *Jesuskirken* (Valby, 1966), 3.

By the time the Church Donation was made official, the preparations for the church building had already begun. In early 1882, Carl contacted Professor Vilhelm Dahlerup (1836–1907)—whom he had already employed as architect of the Ny Carlsberg buildings, including his private villa and the "Old Glyptotek"[16]—and entrusted him with the task of designing the new church. Jacobsen had a strong preference for an architecture rich in details, mixing different styles and motives, and Dahlerup's stylistic ideas were congenial with those of his employer. For Dahlerup, the decorative element in architecture was essential.[17] Before his first meeting with Dahlerup, Jacobsen had collected all the photographs of churches in Ravenna that he could find and asked him to design a church modeled on them, in red brick and with rounded arches. Jacobsen and Dahlerup first planned a magnificent, richly decorated exterior in "monk stone" (a kind of large brickstone used in the Middle Ages), with a huge separate bell tower.[18] His early sketches for the Jesus Church were shown publicly at exhibitions in the spring of 1883 and in 1884.[19] However, this design turned out to be far too expensive; the plans were revised, many decorations were canceled, and the bell tower had to be postponed.

Parallel to the design work, Carl contacted the church ministry in a letter dated 7 February 1884[20] laying down three conditions for the donation: that a fund for the maintenance of the church would be created, that he and his wife would have a decisive influence on the appointment of the pastor and organist, and that there would be "suitable payment" for them. The letter was meant to start a process of negotiations with the ministry and the diocesan authorities. The building of the church started in the same year, and the negotiations went on during the whole building process.

In 1889, the roof was laid on the church; on 6 September 1890, the organ was finished; and on 31 January 1891, the crypt with the family chapel was inaugurated.[21] However, the dedication of the church itself did not take place until more than a year later, on 15 November 1891. Negotiations on the status of the church went on until October 1891, and the ministry's final decree[22] made it an annex church in Hvidovre parish, under the supervision of the Sjælland

16. The "Old Glyptotek" was designed partly by Dahlerup and partly by another of Carl Jacobsen's preferred architects, Hack Kampmann. See Zanker-v. Meyer, *Die Bauten*, 115–27.

17. Dahlerup's work as an architect seems to have been restricted to overall design and decoration. Zanker-v. Meyer (*Die Bauten*, 125) goes so far as to state that Dahlerup in a certain sense should be seen rather as a decorator.

18. Zanker-v. Meyer, *Die Bauten*, 146f.

19. Zanker-v. Meyer (*Die Bauten*, 146f.) also mentions an exhibition as early as 1882.

20. A copy of the letter is in the Regional Archives, Copenhagen, Pastor's Archive (Præstearkiv), Jesuskirken, document no. 5.

21. Glamann, *Øl og marmor*, 142.

22. Regional Archives, Copenhagen, Pastor's Archive (Præstearkiv), Jesuskirken, document no. 12.

diocese, with a board of directors consisting of the pastor, a parish council representative, and Carl Jacobsen as chairman.

The Art and Architecture of the Jesus Church

The ground plan of the Jesus Church, with rows of columns equidistant from one another separating the nave from the aisles, seems to be based on the S. Giovanni Evangelista Basilica Church in Ravenna.[23] The double capitals of the entrance columns recall Ravenna as well, but the exterior also reveals inspiration from other medieval sacred edifices. The exterior is in several respects modeled (although freely) on the cathedral Notre-Dame-la-Grande of Poitiers[24]—for instance, the entrance with the three round-arched openings. Some of the capitals have motives borrowed from the synagogue of Toledo. Among the many other medieval buildings of which traces are found in the Jesus Church can be mentioned Santa Maria de' Frari in Venice, for the so-called Apostles' Wall at the back of the sanctuary,[25] and St. Michael's Cathedral in Hildesheim, for the general design of the nave.[26]

Variety was a guiding principle in the interior design. One year after the completion of the church, a colleague of Dahlerup's wrote: "It must be emphasized to the glory of Dahlerup that no two ornaments, no two pillars, no two capitals, and no two bases in the interior of the church are alike."[27] Even if the realization of this idea bears witness to Dahlerup's "extraordinary imagination,"[28] the original idea was, as always, Carl Jacobsen's: "I also wished that, just as in early Christian churches, every ornament and capital should be different, not one of them should be like another."[29]

The interior of the Jesus Church is quite richly decorated for a northern Protestant church. Carl Jacobsen purchased originals and had reproductions made of already existing works of earlier masters, but he also employed several contemporary Danish artists for its sculptures, reliefs and paintings. The *Genii of Life and Death* of Pietro Tenerani (1789–1869) and the baptismal font occupy oval niches on either side of the choir arch, symbolically marking the transition between the service of the word in the nave and the service of the sacrament in the choir. Tenerani was a student of Bertel Thorvaldsen (1770–1844), the central

23. Anne Marie Nielsen, "Jesuskirken og den oldkristne basilica," in *Carl Jacobsens helligdomme*, ed. A. M. Nielsen (Copenhagen: Ny Carlsberg Glyptotek, 1998), 91.

24. Schiødte, "Jesuskirken," 3.

25. Schiødte, "Jesuskirken," 4.

26. Nielsen, "Jesuskirken," 91.

27. Schiødte, "Jesuskirken," 4.

28. Carl Jacobsen, quoted in Zanker-v. Meyer, *Die Bauten*, 147.

29. Jacobsen's annotations on the creation of the Jesus Church, archive of the Carlsberg Foundation; quoted in Zanker-v. Meyer, *Die Bauten*, 147.

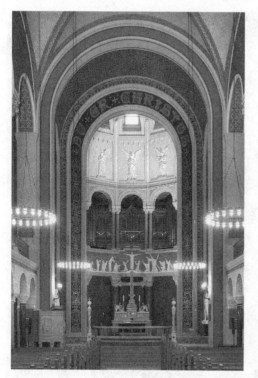

Figure 15-2. Jesus Church, Copenhagen, view of chancel, with Cavaillé-Coll organ and "Pillars of Christianity" frieze by Stephan Sinding. Printed with permission of Ny Carlsberg Glyptotek, Copenhagen.

figure in Danish sculpture, who lived most of his life in Rome and was deeply influenced by classical sculpture and antique mythology. The baptismal font is the work of another Thorvaldsen pupil, Jens Adolf Jerichau (1816–83), who went to Italy in 1838 and worked in Thorvaldsen's workshop, copying sculptures by the masters of antiquity but also creating independent works. In the mid-1840s, Jerichau distanced himself from Thorvaldsen's idealizing, neoclassical style in favor of a more independent, naturalistic approach, as can be seen in the crucifix for the exterior of the Jesus Church.

In contrast to Jerichau, the main interest of the Norwegian sculptor Stephan Sinding (1846–1922) lay in French naturalistic sculpture, often with a strong emotional charge. From 1884, when he settled in Copenhagen, he was strongly supported by Carl Jacobsen, who purchased almost every one of his works. His monumental and expressive frieze *The Pillars of Christianity*, with its central position in the choir, immediately below the organ, is perhaps the work of art that first catches the visitor's attention on entering the church (figure 15-2). The frieze contains forty-eight human figures, including Jesus in the center, opening his arms toward his followers and witnesses: apostles, saints, martyrs, church fathers, *doctores ecclesiae*, and reformers of the church. Although Sinding must have appreciated Jacobsen's continued support, Jacobsen did not content himself

Figure 15-3. Jesus Church, Copenhagen, Apostles' Wall, with paintings by August Jerndorff. Printed with permission of Ny Carlsberg Glyptotek, Copenhagen.

with deciding what figures should be included on the frieze, but also saw fit to give the artist plenty of advice on its realization. Finally Sinding, losing patience with Jacobsen's constant meddling in his work, simply took the unfinished frieze home from the church to his own workshop.[30]

The important painter for the Jesus Church project was August Jerndorff (1846–1906), like Sinding an artist of Carl's own generation. Jerndorff made several portraits of members of the Jacobsen family and leading members of the Carlsberg staff, and he was a member of a small colony of artists living close to the Carlsberg breweries.[31] His chief contribution to the church is the set of paintings of the twelve apostles on the Apostles' Wall at the back of the sanctuary (figure 15-3). The pictures of the apostles are clearly inspired by the icon art of the Orthodox church, and the Apostles' Wall has been likened to the Orthodox

30. Glamann, Øl og marmor, 148.
31. Glamann, Øl og marmor, 303.

icon-covered rood screen called the *iconostasis*.[32] The apostles are depicted with a halo and a Pentecostal flame, and each has his own special attribute. The faces are highly individualized and bear witness to Jerndorff's mastery in portrait painting.

One of the most striking features of the Jesus Church is the wealth of inscriptions decorating its walls, unparalleled in any other Danish church. The first inscription to meet the visitor's eye, above the portico of the Jesus Church, is from Jesus himself: "I am the way; I am the truth and I am life" (John 14:6). On approaching the main door one sees two large gray rectangles flanking it on either side. On them are inscriptions written in golden letters. Imagine the visitor's surprise to discover that they are not biblical but taken from pagan Roman authors of the first century, on the Jewish prophecies about the coming Messiah. On the left, Tacitus reports: "Most of the Jews had the conviction that the Eastern land should now become strong and that men coming from the land of the Jews should gain control of the world," and on the right, Suetonius: "In the orient, an ancient and uninterrupted belief had spread, that in those days the Master of the World would emerge from the land of the Jews." In the entrance hall, there is one quotation from each of the major prophets of the Old Testament: one each from Isaiah, Jeremiah, and Ezekiel, prophesying about the Messiah. A fourth quotation, from Daniel, is on the eternal kingdom.

On the outside of the entrance and in the entry hall we encounter prophecies and testimonies about Jesus, whereas inside the church Jesus himself speaks to His congregation, which responds with prayer and praise in the space where the divine service is celebrated. On the lower walls of the nave, under the balcony, the emphasis of Jesus' teaching is on ethics; higher up, on his identity and mission (Christology); the special theme of the two balcony friezes is the relationship between Jesus and the church. The nave contains only words from the teaching of Jesus; near the choir arch, the emphasis is on sacrament and liturgy. In the choir itself are found words of prayer and praise, mainly from the Book of Psalms; here the song of humans—including praise of the martyrs—unites with that of angels.

The inscriptions on the organ balcony are quite different from those elsewhere. Here one finds neither prophecies nor words of Jesus, but instead expressions of prayer and praise to God. The placement of these inscriptions has an obvious symbolic link to the organ's function in support of the congregation's dialogue with God. This symbolism is further emphasized by the fact that all the quotations are taken from the Book of Psalms.

Concerning the inscriptions as reflections of Carl Jacobsen's own theological

---

32. Zanker-v. Meyer, *Die Bauten*, 152.

convictions, Sylvester Roepstorff has made two important observations: that several of the inscriptions deal with the dangers of worldly wealth and power, perhaps reflecting Carl Jacobsen's own situation; and that there is a discrepancy between Carl's own professed exclusive interest in—and only in—Jesus' human nature, and the presence of several christological statements clearly alluding to Jesus' unique mission and powers, and the special relationship between Jesus and his Father, as well as between Jesus and the church.[33]

Roepstorff suggests that Carl may in reality have been more orthodox in his Christian faith than he professed. Also to be considered is the influence of Carl Jacobsen's wife, Ottilia, who cultivated a more traditional piety. In any case, the choice of quotations, certainly made by the Jacobsens themselves, must have required not only a very good knowledge of both the Old Testament prophets and the Gospels, but also a considerable amount of reflection on the interplay between the inscriptions, the sculptures and paintings, and the functional and symbolical properties of the church building itself.

The Jesus Church is in many respects different from every other Danish church. As we have seen, its inspiration was almost entirely taken from abroad, especially southern Europe, and a connection to the Danish church-building tradition was not intended. The interior, with its wealth of sculptures and paintings, offers a particularly conspicuous contrast to the usually rather austere Danish worship spaces.

Since the characteristic traits of the Jesus Church obviously reflect the views of Carl Jacobsen, it is not surprising that parallels can be found in several of his other buildings. Dahlerup's—and Jacobsen's—strong leaning toward medieval architecture is evident even in the Ny Carlsberg building, with its irregular character and rounded arches. Other parallels between the Jesus Church and other Jacobsen buildings include the variety of ornamentation, the presence of friezes with relief motifs in antique style, the large number of inscriptions (biblical inscriptions are found also in the Glyptotek), and the bold mixture of styles; the two last-mentioned characteristics may, in a wider perspective, be seen as typical of the time, although they were taken to extremes by Jacobsen and Dahlerup. Even Jacobsen's celebration of Jesus is not confined to the church; it is also present in the Glyptotek, where there is a special "Christ room."

The Organ

In one of his few known statements about the Cavaillé-Coll instrument of the Jesus Church, Carl Jacobsen refers to it as "the beautiful organ."[34] His goal of

---

33. Roepstorff, "Jesuskirkens teologi," 19f.

34. Letter to Frederik Rung, dated 3 December 1891 (Regional Archives, Copenhagen. Jesuskirken A3, copybook).

making the church exceed all others in beauty[35] seems to have included music, but despite his connoisseurship of the visual arts, Carl had no expert knowledge of organs. He probably just called for the finest organ builder available, and that, it was widely accepted, was Cavaillé-Coll. It is natural to assume that, for the choice of builder, he sought advice from one or more leading organists: perhaps the French-oriented composer Otto Malling, who later became involved in the project as a supervisor, or Johan Henrik Nebelong, the church ministry's consultant on organ matters. Carl was also an ardent supporter of French modern art. In 1888, during the building of the Jesus Church, he performed the remarkable feat of arranging a large exhibition of French painting and sculpture in Copenhagen, including the construction of a special building for the purpose. Carl visited Paris several times, and in view of his habit of visiting church services on his travels, it is likely that he had personal experience of the sound of Cavaillé-Coll organs.

The organ was originally intended to have 40 stops, distributed on three manuals and pedals.[36] However, at some stage of the planning, the size was halved to 20 stops. It has been suggested that Carl Jacobsen merely followed the advice of Nebelong, who held that 20 stops would be sufficient for the church, a statement that has been described as "strange."[37] Whatever the reason for Nebelong's alleged opinion, one might see a parallel here to the changes of plans for the church itself: general financial problems may well have been a contributing factor.[38] It is important to remember that the building of the organ was never an independent project, and that therefore the cost of the organ must be put in relation to the financial situation of the church-building project as a whole.

The 20-stop organ was extremely expensive by Danish standards.[39] The cost

35. Schiødte, "Jesuskirken," 1. The authenticity of this statement is doubted by Zanker-v. Mayer (Die Bauten, 146).

36. Hansen and Olesen, Jesuskirkens orgler, 14.

37. Hansen and Olesen (Jesuskirkens orgler, 14) suggest an element of professional prestige: Nebelong, who was organist at a 20-stop organ in St. John's Church, would not have wanted the new organ to be larger than the one at St. John's. The information on Nebelong's role in the decision of the size of the organ is based on oral tradition (conversation with Ole Olesen, 15 Oct. 2000).

38. In this respect, I am unable to agree with Hansen and Olesen (Jesuskirkens orgler, 14), who state, "There is nothing to suggest that there were financial reasons for the reduction."

39. The information on the price is contradictory. Bliddal (Jesuskirken, 19) gives the exact sum of 110,520 crowns. A much earlier source is the music critic Gustav Hetsch, who mentions 20,000 crowns, "according to hearsay." (Gustav Hetsch, "Orglet," article in the periodical Hvar 8. Dag, in photocopy in the Danish Organ Registry, in the Museum of Music History, Copenhagen. No date or number of the issue is indicated on the photocopy; the limits are 1904 [the organ of the World's Fair in St. Louis is mentioned] and 1916 [the year when Gustav Helsted, referred to as the organist of the Jesus Church, left this position]. Neither of these prices concurs with the information in the "Grand livre noir de commandes" of the Cavaillé-Coll firm, which gives 38,000 French francs (Gilbert Huybens, Aristide Cavaillé-Coll: Liste des travaux exécutés [Lauffen: Rensch, 1985], 54), which would correspond to aproximately 27,000 Danish crowns, according to the currency rates given in Copenhagen newspapers in September 1890. However, even the lowest of these sums (20,000) would have

for an organ twice that size would have been considerable in relation to that of the whole church, and also in view of the project's financial problems, which caused several reductions and postponements. It must also be remembered that Carl's interest in music could not compete with his passion for the visual arts. It is not clear whether the 40-stop idea was conceived at a stage when the decision had already fallen on Cavaillé-Coll. It may be that it had to be abandoned when Cavaillé-Coll's price became known—it seems logical that Carl Jacobsen, faced with the choice, would have accepted a reduction in size rather than abandoning his standards of quality. However, in spite of its limited size, the organ as it stands today is not inadequate for the room. It is built according to the well-known Cavaillé-Coll concept: with a strong swell division, collective combinations, and a specification with most of the characteristic timbres. The overall sound impression in the church is that of a symphonic instrument, well suited to its acoustical environment.

The organ was completed on 6 September 1890.[40] Félix Reinburg, second in command in the Cavaillé-Coll firm, was responsible for the work, and the final inspection was probably conducted by Otto Malling, although no inspection report is known to have been made.

The Pastor and the Organist

Jacobsen wanted a pastor and an organist of more than average capacities, and it is a telling fact that twenty-five years later, when both left their positions in the Jesus Church, it was to become dean and organist, respectively, of Our Lady's Church, the unofficial cathedral of Copenhagen. The Rev. Henry Ussing (1855–1943) was already well known in Danish church life when he was appointed pastor of the Jesus Church, and his sermons often attracted large congregations. Carl Jacobsen did not know Ussing personally beforehand, but his father, J. L. Ussing, was a well-known archaeologist and philologist who had written an article on the churches of Ravenna with which Carl had become fascinated. From 1887 on, J. L. Ussing was a board member of the Carlsberg Foundation, and in December 1890 Jacobsen wrote to inform him that he knew of his son's interest in the ministry at the new church, adding, "I have heard only good and *very* good

been about three times as large as the price for a Danish organ of the same size. For comparison: the price of the 20-stop organ built in 1890 by Frederik Nielsen for Our Lady's Church in Odense was 6,029 crowns; with a new façade (as was the case in the Jesus Church), the probable cost would have been around 7,000 crowns (Ole Olesen, e-mail to author, 4 Sept. 2000). None of the six firms competing for the commission of building the organ in Højby Church in 1906 asked for more than 2,600 crowns for a 7-stop organ (André Palsgård, *Orgelsagen i Højby Kirke 1906* [Søborg: Eget forlag Andre Palsgård, 1997], 8–17).

40. In the Cavaillé-Coll firm's "Grand livre noir de commandes," 6 Sept. is given as the date of delivery (Huybens, *Aristide Cavaillé-Coll*, 54).

Figure 15-4. Gustav Helsted (1857–1924), first organist at the Jesus Church, Copenhagen.

things about your son, and I will certainly have him in mind."[41] Henry Ussing was theologically conservative, with a tendency toward Reformed (Calvinist) views, whereas Jacobsen was led by his love of visual beauty to feel inclined toward Roman Catholicism; nonetheless, a friendship grew up between the two men, who respected each other's honesty and candidness.

An important requisite for getting an organist with the desired qualifications was a sufficient salary. The payment was set at six hundred Danish crowns a year, equal to several of the large churches in the center of the city, and with opportunities for additional income.[42] Gustav Helsted (1857–1924; see figure 15-4) was chosen as organist, apparently on the basis of his merits alone. Helsted was active as a conductor, violinist, organist, and music pedagogue, but it was mainly in the field of composition that he had acquired his reputation. He was regarded as a radical among Danish composers, and he participated in several initiatives for the promotion of new Danish music. Helsted's compositional output is dom-

41. Letter from Carl Jacobsen to J. L. Ussing dated 15 Dec. 1890 (Royal Library, Copenhagen, letter collection).

42. Julius Foss, *Organist- og kantorembederne i København og de danske købstæder og sammes indehavere i 1905* (København: G.E.C. Gad, 1906).

inated by chamber music—where he was most successful—and orchestral works. He was appointed a teacher at the Royal Conservatory in 1892, first in music theory, then, beginning in 1904, also in organ. Among his pupils was Emilius Bangert, his immediate successor at the Jesus Church and one of the leading figures of the Danish organ reform movement. During his tenure in the Jesus Church, Helsted was noted not only for his eminent organ-playing technique and his skill in using the Cavaillé-Coll's sonorous possibilities, but also for his rich imagination and improvisational skills, which imbued the service with a special atmosphere.

The Brewer and Church Music

Carl Jacobsen was undoubtedly a musical person. As a young man, he enthusiastically took part in male quartet singing,[43] he regularly went to concerts,[44] and he recalled musical experiences from his travels.[45] In 1888, he established a concert hall in a building where he later arranged orchestral concerts.[46] It is therefore not surprising that he also took an active interest in the musical activities in his own church.

The dedication service for the Jesus Church began and ended with contemporary organ music. The first item of the service order was a "prelude" by Helsted himself. No work with such a title is found in his opus list, suggesting that it was an improvisation. The postlude ("Postlude for a Solemn Service") was composed by Gottfred Matthison-Hansen, Helsted's former teacher and a leading Danish organ personality.[47] The other two organ pieces played in the service were by Felix Mendelssohn and Johann Sebastian Bach.[48] The choir of the Caecilian Society contributed a Te Deum on an "old melody" (plainsong?) and Mo-

43. Glamann, *Bryggeren*, 89.

44. Glamann, *Øl og marmor*, 200.

45. See the reference to church music in Germany and Italy in the letter to Frederik Rung, quoted below.

46. Frederik Poulsen, "Jacobsen, Carl," in *Dansk Biografisk Leksikon*, vol. 11 (Copenhagen: J. H. Schultz, 1937), 277–86.

47. No piece of that name ("Efterspil ved en Festgudstjeneste") is found in Matthison-Hansen's opus list. However, a piece by that composer with the German title "Nachspiel bei einem Festgottesdienste" was published in 1921 as no. 33 in the second volume of *Album nordischer Komponisten für Orgel*, ed. Paul Gerhardt and Max Reger (Copenhagen: Wilhelm Hansen). The similarity of the titles strongly suggests that this was the piece that was played at the dedication of the Jesus Church. (For this information, the author is indebted to Jørgen Haldor Hansen, organist of the Jesus Church.)

48. In the program, both pieces are given as preludes to congregational hymns, but there is a strong possibility that they were free works in the keys of the respective hymns. At that time, nonthematic chorale preludes were common in Denmark. See Sverker Jullander, "Matthison-Hansen, dansk organistdynasti, Del I: Hans Matthison-Hansen," *Orgelforum* 21, no. 4 (1999): 174–81.

zart's *Ave verum corpus*, with a new Danish text by the pastor, Henry Ussing, written the night before the service.

After the inauguration, on 3 December 1891, Carl wrote a letter to Frederik Rung, leader of the Caecilian Society in Copenhagen; this choral society gave regular concerts of sacred and early music, normally in a concert hall in the center of Copenhagen. Carl describes the overwhelming impressions that the music in German and Italian churches had made on him: "In divine service this music is done full justice; these are the right settings for which it is intended, and . . . serve to a particular degree to make mind and spirit susceptible to pure musical effect." He then goes on to his concrete proposal: "I have in mind that the Jesus Church might be particularly suited to be . . . the [Dresden] Court Church [of Copenhagen]. It is so that there is a demand from the [church] ministry that this church shall be the home for the development of beautiful church music in the service; the beautiful organ, as well as the excellent acoustics of the church, the whole festive character, make it natural to conduct the experiment here."[49] It is interesting that Jacobsen expressly refers to music within the service—all of the models he mentions are Catholic—and not to concerts. His use of the term "experiment" (*Forsøg*) shows that a rich musical setting of the service, such as that which he had in mind, was unknown in the Danish church. Despite Carl's eloquent plea for a regular participation of the Caecilian Society in the musical life of the church, it does not seem that the letter had much effect. The society continued to perform in the Concert Palace in Copenhagen; despite its many advantages, the Jesus Church may have been considered to be too distant for the Copenhagen audience.

In a letter to the bishop, Jacobsen expressly mentions "organ recitals and organ concerts" as parts of the purpose for the church.[50] To this proposal, the bishop replied that "it goes without saying that the permission of the Bishop must be obtained for arrangements of the aforementioned kind, and that equally the programs of the events must be submitted to his consideration."[51] This reply shows that church concerts, including organ recitals, were still unusual and looked upon with some suspicion; it must have appeared particularly strange to have such activities in a church so far outside the city center.

The first concert in the Jesus Church was not given until 6 May 1893. It had the form, common at the time, of an organ concert, where the organist had

49. Letter of 3 Dec. 1891 to Frederik Rung (Regional Archives, Copenhagen, Jesuskirken A3, copybook).

50. This letter (date unknown) is mentioned by the bishop in his letter of 27 Feb. 1891 (see note 51).

51. Letter of 27 February 1891, in the Regional Archives, Copenhagen, Pastor's Archive (Præstearkiv), Jesuskirken.

occasional assistance of a singer or instrumentalist. The program[52] shows the same mixture of classical and modern repertoire as the dedication. Helsted played César Franck (an unspecified fantasy) and Alexandre Guilmant ("Marche funèbre et Chant séraphique"), but also Bach (a toccata and fugue, probably the famous piece in D minor); the singer performed arias by G. F. Handel and Luigi Cherubini, whereas the oboist played a piece by Alfred Tofft, a contemporary Danish composer, now forgotten. Helsted also performed as a member of a string sextet, which played an adagio of his own composition.

Music Played on the Jesus Church Organ

At the time of the building of the Jesus Church organ, the music of the French symphonic school was not totally unknown in Denmark. Thanks to the activities of the country's leading organ recitalist, Gottfred Matthison-Hansen (1832–1909), pieces by Charles-Marie Widor, Guilmant and Franck (CD track 11) had already been heard for a few years. Matthison-Hansen was organist at Trinity Church, Copenhagen, and professor of organ and piano at the Royal Conservatory.[53] Gustav Helsted had been a pupil of Matthison-Hansen, and the Trinity recitals inspired him to introduce similar concerts in the Jesus Church, where he had the advantage of an organ ideally suited to the French repertoire. With the arrival of the organ reform movement in the mid-1920s, interest in romantic music and the French symphonic tradition faded. However, Finn Viderø (1906–86), a famous performer associated with a later stage of the movement, had first-hand experience of the Jesus Church organ, where he had served as a substitute organist early in his career. At first sight, there seems to be little to connect Viderø's later activities to this organ. He was known primarily for his interpretations of Bach and Dieterich Buxtehude, and his strict, matter-of-fact, "unromantic" style of playing might seem very far from the aesthetics and repertoire associated with the Jesus Church organ. However, in the preface to his organ tutor, he refers to the masters of the French symphonic school as model performers. One may also see his very consistent adherence to the *legato absolu* advocated by Marcel Dupré—in his tutor as well as in his performances—in this light. Finally, in spite of Viderø's very marked northern European and baroque profile, he edited not only music by seventeenth-century masters (see chapter 4), but also Franck's *Trois Chorals*.

In 1890, Helsted wrote a fantasy in three movements—preludium, inter-

---

52. Reviews in *Aftonbladet*, 8 May 1893; *Berlingske Tidende*, 8 May 1893; *Musikbladet* 10, nos. 9–10 (1893); and *Politiken*, 9 May 1893.

53. Emil Reimer, "Johan Gottfred Matthison-Hansen, Professor, Orgelvirtuos og Komponist," parts 1–3, *Medlemsblad för Dansk Organist- og Kantorforening* 6, no. 11 (1909): 149–51; 7, no. 6 (1910): 205–8; 7, no. 7 (1910): 216–17; and Poul-Gerhard Andersen, "Orgelromantik i Danmark," *Orglet*, no. 1 (1974): 10.

mezzo, and fugue—which received its first performance in the Jesus Church with Helsted at the organ.[54] On this occasion, 4 December 1897, a critic wrote: "One is led along the strangest roads, where there is, however, always an element of beauty, or a peculiarity. . . . Mr. Helsted shows himself as a contrapuntist of rank; the severe style has, as it were, gone into his blood, to such an extent that it has become his natural mode of expression. . . . the piece ends with glorious chords, a peculiar piece, in every respect independent."

Helsted's "independence" as a composer shows itself also in his only large printed organ work, the Sonata in D, composed in 1906.[55] Widely different from both Matthison-Hansen and Otto Malling, its harmonic language has little similarity either to Franck or to the more conventional romantic idiom of other French organ composers; it is, however, equally far removed from the neo-German style of Richard Wagner, Franz Liszt, or Helsted's contemporary Max Reger. Rather, it shows some affinity to the transparent, nonromantic style of Carl Nielsen. The sonata is probably the only large work by a Scandinavian composer conceived for a Cavaillé-Coll organ.[56]

In 1905, Helsted wrote a small organ piece that may seem insignificant in itself but is of special interest in this context. Its full title is "Organ Prelude at the Ceremony of Unveiling the Memorial in the Jesus Church, 15 December 1905, of Ottilia Jacobsen." The memorial referred to is probably the epitaph in memory of Mrs. Jacobsen situated on the left side wall in the choir.[57] The piece is divided into four parts: a festive introduction and three sections, each built on a borrowed theme. The first of these themes is taken from Gluck's *Iphigenia in Aulis*, and the second is a Danish congregational wedding hymn. For the third section, Helsted returns to Gluck, this time with a melody from *Iphigenia in Tauris*. A clue to the choice of the second Gluck theme can be found in a letter written on 8 January 1890 by Carl Jacobsen to the eighty-four-year-old composer and organist J.P.E. Hartmann. Jacobsen, who was a great admirer of Hartmann's art,[58] wrote: "My wife and I could not hold back the expression of the emotion that we both felt on Monday on seeing your white-locked head at the organ of Our Lady's Church. It was once again a serene memory connected to our deeply mourned boy, that 'old Hartmann' played Iphigenia's music over his coffin."[59]

---

54. The preserved autograph, a fair copy, dated only "1890," shows no sign of having been used in performance. There are manual indications referring to a three-manual organ, but no specific registration indications.

55. The work remained unpublished in Helsted's lifetime and was not printed until 1929.

56. Helsted does not, however, adopt the French system of indicating registration changes.

57. The epitaph was "donated by friends" (Bliddal, *Jesuskirken*, 20). No date of the setting up of this epitaph is given; Ottilia Jacobsen died in 1903.

58. On 31 Dec. 1888, Jacobsen wrote to Hartmann, asking him for permission to have a marble bust of him made and installed in the Glyptotek.

59. Royal Library, Copenhagen, letter collection.

The "deeply mourned boy" was Carl and Ottilia's son Alf, who died at the age of nine on New Year's Day, 1890. The funeral was held on Epiphany Day. "Iphigenia's music" refers to a piece from Gluck's *Iphigenia in Tauris*, which Hartmann played on the occasion.[60] The somewhat mysterious expression "once again" suggests that the same piece had been played, presumably by Hartmann, at J. C. Jacobsen's funeral in the same church in 1887. Alf seems to have been the most intellectually gifted of Carl and Ottilia's children and shared his father's interest in antiquity; of the four children's deaths, this was probably the most severe blow to the father. It is likely that the theme from *Tauris* in Helsted's composition is identical to that of the funeral piece. Its presence in this memorial work suggests that it was also played at Ottilia's funeral. In any case, it must have carried important symbolic significance for Carl.[61]

Given Helsted's normally rather advanced musical idiom and originality of style, a "potpourri" of this kind is hardly the kind of composition one would expect from him. The context of the piece, the style, and the choice of themes strongly suggest that it was composed at Carl Jacobsen's initiative, probably with detailed instructions on the choice of thematic material, and thereby also on the form of the piece. The piece thus shows us Carl Jacobsen in a new role, perhaps unexpected but not without logic: is it really to be wondered at that a man "the size of a chief, both bodily and spiritually"[62]—the initiator and funder of the church, responsible for the purchase of the most exclusive organ in Denmark after the Compenius organ in Frederiksborg; the chairman of the church's board of directors; the man who selected the organist and who had a great vision for the musical life of the church—that such a man, as the ultimate consequence of all these engagements, should also become involved in the composition of music for his shrine?

Postscript: The Jesus Church Organ and Danish Organ Building

Under the influence of the leading organ consultants Niels W. Gade and J.P.E. Hartmann, both famous composers of the Mendelssohn generation, Danish organ building had remained faithful to classical and postclassical practices, technically and musically, until the 1890s. There was not much, if any, influence from the leading modern continental organ builders or their "symphonic" organ style.

The sound world of the Jesus Church organ was thus very different from what

---

60. Glamann (*Øl og marmor*, 140) refers to the piece as a "funeral march," a term which is not a title but refers to its function in this particular context.

61. The significance of the theme from *Iphigenia in Aulis* remains unclear. Possibly it is connected in some way to Ottilia's birth or childhood: this would fit in with the second theme representing her adult life as a married woman, and the third representing her death.

62. Poulsen, "Jacobsen, Carl," 285.

Danish organists and organ builders were used to. On this organ, "one could experience here at home for the first time a real French swell division, real French reeds and a real French Voix Céleste. This made a tremendous impression, and it had its consequences."[63] However, these "consequences" did not take the form of copying the Cavaillé-Coll concept as a whole, with powerful and effective swell divisions, for instance. In terms of sound architecture, Danish two-manual organs were built according to a concept totally different from that of Cavaillé-Coll, with a powerful first manual and a much weaker second manual (within a swell box), excellently suited to the needs of the liturgy, where congregational hymn singing—which flourished in the nineteenth century—was the most important element. The second manual was for preludes, interludes, and accompaniment of the pastor, while the main function of the first manual was the accompaniment of congregational singing. Composed organ music was not often played, and organ recitals were rare; thus the performance of repertoire was not usually a primary consideration in the planning of organ-building projects.

In one particular aspect, the building of the Jesus Church organ had a significant consequence for the Danish organ scene. The presence of the high level of organ-building skill, represented primarily by Félix Reinburg, led to the realization of a restoration project, unique for its time in its respect for the historical material, of the most remarkable organ in Denmark, the Compenius organ in the Frederiksborg Castle Chapel (see chapter 2). The restoration, initiated by the musicologist Angul Hammerich and the former French consul in Denmark, C. M. Philbert, took place in 1895 under the direction of Reinburg, assisted by a prominent Danish builder, V. H. Busch. One of the most remarkable features of the restoration was that the organ was returned to its original meantone temperament, perhaps stimulating an interest in the baroque organs that paved the way for later developments.

The Danish late-romantic period was short. Not only did it begin late; it also ended early. As early as the mid-1920s, the new organ reform movements began to leave their mark on Danish organ building. Prominent organ-building firms—such as Marcussen & Søn and Frobenius—were attentive to the new trends; in particular, Marcussen, under the dynamic leadership of Sybrand Zachariassen and Poul-Gerhard Andersen, developed the ideas of the German *Orgelbewegung* in a way that was to have a great impact on organ building in other countries as well. This development seemed to mark the definitive end of the influence and attraction of the Jesus Church organ.

One of the leading figures in the Danish organ reform movement was Gustav Helsted's immediate successor, Emilius Bangert, who was organist in the Jesus

63. Andersen, "Orgelromantik," 10.

Church from 1916 to 1919. Bangert was a friend of Albert Schweitzer, and thus close to Alsatian organ reform, whose ideal was not the North German seventeenth-century organs but the Alsatian Silbermann organ of Bach's time, which Albert Schweitzer saw as further perfected in the work of Cavaillé-Coll. Bangert collaborated with Schweitzer in several organ projects, among them the new organ for Århus Cathedral, where he later became organist. The specification of this large organ, built in 1928 (four manuals, 88 stops) shows some French traits, such as a strong swell division with 16', 8', 8', and 4' reeds. At one stage of the planning, the intention was to entrust the French firm Haerpfer with the construction of the reeds, although the organ was otherwise to be built by the Danish firm of Frobenius. It may also be noted that in 1923 Cavaillé-Coll's successor, Mutin, sent in a proposal with a suggested specification.

The Jesus Church organ survived the period of organ reform, in the wake of which the vast majority of late-romantic organs in Denmark were destroyed or extensively rebuilt. Threats to its existence were, however, not absent. In the 1920s, there were proposals that the organ be replaced by a neo-baroque instrument. Sometime between 1927 and 1944, the organ lost one of its most characteristic stops, the Voix céleste, which, at the request of the organist, was replaced by a Borduna 8' (probably to accompany the pastor). In 1947 a leading organist and organ consultant, P. S. Rung-Keller, dismissed the organ, not as a work of art, but as a church instrument; he was especially disturbed by the architecture of the façade. Rung-Keller wanted the organ to be placed in a room at the YMCA or "in a modern school assembly hall in Valby." However, since Rung-Keller realized that it would take some time to replace the organ with a more suitable instrument, he proposed, as an interim solution, that the obnoxious façade be, "for the sake of appearance, concealed by means of curtains between the columns."[64] But the tide turned, and the value of the instrument itself, and of keeping it in its original place, began to be realized. It was a sign of the times when, in 1963, a replica of the original Voix céleste was installed, thus restoring its original specification to the organ. The builder responsible for this work was one of the leading figures of the organ reform movement, Poul-Gerhard Andersen.

---

64. Hansen and Olesen, *Jesuskirkens orgler*, 28.

16

TECHNOLOGY AND THE ORGAN IN THE NINETEENTH CENTURY

BARBARA OWEN

AT THE DAWN OF THE NINETEENTH CENTURY, THE TECHNOLOGY OF ORGAN BUILDING was still based on principles developed in the fifteenth century, but it had been pushed to its ultimate limit. Also by 1800, a general technological revolution was already under way; the organ, once the epitome of cutting-edge mechanical expertise, was rapidly becoming an anachronism. The potential of steam power had been recognized for centuries, but in 1769 James Watt, a Scot, patented the reciprocal-piston steam engine, the first practical device for harnessing this power. By the turn of the century, steam engines were powering watercraft, and by the 1830s the steam locomotive had become a reality, revolutionizing land travel. In a parallel development, the first power-operated loom was patented in 1785. While its engine utilized the same water power that for centuries had turned gristmills, in harnessing it to operate the power loom (and later other types of machinery) the way was paved for the large factory operations of the early nineteenth century, from textile mills to machine shops.

In the world of music, there was another revolution brewing. Increasing from the midpoint of the eighteenth century onward, the old block-dynamic approach to musical expressiveness—most prominently exemplified by the organ—was being challenged by the growing and increasingly flexible symphony orchestra and those who wrote for it, along with a new breed of keyboard instrument that had been under development since the beginning of the century but began to come into its own in the second half: the pianoforte, so named for its capacity for dynamic shading, depending on how strongly its keys were struck. Onetime organists such as Mozart, Haydn, and Beethoven abandoned the organ in favor of this expressive instrument and wrote masterworks for it.

Thus, although the organ market (at least with regard to smaller churches) was increasing, some excellent organs were still being built (but with fifteenth-century technology and very limited expressiveness), and even some serviceable organ music was being written (although largely by minor composers), the period from the closing years of the eighteenth century through the first quarter of the nineteenth represented something of a nadir in the history of the organ. Something had to change if the organ was to recover its former importance as a musical medium.

Some ingredients for change were already there. One was the expression box. As early as the seventeenth century, organ builders had been putting a few sets of pipes in an "echo box" with a movable lid that could be operated by the player, and early in the eighteenth century English builders had begun to put an entire short-compass manual division—the Swell—into a box fitted with sliding or Venetian-type shutters, which, however, could usually be fixed only in the fully open or closed position. Another was the free reed, first incorporated into keyboard instruments in the late eighteenth century, paving the way for the harmonium or *orgue expressif*—expressive in that the dynamic could be altered by increasing or decreasing the wind pressure, which was controlled by the player's feet.

There were also a few turn-of-the-century experimenters, most notably Abbé Vogler, who advocated free reeds, the enclosure of the entire organ in an expression box, new stops imitating modern orchestral instruments, and the abolition of mixture stops. Vogler also attempted to apply "scientific" principles to the use of mutations and advocated extensive "borrowing" of stops.[1] He did persuade a few organ builders to abet his experiments; oddly enough, he seems to have been well received in Sweden, where some organs in which the pedal borrowed stops from all the manuals were built around the turn of the century.[2] But most of his ideas were too radical for the times for Vogler to gain many adherents, and his tendencies toward megalomania probably made him suspect in many circles.

Despite such precursors, the tangible revolution in organ building was not really manifested until the second quarter of the nineteenth century. Once begun, it progressed like wildfire, and technology and expression played major (and mutually supportive) roles. The players in this revolution included both organ builders and organ players, and, in accordance with the theory that things happen universally when the time is ripe, were at work in England, France, and Germany at about the same time.

1. Wolfgang Metzler, *Romantischer Orgelbau in Deutschland* (Ludwigsburg: Verlag E. F. Walcker, 1962); pp. 26–34 give a detailed description and assessment of Vogler's concepts and influence.
2. Peter Williams, *The European Organ, 1450–1850* (London: Batsford, 1966), 122.

Innovations in Key Action

Just as the power of steam had been known for centuries but was not usefully harnessed until the late eighteenth century, so too was the power of air under pressure. It seems somehow ironic that it was not until the early nineteenth century that this source of energy, so obviously available in organs, was not put to any use in them beyond making pipes speak. But organs were becoming larger and their key action more cumbersome; inventive minds began searching for some means of artificially lightening the action in large instruments and inevitably focused on ways to make the organ wind do the job.

As early as 1823, one Joseph Booth, an organ builder in Wakefield, England, used a small bellowslike device to operate some offset bass pipes in an organ in Sheffield, but, according to E. J. Hopkins, "his appliance . . . was not intended for key-movements."[3] That application seems not to have occurred until over a decade later, when David Hamilton of Edinburgh introduced these small assisting bellows pneumatics into the action of an organ of St. John's Church in that city. How long he had been developing this action is not known, but his prototype, which exists in the Royal Scottish Museum of Edinburgh, is said to have been made in 1833.[4] It differs somewhat in design (but not in principle) from the more compact mechanism used by Aristide Cavaillé-Coll and later French builders.

Another builder, Charles Spackman Barker of Bath, was also experimenting with pneumatic action assistance, but he appears initially to have gotten on the wrong track by attempting a pistonlike device. What connection he had with Hamilton is not known, but the mechanism that now bears his name—the "Barker machine," or pneumatic lever—is suspiciously like Hamilton's in its concept.

In 1829–34, William Hill of London, encouraged by the organist W. H. Gauntlett, was building what were then the two largest organs in the British Isles, for York Minster and Birmingham Town Hall. Barker tried to interest Hill in pneumatic assistance for the action in these organs. "Experience, however, in large organs was then wanting in this country," according to Hopkins, and Barker's offer was dismissed.[5] As it turned out, this was most shortsighted of Hill, for in Birmingham at least, his all-mechanical action was so stiff and heavy that in 1846 Felix Mendelssohn declined to play a recital there, fearing that he "would not have the strength to do so," and Cavaillé-Coll compared the Birmingham action to that of a carillon.[6]

---

3. Edward J. Hopkins and Edward F. Rimbault, *The Organ: Its History and Construction* (London: Robert Cocks, 1855), 57.

4. J. I. Wedgwood, "Was Barker the Inventor of the Pneumatic Lever?" *Organ* 14 (July 1934): 49–52.

5. Hopkins and Rimbault, *The Organ*, 58.

6. Nicholas Thistlethwaite, *Birmingham Town Hall Organ* (Birmingham: Birmingham City Council, 1984), 10.

Rebuffed in England, Barker offered the pneumatic lever to Cavaillé-Coll, eventually patenting it in France in 1839. Cavaillé-Coll's own description of the device shows how he quickly seized upon the advantages it provided:

> For each manual key there is provided a small bellows [i.e., wedge-shaped pneumatic], connected to the pull-down of a pallet in the chest. These little bellows are so designed that when a key is depressed, the corresponding bellows fills with wind from the main supply. Since air is elastic, the little bellows immediately fills with wind, and it opens the pallet connected to it. When the key is released, the little bellows collapses, and the pallet immediately closes. This new device not only allows us to decrease the stiffness of the key action; it also allows us to increase the size of the pallets and thus to supply the pipes with all the wind they need to speak with characteristic power. Finally, it will be observed that this device is a valuable resource where the action of coupled manuals is concerned.[7]

For an inventive mind as keen as Cavaillé-Coll's, the use of pneumatic assistance not only solved the action problem, but also opened other doors. Concerned that reed stops on lower pressures had a tendency to lose power in the treble, he could now with impunity provide the reed trebles with higher pressure in the knowledge that the weight of the action would not be affected. This in turn led to the design of a more sophisticated "tiered" wind system made up of multiple horizontal reservoirs that provided steady wind at two or more pressures. Manpower still operated the feeder bellows, however.

Cavaillé-Coll did not invent high-pressure reeds, overblowing flutes, the swell box, the horizontal bellows, combination pedals, or the pneumatic lever. But his genius was that of the alchemist: what he did was to reconcile and transform all this disparate material into something cohesive and unique that was to captivate players and composers and leave a lasting imprint on French organ building and organ music to the present day.

Developments in Germany

Meanwhile, some parallel activity was occurring in Germany, though at first it seemed to be influenced more by the legacy of Vogler than by what was occurring in other countries. One can only speculate as to what role visitors such as Mendelssohn and Sigismund Neukomm played in the seemingly reluctant introduction of the full-fledged *Schwellwerk*; as late as 1855 Friedrich Ladegast—whose youthful contact with Cavaillé-Coll had influenced his tonal ideals—could still construct a four-manual, 81-stop organ in Merseburg Cathedral (dedicated by Franz Liszt) that had no enclosed division.[8] But it would not be long before

7. Fenner Douglass, *Cavaillé-Coll and the Musicians* (Raleigh, N.C.: Sunbury, 1980), 23.
8. Walter Ladegast, *Friedrich Ladegast, der Orgelbauer von Weissenfels* (Stockach am Bodensee: Weidling, 1998), 50ff.

German builders would become aware of the revolutionary technical ideas emanating from France. Organs of ever-increasing size were becoming an obsession all over Europe, but perhaps nowhere more so than in Germany.

In 1821 Eberhard Friedrich Walcker completed his first modest instrument and with it founded the Ludwigsburg firm that still bears his family name. By 1833 he had completed for St. Paul's Church in Frankfurt a 74-stop organ of three manuals (and two pedal boards!) that established his reputation and was the first of a long succession of ever-larger instruments built not only by the Walcker firm, but also by other nineteenth-century German firms such as Ladegast, Sauer, Schulze, Buchholz, and Reubke. The organ in St. Paul's Church boasted a 32′ Untersatz on its Hauptwerk, balanced by a plethora of mixtures and mutations, said to have been based more on quasi-scientific principles than tradition. Vogler's lingering influence is seen in the presence of two free-reed stops (Hautbois and Physharmonica) on Manual 3, which also contained such hints of things to come as an overblowing Hohlflöte and a double-mouthed Lieblich Gedeckt.[9] This third manual of Walcker's Frankfurt organ was an enclosed division, with an extra crescendo device for the free reeds Hautbois and Physharmonica.[10] A four-manual, 63-stop organ built in 1838–39 by the Buchholz firm in Berlin for the Stadtkirche in Kronstadt (Romania) contains two divisions under expression: one, the *Unter-Manual*, a fairly standard *Schwellwerk*, minus reeds; the other, the *Ober-Manual*, a prototype of a Solo division, containing four flue stops and three reeds.[11]

Despite their size, both the Frankfurt organ and the Kronstadt organ (and many other large German organs of the period) had fully mechanical key and stop action. Walcker's 1833 wind system consisted of twelve foot-operated wedge bellows; that in Buchholz's 1839 organ had nine foot-operated wedge bellows. It would seem that despite the adoption of swell enclosures and some of the tonal material associated with the romantic organ, the basic mechanical matrix of these organs was strictly the old fifteenth-century technology—highly sophisticated, it is true, but also pushed to the limit. If there is any explanation of why the Germans clung (rather successfully) to this technology for large organs in this period, it is probably that, having built monumental organs continuously from the seventeenth century onward, they were simply better at it than either the French or the English.

However, the winds of technical change were soon to blow over Germany, and in an aspect of organ construction untouched in other countries. Despite some of the improvements in action assistance and wind supply noted above in

9. Metzler, *Romantischer Orgelbau*, 54ff.

10. Ferdinand Moosmann and Rudi Schäfer, *Eberhard Friedrich Walcker (1794–1872): Zum Gedenken an seinen 200. Geburtstag 3. Juli 1994* (Kleinblittersdorf: Musikwissenschaftliche Verlagsgesellschaft, 1994), 58, 79–86.

11. Uwe Pape, *Die Buchholz-Orgel in der Stadtkirche zu Kronstadt* (Berlin: Pape, 1998), 7.

England and France, both countries clung tenaciously to the old tried-and-true slider (note-channel) chest in their organs. The only variant, the spring chest, had occurred mainly in northern Europe in the seventeenth century, although in Italy some builders were still employing such chests in the early nineteenth century. But this was still a note-channel chest, the spring mechanism having to do only with the stop action.

So it was somewhat revolutionary when in 1840 Eberhard Walcker introduced a windchest of quite different design, based on a very different principle.[12] It was apparently not an entirely new idea, having been experimented with about a half century earlier by an obscure builder named J. S. Hausdörfer.[13] but, like Booth's early "helpers," it required the mind of a clever mechanic to bring it into practical use. Walcker's chest had stop channels, rather than key channels (the stop action simply admitting wind to specific channels via ventils), and wind was admitted from the stop channel to the pipes by small individual valves, one for each pipe. The valves were cone (*Kegel*) shaped, and the chest—actually what would later be generically called a ventil chest—was known as a cone-valve chest or *Kegellade*.

The pipe valves were operated by small pneumatics not unlike those in the Barker machine, which were activated by a primary valve opened, initially, by an ordinary mechanical key action. But because little effort was required to open the primary valve, the key action was light regardless of the number of pipe valves that had to be opened. Barker and Cavaillé-Coll had sought to lighten touch by interrupting the action between the key and the standard slider chest with a "helper" mechanism; Walcker achieved the same end by devising a wholly new type of windchest. The idea seems to have caught on quickly, for before the end of the decade the builders Weigle, Steinmeyer, Rohlfing, and others in central Germany were using some version of *Kegellade*, although some, such as Sauer, did not adopt this type of chest until later.[14]

Registrational Aids

The 1840s were a period of great inventive activity as organ builders sought to harness new technologies to meet the demands of the players and the music. Another area conducive to experimentation was that of registrational aids. Until the beginning of the century, these had been relatively primitive, mainly con-

12. Hermann J. Busch, "Zwischen Tradition und Fortschritt: Zu Orgelbau, Orgelspiel und Orgel-komposition in Deutschland im 19. Jahrhundert." in *Mundus Organorum*, ed. Alfred Reichling (Berlin: Merseberger, 1978), 63–91.

13. William Leslie Sumner, *The Organ: Its Evolution, Principles of Construction, and Use*, 4th ed. (London: St. Martin's Press, 1973), 344.

14. Busch, "Zwischen Tradition und Fortschritt," 63–91.

cerned with putting the higher-pitched chorus stops on or off (the English "machine stop" pedal and the Italian *Tiratutti* knob) or controlling pedal stops (the ventil) or borrowed ranks (the German *Windkoppel*). Baroque registration practices discouraged too-frequent stop changes, but when they were necessary in playing large continental organs, assistants were required.

French organ builders in the eighteenth century dodged the need for registration aids by simply putting frequently used solo stops (Cornet, reeds) on extra short-compass manuals, where they could be left on while the organist used other stops on the two main manuals. Cavaillé-Coll was trained in this tradition, and it is interesting to note that his initial proposal for St.-Denis comprised a five-manual organ with three full-compass divisions and two short-compass "solo" divisions. But changes in organ repertoire, especially the increased use of transcriptions, were challenging this concept, and his final disposition called for four full-compass divisions on three manuals, one of them enclosed.[15] It likewise contained something quite new to French organs, the *pédales de combinaison*. Most of these were couplers of one sort or another, including one coupling all manuals to pedal, and a sub-octave coupler; most interesting were two that coupled the trebles and basses (separately) of the reeds and harmonic flutes to the Positif. Before long Cavaillé-Coll's specifications contained other pedals to control ventils that brought on already drawn stops (usually reeds) located on chest divisions winded from the high-pressure bellows. These became a standard registration aid and were exploited by César Franck and other composers.

Meanwhile, in England, another young builder, Henry Willis, was also seeking improvements. Having visited France in 1848 and 1849 and met Cavaillé-Coll and Barker, he was impressed by the effectiveness of multiple pressures and, not least, Barker's pneumatic lever, which thus finally migrated back to England.[16] In 1851 he found the opportunity to incorporate these and some of his own improvements in his three-manual, 70-stop (22 were in the Swell) organ built for the main hall of the Crystal Palace in London for Prince Albert's "Great Exhibition of the Art and Industry of All Nations." It contained several innovations, including "break-away" pallets in the Choir, four separate wind pressures, double swell shutters, and an odd "roller" valve for pedal pipes, but one stands out above all others: Willis's combination pistons. Pneumatic action had been applied to the stop action, and thus a pneumatically operated combination action requiring only a light touch became feasible. Willis describes it as follows:

> On the key slip, which is of brass, immediately below each clavier, project a number of small studs, each of which corresponds to, and is labeled with, a

15. Douglass, *Cavaillé-Coll and the Musicians*, 13ff, 27ff.

16. William Leslie Sumner, *Father Henry Willis, Organ Builder* (London: Musical Opinion, 1955), 16.

certain combination of stops belonging to the clavier adjoining; when the hands are on the keys, these studs, lying directly below, can be touched easily with the thumbs, and when any one of them is slightly pushed in, in this manner, it draws the combination of stops to which it corresponds, in the same manner as the composition pedals. This is effected by the aid of a pneumatic apparatus, on the same principle as that applied to the keys. The stud, on being touched, admits compressed air into a bellows, which immediately rises with sufficient power to act, by means of rods and levers, on the machinery of the stops, drawing out those which the given combination requires, and pushing in those that are superfluous.[17]

It is obvious that the combinations were fixed ones; a few more decades had to elapse before a means could be found to make them adjustable. But pneumatically operated combinations operable by the thumb were a giant step ahead of cumbersome mechanical combinations, which required the full force of the player's foot to operate them.

The 1851 Crystal Palace Exhibition

Organs had been exhibited at expositions before (witness Abbey's collaboration with Erard on an exhibition organ in 1827), but there had never before been an exhibition like the 1851 Crystal Palace extravaganza. It set the tone for many subsequent events in Europe and America, where the latest glories of the industrial revolution—now in full swing—were proudly exhibited to amaze and enlighten the populace, which responded by attending in droves.

Although Willis's organ was by far the largest and most impressive exhibited in 1851, it was not the only one, and many of the smaller organs also boasted interesting technological innovations ranging from the useful to the bizarre. While several continental builders displayed examples of their work, Cavaillé-Coll was curiously absent. However, his chief competitor, Ducroquet (for whom Barker was then working), exhibited a two-manual, 20-stop organ containing many characteristics first introduced by Cavaillé-Coll that were rapidly becoming standard in French organ-building: Barker machine, multiple wind pressures, sub and super couplers, free-reed stops, and what was becoming the "signature stop" of the French Romantic organ, the 8′ Flûte harmonique.[18] Ducroquet was the only French firm to exhibit an organ, although there was no dearth of harmoniums of various types offered by French and Belgian manufacturers.

There was also only one German entry, by Johan, Friedrich, and Edmund

17. Peter Mactaggart and Ann Mactaggart, eds., *Musical Instruments in the 1851 Exhibition* (London: Mac & Me, 1986), 62.

18. Mactaggart and Mactaggart, *Musical Instruments*, 49.

Schulze of Paulinzelle; the better-known and more technically innovative Walcker was, like Cavaillé-Coll, conspicuous by his absence. Compared to some of the French and English exhibits, Schulze's two-manual, 16-stop organ was rather old-fashioned from a technical standpoint. Its action was straight mechanical, it had no enclosed division, was winded by two wedge bellows, and appears not to have had any registration aids beyond couplers. In addition, only the Hauptwerk could be coupled to the pedal.[19] This coupler was described as an "internal movement," one that did not affect the keys, but it may only have been a *Windkoppel*, known since the eighteenth century, rather than any new device.

Schulze's organ did have one innovation, however, in that its pedal keys were arrayed in a concave rather than flat manner. But even this was seen as capable of improvement, for when Henry Willis pointed it out to the organist S. S. Wesley at the exhibition, Wesley is said to have responded, "It is a pity he did not go further, and make his pedals spread out."[20] And thus was born the Willis-Wesley concave and radiating pedal board, later to become standard in both England and North America. However, if Schulze's organ had little technological impact, it did impress the English with its bold, full-blown tone and contributed the mild, high-cut-up Lieblich Gedact to the developing English romantic tonal palette.

The Organ Factory

Greater expressiveness, new color stops, and mechanical assistance for key and stop action were not the only innovations brought to the organ by the industrial revolution. Until the early nineteenth century, organs had been made with hand tools in fairly small workshops; some portions were actually made on site in remote churches and cathedrals. Many workmen were not even regular employees of the builders, acting more as occasional subcontractors, and on larger organs the decorative casework was often constructed by outside parties.

By the middle of the nineteenth century this was changing rapidly as power-driven woodworking machinery was introduced and the more ambitious builders were converting their operations to the factory system, in which full-time employees specialized in different facets of the work. It would appear that this trend began in England, but by 1860 large organ factories with power-driven machinery could be found almost everywhere. As early as 1846, Forster & Andrews, located in the British industrial center of Hull, could advertise that their establishment

19. Mactaggart and Mactaggart, *Musical Instruments*, 58.
20. Sumner, *Father Henry Willis*, 21.

was "the largest and most completely fitted up manufactory in the United King-dom."[21] In 1858 William Simmons advertised that his new five-story organ factory in Boston was the first in the United States to employ steam-powered wood-working machinery. His major competitors, the Hooks, had built a large factory a few years earlier and would soon also employ steam power.

While many smaller organ-building firms continued to operate in the older manner, they could not pretend to compete with the larger ones. The conversion to the factory system had several advantages for enterprising builders in an era when the market for organs was growing, not the least of which was increased output. Expanding populations meant new churches in the rapidly growing sub-urbs of large cities, while the revival of interest in organ music and concerts during the second half of the nineteenth century drove the market for larger church and concert-hall organs in the cities. The growing demand for organs indeed mandated ever-larger facilities, and some builders, such as Henry Willis, found themselves moving to new quarters every few decades as their workforce and amount of equipment expanded.

Probably the first effect of building organs in a factory setting was the stan-dardization of parts. Samuel Renn, working in the industrial center of Manches-ter, is cited as being one of the first in England to make a practice of this, as early as the 1830s, and Michael Sayer suggests that his contacts with Lancashire manufacturers and mill owners "gave him insights into industrialized methods and experience of . . . early woodworking machinery less accessible to his London contemporaries."[22] However, it was not long before all but the smallest workshops practiced some form of standardization of small action parts, keyboards, and even windchests and pipes made more feasible by improved machinery. It is interest-ing to note that certain other pioneers in converting organ building to a factory operation also worked in industrial centers—Walcker in Ludwigsburg, for ex-ample.

By mid-century, two other effects of industrialization were noticeable. The increasing technical sophistication of larger organs has already been discussed, but the effect upon smaller, simpler organs was quite different. It can be argued that small organs of any builder—from Green's chamber organs to Silbermann's parish church organs—have always tended to fall into similar patterns. But "sim-ilar" and "identical" are not the same thing, and what the factory system made possible was small organs that were virtually identical, made from the same standardized parts to the same common design. From this it was but a small step to marketing them from a catalog, although it was not until almost the last quarter of the nineteenth century that this was actually done.

---

21. Laurence Elvin, *Forster & Andrews, Organ Builders* (Lincoln: Elvin, 1968), 9.
22. Michael Sayer, "Industrialized Organ-Building—A Pioneer," *Organ Yearbook* 7 (1976): 90–100.

In 1862 the Reverend John Baron, an Anglican rector of the Oxford movement persuasion, in reaction to the encroachment of harmoniums into parish churches, proposed some standard designs of very small and basic one-manual organs that he called "Scudamore organs," the smallest of which had but two stops, an 8' Open Diapason and an 8' Dulciana.[23] The first "catalog" Scudamore organs were made by the Willis firm and proved popular enough to be emulated soon after by other builders, including Bevington and Walker, Warren in Canada, and Hook & Hastings in the United States.

In 1871 Hook & Hastings issued the first of a series of several catalogs in which were described six models of small one- and two-manual organs, with stop lists and prices; by the end of the century their catalogs listed up to seventeen models, ranging in size up to three manuals and 27 stops. In 1889 Cavaillé-Coll printed a catalog of *Orgues de tous modèles* ranging in size from a one-manual *orgue du choeur* to a substantial three-manual, 30-stop scheme. It is uncertain when Walcker began advertising catalog organs, but they have continued the practice to the present day. In the rapidly expanding American Midwest, John L. Hinners in 1879 established an organ factory in Pekin, Illinois, that from the outset built little else than catalog organs. Because so many of the smaller catalog organs built in the late nineteenth century in all countries were purchased by small rural churches, a number yet survive in regular use to testify to the practical design, sound workmanship, and musical excellence of such workhorse instruments.

New Technologies for Organ Blowing

By the middle of the nineteenth century, technology and industrialization were making organ building more efficient and organs easier to play, more expressive, and more manageable, but one element still harked back to the Middle Ages: large organs, such as those previously mentioned in Paris, Frankfurt, and Birmingham, were still blown by the arms or legs of strong men. Improvements in the design of bellows, reservoirs, and feeders may have made their job a bit easier, but even the smallest organ required one person to supply the wind, and the largest ones needed several: four blowers were required by Willis's 70-stop organ at the 1851 Crystal Palace exhibition, and some large German organs required even more. Technology still had a bit farther to go.

At a symposium in 1998, a panel was asked: What technical development in the recent history of the organ has had the greatest impact on the instrument and its players? Several suggestions were made, but the one that generated the

23. John Baron, *Scudamore Organs, or Practical Hints Respecting Organs for Village Churches and Small Chancels, on Improved Principles* (London: Bell and Daldy, 1862).

greatest amount of agreement was mechanical blowing. This invention not only allowed organists to practice long hours on the organ (rather than on the clavichord, harpsichord, or piano), but also opened the door to higher wind pressures, greater use of pneumatic devices in the action, and the monster organs of the early twentieth century.

Many organ builders at the midpoint of the nineteenth century seem to have been acutely aware of this need. Steam seemed at first the logical path to explore. In 1853 William Hill built a large four-manual organ for a hall in London called the Royal Panopticon of Science and Art. It had high-pressure Tuba stops at 8' and 4' pitches and seven bellows providing multiple pressures. But a steam engine, rather than a team of men, operated the feeders.[24] Hill's rival, Willis, was not far behind: his even larger organ, built a year later for another public place, St. George's Hall in Liverpool, was winded by "two immense bellows, each with three feeders driven by an eight horse-power steam engine" in the vaults below the organ. The system remained in use until 1924, when it was superseded by a centrifugal fan blower, making it no longer necessary to have to notify the engineer and stokers hours in advance of any performance on the organ.[25] Later, in the 1870s, Willis substituted a system of pistons for the feeders, but these were still driven by steam; indeed, inconvenient as it was, steam seemed to be the power of choice for many of England's large secular organs (and a few in cathedrals) until the early decades of the twentieth century.

Another, less costly and inconvenient source of blowing power soon began to come into use, however: the hydraulic engine or water motor. Utilizing the pressure in water mains to operate a reciprocating piston device attached to the feeders under the bellows, it was first patented in England in 1857 by David Joy, an engineer, and William Holt, an organ builder,[26] and by 1859 had been applied to the large organ in London's Temple Church.[27] Water motors soon came into widespread use in urban areas in England, as well as in the United States and Canada, where steam power had largely been bypassed. When a four-manual Walcker organ was installed in the Music Hall in Boston in 1863, the wind was furnished by a two-horsepower water motor operating six large feeder bellows, but because this technology was so new it was perhaps a bit suspect, and if necessary the organ could also be blown by four men.[28]

Water motors had only recently begun to appear in Boston—Hook's 1863 organ in the Second Church utilized one—and the Music Hall water motor was

24. Laurence Elvin, *Organ Blowing: Its History and Development* (Lincoln: Elvin, 1971), 34.
25. Elvin, *Organ Blowing*, 34.
26. Elvin, *Organ Blowing*, 38ff.
27. Sumner, *The Organ*, 160.
28. *The Great Organ in the Boston Music Hall* (Boston: Ticknor and Fields, 1866), 59.

probably the Bostonians' idea, for many large organs in Germany were still manually blown, including Walcker's even larger 1856 organ in Ulm Cathedral. However, when this instrument was enlarged to over 100 stops in 1886, it was blown by a four-horsepower gas engine with automatic regulation.[29] France, which had led the way in so many early innovations, seemed content to continue to have a substantial number of its largest organs blown by manpower, often well into the twentieth century. One possible reason for this may be simply that the French tended to eschew excessively high wind pressures and unusually large organs. Stephen Bicknell has noted that "For Cavaillé-Coll an organ with a 32′ stop was a landmark instrument. For Willis such an organ was commonplace."[30]

In England and North America, water motors were generally the power source of choice for churches, at least in urban areas where a municipal water supply was available and churches were exempt from water taxes; organs in rural areas continued to be hand blown, some until quite recent times. A bewildering variety of water motors was in use by the end of the century and accounted for a substantial number of patents for improved models touted for their silent or jolt-free operation. Similar claims were made for the only real competitor, the gas engine, which, however, never achieved the widespread use of the water motor. By 1889 the Roosevelt firm of New York was using electric motors,[31] which around the same time also began to make their appearance in England; an early (1891) application was in Holy Trinity Church, Chelsea, London.[32]

All of these power sources had one thing in common, however: they merely substituted for the human blower in operating the feeders that actually supplied the wind to the bellows. Reciprocating motors (sometimes simply bolted to the old blowing handle) operated double feeders, but triple feeders attached to a crankshaft came increasingly into use and could be run by a wheel belted to a two-cylinder water motor or a DC electric motor regulated by a rheostat attached to the bellows top. As long as the crankshaft was kept greased and the feeders did not creak, the latter system could be remarkably quiet.

The real break with the concept of simply substituting steam, water, gas, or electric power for manpower in operating feeders did not come until the very end of the nineteenth century, when the introduction of enclosed centrifugal fan blowers finally made the feeders obsolete. Fan blowers had, in fact, already been around for a few decades; such blowers were exhibited as early as 1862 at the International Exhibition in London and were used as forge blowers and venti-

---

29. *Beschreibung der Münster-Orgel zu Ulm* (Ludwigsburg: Walcker, 1900).

30. Stephen Bicknell, *The History of the English Organ* (Cambridge: Cambridge University Press, 1996), 257.

31. Orpha Ochse, *The History of the Organ in the United States* (Bloomington: Indiana University Press, 1975), 268.

32. Elvin, *Organ Blowing*, 79.

lators. At first fan blowers were not thought to be practical for organ blowing, but a successful application of a forge blower to a four-manual Abbott and Smith organ was reported in 1895, and, their design having subsequently been modified by Robert Hope-Jones and other engineers, purpose-built centrifugal fan blowers for organs soon began to be manufactured.[33]

The advantages of the fan blower soon became apparent. By eliminating the feeders and their attendant mechanism, a source of potential noise and maintenance was also eliminated. True, the early fan blowers were themselves rather noisy, but they could be located in a cellar or other remote location and the wind conveyed up to the reservoir bellows of the organ, even if the organ was located two stories up in a gallery. And regulation of wind, at first thought to be a handicap to the use of fan blowers, turned out to be easily accomplished by the use of a curtain valve or "butterfly" valve located between the blower and reservoir and attached to the top of the latter. Several firms were soon making blowers especially designed to provide low-pressure wind for organs, including Kinetic in England (which soon opened an American branch) and Spencer in Hartford, Connecticut (where a ready market existed in John T. Austin's newly established organ factory).

These fan blowers were simple, rugged machines, requiring only minimal maintenance; a large two-stage Kinetic blower installed in 1906 in a Boston church was still running reliably in 2000, although its original DC motor had been replaced with a new AC motor a few decades earlier. At the end of the twentieth century, centrifugal fan blowers, although now made to improved and quieter designs, still provide wind for most of the world's organs. But we should not forget that they are the result of a half century of experimentation in mechanical organ blowing technology prior to 1900.

Further Developments in Key, Stop, and Combination Actions

The same half century also saw a continuing exploration of new technologies applied to organ action and registration aids. The Barker machine had opened up other possibilities utilizing pneumatic technology. As early as 1835 the French builder Moitessier had experimented with an action in which an impulse of air running through a small-diameter tube was substituted for the mechanical connection between key and chest, but he did not successfully apply it until 1850, in an organ in Toulouse. Another French builder, Fermis, developed a more advanced form of tubular-pneumatic action in 1866 and exhibited it at the Paris Exhibition of 1867. There it was noted by Willis, who patented his own version

---

33. Elvin, *Organ Blowing*, 97.

in 1868. In 1872 Willis found a use for it in his divided organ for St. Paul's Cathedral, where a tubular action running under the chancel floor from the console activated the Barker machine in those parts of the organ on the south side of the chancel.[34]

This adaptation did not go unnoticed and soon led to a proliferation of divided organs in the British Isles, as well as detached consoles. Indeed, tubular-pneumatic action quickly became far more popular in England and Australia than in France and was used in organs of all sizes. It would seem that Cavaillé-Coll and his growing school of Parisian followers had, after their initial ground-work, become rather conservative in their approach to action design. A Parisian organ of 1890 was not vastly different from one of 1850 in either its tonal or mechanical appointments; the same could not be said of organs in England, Germany, or America.

The Germans, meanwhile, continued to perfect the individual pipe-valve chest, which was extensively used by Walcker and other builders such as Sauer and Weigle, especially in larger organs, and eventually began applying pneumatic action to it. Gustav Sander of Liegnitz may have been the first German builder to patent a tubular-pneumatic action, in 1867.[35] Walcker patented its version in 1889, and Carl Weigle developed his own variant at around the same time.

In North America, tubular-pneumatic action did not win the wide approval and use that it had in England and Australia, simply because it arrived too late. Already an even newer technology was beckoning. In 1826 an Englishman, William Sturgeon, invented the electromagnet, and it was not long before the idea of utilizing it in organ action took root. In 1851 Henry Gauntlett, a prominent English organist, conceived the then rather fantastic idea of using electricity to play the eight organs at the Crystal Palace exhibition simultaneously; while this was clearly impossible at the time due to the primitive state of the technology, he did patent a concept of opening the pallets in a windchest by magnetic means. In 1855 Stein and Son exhibited an organ played by electricity at the Paris Exhibition, but according to J. W. Hinton, who saw it there, it "contained many defects."[36]

At around the same time two French scientists, Du Moncel and Froment, were also making attempts to harness the electromagnet to organ action. However, it was another French scientist, Albert Peschard (who was also an organist in Caen), who in 1864 patented the first really workable application of the electromagnet—a rather simple device in which the magnet opened a small primary

34. Bicknell, *The History of the English Organ*, 268.
35. Hans Gerd Klais, "War die Kegellade ein Irrtum?" in *Mundus Organorum*, 171–185.
36. J. W. Hinton, *Story of the Electric Organ* (London: Simpkin, Marshall, 1909), 25.

valve, which exhausted air from a larger pneumatic inside the pallet box of a slider chest. This collapsed and pulled down the pallet. Peschard later worked with Barker in applying electricity to the older Barker machine action.[37]

The French builder least interested in electricity was the aging Aristide Cavaillé-Coll. During the 1860s both Peschard and Barker attempted unsuccessfully to interest him in the use of electricity, and he remained unimpressed even when his chief competitor, Merklin, began building some organs with electric action in 1888. Indeed, he never used it, and in 1898, near the end of his working life, he even saw fit to replace the unreliable electro-pneumatic action in an organ built by Peschard and Barker for St. Augustin's Church, Paris, with his own tried-and-true mechanical Barker machine action.[38]

During the 1860s also, experiments with electric action were underway in England, where Bryceson Brothers began building fairly successful organs with a form of the Peschard-Barker action in 1869, but it was not until 1885 that Willis built an organ with a reliable electro-pneumatic action, for Canterbury Cathedral.[39] At the same time in the United States, young Hilborne Roosevelt, while still a nineteen-year-old apprentice, designed and patented an electric action in 1868. He exhibited a small organ with this action at a New York industrial fair in 1869, winning a gold medal for his invention. However, it was apparently not until his 1872 travels in Europe that he learned of the French experiments with electricity.[40]

With such an auspicious beginning, it was inevitable that the Roosevelt firm would become the standard-bearer for electro-pneumatic organ action in the United States, and it ultimately built several large and influential instruments with this action. But Hilborne and his brother Frank also became pioneers, along with the Casavant firm of Quebec, in the development of adjustable combination actions, which took registrational aids one more giant step toward the twentieth century. The first such actions seem indeed to have been devised in collaboration between Roosevelt and Casavant, largely to designs by Salluste Duval, who also assisted the Casavant brothers in building their first large electric-action organ in 1890 for Notre-Dame Church of Montreal.[41]

The final years of the nineteenth century and the opening years of the twentieth saw a flurry of inventions and patents everywhere, all having to do with aspects of electro-pneumatic action and improvements in chest design and registrational aids. Many builders still made small tracker-action organs for country

37. Reginald Whitworth, *The Electric Organ* (London: Musical Opinion, 1948), 13.

38. Fenner Douglass, "Cavaillé-Coll and Electricity in Organ Building," in *Visitatio Organorum* (Buren: Frits Knuf, 1980), 103–115.

39. Bicknell, *The History of the English Organ*, 287.

40. Ochse, *The History of the Organ in the United States*, 265–67.

41. Antoine Bouchard, "Canada's Oldest Organbuilding Firm," *Tracker* 43, no. 2 (1999): 9–20.

churches (some of which as yet had no electricity), and tubular-pneumatic action was still used by some builders, especially in Australia, along with electro-pneumatic action. Generators belted from centrifugal fan blowers provided reliable action current, doing away with the need for batteries to power the action. Fast-acting adjustable combination pistons allowed organists to make lightning-fast stop changes when playing the increasingly popular orchestral transcription literature. Multiple easily controlled swell boxes made possible more expression than Abbé Vogler ever dreamed of.

The English-trained John T. Austin introduced a radical new type of walk-in windchest and established the business that still bears his name in America; young Ernest Skinner, working at first for George Hutchings's Boston firm, developed the prototype of the now-ubiquitous "pitman" chest. In England, Robert Hope-Jones devised chest actions and switching mechanisms to allow ranks of pipes to be electrically "borrowed" at different pitches and on different divisions, a technique that, in the early decades of the twentieth century, resulted in the cinema organ (or, as Hope-Jones preferred to call it, the "unit orchestra"). And all of the new technologies combined to make possible the early-twentieth-century monster organs of 100-plus stops built in England, Germany, North America, and elsewhere.

Indeed, the story of organ technology during the twentieth century is no more or less than a story of refinements and experiments based on the technologies developed and tested in the nineteenth century. Only at the very end of the twentieth century did a truly new technology—electronics—emerge to challenge once again the inventive and adaptive powers of organ builders.

But perhaps the greatest paradox of these latter days is that most of the old technologies still survive in restored and entirely new organs. Although they may utilize the latest in power tools and computer-assisted drafting, builders world-wide can still build mechanical-action organs with fifteenth-century technology, right down to the human-powered wind supply (although usually with an electric fan-blower backup). Lately, the Barker machine has been revived—a notable example being the 1998 Verschueren organ in the School of Music at Göte-borg—and even improved upon.

Many large organs today exhibit what could almost be called a confusion of technologies, were it not for the fact that in most instances the use of each has been carefully and intelligently planned. Mechanical key actions, electrical stop actions, and electronic combination actions can comfortably coexist in the same instrument, which may, in addition, contain tonal elements from the Middle Ages through the early twentieth century. Confused eclecticism? Perhaps, or perhaps not. Unlike the nineteenth century, the twentieth is yet too close to us to be dispassionately sorted out and analyzed, and the organ—as the most complex of all musical instruments—continues its evolution tonally and technically.

17

ARISTIDE CAVAILLÉ-COLL: MASTER OF MASTERS

JESSE E. ESCHBACH AND LAWRENCE ARCHBOLD

Paris: The Capital of the Nineteenth Century

When in 1935 Walter Benjamin memorably proclaimed Paris to be "the capital of the nineteenth century," he crystallized an idea that, in itself, was not new: as early as 1901 Charles Simond, in a remarkable essay entitled "Cent Ans de Paris: 1800–1900," had noted that while trends in the nineteenth century toward development, energy, and the production of both material and intellectual property were worldwide phenomena, they had as their center the city of Paris.[1] Paris in the nineteenth century, however, is more likely to be remembered now as that century's "capital of pleasure, fashion and luxury," as Ralph Locke has suggested, qualities by which Paris specifically, and France generally, became epitomized.[2] Such was certainly the case for the Swedish Baron and Baroness de Gondremarck who, in Jacques Offenbach's *opéra bouffe* of 1866, *La Vie parisienne*, visit Paris and, amidst scenes of conspicuous consumption, are drawn into romantic intrigues. More recently, a Scandinavian perspective on the culture of later nineteenth-century Paris can be found in the 1987 film *Babette's Feast*, in which members of the Danish upper class, toward the end of the century, are seen to savor the delicacies of French gastronomy from the hands of one of its most distinguished Second Empire practitioners.

The title of the chapter is taken from a remark made by Alphonse Mailly, professor of organ at the Conservatoire Royal de Musique in Brussels, around 1875: "Cavaillé-Coll est le maître des maîtres." Quoted in Maison A. Cavaillé-Coll, *Orgues de tous modèles* (1889; facsimile reprint as *Maison A. Cavaillé-Coll: Paris 1889*, ed. Alfred Reichling, Documenta Organologica, vol. 2 [Berlin: Merseburger, 1977], 13).

1. See Graeme Gilloch, *Myth and Metropolis: Walter Benjamin and the City* (Cambridge: Polity Press, 1996), 97–98; and Charles Simond, "Cent Ans de Paris: 1800–1900," in *Paris de 1800 à 1900: d'après les estampes et les mémoires du temps* (Paris: Librairie Plon, 1901), 619.

2. Ralph P. Locke, "Paris: Centre of Intellectual Ferment," in *Music and Society: The Early Romantic Era* (Englewood Cliffs, N.J.: Prentice Hall, 1990), 78.

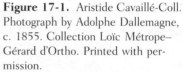

Figure 17-1. Aristide Cavaillé-Coll. Photograph by Adolphe Dallemagne, c. 1855. Collection Loïc Métrope–Gérard d'Ortho. Printed with permission.

Offenbach's *La Vie parisienne* was written in anticipation of the 1867 exhibition, reminding us that to regard the government of Louis Napoléon as merely a "carnival empire"—as some have done—misses a point: throughout the second half of the century a series of notable exhibitions (that in 1889, perhaps the greatest, left as its enduring monument the Eiffel Tower) brought together science, industry, and the arts to assure the world that Paris was not merely a capital of fashion but also one of technology. Of all those in the musical world, perhaps instrument builders—whose creativity inevitably draws upon science, industry, and the arts, all three—would have been in the best position to appreciate such extravaganzas.

The Paris of Hector Berlioz and Georges Bizet was "a city unsurpassed in its musical resources."[3] With respect to organs, by the era of the Second Empire, many of the most notable ones were the work of Aristide Cavaillé-Coll (1811–99; figure 17-1), whose rise to international fame as an organ builder is related to his being located in Paris. Drawing on traditions and innovations from Spain, Germany, and England, as well as the prerevolutionary French style, Cavaillé-Coll achieved a distinctive synthesis of various elements of progressive European organ building that responded to the increased emphasis on the symphonic orchestra in European musical culture without rejecting basic premises of the

3. Locke, "Paris," 32.

organ that he had inherited. (Indeed, as Kurt Lueders has shown, Cavaillé-Coll was essentially a conservative builder, especially in his later years, and particularly so when seen against his competitors and their innovations, of which many now seem dubious.)[4] Cavaillé-Coll's relationships with the leading organists of his time and place were sometimes complex, yet the best such organist-composers, including César Franck, Charles-Marie Widor, and others, benefited from his influence and in turn gave to his instruments distinctive musical styles; together they made Paris the most exciting venue for organ culture in the last decades of the century.

Cavaillé-Coll organs were purchased not only throughout France, but abroad, and were widely influential. The allure of *cailles en sarcophage* to the connoisseurs at Babette's table may not, in the end, have been all that different from that of one of Aristide Cavaillé-Coll's more rarified stops, such as the Flûte à Pavillon. Indeed, to purchase a Cavaillé-Coll organ in the latter years of the nineteenth century was not simply to buy an instrument of unsurpassed quality; it was also to acquire something of the magic of the French organ school and the prestige of the capital of the century. To understand why, it is necessary to turn to the details of Cavaillé-Coll's career.

The Early Years

As documented in his correspondence, and later by his daughter Cécile, the early years of Aristide Cavaillé-Coll were indeed enchanted.[5] How many provincial organ builders, after all, would be likely to have an opportunity to meet Rossini, one of the most popular composers of his day, and to make such an impression that Rossini supplied him with letters of introduction to some of the leading luminaries of Paris in the early 1830s? How likely was it, after all, that a young man of twenty-two years with little formal education, largely self-taught, could "rise" to Paris, present his credentials, and be just in time to compete in the bidding process for one of the most prestigious instruments to be built in France in nearly a hundred years? And just how likely was it that this bumpkin, most recently from the Dordogne, whose French must have been accented at best, would actually be awarded the contract, competing against some of the best-known, established builders of the day? Pierre Dallery, successor to François-Henri Clicquot, had restored several important organs after completing

4. Kurt Lueders, "Reflections on the Esthetic Evolution of the Cavaillé-Coll Organ," in *Charles Brenton Fisk: Organ Builder: Essays in His Honor*, ed. Fenner Douglass, Owen Jander, and Barbara Owen (Easthampton, Mass.: Westfield Center, 1986), 1:136.

5. The early years of Aristide Cavaillé-Coll are admirably documented by his daughter and son, who possessed what is now known as the Lapresté collection. Fenner Douglass retold the story and provided rich documentation in his *Cavaillé-Coll and the Musicians* (Raleigh, N.C.: Sunbury, 1980), 8–12.

the latter's work at Poitiers Cathedral at the onset of the French Revolution and was responsible for a small instrument built in the chapel of the Tuileries Palace for Louis XVIII. Pierre Dallery and his son Louis-Paul, as well as Sébastien Erard and John Abbey, were well established in the eyes of the French government.

Seven years later, the Cavaillé-Colls were close to finishing the instrument at St.-Denis. Aristide had promised, in the original contract, a very large organ capable of being played with all of its five manuals coupled. True, after his father arrived on the scene the contract was rewritten and the number of manuals eventually reduced to three (playing four divisions), but Aristide persisted in promising that an organist could play all manuals coupled. It is clear, however, that at the time of these unprecedented brash promises, the young Cavaillé-Coll had little idea just how this technical feat would be realized. Only when the organ was nearly complete did the Englishman Charles Spackman Barker travel to France in hopes of discovering a market for his new pneumatic lever, which was capable of lightening key action, especially for coupled manuals. One wonders just how far Aristide's career might have progressed without Barker's fortuitous visit. Imagine, for instance, the reception committee as it reviewed the terms of the contract and tested the Grand-Choeur of the organ with its manuals coupled. They would have found an abundance of wind, but surely an unwieldy key action, essentially unplayable when coupled. The furor would have been enormous, and the established builders of Paris would certainly have wasted no time in denouncing the youngster from Toulouse as brash and incompetent, if not dishonest. Aristide and his family would certainly have beaten a hasty retreat back to their native Dordogne and at most occupied a paragraph or two in the history of the French organ.

Enchanted? Most assuredly. Aristide Cavaillé-Coll's situation in the 1830s was not unlike that of a young performer today who wins a major international competition. No doubt there were several artists at the same level, and depending on the tastes (if not whims) of the judges, the prestigious prize could have gone in a number of directions. The winner profited from a measure of luck. The name has suddenly gained recognition, leading to concerts and recordings for the immediate future. For Aristide, the influential contract at St.-Denis was his first prize. It propelled him to instant fame and assured him of numerous contracts over the next few years. Luck clearly played a major role in establishing Aristide's young career, but had the builder relied exclusively on his first good fortune, his career would have been extremely short lived.

Trained from his earliest years in the multiple skills required to be a successful organ builder, Aristide was well versed in the traditional French postclassical organ of the late eighteenth and early nineteenth centuries. Because of the family's close ties to Spain (specifically Catalonia), young Aristide also inherited a broader vision of stylistic possibilities. Rossini's letters of introduction make it abundantly clear that Aristide was a hard worker. His credentials in mathematics were beyond reproach, but his background in music appears essentially nonexistent. He apparently played no instruments and never studied solfège or music history. Yet, he intuitively understood that the styles of his grandfather and father were rapidly going the way of the harpsichord. The new musical styles, especially the quest for "expression" on keyboard instruments, became the overwhelming concern of the younger generations, and Aristide experimented not only with the Venetian swell, probably only known in two locations in France by the 1830s,[6] but also with the new free-reed stops so valued in Germany and championed by Abbé Vogler.

He also understood, when designing his first instruments in the 1830s, that the old Grand-Jeu (now called Grand-Choeur) had to be rethought. Previously, few if any foundation stops had been mixed with the Trompette-Clairon-Cornet registration, but Aristide understood that this sound needed more support and breadth, especially in the treble, to support the massive homophonic textures rapidly making their way in the more progressive Parisian *tribunes*, borrowed from the opera, symphony, and piano. He experimented with new winding systems and quickly solved the problem of insufficient wind in the key channels, which had been partly responsible for organists' never drawing much foundation support with the old Grand-Jeu. By the time his first instrument in Paris was completed (Notre-Dame de Lorette, 1838), Aristide had come up with the idea of separate key channels for the foundations and reeds, thus supplying them with copious wind and allowing the two groups of stops to be united when desired in order to form the new Grand-Choeur. This radical development was yet again happenstance. Although Aristide had concerned himself with wind supply and pressures generated at the reservoirs throughout the 1830s, modifying or even abandoning the sacrosanct key channel chest had apparently not been a part of his original scheme. Owing to a last-minute change in the design of the organ case imposed by the architect of Notre-Dame de Lorette, Cavaillé-Coll was required to furnish a Positif de dos, resulting in the deletion of the internal Positif, originally intended to be on the same chest as the Grand-Orgue.[7] Suddenly, Aristide found himself with fifty-four free key channels and quickly came to the conclusion that by moving the Grand-Orgue reeds to the free channels and giving the Grand-Orgue key action additional backfalls, activated by a pedal at the key desk, the second set of pallets could be activated or deactivated at will by the performer. This essentially marks the birth of *anches préparées*, originally intended as a means of nourishing the chest with an abundance of wind, but within fifteen

6. Beauvais Cathedral (Hamel, 1827) and the Légion d'Honneur, St.-Denis (John Abbey and Sébastien Erard, 1826–27).

7. Aristide Cavaillé-Coll, "Etats d'orgues avant et après travaux (1838–1858)," MS, Bibliothèque Nationale de France, Département de la Musique, 5–14.

years giving rise to the famous French crescendo of the middle and late nineteenth century, still today a sine qua non of French organ repertoire.

Keys to Cavaillé-Coll's Success

Cavaillé-Coll's providential early training, his ability to find himself at the right place at the right time, and his clairvoyance in sensing the direction of musical style, not to mention its ramifications in organ building, were indeed key ingredients for his eventual international reputation, established at the very latest by the early 1860s and tenaciously held throughout the duration of his career. The voluminous correspondence from 1833 to 1859, scrupulously maintained in the Lapresté collection, gives the impression that Aristide frequently traveled about France and could almost manage his growing business from virtually any location. Lengthy trips away from the shop were the rule of the day. After all, transportation was slow (even with an emerging railroad), and contractual negotiations with both the government and the local parishes were highly formal, as was the "proofing," mandatory before final payment could be rendered. In fact, Aristide surrounded himself with a legendary team of coworkers, many of whom spent their entire professional careers working in his shop. At first, the business consisted largely of his father Dominique and his brother Vincent, occasionally assisted by other relatives in the south of France, notably his uncle, Martin Cavaillé-Coll. Aristide chose his disciples carefully. There are few accounts in the almost thirty years' worth of detailed correspondence alluding to any kind of problem with workers. On the contrary, numerous letters, addressed to customers in Paris, in the provinces, and abroad, attest to the trust and admiration Aristide demonstrated for his team. Over the years, Jean Puig, Sauvage, Parisot, Gabriel and Félix Reinburg, Kieffer, Glock, Bernard Thiemann, Charles (Carlos) Carloni, Pierre Veerkamp, Auguste Neuberger, and Alphonse Simil (architect) formed an impressive *pléiade* of collaborators who made important decisions, not to mention contributions, in the realms of design, voicing, and action. With the rapid economic and demographic growth under the Second Empire of Louis Napoléon, business all but exploded, requiring Aristide to rely more and more on his coworkers. Had he chosen poorly or treated them tyrannically, Aristide's success would have been at the very least compromised. His modus operandi, however, consisted of treating trusted employees with deference and respect. Indeed, his niece Berthe (Vincent's daughter) married Gabriel Reinburg in 1867.[8]

Aristide Cavaillé-Coll possessed no less prowess in dealing with the cumbersome government bureaucracy of his day. From the time of Napoléon's *Concordat*

---

8. Cécile Cavaillé-Coll and Emmanuel Cavaillé-Coll, *Aristide Cavaillé-Coll* (Paris: Librairie Fischbacher, 1929), 70.

of 1801, the Roman Catholic Church became the official state church, and its finances were administered in part by the *Ministère des cultes* (religious affairs department) in Paris; Protestant churches also had some standing and could appeal for funding as well. Cathedral churches were eligible for considerable subsidies, including work on organs. Thanks to the devastation of the revolution, important work still needed to be done throughout France in the 1830s and 1840s, just at the beginning of Aristide's career. The government office responsible for allocating funds could essentially make or break a career. True, the choice of a builder was left to local authorities, much to the government's credit.[9] But the payment schedule was another matter. Cavaillé-Coll's correspondence is full of pleas to both local and government officials asking that decisions be made and accounts paid. Paris was especially sluggish in settling accounts after the turmoil of 1848. This, coupled with problems with his father, Dominique, almost resulted in complete financial failure for the shop. Aristide barely survived, but he would know similar hardships at least two more times in his lengthy career.

The ability to deal adroitly with government ministers, other government leaders, local church council members, and parish priests was absolutely essential in the post-Napoleonic era in France. Cavaillé-Coll proved himself to be a consummate master. He developed strong ties with personnel in the *Ministère des cultes*, the most important contact being Hippolyte Blanc. There is no evidence to suggest that Blanc ever engaged in any practices directly favoring one builder over another, but he did keep Aristide apprised of developments and, when certain decisions were to be made, occasionally gave advice on when an inquiry could be timely. The contract with the cathedral of Perpignan is one such example. The question of funds sufficient to rebuild the large organ lingered at the ministry for five years. Despite repeated letters to the clergy and ministry officials, decisions were slow in coming, and the contract was all but forgotten. Blanc assisted Aristide by reminding the minister of the Perpignan business at the opportune time, and eventually Cavaillé-Coll signed one of his most beautiful masterpieces in 1858.[10] Aristide's ties with the bureaucracy, however, were practically formalized in 1854 when, in February of that year on his forty-third birthday, Aristide married Adèle Blanc, Hippolyte's sister. Although there is no evidence to suggest that Aristide married for anything but the most legitimate reasons, the new family associations surely did not compromise his standing in the ministry office.

Government officials were not alone in their power to make or break a career for craftsmen doing business with the churches of France. Organists have always played a pivotal role in acceptance of new trends, and nineteenth-century France was no exception. The close association of the young Louis-James-Alfred

9. Michel Jurine, *Joseph Merklin, facteur d'orgues européen: Essai sur l'orgue francais au XIXe siècle* (Paris: Aux Amateur de Livres, 1991), 2:128–56.

10. Aristide Cavaillé-Coll, "Lettres. 1851–1855," MS, Bibliothèque Nationale de France, Département de la Musique, 320–21.

Lefébure-Wély and Aristide Cavaillé-Coll has been documented elsewhere.[11] Suffice it to say that Lefébure-Wély was probably the first to encourage and applaud Cavaillé-Coll's bold move to unite foundations and reeds, resulting in a new Grand-Choeur, and was clearly at the very threshold of understanding and mastering the various mechanical accessories normally brought into play by his famous *pédales de combinaison*, which garnished all organs newly constructed or rebuilt by Aristide. The close association between the builder and musician was pivotal in the 1840s, for Cavaillé-Coll's work was under close scrutiny and at times severe criticism. Eventually, with the arrival of the Belgian organist Jacques-Nicolas Lemmens on the Parisian scene in 1850, the builder again had the perspicacity to foresee the organ works of J. S. Bach as the eventual capstone of the French school. He began championing the young Belgian's career in France, without, however, completely abandoning his old friend Lefébure-Wély. Within ten years of Lemmens's first recital in Paris, young French organists began studying the German contrapuntal tradition in Brussels, bringing back their virtuosity and new legato technique to France.

Cavaillé-Coll's Smaller Organs

The absolutely sumptuous quality of Aristide Cavaillé-Coll's organs, due in part to some of the factors enumerated above, surprise no musician acquainted with such masterpieces as St.-Ouen, Rouen; St.-Etienne, Caen; St.-Sernin, Toulouse; St.-François de Sales, Lyon; or the Cathédrale Ste.-Croix, Orléans. But what of smaller instruments? What of the "workhorse" organs, those instruments that accompanied the liturgy from beginning to end throughout all the feasts of the liturgical year? These instruments, known as *orgues de choeur*, have fared about as well as nineteenth-century *grandes orgues*: many have been rebuilt beyond recognition. However, enough examples survive both in France and abroad, not to mention smaller *grandes orgues*, to give the searcher of the twenty-first century a clear idea of the "meat-and-potato" organs constructed by the Cavaillé-Coll shop. In fact, they demonstrate the same quality of workmanship and materials apparent in the largest, most prestigious organs. Few musicians today would dream that the largest percentage of these choir organs, and often smaller *grandes orgues*, are actually stock models, carefully specified in the shop notebook with their complete stop lists and windchest design numbers.[12] Elsewhere in the same record appears an inventory running from 1850 to the late 1880s that details all windchests constructed new by the Cavaillé-Coll firm, supplying location, number of stops, compass, number of pallet boxes, number of sections, measure-

11. Nicolas Gorenstein, "Le tutti: Une registration qui n'existe pas," *L'Orgue* 236 (1995): 14–15. Also, Douglass, *Cavaillé-Coll and the Musicians*, 71–82.

12. Aristide Cavaillé-Coll, shop notebook, "Composition des Jeux de nos divers modèles d'Orgues," MS, Oberlin University Libraries, Special Collections, 135.

ments, chest design numbers, and stick numbers. Putting the two sections of the notebook together reveals just how many of these "standardized" stock models were built and exactly where they went. Few of their *titulaires* today would guess that their instruments were anything other than custom designed. The advantage was that such organs could be sold at a fraction of the price of an individually designed one, thereby placing a genuine Cavaillé-Coll in the hands of even the most modest parish. In fact, the firm published a catalog in 1889 of its most successful stock organs, ranging from a modest 6-stop instrument on one manual for 6,000 francs to a small three manual of 30 stops for 60,000 francs.[13]

Such may have been the case at the Jesus Church in Copenhagen, the only church in Scandinavia to purchase an organ from Cavaillé-Coll. Its stop list closely resembles no. 10 from a document maintained in the shop entitled "Composition des jeux de nos divers modèles d'orgues," a section of the shop notebook cited above (see specification 17-1). This was not one of the models included in the published catalogs. With the exception of the Récit Clairon (specified as a Voix Humaine in the manuscript), the stop list closely matches the manual specification of organ no. 10; the catalog model, however, specifies borrowed pedal stops, while the Jesus Church funded four independent registers. This independent pedal represents the most significant departure from the stock model and may have been a concession to the tradition of the Nordic organ, with its propensity for independent pedal divisions.

SPECIFICATION 17-1.

A. Cavaillé-Coll, Specification no. 10 from MS Shop Notebook

N° 10. Orgues de 16 jeux de 56 notes à 2 Claviers avec un Pédalier de 4 jeux empruntés

1ʳᵉ Disposition

1ᵉʳ Clavier, 56 notes	2ᵐᵉ Clavier expressif de 56 notes
1. Montre 8 p	9. Flûte Traversière 8 p
2. Prestant 4 p	10. Viole de Gambe 8 p
3. Salicional 8 p	11. Flûte octaviante 4 p
4. Bourdon 16 p	12. Voix céleste 8 p, 44 notes
5. Flûte harm: 8 p	13. Octavin 2 p
6. Bourdon 8 p	14. Trompette 8 p
7. Flûte douce 4 p	15. Basson & Hautbois 8 p
8. Doublette 2 p (ou Pleinjeu 2 à 5 rangs)	16. Voix humaine 8 p
(p = pieds [feet])	

---

13. Maison A. Cavaillé-Coll, *Orgues de tous modèles*, 28, 47. Another catalog was published under the same title in 1891, with different specifications and a greater degree of flexibility; it is reprinted in *Les Orgues de Cavaillé-Coll en leur temps* (Saint-Geniès-des-Mourgues: Editions de Bérange, 1999).

Builder for His Time and Inspiration for the Future

The confluence of factors enumerated above certainly contributed to Aristide Cavaillé-Coll's international reputation during much of the nineteenth century, but it does not necessarily account for the immense interest in, if not veneration for, his work that younger generations of organists profess today. True, he founded a style that permitted the flowering of the late-nineteenth-century school of organ playing and composition so celebrated today, and that lies at the very root of much of twentieth-century French organ composition as well. But the profound respect Cavaillé-Coll's name commands today among builders and musicians alike may well be linked to the delicate balance this builder maintained between tradition and innovation.

As noted earlier, Aristide Cavaillé-Coll was the fourth generation of his family to build organs. The work of his grandfather Jean-Pierre and his father, Dominique, was highly regarded in the south of France, and it is in this postclassical style that Aristide was steeped as a child and adolescent. He understood intuitively that musical style was changing and that the organ had to evolve as well, and his writings throughout the 1830s bear witness to the intense creativity he lavished on addressing these issues. Wind supply was his first concern, and he adopted Cumming's parallel reservoir almost immediately. He delighted in the development of multiple wind pressures by means of superimposing reservoirs, which allowed him to place the trebles under higher pressure, a situation especially beneficial for his development of harmonic reeds and flutes. In the old Grand-Jeu registration, the Cornet is essential, its function being to bolster the reed trebles in an attempt to balance them with the basses. Cavaillé-Coll's concept was to allow the harmonic trebles themselves to balance with the powerful basses without relying on the Cornet sonority. Additionally, these trebles allowed his new Grand-Choeur to soar in the higher ranges; this was essential for the new homophonic styles pervasive at this time. With respect to the key channel (slider) chest inherited from older work, it was never a question of abandoning the classical design. Here, he was content to add a second pallet box, in most instances allowing the first half of the division's stops, located on the front side of the chest, to be winded by one groove, while the second half, consisting usually of mutations, mixtures, and reeds, was nourished by a second pallet box on the back side of the chest. The famous division observed on so many of his instruments—with 16', 8', and 4' foundations grouped on the *fonds* side of the chest and played without the ventil, while the 2', mixtures, and reeds played only with the *appel* depressed—was merely an outgrowth of old French classical chest design. Key action was reconsidered as well, and as noted in the story of the St.-Denis contract, Aristide Cavaillé-Coll was indeed fortunate in meeting Charles Spackman Barker just before the completion of that organ. Barker's invention became a stable element on the primary manual in organs over 25 stops: the practice was followed from St.-Denis (1841) through his last instruments in 1898.

The most essential components of his style were in place by the time the St.-Denis organ was inaugurated in September 1841. Throughout Cavaillé-Coll's career, which embraced several style periods, these innovations remained solidly intact. He perfected them, reconsidered mixture compositions, and worked with various tonal schemes before arriving at his mature symphonic style around 1880. Nonetheless, the most decisive departures from traditional organ building were made in the 1830s and remained essentially constant throughout the next sixty years. What is even more revealing, however, is not the "inventions" and developments of Aristide Cavaillé-Coll, but rather the nineteenth-century developments eschewed by the builder. Although it is beyond the scope of this effort to review the entire evolution of German, English, and American organ building during Cavaillé-Coll's lifetime, suffice it to say that he remained staunchly faithful to the old slider chest and to mechanical action, assisted by the Barker lever on the primary manual. These two items go far in defining any organ style, and their use throughout the entirety of his career admirably demonstrates an important aspect of his perfect equilibrium between old and "new" French work.

As with the majority of pivotal figures in the evolution of musical style and instruments, Aristide Cavaillé-Coll's legacy fell into a kind of purgatory shortly after his death in 1899. The neoclassical aesthetic first made its presence felt in France in the 1920s following World War I. It became an absolute tidal wave following World War II, and much of the irreplaceable legacy of the nineteenth century was sacrificed to a style of instrument that attempted to serve both baroque and romantic styles of music. Unfortunately, organs from any previous style period, be they baroque or romantic, that needed repair or overhaul were invariably rebuilt in the new style advocated by the French government's advisory committee on organ restoration. Although the professional journals of this period decry the "decadent" aesthetic of almost every aspect of nineteenth-century work, the occasional voice in the wilderness (such as Marcel Dupré, and later Daniel Roth, Marie-Claire Alain, and Kurt Lueders) transmitted sufficient respect and admiration for the work of Cavaillé-Coll that younger generations coming into prominence in the early 1980s began to reverse old policies, and today, once again, many organists take great pride in their appointments to *tribunes* where a reasonably authentic organ of Aristide Cavaillé-Coll is found.

No one factor determined the brilliant career of Aristide Cavaillé-Coll. Indeed, history witnessed a delicate, rare combination of raw talent, honed and perfected at a very early age, and consisting of prowess in mathematics and physics, perspicacity, the ability to sustain long, hard hours, and an excellent ear (if untutored musically), combined with a cultural and political environment rife with opportunities. Just as with other styles of organ building studied and emulated today, Cavaillé-Coll's organs worked with and for the performer and composer. The beauty he conceived and realized was quickly recognized by the greatest artists of the period, be they musicians, painters, sculptors, or writers. Musicians responded, and a cohesive style soon evolved. In the case of the symphonic organ repertoire of nineteenth- and twentieth-century France, the age-old question of the chicken or the egg was answered years ago when Aristide Cavaillé-Coll's favorite organist at the end of the nineteenth century, Charles-Marie Widor, proclaimed that the paths followed by his friend Cavaillé-Coll were completely responsible for the wealth of masterpieces composed in France during the nineteenth century.

18

WALCKER AND CAVAILLÉ-COLL:
A FRANCO-GERMAN COMPETITION

PAUL PEETERS

IF PARIS WAS THE CAPITAL OF THE NINETEENTH CENTURY, AND IT CERTAINLY WAS, Berlin was "hardly a city" in 1828, according to the writer Heinrich Heine, who wrote: "Berlin is more like a spot where a mass of people has gathered, and although there happen to be many educated people among them, they could care less about where."[1] Not Berlin, but Frankfurt am Main was the city where the Deutsche Bundestag, the official body of the German Confederation, had met since 1817. This was not a parliament, but a congress of representatives of the confederation's states and cities. In 1848–49, Frankfurt also hosted the first meeting of the German Nationalversammlung, the first national German parliament, and it was there, after the Franco-Prussian War, that the Peace of Frankfurt was signed between France and Germany, on 10 May 1871.

The meetings of the Nationalversammlung were held at St. Paul's Church in Frankfurt am Main (figures 18–1 and 18–2), where the organ-building career of Eberhard Friedrich Walcker (1794–1872) had its breakthrough with the completion in 1833 of his first masterpiece, a truly remarkable instrument with three manuals, two pedals, and 74 stops, his opus 9 (figure 18-3). In that same year Aristide Cavaillé-Coll's career really began with his first trip to St.-Denis near Paris, where he would also build a three-manual organ, with 69 stops. Nineteenth-century French and German organ builders produced a dazzling variety of instruments, despite what is commonly assumed about the effects of nineteenth-century mass production. But it is beyond doubt that these two

I would like to thank Prof. Dr. Hermann J. Busch (Siegen), Dr. Sverker Jullander (Göteborg), Koos van de Linde (Geel), Prof. Dr. Uwe Pape (Berlin), and Christoph Macke, of Orgelbau E. F. Walcker GmbH (Kleinblittersdorf), for their kind help.

1. Heinrich Heine, *Reisebilder, Dritter Teil, 1829–30: Reise von München nach Genua*, vol. 5, *Sämtliche Werke*, ed. Hans Kaufmann (Munich: Kindler Taschenbücher, 1964), 173.

Figure 18-1. Frankfurt, St. Paul's Church, exterior, 1848. Historisches Museum Frankfurt am Main. Printed with permission.

Figure 18-2. The opening of the *Nationalversammlung* in St. Paul's Church, Frankfurt, 18 May 1848. © Bildarchiv Preußischer Kulturbesitz, Berlin.

Figure 18-3. Frankfurt, St. Paul's Church, interior with Walcker organ (1833). Printed with permission of Bärenreiter Verlag, Kassel.

builders personify French and German organ building during the nineteenth century.

Eberhard Friedrich Walcker

Eberhard Friedrich Walcker (figure 18-4) was born in 1794 in Cannstatt, Baden-Württemberg. During the summer of 1807, Abbé Georg Joseph Vogler's visit to Cannstatt was perhaps the catalyst for Walcker's decision to become an organ builder. At the very least, some of Vogler's ideas influenced his concept a great deal. His father, Johann Eberhard, who had started to build organs in 1780, began training Eberhard Friedrich in 1808, when he was fourteen years old. He in turn developed his own ideas and founded a new company in 1820 in Ludwigsburg. His first organ project (Kochersteinsfeld, 1820) was too large for his new shop and had to be built in his father's workshop. His fourth opus, an instrument for the Garnison Church in Stuttgart (1824), soon became known for its quality and would bring several orders for new instruments. The breakthrough came with the new organ for St. Paul's Church in Frankfurt,[2] commis-

2. The information about this organ is based on Ferdinand Moosmann and Rudi Schäfer, *Eberhard*

Figure 18-4. Eberhard Friederich Walcker. Printed with permission of Bärenreiter Verlag, Kassel.

sioned by the city council. Only the insistence of a friend convinced Walcker to compete for the contract "and primarily because this new work . . . would give [him] the chance to establish [his] reputation as an organ builder . . . abroad."[3] The proposals were judged by a Dr. Hoch, who presided over the council. He stated "that amongst all the competitors who have applied, from the beginning Mr. Walcker has proven to be a scientifically educated and not merely mechanical organ builder."[4]

A specification was proposed by the St. Paul's organist, together with the organist and composer Christian Heinrich Rinck and the music publisher Johann Anton André from Offenbach, that Walcker found too traditional:

> The better modern opinion discards this entanglement of tones and abides by that which makes the tone pure . . . one prefers to have many stops, of which the player also can use each individually to bring forth a melody, but by combining them can also provide a rich variety in character. The beauty of an organ

Friedrich Walcker, 1794–1872 (Kleinblittersdorf: Musikwissenschaftliche Verlagsgesellschaft, 1994), 79–86. See also Joseph Burg and Hans-Otto Jakob, "Cavaillé-Coll et Francfort-sur-le-Main: Notes sur un échange artistique," *L'Orgue* 193 (1985): 6–21.

3. Wilibald Gurlitt, "Die Frankfurter Paulskirchen-Orgel von 1827," *Zeitschrift für Instrumentenbau* 60 (1940): 89ff.; quoted in Moosmann and Schäfer, *Walcker,* 79.

4. Gurlitt, "Paulskirchen-Orgel," 89ff.; quoted in Moosmann and Schäfer, *Walcker,* 80.

hardly consists of screaming, especially confused screaming; we have turned away from that idea. It is rather found when the tone has a great and, I would even dare to say, a holy character.[5]

The organ took three years to build in the workshop and another two and a half years to install and voice in the church.

Walcker would remain in Ludwigsburg until his death in 1872. For many years, Walcker was a member of both the Ludwigsburg town council and the church council. Ludwigsburg is a county seat north of Stuttgart in southern Germany, some eighty miles from Strasbourg. Now it has about 85,000 inhabitants, but in 1832 it had no more than about 10,000. Its castle, built between 1704 and 1733 during the reign of Count Eberhard Ludwig, was the Württemberg residence at various times.

Walcker remained a man of the country; he enjoyed being with his family, he was very religious, and his lifestyle was deeply influenced by his childhood poverty and the difficult first years of building up his own business. He was neither fashionable nor worldly, and when asked once about the rewards of being an organ builder, he said, "The most important reward is the effort itself and the knowledge that one has applied the strength of one's life toward a profession, given by God."[6] He once summarized his creed as an organ builder as follows:

> I inherited . . . the love of organ building from my father, who was at the time a skillful organ builder in Cannstatt. . . . Wartime did not favor the art; the congregations themselves cared too little for the church to spend much money on worship; with respect to the organ, one was mostly limited to repair work. Nevertheless, I did not let this deflect me from my decision to devote myself to this art. I lived in the hope that I might be able to lift it beyond its shortcomings and develop the instrument to such a level that it could fulfill its main purpose, in contributing to worship in a worthy way. It was (and remained so during my whole life) a cherished idea that I, who am not ashamed to confess the Gospel, could serve the church of Christ through my occupation, if only indirectly.[7]

Is this not a clear confession of a Protestant believer? Quite different from his Roman Catholic French confrère, as we shall see.

Aristide Cavaillé-Coll

Aristide Cavaillé-Coll (see figure 17-1) was born in Montpellier in 1811. At the age of eighteen he was sent by his organ-building father to Lerida, Spain, in

---

5. Gurlitt, "Paulskirchen-Orgel," 89ff.; quoted in Moosmann and Schäfer, *Walcker*, 80.

6. Karl Friedrich Klaiber, "Orgelbauer Walcker von Ludwigsburg," *Daheim* 5 (1869): 415; quoted in Moosmann and Schäfer, *Walcker*, 22.

7. Klaiber, "Walcker," 412.

order to finish an organ there. He not only managed to finish the job in a splendid way, but even applied some new ideas of his own, evidence of an ingenious mind. In September 1833, at age twenty-two, Cavaillé-Coll left the south of France and traveled to Paris, where he would stay for the rest of his life. Aristide became a man of the world and citizen of the "capital of the nineteenth century." He moved in influential circles—politicians, artists, scientists, musicians, and Catholic clergymen—and was involved in the organ world in Paris and abroad whenever the opportunity presented itself. His correspondence reveals a fascinating personality and a versatile mind.

Cavaillé-Coll's relationship to his father (as well as his brother) must have made it more difficult for him to pursue his personal goals than it probably had been for Walcker, whose own father gave up building new instruments in 1820. The firm A. Cavaillé-Coll, Père et Fils was not dissolved until the end of 1849, when Aristide was thirty-eight years old.

Both lives were marked by Franco-German antipathies, wars and revolutions: Walcker's childhood and early youth were affected by the French Revolution, his adult years by the battles to defeat Napoléon; in 1870, three of his sons were mobilized for war with France. Cavaillé-Coll's company suffered from the Revolution of 1848 and the Franco-Prussian War of 1870–71. In the autumn of 1870, his foreman and voicer Félix Reinburg left for England to direct the installation of a large organ at a private residence; Cavaillé-Coll could not leave until March 1871 and missed its inauguration.

Walcker's career was hindered by the difficult economic times for congregations in Germany, and this might have been one of the reasons that his production did not reach the same level as that of Cavaillé-Coll, who benefited from the fact that the French state had begun to take an active role in organ building after it signed a Concordat with the pope in 1801 giving it control of the churches and their inventory.

Two Similar Careers

Apart from these contrasts, there were also similarities in their careers. Both had their roots in a classical organ-building tradition, and even if there are many classical features to be found in their respective concepts, each of them eagerly experimented, searching for a modern organ concept. The success of their early achievements motivated them to continue looking for opportunities to build spectacular instruments. The high quality of their products and professional organization of their workshops were keys to success. Distribution of different tasks among specialized groups of workers and halls where complete (and even very large) instruments could be assembled, as well as new achievements through the Industrial Revolution, were all changing the craft of organ building in several respects. Walcker had a welfare system for his personnel; Cavaillé-Coll's sense of social welfare can be seen in his practice of employing several members of the same family. Eberhard Friedrich's sons all were involved in the company and inherited the business, while Aristide's son Gabriel became a competitor and even tried to take advantage of his father's severe financial problems in 1892. Neither Cavaillé-Coll nor Walcker was a good businessman; their ideals of quality kept them from prioritizing the economic sides of their companies. They were very successful in developing their organ-building concepts, and even though they were not successful financially, they both taught many young organ builders, guaranteeing that their ideas were spread far and wide.

Throughout both careers there are landmarks, but none greater than Walcker's organ in Ulm (1849–56), with four manuals, two pedals, and 100 stops, and Cavaillé-Coll's for St.-Sulpice in Paris (1857–62), with five manuals, one pedal, and 100 stops.[8] It was probably competition with the Ulm instrument that made Cavaillé-Coll extend his organ for St.-Sulpice to the same number of stops.[9]

We do not know whether Walcker was eager to build an even larger instrument, but Cavaillé-Coll clearly was. Cavaillé-Coll published in 1875 a plan for a huge instrument to be built for St. Peter's in Rome. It would have had five manuals and pedal, 124 stops, and 8,316 pipes. Sadly, it was never built. In November 1878 Jacques-Nicolas Lemmens was in Rome, where he was granted two audiences with the pope. He reported to Cavaillé-Coll that although there were many supporters for the project, there were also others who doubted whether St. Peter's was a church suitable for the proposed organ.[10]

Walcker's sons did build an organ in 1884 for Riga Cathedral in Latvia: four manuals, pedal, with (coincidentally?) 124 stops, exactly the same number as the instrument Cavaillé-Coll proposed for St. Peter's. The Riga organ, however had only 6,826 pipes, because it had a smaller compass and fewer mixture ranks. Cavaillé-Coll planned to build manual keyboards of 61 notes, and a pedal with 30 keys for St. Peter's, whereas Walcker's sons built 54-note manuals and a pedal with 27 keys for Riga.

Meetings, Opinions, and Judgments

Aristide Cavaillé-Coll took two extended study trips through Europe and made a point of visiting Walcker on both occasions. In 1844 he visited Strasbourg and

8. The number of 100 stops must have set a kind of a magic limit. It was, however, an organ builder from England, Henry Willis (1821–1901), who was the first to complete an organ with that many stops: the instrument at St. George's Hall in Liverpool, 1855.

9. Fenner Douglass, *Cavaillé-Coll and the Musicians* (Raleigh, N.C.: Sunbury, 1980), 137, 160. The instrument at Ulm no longer exists.

10. Two letters from J. N. Lemmens to A. Cavaillé-Coll, dated 13 Nov. and 22 Nov. 1878; cited in Norbert Dufourcq, ed., "A propos du Cinquantenaire de la mort de Cavaillé-Coll 1899–1949: Lemmens et Cavaillé-Coll (Publications de lettres)," *L'Orgue* 67 (1953): 60–61.

Rouffach in France; Bern, Freiburg, Zürich, and Winterthur in Switzerland; Stuttgart, Frankfurt am Main, and Cologne in Germany; Haarlem, Rotterdam, and Utrecht in the Netherlands; and the city of London. On his 1856 tour of Germany he planned to visit only Cologne, but he ended up visiting Berlin, Potsdam, Weimar, Frankfurt am Main, Stuttgart, and Ulm as well. It is known that Walcker got to Paris at least once, met Cavaillé-Coll there, and most likely saw some of his instruments. Walcker's firm had an exhibition at the Exposition Universelle in 1855, but there is no proof that he himself made the journey.[11] According to Cavaillé-Coll's letter to Lemmens, Walcker might also have planned to come during the autumn of 1856, after the examination of his organ in Ulm, but he definitely visited Paris on his way to London in the beginning of February, 1857. In connection with the negotiations for a new instrument to be built for the Music Hall in Boston, Dr. Jabez Upham, president of the Boston Music Hall Association, wanted Walcker to study the latest developments in organ building in France and England, "with the proviso that Herr Walcker himself should meet me in Paris, and go thence with me to London, in order to learn and engraft upon his schedule such improvements as the best works of the French and English makers might suggest."[12]

Walcker's son Karl (1845–1908) worked for some time in Paris as a businessman, but in 1868 Walcker urged him to come back to Ludwigsburg to join the company.[13] Walcker's few trips always seem to have been related either to orders for instruments or an occasional visit to a spa.

On Cavaillé-Coll's first study trip in 1844, he wrote his father about the instruments he visited and the organ builders and organists that he met, commenting on what he found in those organs and comparing them to his own organ-building style. He called Walcker a "builder of merit and genius"[14] and classified him "with his genius and painstaking work, as the best builder among all those I visited,"[15] but he did have some critical words to express privately about Walcker's famous organ in St. Paul's Church:

11. Michel Jurine, *Joseph Merklin, facteur d'orgues européen: Essai sur l'orgue français au XIXe siècle* (Paris: Aux Amateurs de livres, 1991), 1:68, 78. To my knowledge, the Walcker firm did not participate in any other Paris exhibition.

12. Jabez B. Upham, "Narration of My Organ Tour: Remarks at a meeting of the Harvard Music Association, January 1858," in "Methuen," part 1, *The American Organist* 45, no. 3 (March 1962), 14. The trip is also documented by letters from Walcker to his wife, dated 8 February and 10 February 1857, and in Walcker's "Notizbuch from 1857 (Walcker family archive, kindly made available by Gerhard Walcker-Mayer, Bliesransbach, Germany).

13. Johannes Fischer, *Das Orgelbauergeschlecht Walcker: Die Menschen, die Zeiten, das Werk* (Kassel: Bärenreiter, 1966), 60; Moosmann and Schäfer, *Walcker*, 17. It is not known when Karl moved to Paris, but from letters in the Walcker family archive we know that he was there at least from 1866 to 1868 and also that he forwarded letters from Walcker to Cavaillé-Coll during his stay in Paris.

14. Douglass, *Cavaillé-Coll and the Musicians*, 207: letter to Monsieur Callinet Sr., organ builder in Rouffach, 28 Jan. 1845.

15. Douglass, *Cavaillé-Coll and the Musicians*, 205: letter to Carl Gottlieb Weigle, organ builder, Stuttgart, 15 Nov. 1844. Weigle, the son of Eberhard Friedrich's brother-in-law, studied with Eber-

This morning I saw the famous organ of St. Paul's Church. It is very beautiful, but it is always cold, like a German. There is majesty in its foundation stops, leanness in the reeds, softness in the solo stops, a bit of hesitation in the ensemble; the lungs lack strength: it is because of this that the musical effects of the instrument are so indifferent and lukewarm.

75 stops, three manuals, two pedal keyboards; all this impresses by its number. But, in the same way that a French soldier is equal in value to five soldiers of other nations, an organ with 15 stops at different pressures offers more power and more nuances in the sound effects than this immense instrument. Nevertheless, there are good things, but the lungs are weak; it is like a fine man suffering from tuberculosis.[16]

After visiting Ulm on his second study trip in 1856, he wrote to Walcker:

My dear Sir and honored colleague: I should thank you for the letter of introduction you gave me to your son, and for the kindness he showed by allowing us to see and hear your magnificent organ in the Cathedral of Ulm. It was with the greatest interest that we examined that immense organ, in which you applied your new construction principle, enabling you to give the organ dimensions heretofore unknown, and making this instrument the largest and most complete, I believe, of any that exist in Europe. May I congratulate you on this magnificent work.[17]

It is clear that Walcker was not in Ulm on the occasion of Cavaillé-Coll's visit. Cavaillé-Coll's private opinion of Walcker's organ at Ulm is, once again, quite critical and shows that he believes in the superiority of his own concept. Nevertheless, he also gives Walcker credit for high artistic standards, the quality of the execution, and of the handicraft:

The façade Principal is of 32' pitch; the largest pipes have a diameter of 2 feet and a length of c. 40 feet. It is monstrous, but the church is so large that the pipes, seen from a distance, give the impression of normal 16-foot length. I do not like the façade. It lacks proportions; next to those large pipes, there are small pipes with a diameter of 3–4 inches, which are in disproportion with the others. Here, the architect lacked good sense: the woodwork itself is too slender for the pipes and the place. One would need wings in order to be able to walk along the façade and to appreciate the fine craftsmanship, which gets completely lost at a distance. The work inside is more impressive. It is a forest of tall pipes in all kinds of forms and dimensions. M. Walcker seems to have

hard Friedrich Walcker from 1825 onward and then became one of his workers. Weigle was very much involved in Walcker's first large organ with cone chests at the Stiftskirche in Stuttgart. As soon as that instrument was finished (1845), Weigle founded his own company in Stuttgart.

16. Letter from Aristide Cavaillé-Coll, Frankfurt, 10 Oct. 1844; cited in Cécile Cavaillé-Coll and Emmanuel Cavaillé-Coll, *Aristide Cavaillé-Coll* (Paris: Librairie Fischbacher, 1929), 62.

17. Douglass, *Cavaillé-Coll and the Musicians*, 359: letter to M. Walcker, organ-builder in Ludwigsburg, 2 Sept. 1856. Obviously Cavaillé-Coll was not yet aware of Willis's 100-stop organ at St. George Hall in Liverpool, completed in 1855 (or did he not want to mention it?).

wished to include all that modern art possesses of the highest perfection and of which he himself has widened the domain. The manuals are well located in the center of the instrument, in such a way that the organist can look at the altar (if there had been one, since it is a Protestant church). In this instrument, his new system of windchests, which your builder Merklin displayed during the latest exposition, is applied on a very large scale. The free reeds are very much varied and rather beautiful. I say rather beautiful, because I prefer the straightforwardness of the beating reeds, which we make better than the Germans. He also has made good use of the pneumatic Barker lever, with a modified construction according to my ideas.

One finds here also an original device, a pedal producing a crescendo by adding successively all the stops of the organ; a pedal for which M. Merklin seems to credit himself in the article which M. Fétis has written on the organ at Murcia. I learned that it is one of my former pupils who directed this famous construction of which M. Merklin has made so much ado. So I should have contributed to it in one way or another.[18]

German Comments on French Organ Building

Unfortunately, no similar collection of correspondence exists from Walcker, so we cannot hear Walcker's personal critical voice in the same way.[19] From the organist Carl Franz's report on his journey to Paris in May of 1880, we can at least get a German view of Cavaillé-Coll's style.[20] Franz gave a concert on Cavaillé-Coll's large organ in the Trocadéro and visited the instruments of St.-Sulpice, Notre-Dame, and Ste.-Clotilde. He met Cavaillé-Coll personally as well as other organ builders.

In many respects, Franz considers French organ building to be conservative, or at least more conservative than in Germany. He believes that there have been no experiments in France with tubular-pneumatic or electric action, no pneumatic-operated pistons, no roller crescendo, no concave pedal boards, and so forth. But Franz is a supporter of the conservative French slider chests; although he sees their disadvantages, the main one is corrected by Cavaillé-Coll's pneumatic stop action in St.-Sulpice and Notre-Dame. Franz describes experiments Cavaillé-Coll was carrying out with the harmonics of a fundamental and

18. Letter to Jacques Lemmens, dated 11 Sept. 1856; cited in Norbert Dufourcq, ed., "Lemmens et Cavaillé-Coll," *L'Orgue* no. 57 (1950): 111–12. Cavaillé-Coll refers here to Charles Spackman Barker, who worked for Merklin at that time and who apparently had designed this construction; see Jurine, *Merklin*, 1:164–65. Moreover, Jurine points out that Cavaillé-Coll is mistaken with respect to the kind of construction.

19. The Walcker family archive (kindly made available by Gerhard Walcker-Mayer, Bliesransbach, Germany) does contain some correspondence from Eberhard Friedrich, but there is no complete inventory.

20. Carl Franz, "Einige Beobachtungen über den Orgelbau und die musikalischen Zustände in Paris," *Die Orgelbauzeitung* 2 (1880): 145–48.

is enthusiastic about the demonstration that Cavaillé-Coll gave him of his device with thirty-two pipes, representing a fundamental with its thirty-one harmonics, and mentions the use of the seventh harmonic in the Notre-Dame organ.

At first sight, he finds the French consoles more difficult to handle, but he also notices advantages of the combination pedals and the stop action such as that of St.-Sulpice and Notre-Dame, once one has become accustomed to it and understands how to use the organ's features. French organ building is more modern with respect to the compass (fifty-six keys for the manuals, thirty for the pedal, while the compass in Germany is still fifty-four and twenty-seven), and he observes differences in the width of the keys.

He finds the enclosed divisions of the French organs by no means weak in sound; on the contrary, their effect is even audible when used in the full organ. There are many reed stops, all of high quality, and all with very precise speech, even when played staccato. The Oboe and the Clarinet are very much like the instruments of the orchestra, and Franz is astonished that one can achieve this by using beating reeds. He criticizes the crackling sound of the lowest three notes of the Bombarde 32′, but this disappears when the full organ is used. In France it has been proved that one can build a Clairon 4′ stop as a reed stop up to g‴.

Strangely enough, he does not say much about the flutes; he mentions the 8′ and 4′ flutes, which often are built as harmonic stops, but he ignores the 2′ harmonic flute, even though this trio of stops is very characteristic of Cavaillé-Coll organs. Franz found the Principals and stopped pipes, as well as the Subbass in the pedal, lacking in character. String stops such as the Gamba and Salicional ranged from rather good to mediocre. He was impressed however, by a Principal 8′ in Notre-Dame and by open wooden 32′ stops that produced a mighty effect. No French organ lacked an undulating stop such as the Voix céleste or Unda maris. He reported that Frenchmen were fond of undulating and trembling sounds, and added a tremulant to the Vox humana so it would sound similar to the voice of a French singer. The full organ sounded mighty and noble, and the mixtures lent brilliance to it.

Franz also attended a lesson at the conservatory, given by César Franck. The students could become familiar with the French organ type, even though the instrument at the conservatory was small. Two students played works by Bach, but the most important part of their education consisted of improvisation, high-lighting the role of the organ in the Roman Catholic service. Even as he admired the French art of improvisation, he considered it unsuitable for the services in his own Protestant church.

Franz was also very impressed by the organ playing of Alexandre Guilmant at the Trocadéro. He admired his beautiful "half-staccato" technique, which preserved the clarity of the organ sound even in the huge reverberant hall. The French organists handled the organ at such occasions more like an orchestra (an interesting perspective, in view of the general perception that the German organ was the preeminent imitator of the orchestra during the last quarter of the nineteenth century). What he did not like, however, was the too-colorful way the French organists played Bach, and he therefore chose not to play Bach at the Trocadéro himself.

Even if some of Franz's comments reveal that he was not well informed about all aspects of organ building, his account still provides an interesting window into the average German experience of French organ culture.

Cavaillé-Coll in Germany and Walcker in France?

Cavaillé-Coll never built an organ in Germany, but he did make the attempt. In 1856 he went on an exploratory trip to Cologne to plan for a new organ to be built for the Gürzenich Concert Hall,[21] and apparently also to explore the possibility of building an instrument for the cathedral. Jacques Ignaz Hittorf, a Cologne native, an archaeologist, and an architect to the French court, wrote a letter of recommendation for Cavaillé-Coll with which he could introduce himself to Ernst Friedrich Zwirner, the architect of the cathedral in Cologne. Hittorf was the architect of the church of St.-Vincent-de-Paul in Paris and had also designed the façade of Cavaillé-Coll's organ in that church. Hittorf stated in his recommendation that he hoped that Zwirner could do his part in helping Cavaillé-Coll to get the order for the new organ.[22] After his arrival in Paris, Cavaillé-Coll wrote to Zwirner, referring to the acoustical situation in the cathedral at Ulm with respect to that in Cologne,[23] but neither possibility materialized.

The only Cavaillé-Coll organ in Germany during his lifetime was the house organ built for the famous singer Pauline Viardot-Garcia in 1851. It was moved to the Viardot family villa in Baden-Baden in 1864 but returned with them to Paris in 1872.[24] Since 1999, the Church of St. Bernhard in Mainz-Bretzenheim has housed a small two-manual Cavaillé-Coll organ with 15 stops,[25] the only Cavaillé-Coll organ presently in Germany.

Although several German organ builders (Wilhelm Sauer, Friedrich Ladegast,

---

21. Cavaillé-Coll's letter to Franz Weber, organist at the cathedral in Cologne and director of the Choral Society of Cologne; cited in Douglass, *Cavaillé-Coll and the Musicians*, 359. Weber had visited Cavaillé-Coll in Paris on the occasion of a concert tour that had brought him and his choir to Paris.

22. See Hans Steinhaus, "Deutsche Orgeln im Urteil von Aristide Cavaillé-Coll," *Acta Organologica* 14 (1980): 218–19.

23. See Douglass, *Cavaillé-Coll and the Musicians*, 359–60.

24. Carolyn Shuster-Fournier, "Les orgues de salon d'Aristide Cavaillé-Coll," *Cahiers et mémoires de l'orgue* 57–58 (1997): 25–40.

25. Peter Reifenberg, "Abriß der Geschichte der Cavaillé-Coll-Orgel von St. Bernhard, Mainz-Bretzenheim," in Reformer, Genie, Visionär: Internationales Symposium zum 100. Todestag des französischen Orgelbauers Aristide Cavaillé-Coll (1811–1899) (Mainz: Akademie des Bistums Mainz, Erbacher Hof, 1999), 8–9.

and Carl Friedrich Buchholz) either studied with Cavaillé-Coll or visited him, none adopted Cavaillé-Coll's style as such; his influence in Germany is therefore limited. Cavaillé-Coll's sound concept was accepted only in an extremely modified form, owing mainly to the influence of German organists and consultants who considered the French concept to be too profane and too much concert oriented.[26]

Did Eberhard Friedrich Walcker build organs for France? The answer is yes and no. Before 1870, the year of the Franco-Prussian war, Walcker had built four organs in France: Wesserling (Roman-Catholic Church, 1857), Mulhouse (St. Steven [Etienne], 1865), and a main organ and a choir organ in Haguenau (St. George, 1866).[27] However, all of these are in the Alsace region. The Alsace—also known for its own strong organ-building tradition—though politically part of France, was ostensibly an autonomous region between the two countries that was heavily influenced by German culture. Between 1870 and 1899, the Walcker company delivered fifteen more organs, all but one for the Alsace and Lotharingen region, which would both be a part of Germany until the end of World War I;[28] the remaining instrument, a house organ, was built for a private individual in Toulouse in 1895.

Competitors in Antwerp

When a new organ was to be built for the Antwerp Cathedral in Belgium in 1888, three companies were selected to submit a proposal for a fixed price of 150,000 Belgian francs:[29] Aristide Cavaillé-Coll, E. F. Walcker und Cie., and Pierre Schijven.[30] It is very interesting to compare these plans, each for an instrument with four manuals and pedal, and to read the comments of the organ committee. Cavaillé-Coll submitted a plan with 75 stops, Walcker 102 stops (in fact 100 real stops) and Schijven 87 stops.

26. Hermann J. Busch, "L'influence d'Aristide Cavaillé-Coll sur la facture d'orgues en Allemagne dans la deuxième moitié du XIXe siècle," *Cahiers et mémoires de l'orgue* 48 (1992): 89–96.

27. These data are taken from the original "Opusbuch" of the Walcker company, of which Christoph Macke, of Orgelbau E. F. Walcker GmbH, Kleinblittersdorf, kindly provided photocopies.

28. In the Walcker company's catalog from 1874, all their organs in the Alsace were listed under "Deutsches Reich." *Catalog von E. F. Walcker & Cie. in Ludwigsburg* (Stuttgart: Stuttgarter Vereins-Buchdruckerei, 1874).

29. This paragraph is based on Koos van de Linde, Jeroen Deriemaeker and Gerard Pels, *Het Schijvenorgel van de Kathedraal te Antwerpen* (Antwerpen: Antwerpse Kathedraalconcerten vzw, 1988). Koos van de Linde kindly provided photocopies of Walcker's proposal and of the minutes of the meetings of the organ committee, stored in the archives of the church (Antwerpen, Kathedraal; archief kerkfabriek, no. 6).

30. Pierre Schijven worked for Joseph Merklin from as early as 1843 and later became the foreman in Merklin's workshop in Brussels. In 1873 he founded his own organ company (i.e., he continued Merklin's workshop, but under his own name and for his own account). It is said that Cavaillé-Coll highly respected Schijven.

The organ culture in Belgium was highly influenced by France. For that reason, the committee had its doubts with respect to Walcker's proposal. The committee's members judged that Walcker's organ had too many stops, of which rather many were made out of wood; the number of stops that Schijven proposed was sufficient. They also thought that the cone chests were not durable enough in the humid climate. The committee undertook a journey to Düsseldorf to visit a recent organ by Walcker;[31] the general opinion was that the flue stops were good but a bit monotonous, that there were too many wooden pipes in the organ, and that there were too few reeds, which also left much to be desired (no more than 7 out of 50 stops were reeds, which they attributed to the fact that it was an instrument in a Protestant church). They criticized the interior of the instrument and found the wind supply difficult to handle, and they observed problems with the stop action. Altogether, the organ left much to be desired; however, it was cheap.

The committee judged that Cavaillé-Coll proposed too few stops, especially in relation to his price. In order to enable a comparison of Cavaillé-Coll's and Schijven's proposals, they asked Cavaillé-Coll to add 11 stops to his specification and to do it within the given budget. This Aristide refused to do, stating that his organs could easily compete in strength with larger organs from other companies.

Apart from the organ in Düsseldorf, the committee also visited Cavaillé-Coll's organs in Gent (St. Nicholas) and at the Brussels Conservatory, which both were highly praised. Schijven's organ in Kortrijk (St. Martin) was visited as well and found to be in bad condition; one of the manuals was completely unusable, and the stop knobs could be drawn only with great difficulty. Two more Schijven instruments were investigated: one in Schijven's shop as well as his large organ in Our Lady's Church (Onze Lieve Vrouw) in Laken near Brussels (built 1872–74); both were considered to be good instruments.

Although some of the members concluded that Cavaillé-Coll's work was of a superior quality, the committee found it difficult to choose between Cavaillé-Coll and Schijven. When the votes were counted, three out of five went to Schijven, two to Cavaillé-Coll.

A comparison of the specifications reveals the following interesting features. Cavaillé-Coll has not only the fewest 8' flue stops of all (which is not surprising), but also the fewest reed stops, since both Walcker and Schijven had so many of them. Walcker proposed 27 reeds out of 100 real stops (27 percent); Schijven, 23 of 87 stops (26.5 percent); and Cavaillé-Coll, 19 of 75 stops (25.3 percent). Cavaillé-Coll's specification is typical for his late work: a relatively small but

31. It must have been opus 375 (1880) for the New Protestant Church, an organ with 48 stops on three manuals and pedal, cone chests, mechanical action, and a Barker machine for the Great and the couplers (Walcker, "Opusbuch"). Either two more stops were added before installation in Düsseldorf, or the committee members miscalculated the number of stops.

extremely powerful concept within the frame of a specification according to his approved principles.

Walcker's specification contained many French elements; this was unusual for them, but they were aware, of course, of the Belgian taste. The proposal is written completely in French, and many of the stop names are in French as well, although we also find German stop names, and even several Franco-German, such as "Rohrflûte." There are combination pedals in the French manner, and they even propose an extra division over and above the 102 stops, called "Bombarde," to be played from the Great and the Pedal, with 6 stops at a pressure of 150 mm. (five of them reeds, one a flue stop), which could "produce an absolutely grandiose effect in the services of the important festivals."

Schijven represents both German and French elements. He proposes 2 free-reed stops (Walcker has 6 free-reed stops, Cavaillé-Coll none), and his system of combination pedals enables the organist to prepare and introduce three categories of stops: foundations, mutations, and reeds.

Walcker's Hypothetical Instrument for the Jesus Church in Copenhagen

Considering Cavaillé-Coll and Walcker to be the most important organ builders on the European continent during the nineteenth century, one could hypothesize about the type of instrument the Walcker firm might have built for the Jesus Church in Copenhagen if they had received the order. Cavaillé-Coll's instrument is rather small (20 stops), but it was expensive: it cost 38,000 francs, which was about 27,400 Danish crowns in 1890.[32]

In Walcker's opus list one finds two new organs built in 1890 that are comparable in size to Cavaillé-Coll's instrument: opus 541 for the Protestant City Church in Pfullingen (2 manuals, pedal, and 24 stops: 11 + 8 + 5; the second manual is in a swell box), and opus 570 in the Protestant Church of Trossingen (2 manuals, pedal, and 24 stops: 11 + 8 + 5; the second manual, however, is not in a swell box). The instrument in Trossingen may be compared to the Cavaillé-Coll organ delivered to Copenhagen (see Table 18-1).

Both Walcker organs in Trossingen and Pfullingen are the same size and probably had similar, standardized windchests. The instrument in Pfullingen has no fewer than six 8′ flue stops on Manual 1 and four 8′ flue stops on Manual 2; no reed on Manual 1, only one (Trompete 8′) on Manual 2,[33] and three 16′ and two 8′ flue stops in the pedal.

---

32. Gilbert Huybens, *Aristide Cavaillé-Coll: Liste des travaux exécutés* (Lauffen am Neckar: Rensch, 1985), 54–55. According to the *Kjøbenhavns Børs-Tidende* for the period 2–7 Sept. 1890, 100 French francs equaled 72.05 or 72.15 Danish crowns. (But see chapter 15, note 39.)

33. In the Walcker company's "Opusbuch" a change has been made: the 8′ Trompete had originally been located on Manual I, but was exchanged with the 8′ Gemshorn from Manual II.

TABLE 18-1.

Comparison of Small Organs by Cavaillé-Coll and Walcker

Cavaillé-Coll, Jesus Church Organ 20 stops, slider chests, swellbox **Grand Orgue** (I) C-g''' (56 keys)		Walcker, Trossingen Organ 24 stops, cone chests, no swellbox **1st Manual** C-f''' (54 keys)	
Bourdon	16'	Bourdon	16'
Montre	8'	Principal	8'
Bourdon	8'	Gedeckt	8'
Flûte harmonique	8'	Hohlflöte	8'
Salicional	8'	Viola di Gamba	8'
Prestant	4'	Octav	4'
Flûte douce	4'	Rohrflöte	4'
		Octav	2'
Plein-jeu	IV	Mixtur	V
		Trompete	8'
Récit expressif (II) C-g''' (56 keys)		**2d Manual** C-f''' (54 keys)	
		Geigenprincipal	8'
Flûte traversière	8'	Gemshorn	8'
Viole de Gambe	8'	Salicional	8'
Voix céleste	8'	Voix celeste	8'
		Lieblich Gedeckt	8'
		Aeoline	8'
Flûte octaviante	4'	Flauto dolce	4'
		Fugara	4'
		Cornett	V (from c)
Octavin	2'		
Trompette harmonique	8'		
Basson-Hautbois	8'		
Clairon	4'		
Pédale C-f' (30 keys)		**Pedal** C-d' (27 keys)	
Soubasse	16'	Subbass	16'
		Violonbass	16'
Basse	8'	Octavbass	8'
Bourdon	8'	Violoncello	8'
Bombarde	16'	Posaunenbass	16'

Couplers: Récit-G.O., G.O-Péd., Récit-Péd.
Combinations:1) Tr 8' + Cl 4';
  2) M 8' + P 4' + Pl-jeu
Expression Récit
Orage

Couplers: Man. 2-Man. 1, 1-Ped., 2-Ped.
Combinations: Tutti, Forte, Mezzo-forte, Piano

Unfortunately, we do not know the prices of either of these two instruments. But we can find prices of comparable Walcker organs; according to Walcker's catalog from 1874, an instrument with 24 stops (and a specification almost identical to that of Trossingen) would cost 12,900 German reichsmarks without the case; the tubular-pneumatic Walcker organ with 30 stops, built for a church in Poznan (Poland) in 1899, cost 11,900 German reichsmarks.[34] These amounts in Danish crowns would be 11,508 and 10,616 respectively.[35]

When we look at Cavaillé-Coll's organ in the Jesus Church and compare this to an instrument by Walcker of a similar size, it becomes apparent that Cavaillé-Coll had developed a very simple but most ingenious concept that functions in both a small and a large context. Thus, one can perform a large part of the repertoire written for that concept on every instrument that has 20 or more stops.

Walcker's concept, however, requires a larger instrument in order to meet the demands of most of the repertoire; all the different sound layers and fine sound gradations, most of all in the soft registrations, as well as the real effect of the roller crescendo, are successful only in Walcker's larger instruments.

The combination of Cavaillé-Coll's strong concept, his influential connections, the important position of the organ in nineteenth-century France, and Paris's central role enabled a development of organ culture in France that explains why the French nineteenth-century organ aesthetic still exerts supremacy over the German. And in glaring contrast with Germany, although many of Cavaillé-Coll's organs have been threatened in various ways, many have survived interventions by the organ reform movement.

After he had heard and inspected a new instrument by Cavaillé-Coll in 1843, Rossini is said to have remarked, "Dear Sirs, for such instruments one should compose new music."[36] As late as in 1887, Alexander Wilhelm Gottschalg observed with respect to composers from German-speaking countries "that, in fact, no fully equivalent compositions are yet available for organs that have been equipped with all modern achievements."[37]

It is also interesting to observe Cavaillé-Coll's tendency toward the end of his life to reduce the size of his instruments—even for very large churches—to the smallest acceptable limit, thus enforcing and condensing his concept. His proposal for the Antwerp Cathedral contained 75 stops, and his organ for the

34. Walcker, *Catalog 1874*, 22; Franz-Josef Vogt, "Die Walcker-Orgel der kath. Pfarrkirche Herz-Jesu und St. Florian zu Poznan-Jezyce (Posen-Jersitz)," *Ars Organi* 48 (2000): 160. Observe that tubular-pneumatic instead of tracker action made the instruments much cheaper.

35. Berlin, Foreign Exchange Market, 1 Sept. 1890: 112.10 reichsmarks equals 100 Danish crowns.

36. J. G. Töpfer, *Lehrbuch der Orgelbaukunst*, 2d ed., published as *Die Theorie und Praxis des Orgelbaues*, ed. M. Allihn (Weimar: B. F. Voigt, 1888), 13. Rossini may have said this after having inspected and heard Cavaillé-Coll's organ for the church of St.-Jerôme in Toulouse on the occasion of its presentation in Cavaillé-Coll's workshop.

37. A. W. Gottschalg, "Die moderne Orgel in orchestraler Behandlung," *Urania* 44 (1887): 99.

Church of St.-Ouen in Rouen only 64. By contrast, in Walcker's organs and those of other German builders toward the end of the nineteenth century, there is a clear tendency to increase the number of stops.

Michel Jurine has proposed a most interesting thesis. He concludes that while all of the organ builders during the nineteenth century envisioned the combination of art and industry, Aristide Cavaillé-Coll invented a new relationship between art and science.[38] Might we (mis)use that quotation to describe the competition between France and Germany as a matter of art and science versus art and industry?

38. Jurine, *Merklin*, 2:383.

19

ON THE ORGAN PROBLEM [AS SEEN IN 1930]

FRITZ HEITMANN

Professor at the Staatliche Akademie für Kirchen- und Schulmusik, Berlin

Fritz Heitmann (1891–1953) was one of the teachers of Alf Linder (see chapter 22). The following article originally appeared under the title "Zum Orgelproblem" in Deutsche Tonkünstler-Zeitung, *published by the Reichsverband Deutscher Tonkünstler und Musiklehrer E. V., Berlin, in its issue of 5 June 1930.*

ASSISTING MY FATHER IN MY YOUNG YEARS AT THE PANKRATIUS CHURCH IN OCHsenwärder (near Hamburg) by pulling stops when he played the Arp Schnitger organ in worship service, I could not have imagined that two decades later the name of this organ builder would rise to such preeminence. But how difficult it was to render service at this instrument of ours, two hundred years old! It was always not just the organist that was needed—the man to work the bellows in his little chamber, the one who would come down from the tower after ringing the church bells to impart life breath to the instrument in the sweat of his brow, seemed much more important. Only he would truly activate the sound—and the service. On high holidays when the organ, in all its glory, was to sing the Creator's praise with cymbals, mixtures, trumpets, and trombones, it would take two generations to work in front and back of the console: I helped my father in pulling and closing stops to involve or disengage the plenum, and the bellows treader similarly needed the support of his son to supply enough wind. When the organ had enhanced such a special service, all participants would depart in just pride of their accomplishment. It had sounded so mighty and so powerful! When later I took to the organ bench to substitute for my father, I came to feel what it meant "to reach deeply into the jaws of such an instrument, for not only the hands but indeed the feet were to be applied" (Michael Praetorius, *De Organographia*). The resistance of the keys made one work hard. But one also felt "true substance" to challenge one's fingers, and felt to have grown to be one with the organ.

In my Leipzig student years, I became acquainted with large modern instruments. On these, everything worked with such ease that, at first, the keys seemed to "run away" under the fingers—the mechanical action had been supplanted by a pneumatic transmission of the finger weight upon the keys, with the result of a totally unaccustomed ease of playing that appeared to me at first unnatural. The wind was supplied by an electric fan blower, and everything in these instruments—the console and its apparatus, with small, elegantly moving levers instead of heavy wooden draw stops, noiseless functioning of the register and key action instead of unavoidably rumbling clatter, the possibility of changing stops with lightning speed, crescendo pedal and swell shutters, all features entirely unknown to me—made these instruments appear incredibly progressive and desirable. Here, finally, the goal had been achieved: one could rule the sound of the organ without any assistance and with complete independence. I must confess that, under the impression of a grandiosely performed recent composition on the modern instrument, and the thousandfold shadings accomplished with such ease, this eager young musician recalled the small village organ at home as rather dwarfed and limited.

In the course of twenty years of my professional activity, both in Germany and abroad, I have gained experience with many old as well as many modern organs, and as a result I now consider each of these types, used in its proper place, equally suitable and justified from the point of view of serious and artistic practice; what they have in common is much more than has usually been assumed.

But the organ has its own secrets. Zelter wrote on one occasion to Goethe: "With your very superscription ('Cathedral, Service, Organ, Singing') you have hit the nail on the head—as if the organ had gripped your own feelings. It has a somehow accusing, satanic quality." He wanted to express that the sound of the organ affected him in a very special manner, quite different from other musical impressions. The effect of mixtures is a dominant one, and the entire sound of the organ is subject to it. Performance on the organ cannot be judged by the usual musical standards. Much that has been written for the organ (including quite valuable works) is not equal to the exalted severity of the mixtures and will thus sink into obscurity before long. This exalted severity of the mixtures was not perceptible at all times. The insight about the special quality of organ sound that Arp Schnitger's organ gave to my musical life has recently been shown to a wider public by another North German organ—that in the St. Jacobi Church in Hamburg—as well as by the organs of Gottfried Silbermann in central Germany.

It was here that the "organ problem of our time" became apparent! The tart freshness, the highly original quality of characteristic dispositions became a revelation to many. It was as if the phenomenon of organ sound had found its purest embodiment in those instruments long before our time and as if we had strayed all too far from its ideal expression. The magic of the "primitive" in sound and music had a powerful effect. We seemed to have arrived at an irrevocable verdict: Not only modern instruments, but also modern organ composition seemed to have been weighed and found wanting. Should we not throw the ballast of all organ music after Bach's time overboard and remove all new organs from our churches, replacing them with more suitable ones?

The fanatics thought so. Those whose view reaches further will be guided by the following considerations:

We live in the twentieth century. We neither should nor want to withdraw from our surroundings in order to live in a period that has gone and will not return. We want to face the tasks of our time squarely; its frame of reference in many ways conforms to that represented by the names Schnitger and Silbermann. As glorious as it is to play and hear the organs of the past in the great cathedrals and as much as we wish to adhere to this organ ideal, we—organ builders and organ performers—must try to direct this fountain of youth into our time and use it creatively for contemporary tasks.

Contemporary tasks: first of all—we affirm all the strong virtues of the organ. It may seem as if the primal serenity of Vincent Lübeck and Buxtehude negates and precludes northern heaviness, the modern complications of such organ music as Reger's. Yet we sense in Reger's work a strong commitment to the mixtures; they allow a realization of Reger's bent toward mysticism. In spite of all modern longing and tendencies of an almost supersensitive nature, he was a primordial, strong musician. His work, despite all that recent times have been able to revive in the way of hitherto unknown wonderful early organ music, stands as a rock next to the summit of Bach's work—a rock, though exposed to many storms, yet not truly endangered by modern developments. The challenges of our time further include support for the efforts our generation is showing in the creation of new substantial organ music. Here, too, there is a strong tendency to return to strict and elemental values. As people of our own time may not command the "wholeness" of the old masters, yet there is nevertheless a certain correspondence between the oldest and the most recent styles. But there is strong interest, and musicians of our time have responded to the true quality of the organ much more readily than the romantics who composed organ music.

Why is it that recent works do not easily lend themselves to performance on the old organs? Was such a radical change of the old organs necessary to satisfy modern demands? The experience from my young years and my student years offers some comment. We need *more manageable instruments* in order to be able to master such works as Reger's *fancifully* roving compositions. We need the modern technical assistance (consider also the contemporary tasks for the organ as an accompanying instrument!): ready response of keys through pneumatic and electro-pneumatic action, a number of free combinations, a crescendo pedal to be used carefully by the player to introduce stops gradually in place of the formerly required registration assistant, the swell-shade for dynamic enlivenment of sporadic expression of a romantic nature. Modern practice requires a certain reduction of blunt organ dispositions, without endangering the luminous brilliance of mixtures. One might define the difference between old and new organ sound in a formula: the modern organ offers "musical refinement" against the more sharply defined characteristics of the old organ. The Silbermann organ in the Cathedral of Freiberg, for instance, would be impossible in a modern church, and particularly in a modern concert hall, due to the sharpness of its mixtures and the unsuitable acoustic situation.

The changed conditions, however, are not of a kind that would justify us in referring to modern organs as a "falsification." If the modern means are used judiciously, and according to a proper stylistic distinction, there is no danger that the richly varied disposition of an instrument would do damage to either a chorale setting of Samuel Scheidt or a contemporary composition. The fact that the classical literature of the time before Bach as well as Bach's own organ music should remain in the foreground of organ performance, as well as the fact that our instruments should be suited for them, particularly, is in no way to the disadvantage of modern works; all of them are guided by the wish for the mixture, that mystical phenomenon of sound.

It is indeed one of our most pressing obligations that we deal with the great masters of organ music before Bach's time. In numerous editions their work has become accessible to a wider community, and we should see to an enlargement of the working basis in both directions. It is up to modern organ construction to revolutionize smaller organ dispositions that heretofore had mainly been standardized in an uninteresting manner. This has called for a new beginning, since many instruments with fewer than 10 or 20 stops have been slighted in their supply of mixtures and thus have been made unsatisfactory for the rendition of classical organ works.

A further challenge is both a more thorough education and experience for our young organists, who need a better acquaintance with the sources of all true organ literature—the organ music of the fifteenth, sixteenth, and seventeenth centuries in North and South Germany and other countries, with its summit in Bach's work—while they must also gain a better understanding of Reger's great art and the trends of our time. With all their general agreement among one another, the different elements of the "main epochs of organ music" require a strict stylistic discipline of the performer. As in the other arts, the force of the interpreter and his inherent ability are at the root of artistic strength. Without them, even the most beautiful organ is a dead instrument. May a new organists' generation, under the influence of models in our day and the future, grow without fear of individual problems that only reflect more general ones of our time, and serve the masterworks of our literature with genuine artistic discipline and freedom!

Translated by Alfred Mann

ᚠART IV

REVIVAL AND RENEWAL

20

EXORDIUM: THE MARCUSSEN ORGAN IN OSCAR'S CHURCH, STOCKHOLM (1949)

THE TWENTIETH CENTURY WITNESSED AN AMAZING ARRAY OF MUSICAL DEVELOP-
ments, among which two opposing tendencies stand out: an unprecedented interest in music of the past, and the cultivation of new compositional styles that
departed radically from those of the common-practice era. The organ reform
movement, which began in Germany during the 1920s, belongs to the first of
these. It was carried forward in Denmark chiefly by the firm of Marcussen and
Søn, which had been founded by Jürgen Marcussen in 1806 and was led during
these years by his great-great-grandson, Sybrand Zacharissen (1900–1960). His
1949 organ for Oscar's Church in Stockholm is built on the *Werkprinzip*, with
each of its divisions clearly separated both spatially and sonically. This makes it
ideally suited to the performance of baroque music, but from the very beginning
it inspired avant-garde music as well, thanks to the encouragement of its eminent
organist, Alf Linder. One of his students, Bengt Hambraeus, began to attend the
Darmstadt summer courses in 1951, where he met Olivier Messiaen and György
Ligeti and helped to forge a new style with the introduction of clusters and
serialism into organ music. Hambraeus later emigrated to North America and
became professor of composition at McGill University in Montreal.

Hambraeus introduces us in chapter 21 to two organs of Oscar's Church: the
Åkerman & Lund instrument that was installed in 1903 when the church was
built and which he played as a student, and the Marcussen organ that replaced
it in 1949. In chapter 22 Kimberly Marshall discusses Alf Linder: his life, his
recordings, and his performance technique. Martin Herchenröder tracks the
emergence of the new compositional style for organ in chapter 23. And in Chapter 24 Joel Speerstra weaves together interviews with Harald Vogel, Cornelius
Edskes, and Axel Unnerbäck to trace a trail from the organ reform movement
of the 1920s to our present culture of organ historicism.

The 1949 Marcussen organ in Oscar's Church (figure 20-1) was greeted with
enthusiasm by many, but it also gave rise to an intense debate, mainly among

Figure 20-1. The Marcussen and Søn organ (1949) in Oscar's Church, Stockholm. Printed with permission of Antikvarisk-topografiska arkivet, ATA, Stockholm.

church musicians, because of its rather extreme voicing. In 1980 the organ builders Bruno Christensen & Sønner added a register crescendo and a set of 240 digital free combinations. The church celebrated the fiftieth anniversary of the organ in 1999 by commissioning a new work from Bengt Hambraeus, *Riflessioni*, which the current organist, Erik Boström, premiered on 5 September 1999.

SPECIFICATION 20-1.

Oscar's Church, Stockholm, Marcussen and Søn, 1949, with additions by Bruno Christensen & Sønner, 1980

Huvudverk (Manual II)	Ryggpositiv (Manual I)	Bröstverk (Manual III)
C-g'''	C-g'''	C-g'''
Principal 16'	Principal 8'	Gedackt 8'
Quintadena 16'	Gedackt 8'	Träprincipal 4'
Principal 8'	Quintadena 8'	Rörgedackt 4'
Spetsflöjt 8'	Oktava 4'	Oktava 2'
Oktava 4'	Gedacktflöjt 4'	Blockflöjt 2'
Rörflöjt 4'	Gemshorn 2'	Quinta 1⅓'
Spetsquint 2⅔'	Sivflöjt 1⅓'	Oktava 1'
Oktava 2'	Sesquialtera II	Sesquialtera II
Flachflöjt 2'	Scharf IV–V	Cymbel II
Rauschquint III	Dulcian 16'	Vox humana 8'
Mixtur VI–VIII	Krumhorn 8'	Regal 4'
Cymbel III	Tremulant	Tremulant
Trumpet 16'		
Trumpet 8'		

Crescendoverk (Manual IV)	Fjärrverk (Manual IV)	Pedal
C-g'''	C-g'''	C-f'
Spetsgedackt 16'	Dubbelflöjt 8'	Principal 16'
Principal 8'	Principal 4'	Subbas 16'
Rörflöjt 8'	Flöjt 4'	Quinta 10⅔'
Spetsgamba 8'	Quinta 2⅔'	Oktava 8'
Unda maris 8' (1980)	Waldflöjt 2'	Gedackt 8'
Oktava 4'	Flageolet 1'	Oktava 4'
Traversflöjt 4'	Mixtur III	Koppelflöjt 4'
Koppelflöjt 4'	Tremulant	Quintadena 4'
Quinta 2⅔'		Nachthorn 2'
Oktava 2'		Rörflöjt 1'
Terz 1⅗'		Rauschquint IV
Waldflöjt 1'		Mixtur VI
Mixtur IV–V		Fagott 32'
Cymbel III		Basun 16'
Trumpet 8'		Fagott 16'
Oboe 8'		Trumpet 8'
Clairon 4'		Trumpet 4'
Tremulant		Cornet 2'

Manual couplers:
Ryggpositiv/Huvudverk, Bröstverk/Huvudverk, Crescendoverk/Huvudverk, Crescendoverk/Bröstverk
Pedal couplers from Ryggpositiv, Huvudverk, Bröstverk, and Crescendoverk
General coupler pedal

(continued)

SPECIFICATION 20-1.
Continued

Swell for Crescendoverk
240 free combinations (Setzer) (1980)
4 pedal combinations (1980)
General crescendo (1980)
Tutti

Mechanical key action for manuals I, II, and III, and for the pedal
Electrical key action for manual IV
Electrical stop action

Recording

CD track 12: Erik Boström playing the premier performance of Bengt Hambraeus, *Riflessioni*.

Literature

Boström, Erik. *Marcussenorgeln i Oscarskyrkan Stockholm: Historisk och beskrivning till 50-års jubileet 1999*. Stockholm: Oscars församling, 1999.

TABLE 20-1.

Erik Boström's Registration for Bengt Hambræus, *Riflessioni*
Marcussen Organ in Oscar's Church, Stockholm

Time	Action
0:01	SW: Spetsgedackt 16′, Waldfl. 1′, Cymbel
0:14	Ped: Subbas 16′, Nachthorn 2′, Cornet 2′
0:18	Ped: − Cornet 2′
0:22	Ped: + Cornet 2′
0:28–0:35	stop cresc. to 10 (= Tutti)
0:58–1:06	stop dim. to initial registration
1:14	+ Ped (only Subbas 16′ + pedal couplers)
1:20–1:24	stop cresc. to 10
1:42–1:51	stop. dim. to HW: Spetsfl 8′, Rörfl 4′, Flachfl 2′
1:51–2:04	stop crescendi and diminuendi: 0–5–8–5
2:15–2:16	stop cresc. To 10
2:25–2:27	stop dim. to 4
2:52	Tutti
3:00	− Tutti
3:04–3:07	stop dim. to 0
3:07	Ped: + Cornet 2′
3:14	Ped: − Cornet 2′
3:20–3:27	stop cresc. to 10
3:42	SW: Gedackt 16, Rörfl 8, Tremulant Ped: Subbas 16, SW coupled
4:27	solo: RP: Quintadena 8′ Tremulant
4:47–4:50	SW: stop cresc. and dim. 0–4–0
4:51	solo: RP: Quintadena 8′, Gedackt 8′, Gedacktfl 4′, Tremulant Accompaniment SW: Tremulant
5:03	SW: Rörfl. 8′, Koppelfl. 4′
5:07–5:17	stop cresc. to 8
5:28	Tutti
5:41–5:46	stop dim.
5:46	Solo. HW: Spetsfl 8′, Rörfl 4 ′, Flachfl 2 ′ Acc. RP: Quintadena 8′, Gedackt 8′, Gedacktfl 4′, Tremulant
6:10–6:14	stop cresc. to 4
6:24–6:28	stop cresc. to 8
6:52–6:54	stop cresc. to 10

(*continued*)

TABLE 20-1.

Continued

Time	Action
8:25–8:35	stop dim. to 5
8:54	Crescendo pedal at 3
9:08	HW: Spetsfl 8', Rörfl 4', Flachfl 2'
9:15	HW: + Quintadena 16', Rauschqvint
9:28	Hw: − Rauschqvint, Pedal without Quinta 10⅔'
9:58	Pedal with Quinta 10⅔'
10:15–10:18	stop cresc. to 8
10:56–10:58	stop dim. to 4
11:04–11:10	stop cresc. to 7
11:23–11:28	stop cresc. to 10
11:45–11:51	stop dim.
11:54	FW: Dubbelfl 8', Tremulant
12:41	+ SW: Unda maris 8', Tremulant, FW coupled
13:17	+ Rörfl 8' (SW), Fl 4' (FW)
13.22	solo: BW:Vox humana 8', Tremulant
14.11	FW: Dubbelfl 8', Mixtur, Tremulant
14:30–15:18	Solo (lower voice, occasionally): BW: Vox humana 8', Tremulant
14:54	+ Ped: Subbas 16' (only)
15:25	RP: Dulcian 16', Scharf
15:30	HW: Rörfl 4', Spetsquint 2⅔' only (no coupler)
15:37	FW and HW as before; BW (occasional chords): Vox humana 8', Tremulant
16:11	RP: Dulcian 16', Gedacktfl 4', Scharf, HW as before
16:18	RP: + Krumhorn 8'
16:27	Ped: + Cornett 2'
16:48	HW: Principal 8', RP coupled
17:06	+ Ped: with Trumpet 8'
17:16–17:20	stop cresc. to 10
17:32–17:48	stop dim. and cresc. 10-0-5-3-4-0-6-0-8-0-10
18:33–18:52	stop dim. to SW: Unda maris, Trem., with FW (Dubbelfl 8', Trem) coupled
18:54	Ped: Subbas 16'
19:10	only SW: Unda maris, Trem.

21

THE ORGANS IN OSCAR'S CHURCH: SOURCES OF
INSPIRATION—AND SOME CONTROVERSY

BENGT HAMBRAEUS

WITHOUT A DOUBT, THE RENOWNED DANISH ORGAN-BUILDING FIRM OF MARCUSSEN & Søn has had a trendsetting impact in Sweden since the mid-1930s. The magnificent instruments built in the Lund Cathedral (1934) and the Göteborg Concert Hall (1936) were followed by many other organs in the succeeding years. Those in Our Lady's Church (Vårfrukyrkan) in Skänninge (1939) and in Oscar's Church (Oscarskyrka) in Stockholm (1949) have won international acclaim, especially through Carl Weinrich's recordings of Bach, and Alf Linder's of Buxtehude, both in Skänninge, on the Westminster label. For these instruments, Sybrand Zachariassen—head of the Marcussen company—was in charge of layout and tonal design, assisted by his close collaborators Poul-Gerhard Andersen, Adolf Wehding, and, in Oscar's Church, Alf Linder. The instrument in Oscar's Church, Skänninge, and the Växjö Cathedral (1940), were, on the whole, built in accordance with the historicizing principles that marked the organ reform movement during the 1920s and 1930s, particularly the *Werkprinzip* of German Renaissance and baroque organs, with its clearly identified sound characters in different divisions (Hauptwerk, Rückpositiv, Brustwerk, and pedal). But the Marcussen sound often adhered as well to basic principles typical for Cavaillé-Coll, with an organic balance between fundamental stops, overtone mutations, and mixtures, and between flues and reeds. The spirit of Cavaillé-Coll was easy to recognize in the Göteborg Concert Hall organ (which was not explicitly built on the *Werkprinzip*) before it was renovated by another company in the 1980s. Such sonic criteria may explain why the "Marcussen sound" was perceived as an organic whole—even the company's most typical *Werkprinzip* instruments had little in common with those neo-baroque instruments that were built by other organ makers in northern Europe during the 1920s through 1940s with similar stop lists; or, to state the obvious: if not translated into artistically conceived scaling and voicing, the most impressive stop list has no real significance for any repertoire.

On the day before Oscar's Church organ was inaugurated (4 September 1949), one of the leading Stockholm newspapers, *Svenska Dagbladet*, published a long illustrated article on the instrument signed by I. B-n. This was Ingmar Bengtsson, who was at that time the chief music critic there, before he was appointed professor of musicology at Uppsala University. Based on interviews with Sybrand Zachariassen, Bengtsson emphasized the importance of a versatile instrument, capable of conveying any repertoire, early as well as modern. In spite of the classical *Werk* design, he found the Oscar's Church organ to be a modern instrument, not a period instrument with narrow limits. During the Sunday High Mass, when the new organ was dedicated, the first organ solo was Bach's E♭-Major Prelude from book 3 of *Clavierübung* (BWV 552,1); the postlude was Enrico Bossi's *Cantate Domino*, where the organ accompanied the church's choir and a brass ensemble. In a recital later the same day, Alf Linder presented music by Bach, César Franck, and Max Reger. Bach, Bossi, Franck, Reger—are these composers consistent with the concept of *Werkprinzip*, as it has been promulgated by the organ reform movement? Would this music, for example, have been an obvious choice of the many narrow-minded organists who excluded Franck and Reger from their neo-Renaissance and neo-baroque organs in favor of Jan Pieterszoon Sweelinck, Samuel Scheidt, Johann Pachelbel, Hugo Distler or Hans Friedrich Micheelsen? Such questions may actually lead us to other topics closely related to the new instrument, namely, the music tradition in Oscar's Church, the history of the church itself (its architecture and location in the city), and the social structure of the Oscar's Church parish, particularly between 1900 and 1950.

Praeambulum: Oscar's Church and Its First Organ

The Oscar's Church parish is one of the youngest in the city of Stockholm. It was established in 1906, in a relatively new area in the city's east end (Östermalm), which, in contrast to London's East End, had recently become dominated by a mostly affluent, conservative, and royalist upper class, and especially by the country's main military organizations (barracks, drill grounds, and high- and middle-ranking officers). The parish got its name from the neo-Gothic church that was built, almost in the middle of the regimental district, between 1897 and 1903 to commemorate the twenty-fifth anniversary (1897) of the reign of the Swedish king Oscar II (1829–1907). It is in the shape of a Latin cross, with a short transept, a wide central nave, and two narrow aisles; these last are actually in two stories, of which the upper ones are galleries, continuing from the organ loft on each side toward the choir. The solid oak pews can easily accommodate fourteen hundred people. From the beginning, the church has been regarded acoustically as one of the finest in the country, regardless of the number in attendance. This was true even after changes were made to the interior, mainly during the 1920s, and later in connection with the installation of the Marcussen organ.

The first organ in Oscar's Church—three divisions, 33 ranks—was installed in 1903 while the building was being finished. It was built by the renowned Swedish company P. L. Åkerman & Lund in Stockholm and closely followed the sonic criteria of Cavaillé-Coll's best instruments. P. L. Åkerman (1826–76), who, in 1866, established the organ-building company Åkerman & Lund (still in existence today), had finished his professional training in Cologne and Brussels between 1854 and 1857. After returning to his native country, he soon became famous for many excellent instruments—for example, those in the cathedrals in Strängnäs (1860) and Uppsala (1871), which were immediately acclaimed by international experts. Like most organs from those years, they underwent various alterations in their tonal design as a result of organ reform ideology. However, both in Strängnäs and in Uppsala, many of Åkerman's registers were retained. They remain exceptional: most other romantic instruments were simply destroyed in the 1930s and 1940s.[1]

In 1922 and 1923, Oscar's Church underwent renovations; at the same time, the organ was enlarged (by Åkerman & Lund) to 86 ranks—albeit with quite a few borrowings—to make it more versatile in its many functions as a liturgical as well as a concert instrument. The church had long since been in demand for fashionable weddings and funerals in the upper social echelons, partly because of its location. But the organ's tonal and architectural design remained essentially what it had been in 1903. All speaking pipes were still hidden behind a neo-Gothic organ façade. Bertil Wester (1902–76), an art historian who published extensively on the Åkerman & Lund organ,[2] had a special interest in organ architecture; he earned his doctorate in 1936 with a dissertation entitled "Gotisk resning i svenska orglar" (Gothic Monuments of Swedish Organ Building). He wrote many important studies on early Swedish organs and organ builders and fought to save valuable instruments that had been declared unfashionable and

---

1. In 1976, the Uppsala Cathedral organ was actually retrofitted and corresponds today—with some minor changes and additions—to the 1871 original. This can be seen as an example of a general trend in Swedish organ building after about 1970, namely, a rediscovery of "romantic" instruments after the too-emphatic promotion of neo-Renaissance and neo-baroque styles during the previous decades under the spell of organ reform.

2. For more information on the Åkerman and Lund organ (1903; 1922–23), see Bertil Wester, *Kristine kyrkas orgel: Orglar i Rättviks tingslag samt en exkurs över Oscarskyrkans orgel, Stockholm* (Stockholm: Generalstabens Litografiska Anstalts Förlag, 1946). Owing to a printing error the book may be erroneously cataloged as *Kyrkorglar Sverige. Dalarne. Falu Domsagas norra tingslag och Falu stad II. Samt Rättviks tingslag.*

useless for various stylistic reasons. Unfortunately, his 1946 study on the Oscar's Church organ is not an entirely trustworthy source, marred as it is by numerous inaccuracies (not merely misprints).[3] However, the numerous photos by themselves are a unique document of this lost instrument, which had been designed as an integral part of the church's architecture.

From the very beginning, efforts were made to establish a solid church music program in the new Oscar's Church parish with both vocal and instrumental resources (mainly choir and organ respectively). When it was officially launched in 1909, it was regarded as the first of its kind in modern times in Sweden. Between 1907 and 1943, the versatile French-inspired composer, organist, and writer Patrik Vretblad (1876–1953) was in charge of planning and performances, together with the church's choral directors Oscar Sandberg and (after 1926) Carl-Oscar Othzén. A booklet was published to celebrate the tenth anniversary of the so-called *Motettaftnar* (Motet Evenings), that is, church concerts, which were given at least four times every year between October and June.[4] This booklet includes a short history of how the initiative materialized and gives interesting insight into social, economic and liturgical-clerical discussions in the young parish. The booklet also includes the names of every clergyperson, musician, and singer involved during those ten years, and most importantly, an impressive list of vocal and instrumental works performed. Numerous composers from many countries are represented—Belgium, England, France, Germany, Italy, Norway, Sweden, and others. On the whole, the repertoire demonstrates a surprisingly wide scope for its time, which may have been unique in Sweden in those days. To give an example: both choral and organ works by Max Reger were performed repeatedly beginning in 1910, only a few years after they had been written and published (the composer was at that time regarded as rather controversial in some circles). This may be seen as evidence of Sandberg's and Vretblad's efforts to introduce new music to listeners, contrasting with earlier established works; among many rare items, we also find motets by Hugo Wolf.

In my opinion, it is important to get an idea—from the short survey above—about the building as a center for social and musical activity ever since the founding of the Oscar's Church parish in 1906. When Alf Linder was elected with an overwhelming majority as the new permanent organist on 23 February 1945, after having served as a deputy since Vretblad's retirement in 1943, he became involved with an established church-music organization. At the same

---

3. Because I am very familiar with this instrument (and have been since 1933), both as a student and occasionally also as a deputy organist, it has been quite easy for me to spot all these various errors.

4. *Festskrift vid Oscars-kyrkans Motettaftnars 10-årsjubileum den 10 december 1919* (Stockholm: Oscarskyrkan, 1919). This booklet was prepared by and sold within the parish; the chapter dealing with social, practical and musical aspects is written by Oscar Sandberg.

time, he brought many new ideas and was able to change the profile of program policy. Even if there was, generally speaking, no drastic change, the emphasis shifted toward a more systematic presentation of the organ repertoire, beginning with a monumental rendering of Bach's complete organ works during twenty-six Saturday evening recitals in 1944. Although this took place at the Åkerman & Lund organ, we listeners could immediately recognize another approach to Bach, one different from what had been heard in previous years. While Vretblad adhered more to a French-inspired, romantic style, Linder demonstrated, in a personal and convincing way, what he had learned during recent studies in Germany, notably with the organists Fritz Heitmann in Berlin and Günther Ramin in Leipzig and composer-theorists such as Hermann Grabner and Johann Nepomuk David. With Grabner, a former Reger student, he had analyzed the works of Reger, which he performed under Heitmann's guidance. This knowledge, acquired from leading German experts, became even more evident when Linder's Saturday evening recitals continued with magnificent performances of Reger's major organ works. But, as we have seen earlier, the first musical events in connection with the new Marcussen organ featured Bach, Bossi, Franck and Reger—all of them long since well established on the premises.[5]

At this point, the question may be asked: Was there any need to replace the existing Åkerman & Lund organ if it was capable of conveying appropriate sounds, and different performance practices, with rather convincing results, such as Vretblad's and Linder's? And hence a second question: Which instrument was the source of controversy—the old organ or the new Marcussen? Was the controversy partly rooted in nostalgia?

Because any instrument (not only the organ) has as its raison d'être a function in a certain environment, society, and time, and in particular in a performing context (i.e., composed or improvised music), one of the most important, even inevitable criteria is that the instrument be reliable from a technical point of view, sonic aspects notwithstanding. Unfortunately, the old Oscar's Church organ was malfunctioning, constantly and extensively. The electro-pneumatic action that had been installed in 1923 when the instrument was enlarged had gradually deteriorated over the years, causing numerous unpleasant surprises, including frequent loud bangs from worn magnets, short circuits in the wiring, and ciphers (unwanted sounding of pipes) from leaking windchests, just to mention a few. Because it would have been costly to do a complete renovation, an organ technician visited occasionally to patch it up in moments of catastrophe. I was a student of Alf Linder from 1944 through 1948, and at the same time

---

5. The Italian composer Enrico Bossi (1861–1925) was known in Sweden through important choral and organ works. As the organist for the Stockholm Philharmonic orchestra, Linder had been the soloist in Bossi's Organ Concerto in the early 1940s.

his assistant during recitals and live broadcasts; my assignment included not only registration and page turning, but also to be constantly alert so that if a certain stop or coupler decided to make an unexpected entry on its own, it could be removed immediately. Linder always kept his cool; I never remember his being nervous before or during any performance. Only once I heard him mutter "För-baskade basun!" (blasted trombone!) when this loud 16' pedal register suddenly blared out of nowhere into a very quiet *Legend* by the Swedish romantic com-poser Emil Sjögren. Linder, of course, did not interrupt his playing—it was just up to me to cancel the stop on the spot. Many such problems were perhaps unknown to those listeners who came to enjoy and learn from Linder's playing. But for the organist (and the assistant), the conditions for performance were not always predictable. Anything could happen—even complete silence, if the organ blower's antiquated power source did not respond to the switch; in such cases somebody had to rush through corridors and galleries and up a long spiral stair-case to a chamber in the church's attic and "stimulate the generator" by quickly turning a huge knob back and forth until igniting sparks triggered the fan motor.

Other problems were related to the borrowings, which were also a result of the 1923 renovation. There may be practical economic and space-saving reasons to borrow pipe ranks, or extend a certain 8' compass with one or more octaves up or down. It is, however, deceiving (and a nuisance to a guest organist, who is not familiar with these peculiarities) when much of the same register appears under different names.[6] Needless to say, this had nothing to do with P. L. Åk-erman's philosophy or with the original 1903 Åkerman & Lund organ; perhaps it can be excused because the instrument became more versatile after 1923, in spite of misleading nomenclature. There were, among many others, two inter-esting cases in the Echo division of the Oscar's Church organ. Installed in 1923 in the church attic, far away from the main organ, its sound was transmitted via a long wooden tunnel to an opening in the choir, above the altar. These two registers were known as the Cremona 8' and Clarabella 4'; according to a popular organ handbook written by Patrik Vretblad, they were unique in Sweden, having actually been introduced there for the first time in this organ.[7] As a matter of

6. Perhaps the most drastic example in the Oscar's Church organ of 1923 was the 8' Corno in the second manual. It also appeared in *five* other contexts, and under different names: as an 8' Trumpet in the pedal; as a 4' Clairon, both in the pedal and on the first manual, where it was also part of a 16' Trumpet; and lastly as part of the 32' Kontrabasun (together with its extension in the 16' Trumpet). I may add that I personally checked every detail of every stop transmisison in the old Oscar's Church organ, simply out of curiosity.

7. Patrik Vretblad, *Orgelregistren: Uppslagsbok för organister, orgelbyggare, och orgelns vänner* (Stock-holm: C. E. Fritzes Kungl. Hovbokhandel, 1932). According to Vretblad, a Cremona 8' was also featured in the Stockholm Concert House organ (built in 1926 by Åkerman and Lund). The Clar-abella, he writes, is common in English and American organs, but in Sweden is found only in the Oscar's Church organ.

fact, the pipes in the respective ranks were inscribed with far more common names: Gamba 8' and Flute octaviante 4'.[8]

With all this came another problem. The sound of individual registers and divisions, well balanced for its time (1903), had been changed in many different ways, beginning with the major rebuilding in 1923. What was done in that year did not drastically alter the French touch of the instrument per se (in spite of the English-American Clarabella); Vretblad was still the organist. One of the additions was a seven-rank Grand Cornet, where one of the ranks was borrowed, and the others mounted as in French instruments. Around 1940 this Grand Cornet was removed, and with it also a three-rank Cornet that had been part of the greater one. They belonged to the first and second manual (Great and Positiv) respectively, with the seven-rank cornet of course on the Great. The Grand Cornet windchest was used for a two-rank Rauschquint (2⅔' and 2'), and a 1' Sifflöte, on the respective manuals; but no change was made to the stop knobs. At the same time, a 5⅓' Fifth became a 4' Flute on the Great. No information about this is given in Wester's book, although it was published in 1946, several years after the change. He must have been aware of the problem; I met him many times in the Oscar's Church organ loft between 1944 and 1946, but, strangely, he would not talk about the loss of his beloved French sound and insisted that the Grand Cornet was still there. Most likely, the changes were made to conform to the new ideals established by the German organ reform movement, where a French-inspired Cornet sound would hardly fit in. It would be far beyond the scope of this article even to summarize the animated debates during those years among Swedish organists and church musicians.[9] At the same time the Oscar's Church organ lost its Cornet(s), it also lost its only Third (3⅕') and Seventh (1⅐'). No 1⅗' was ever built, and a planned 6⅖' in the pedal was never installed.

Considering the many annoying and steadily increasing problems with the old Oscar's Church organ, it is amazing how Alf Linder managed to cope with the decaying instrument in such an artistically supreme way. Almost like a magician, he was able to find appropriate light registrations for Bach's Trio Sonatas (I especially remember the first one, in E♭ major, and the fifth, in C major); a Liszt-

8. This is based on my own thorough examination of the Oscar's Church organ in 1945 and 1946, when the condition of the existing pipe material was scrutinized in connection with the upcoming discussions about replacing the instrument. Details were penciled into my personal copy of Wester's book, where the many above-mentioned inconsistencies in his text are also corrected.

9. For an excellent account of these debates, see Göran Blomberg, *Liten och gammal—duger ingenting till. Studier kring svensk orgelrörelse och det äldre svenska orgelbeståndet ca 1930–1980/83* (Uppsala: Swedish Science Press, 1986). A brief resumé of some controversial questions about the 1949 Marcussen organ in Oscar's Church is presented in Blomberg's book, pp. 94–95; see further below.

Wagnerian force field in the Reubke Sonata; a buoyant verve in works like Bach's D Major Prelude and Fugue, the sense of swing in Ernst Pepping's Concerto no. 1, or the energetic drive in Hermann Grabner's Sonata and Toccata. He was also able to effect an enormous contrast between the meditative and the dramatic vehemence in his rendering of Reger's major works, such as the B-A-C-H Fantasy and Fugue; the Second Sonata; the F-minor Introduction and Passacaglia from opus 63; the D-minor Fantasia and Fugue, opus 135b; and the chorale preludes, opus 67. For me, all these works and many more in Linder's repertoire are ineffaceably connected with the sound that he managed to evoke from the old Oscar's Church organ. It was also interesting that he managed to prepare alternative registrations for the same piece, depending on whether it was performed in a public recital or as a live broadcast. He was one of the few organists in Sweden in those days (perhaps the only one) to apply in practice what is metaphorically expressed in the well-known title of Marshall MacLuhan's book *Understanding Media*. In those days, because of limited frequency range and monaural microphones and radio receivers, broadcast technology was still not able to transmit, in a comprehensible way, the sound of a full organ tutti. Linder was intuitively aware of the need to select the right sound for any composition, depending on the medium in which it was to be presented. For broadcast and the noncommercial recordings he made for the Swedish Broadcasting Corporation's special programs (for example, CD tracks 8–10), he always chose transparent registrations, even for typical organo pleno (Bach) or tutti (Reger) movements, which required a more voluminous sound in recital. Needless to say, such problems mostly disappeared with more advanced radio and recording technology after about 1960 in Sweden.

Although this fourth part of the book has as its focus the 1949 Marcussen organ, I immediately felt it necessary to write this praeambulum in order to make the reader aware of the social environment in which the Marcussen creation emerged and the rationale behind the decision to let it happen. It is obvious that the personality of Alf Linder was extremely important in the history of Oscar's Church, its parish, and its organs. His artistic integrity was recognized from the very beginning by clergy and the parish church council at large, and his expert criticism of the organ's poor condition was immediately seen as a serious problem for the reputation of the parish. Personally, I regard him as a human bridge, leading from one organ landscape to another (see chapter 22).

I also felt it important to reveal, as an insider, some of the many technical deficiencies that accumulated between about 1940 and 1948 in the old organ's action. Such snapshots, taken from ongoing workaday activities, certainly hint at the problems and explain why a completely new instrument had to be the only logical and final solution, even if some of the old pipe ranks would still be used.

The 1949 Marcussen Organ

For the fiftieth anniversary of the 1949 Marcussen organ, which was celebrated on 5 September 1999 with a special morning service and later the same day with the first in a series of Jubilee Concerts, a beautiful booklet was published by the Oscar's Church parish.[10] The author, Erik Boström, became the new organist when Alf Linder died in 1983.[11] Here we can read the story of the conception and birth of the new instrument. With quotations from various minutes of meetings of the parish church council, beginning in 1945, Boström guides us through discussions and Linder's eloquent memoranda (and demonstrations of the decrepit old organ) to those important days in 1949: 7 February, when the church was closed to visitors and work began to remove the old organ, and 4 September, when the new Marcussen instrument sounded for the first time. Informal discussions between Linder and Sybrand Zachariassen had in fact already begun in the spring of 1945. I was actually present at those first meetings in Linder's home, when the first sketches and dispositions were drawn up by Zachariassen, Poul-Gerhard Andersen, and Linder, and I was asked by Linder to assist the Danish guests when they examined, in detail, the motor, blower, windchests and pipes. I could not help feeling nostalgic when the final decision came—but I also realized that not even an instrument's life is eternal; something new must always come. My encounter with these Danish organ experts gave me a unique opportunity to learn something new. I had listened on the radio to Gotthard Arnér's performance, on the Marcussen organ in Växjö Cathedral, of Carl Nielsen's *Commotio* and Kurt Thomas's *Es ist ein Schnitter heisst der Tod*. I remember asking Zachariassen, "Will the Oscar's Church organ be similar to the one at Växjö?" And he answered, "Yes, but bigger and better, if we get the offer to build!" Already at that time (I was only seventeen!) I got the feeling that something very new, exciting, and inspiring was about to blossom.

At the beginning of this chapter I referred to Ingmar Bengtsson's enthusiastic words in the newspaper article of 3 September 1949; a little later I also raised the question about which one of the two organs would be seen as more controversial, the old instrument or the new. There is an interesting sequel to Bengtsson's review. In his above-mentioned dissertation, Göran Blomberg quotes from a letter that he had received from Ingmar Bengtsson on 10 January 1978 (almost

10. Erik Boström, *Marcussenorgeln i Oscarskyrkan Stockholm: Historik och beskrivning till 50-års jubileet 1999* (Stockholm: Oscars församling, 1999).

11. Erik Boström, born in 1947, studied with Alf Linder at the State Academy of Music in Stockholm and later with Olivier Messiaen and Marie-Claire Alain. He belongs to the elite of Swedish organists and was the first in the country to present—on the Oscar's Church organ—Messiaen's *Livre du Saint Sacrement*, which also concludes his CD series of the composer's complete organ works on the Proprius label.

thirty years after the review).[12] In this letter, Bengtsson commented on what he had once written "with such enthusiasm" about the new instrument. He remembered that for certain reasons he had abstained from saying anything negative, even though his immediate impression when he first heard the new instrument was a bit disappointing: he perceived the phenomenal new sound as loud and harsh—in the letter he even uses the word *omogen* (immature). He explained the reason for keeping such thoughts to himself in 1949 by referring to the intense controversy in the 1940s and 1950s between opposing factions of organists and church musicians centered around "romantic organs" versus "organ reform instruments." Bengtsson simply tried to avoid involvement in those emotional and affected debates by not criticizing Marcussen and Zachariassen, who were regarded by many as elite exponents of the organ reform movement. Blomberg also includes some critical statements about the Oscar's Church organ, written by the authoritative, distinguished Danish organist and musicologist Finn Viderø.[13] Viderø's comments—made after more than thirty years—are especially surprising. He describes how the organist "almost felt as if he were being blown off the organ bench because of the violently voiced registers, with their wide-open pipe feet"; he pronounces the same negative verdict upon the huge 1951 Marcussen organ in St. Petri in Malmö (Sweden). Surprising indeed, because around 1950 Viderø was not really known as an anti-organ reform musician; for example, his well-known interest in early Spanish organ music—he seems to have been the first Nordic organist to perform music by Francisco Correa de Arauxo with scholarly understanding of the typical sound of old Iberian instruments—corresponded with his interest in those bright-sounding Spanish Trumpets that protruded horizontally from some of Marcussen's organs in the 1940s (cf. Cavaillé-Coll's *chamades*).

There were, at least in the beginning, some negative opinions about the new Oscar's Church organ, mixed with almost overwhelmingly positive reactions. From an architectonic, visual point of view, there was a tremendous difference from the old organ case, whose gray-stained oak was identical to all the surrounding woodwork in the organ loft and the galleries. With the new organ, a completely new design and the radiant appearance of the bright, natural color of oak was introduced into the building; the former neo-Gothic style from the turn of the century got a "back to the future" face-lift with the huge organ case, inspired by the organ reform movement, where different divisions were functionally exposed. In the old organ, the sound on the whole had been concealed within the neo-Gothic case, with its silent decorative pipes in the front. After

---

12. Blomberg, *Liten och gammal*, 94.

13. Finn Viderø, "Orgelbevaegelsen og Norden" in *Strengen er av gull: Festskrift Rolf Karlsen* (Oslo: Oslo &c., 1981), 107–16. See also Blomberg, *Liten och gammal*, 95.

the summer of 1949, this was no longer the case. The new instrument added a visual element to the church, so that visitors no longer had to guess what was sounding behind the former neo-Gothic screen. Instead of the former "collected symphonic" sound, a diverse sonic spectrum was revealed from spatially separated divisions with distinct characters. The incredible directness with which the front pipes addressed the listeners was also surprising to many people; one listener even perceived the powerful sound as voices from the cosmos, as an epiphany, and as laudations of the archangels! Seen in hindsight, it is only natural that a break with tradition would trigger widely varying opinions, such as Viderø's quoted negative remarks about loudness versus the other listener's association with the powerful voices of angels. A statement by the composer Edgard Varèse[14] comes to mind; he compared a traditional symphony orchestra with a swollen elephant, and a jazz band or big band with the pounce of a tiger; many phrases in the debates exchanged between opposing camps about the earlier and the new Oscar's Church organs were strikingly similar to Varèse's dramatic wording.

One of Sweden's leading church musicians at the time when the Oscar's Church organ was being built and inaugurated was Henry Weman, long since appointed organist at the Uppsala Cathedral. He had been chosen by the Oscar's Church parish council to be the chief inspector of the instrument, where Alf Linder was the supervisor *ex officio*. Weman's final report, after a meticulous inspection of the instrument, is dated 15 September 1949. He gives the organ an A-plus, writing in superlatives about the splendid craftsmanship of Zachariassen and his assistants: "In the country's history of organ building, one has to return to the glorious era of people like Johan Niclas Cahman to find an equivalent in the construction of something where functional organization of sound sources are combined with architectonic elevation . . . in such a way, that the church has been enhanced with its most beautiful fixture up to the present day."[15]

Nowhere in Weman's report, and never in any of Linder's own comments, do we find any negative remarks about excessive loudness. As usual, most controversies emanate more from emotional opinions about taste than from more substantiated and pragmatic considerations. On the whole, beginning in 1949 the organ became in many ways a center for Swedish organ culture far beyond its location in Östermalm. A strong contributing factor was that Alf Linder had been appointed the main organ teacher at the Royal Swedish Academy-College of Music in Stockholm in the same year (1945) that he had been elected tenured organist at Oscar's Church. Because the college was at that time the country's

---

14. Varèse (1883–1965) regarded Charles-Marie Widor as his most important composition teacher after Ferruccio Busoni.

15. Boström, *Marcussenorgeln*, 16.

only professional institute for the advanced training of church musicians and organists—until this training was decentralized in later decades—the new organ attained special status as an educational factor in the church music program of the entire country. Again, Linder's role was extremely important in every respect. He remains in my memory one of the most ethical educators and artists that I ever met. This ethos constantly guided his different activities in everything from questions related to copyright to performance, teaching, and service playing. He knew his métier thoroughly, but was also constantly following new trends, widening his awareness and learning. I think that most of us under his guidance learned by observing his serious and musical attitude to the art of the organ and its role in society. His earlier years as a jazz pianist may also explain his vibrant, infectious approach to Bach's music, which he performed with a healthy touch of swing. In any case, his concern for educational matters, combined with his internationally recognized artistry, made it possible for everybody—students, colleagues, and clergy alike—to have the greatest respect for his personal integrity.

From the practical viewpoint of a musician, it is most important to be able to use an instrument that both sounds good and is technically reliable. It must have been a blessing to Linder—and the church authorities—to have a definitive solution to the many nerve-wracking technical calamities of the past. It was also good for the organist (and especially guest artists) to know that the name of a register, as shown on the knob on the console, corresponded with the expected sound and was not a pseudonym for something else. In contrast to Linder's long experience from broadcast recitals, the new instrument offered numerous new ways to showcase a richer sound spectrum than what had been possible before: briskly vibrant registrations in works such as Bach's trio sonatas provided new perspectives with the distinctly spatially located divisions, something that became even more apparent with the development of stereophonic techniques (which were actually not introduced into the Swedish Broadcasting system until 1957). Because of Zachariassen's scaling, even a massive tutti did not sound thick (even if some people had found it too loud); the music of Max Reger had a new dimension, which it might not have had if performed on a more "fundamentally orthodox" reform organ. Also here, the collaboration between Zachariassen and Linder had made it possible to get a versatile instrument, one on which most styles could be properly interpreted. I quote here from Erik Boström's presentation of the instrument in the jubilee booklet: "As Alf Linder's follower since 1983, I have used the organ in interpretations of Messiaen's complete organ works; and despite the fact that the instrument is not exactly a typical Messiaen organ, it has been possible to achieve interesting sounds for his music."[16]

Erik Boström took over his position three years after the Danish organ-building

16. Boström, *Marcussenorgeln*, 20.

company Bruno Christensen & Sønner had done a major renovation and updating of the instrument; Christensen had actually been one of Zachariassen's assistants in 1949. There had been some minor changes already in 1963, when Linder recommended that some registers in the Rückpositiv and Pedal be changed by Marcussen & Søn. On 2 October 1976 Alf Linder presented a memo to the parish committee that deserves to be quoted here (in my translation) because it provides at the same time striking evidence of Linder's never-ceasing interest in opening windows and doors to new regions (without losing links with valuable traditions); he writes, as a basic statement, the following:

> After more than 25 years, the organ needs a major overhaul, which includes certain technical and musical changes. Since the organ was installed in 1949, much has happened on the organ front: modern organ compositions with "clusters," etc., require another "technique" than the traditional one, and the organ has been put on trial heavily. Parallel with this modern trend, we can also witness a romantic wave in organ music, something that likewise makes changes in sound and technique necessary.[17]

Besides the organ-building aspects, one of the most interesting features of Linder's memo is that unlike many other church musicians, he was always aware of the fact that society and music are not static but in permanent transition. We must remember that he wrote this at the age of sixty-nine, after having followed with great interest the remarkable innovations in his former student Karl-Erik Welin's (1934–92) performances of the avant-garde repertoire (see chapter 23), and his colleague Torsten Nilsson's (1920–99) interpretations of his challenging new compositions. Although in such cases many organists would forbid the performance of that new repertoire and make the music and its interpreter appear ridiculous and a physical threat to their instrument, Linder went the opposite way: if the organ could not convey the repertoire properly, something might have to be changed with the instrument, not with the music and the musician.

Postludium

I have written this chapter, to a great extent, on the basis of my personal experience of the two Oscar's Church organs, their organists, and their repertoire. Alf Linder invited me to play in his Saturday evening recital series, both on the old organ (1945 and 1947) and several times on the new organ. In 1959, I made a recording of Bach's *The Art of Fugue* for the Swedish Broadcasting Corporation programs. During those years, I had regular contacts with Alf Linder as his registrant from 1944 through 1948, and between 1957 and 1972 I was often responsible as a broadcast producer for public organ concerts arranged by the

17. Boström, *Marcussenorgeln*, 18.

Swedish Broadcasting Corporation, and for regular recordings, produced by me or some of my broadcast colleagues (one of whom was Karl-Erik Welin).

As a composer, I have been invited twice to write works to be premiered on the Marcussen organ. In 1974, when I had been living in Canada for two years, I wrote *Ricercare* (the third of my *Five Organ Pieces 1969–75*, published by Nordiska Musikförlaget). It was commissioned by the Swedish Broadcasting Corporation and premiered by Erik Lundkvist. In 1999, I received from the Oscar's Church parish one of my most interesting and emotionally most challenging commissions ever: to write a work for the celebration of the Marcussen organ's fiftieth anniversary, to be premiered by Erik Boström. My immediate and obvious idea was to let the composition be a memorial tribute to Alf Linder, based on transformed reminiscences from his repertoire as I remember his performances, for example, of Bach, Reubke, Bruhns, Reger and Buxtehude—with modulating cross-references and associations of ideas turning unexpectedly into other composer's work. I also imagined that the Oscar's Church organ would perhaps have remembered by itself and stored, as if in a huge data bank, all music and all sounds that had been performed in the church during Linder's forty years as organist. This also gave me an opportunity to use new technical facilities in the new work, *Riflessioni*, premiered at the first jubilee concert on 5 September 1999. These new technical facilities were installed by Bruno Christensen in 1980 after Linder's suggestions and were not available when I composed *Ricercare*. The style of the two compositions is rather different; the earlier one is structured according to the *Werkprinzip*—the score is actually written with one system for each keyboard, so that the organist can easily identify respective manuals. For *Riflessioni*, it was possible to develop completely different dynamic structures, crescendi, diminuendi, rapidly shifting contrasts—something that did not exist before 1980. Let me take the opportunity to thank my friend Erik Boström for a superb premiere performance (CD track 12).

So, finally: Were the Oscar's Church organs sources of controversy? Perhaps they were, for the different reasons briefly related above. Regarding the alleged controversy around the Marcussen organ, it seems to be more a question of subjective opinion and individual taste than an attempt at more pragmatic criticism. In any case, the 1949/1980 instrument never left lukewarm impressions, neither could it be classified as a "neo-baroque screamer" with the kind of piercing, pungent sound that was heard too frequently in other builders' instruments in the 1940s and 1950s. The Marcussen-Zachariassen-Christensen Oscar's Church organ was, from the very beginning, a source of dynamic power, realized in excellent scaling and voicing, which made the best possibilities for contrasts of timbre. It could be soft, but never indifferent; it could be very loud, but with great authority. A source of inspiration? Yes, indeed, for interpreters as well as for composers—and for those listeners who are not afraid of sonic challenges!

22

THE TACITURN CHARISMA OF ALF LINDER

KIMBERLY MARSHALL

*I remember meeting Alf Linder when I was sixteen, auditioning for my
first church music diploma in Lund. He was on the jury, and by
coincidence we were staying in the same residence, so we had breakfast
together every morning. He never said anything, which was a bit
disconcerting, but the morning after I had passed the exam he looked
at me and remarked, "You're going to be a musician, aren't you?"*

HANS HELLSTEN, ORGAN PROFESSOR, MALMÖ MUSIKHOGSKOLA

*During the mid-1970s, I spoke before the National Board of
Antiquities to defend several pneumatic organs from the 1930s and
1940s in Småland that were in danger of being altered to suit
changing tastes. I was perhaps a bit brash in asserting that these
instruments were better for Otto Olsson's music than the newer organs
in Stockholm, and no one on the committee seemed to be influenced
by my arguments. Then, at the very end of the meeting, Linder, who
had been silent the whole while, simply stated: "These organs are
magnificent. They should be saved." And they were.*

COUNT CARL-GUSTAF LEWENHAUPT, ORGAN DESIGNER AND CONSULTANT

THESE ANECDOTES TYPIFY THE REMEMBRANCES OF BOTH ORGANISTS AND ORGAN
builders who came into contact with Alf Linder (1907–83; figure 22-1). Through
his weekly recitals at Oscar's Church, his frequent vespers radio broadcasts, and
his teaching at the music conservatory in Stockholm, Linder became an icon of
the Swedish organ world. Despite his reserved and taciturn manner, his opinions
exerted significant influence on the development of organ performance in Sweden for over forty years, from his first broadcasts on Swedish radio in 1940 until

Figure 22-1. Alf Linder at the Oscar's Church organ. Printed with kind permission of Judith Linder.

his death in 1983. Having studied with Otto Olsson in Stockholm, with Günther Ramin in Leipzig, and with Fritz Heitmann in Berlin, Linder learned the performance style of the great romantics as well as the tenets of the burgeoning neo-baroque movement in Germany, which led him to become a champion of early music in Sweden. In his recordings of Dieterich Buxtehude, Linder displays a clarity and sense of gesture that foreshadow later developments in the performance practice of baroque music. The many types of repertoire he performed dictated his views on organ building, as evidenced in the eclectic design he sanctioned as consultant for the Marcussen organ that was installed in Oscar's Church in 1949. His broad interests also encompassed the organ works of Swedish composers, including Emil Sjögren, Otto Olsson, Oskar Lindberg, and Hilding Rosenberg, whose sixtieth birthday Linder celebrated with a concert in Oscar's Church that was broadcast live on Swedish radio. This man of few words was a revered performer and teacher, and his commitment and charisma inspired many of Sweden's finest performers to expand the horizons of the organ through both early and contemporary music.

Building a Repertoire

Linder was born on 28 July 1907 in Hammerö, near Karlstad.[1] His father, who gave him his first lessons, was the cantor and organist in the local church, so he

1. The biographical information in the following paragraphs has been culled from several sources,

grew up hearing the organ. As his proficiency on the instrument increased, he studied with the organists of Karlstad Cathedral, Claes W. Rendahl and Otto Nordlund. Already at this early stage in his training as an organist, he developed a special affinity for the two composers that were to remain his favorite through-out his career, J. S. Bach and Max Reger. He is reported to have bought the complete organ works of Bach as a ten-year-old boy, and in 1921, at the tender age of fourteen, he performed Bach's G Minor Fantasy and Fugue (BWV 542) in Karlstad Cathedral, reportedly bringing tears to the eyes of his listeners. Also included on that program was Max Reger's Second Sonata, a real tour de force for such a young organist and an early demonstration of Linder's predilection for Reger's music.

His audition piece for entry into Stockholm's Royal Academy of Music was the Prelude and Fugue in C♯ Minor of the professor with whom he would study, Otto Olsson. This may well have been the first time that Olsson ever heard the piece performed, and he must have been impressed by the young Linder, who became his first organ student at the Royal Academy. (Linder had been unsuc-cessful in his audition for the academy the previous year to study with Olsson's predecessor, Gustaf Hägg.) Thanks to Olsson's scrupulous reports, we can trace Linder's repertoire from the autumn of 1925, when he learned the Bach Canzona (BWV 588) and Pièce d'orgue (BWV 572), through 1926, when Gustav Merkel's G Minor Sonata, the middle movements of Charles-Marie Widor's Symphonie Romane, and Olsson's own C♯ Minor Prelude and Fugue were added to the Bach Toccata and Fugue in D Minor (BWV 565), the Passacaglia and Fugue (BWV 582), and the Prelude and Fugue in D Major (BWV 532). During the spring of 1927 Linder completed the Widor Romane.[2]

Interestingly, there is no trace of either Buxtehude or Reger in his curriculum at this early stage. Buxtehude was not a part of the organist's standard repertoire in Sweden during the 1920s, although Olsson pioneered the performance of baroque organ music in Sweden. As early as 1914, he performed a chorale ar-rangement of Samuel Scheidt's Christ lag in Todesbanden for a concert in Gustaf Vasa Church arranged by the Friends of Church Music, and he advocated play-ing pre-Bach repertoire during the worship service.[3] In 1927, the year in which Linder passed his organist's examination at the music academy, Olsson per-

most notably from Mark Falsjö's article, "Alf Linder—en av 1900-talets stora orgelkonstnärer," Kyr-komusikernas tidning 65, no. 4 (1999): 4–11. Much of this has been corroborated in interviews with Linder's widow, Judith Linder, and his other former students Bengt Hambraeus, Henrik Cervin, and Erik Boström, as well as younger organists who had occasion to meet Linder before his death, such as Hans Davidsson and Hans Hellsten.

2. Falsjö, "Alf Linder," 5.

3. Sverker Jullander, Rich in Nuances: A Performance-Oriented Study of Otto Olsson's Organ Music, Skrifter från Musikvetenskapliga avdelningen, no. 50 (Göteborg: Göteborg University, 1997), 131 and n. 84.

formed a recital consisting exclusively of music composed before Bach. None of this appears to have been included in Linder's studies with Olsson, although the young student cannot have been unaware of his teacher's pursuits in this regard.

Olsson's dislike of Reger probably prevented Linder from studying this repertoire with him. Olsson is reported to have expressed contempt for the complexity of German romantic music, and it is clear from the annotations of performed repertoire in his notebook that he greatly preferred the French style.[4] He did, however, play works by the more classical of the nineteenth-century German composers, such as Mendelssohn and Rheinberger, and it is likely that he was targeting Reger with his criticism of "German" music,[5] perhaps because Reger's style conflicted with Olsson's ideal of "clarity." While Olsson played some of the smaller Reger pieces, his students at the academy did not usually play the large Reger works while studying with him, and Linder's repertoire reflects this.

Having passed his organist's examination in 1927, his music teacher's examination in 1931, and his church music examination in 1933, Linder made his debut on 6 December 1933 in a recital at the Gustaf Vasa Church in Stockholm. He performed a program that included Bach's D Major Prelude and Fugue and Passacaglia and Fugue, as well as Olsson's Prelude and Fugue in D♯ Minor. The concert was very favorably received by the press, where Linder was congratulated for his technical skill and use of registration. The Olsson, with its "rich nuancing and registration," was felt to be the high point of the concert.[6] Linder's programming would change significantly after this debut concert, with Reger figuring prominently in his concerts and Olsson's music becoming more rare. His studies in Germany during the summer of 1938 may be responsible for the inclusion of works by Buxtehude and Reger on the program for a concert at St. John's Church in Stockholm on 8 December 1938. This appears to be the first public occasion on which Linder juxtaposed music by these composers, including Buxtehude's Praeludium in F♯ Minor and Reger's Second Sonata, both works that became staples of his repertoire.[7] This concert also included the premiere performance of Olsson's Prelude and Fugue in D♯ Minor, Op. 56, a fitting tribute to Linder's former teacher.

---

4. See the table of performed repertoire for the period 1899–1912 in Sverker Jullander, "French and German Influences in the Organ Music of Otto Olsson," in *Proceedings of the Göteborg International Organ Academy*, ed. Hans Davidsson and Sverker Jullander (Göteborg: Göteborg University, 1995), 472–73.

5. Jullander, "French and German Influences," 473.

6. Falsjö, "Alf Linder," 5.

7. Falsjö, "Alf Linder," 6.

Study in Germany

One cannot overemphasize the importance of Linder's study in Germany for the directions in which he would develop as an organist.[8] During June and July of 1938, he went to Leipzig for a seven-week summer course with Günther Ramin, during which he had twenty-five organ lessons and the chance to study conducting with the Gewandhaus choir. He also played the Silbermann organs in Rötha and performed works by Emil Sjögren, Oskar Lindberg, and Olsson in a concert at the Dresden Kreuzkirche on 2 July that was attended by over four thousand people. In a letter to his parents, he wrote that he had learned more in this course than in all his time at the Royal Academy in Stockholm. He now saw Bach and Buxtehude in another way. Ramin was apparently a wonderful teacher for Linder, and Linder returned to work with him the following year for three weeks in January, for academies in April and July, and for more private organ lessons in the autumn.

In January 1940 Ramin proposed that Linder continue his studies in Berlin under Fritz Heitmann, and that summer Linder made a sojourn to work with Heitmann on his organ playing while pursuing studies in theory with Hermann Grabner and Johann Nepomuk David. This study trip also included concerts in Potsdam and for the Berliner Rundfunk, which further contributed to his reputation back home in Sweden. He had made his first recordings for Swedish Radio in the Stockholm Concert Hall in January and March of 1940, and he was billed as "Stockholm Radio's Organist" for his concert on the Schnitger organ in Berlin's Charlottenburg Castle on 29 June 1941. In June and July of 1942, Linder returned to Berlin for more concerts, radio broadcasts, and an interview with Berliner Rundfunk, and he was invited back to Berlin the following September to represent the Scandinavian countries in a Nordic Week celebration, during which he gave fourteen concerts in as many days throughout Germany. Heitmann was vastly influential in securing him these concerts and in helping him prepare large Bach works for public performance. (Heitmann was famous for his Bach interpretations, and in 1938 he had recorded parts of book 3 of *Clavierübung* for Telefunken on the Charlottenburg Schnitger.) During his studies with Heitmann, Linder gave the first modern Swedish performances of *The Art of Fugue*, in the Stockholm Concert Hall in 1941, and of book 3 of *Clavierübung*, at the Royal Academy of Music in 1943, the same year in which he became the acting organist at Oscar's Church in Stockholm. There he instituted a series of forty-five-minute organ devotions on Saturday evenings from January through May and from September through December, presenting Bach's com-

---

8. Information about Linder's German studies was generously supplied to the author by Judith Linder, who is currently preparing a biography based in part on her husband's surviving correspondence.

plete organ works during these devotions in 1944–45. The Swedish press was ecstatic over Linder's mastery of Bach, and despite the political enmity engendered by the war, his interpretations seem universally to have benefited from his association with German organs and organists.

It is very difficult to assess the political implications of Linder's presence in Germany at this time. Neither Ramin nor Heitmann was a member of the Nazi party, although both performed for political events. Ramin played frequently at the *Parteitage* in Nuremberg and on similar occasions,[9] and he seems to have mingled with leading Nazis, although one of his students reminisced that "as his student . . . I never heard a positive word concerning Hitler."[10] Heitmann also had important connections to the Nazis: in the early 1930s he joined the Kampfbund für deutsche Kultur (KfdK), created by Alfred Rosenberg (later convicted in the Nuremberg trials);[11] he was a member of the Orgel-Arbeitsgemeinschaft der Hitler-Jugend;[12] and he is reported to have described the organ as "simply the instrument of the Hitler Jugend."[13] Although some may speculate that Heitmann refused to play for Hermann Goering's wedding in the Berlin Cathedral on ideological grounds,[14] his official stance was one of cooperation with the ruling regime, which is not surprising, since he certainly would not have retained his position as cathedral organist had he openly opposed the Nazis. Linder appears to have maintained a neutrality vis-à-vis the German political climate, focusing upon his musical studies with Ramin and Heitmann and developing his personal style of playing German organ music under the guidance of these two experts.

A clear line of influence can be drawn between Ramin and Linder's innovative approach to registration. Ramin, a pupil of Straube's, followed his teacher as an early proponent of early music in Germany, and he was directly involved in the "rediscovery" of the Schnitger organ at St. Jacobi, Hamburg. In 1929, the same year that Straube's *Neue Folge* to the *Alte Meister* were published, Ramin wrote that "the most significant event in my efforts to gain clarity concerning seventeenth-century organ music came in the year 1923, when I became acquainted with the Arp Schnittger [sic] organ in the Jacobi Church through Jahnn (Hans Henny Jahnn, playwright and philosopher; see chapter 24), and thereafter

9. Günter Hartmann, *Karl Straube und seine Schule: "Das Ganze ist ein Mythos"* (Bonn: Verlag für systematische Musikwissenschaft, 1991), 91, 109, 115. On 109, Hartmann refers to Ramin as "Parteitagsorganist."

10. Originally published in *Musik und Kirche* 59 (1989): 291; quoted in Hartmann, *Straube*, 27.

11. Hartmann, *Straube*, 76.

12. Michael Gerhard Kaufmann, *Orgel und Nationalsozialismus* (Kleinblittersdorf: Musikwissenschaftliche Verlags-Gesellschaft, 1997), 318.

13. Hartmann, *Straube*, 102: "Instrument der Hitlerjugend schlechthin."

14. Hartmann, *Straube*, 115, recounts that Ramin played at Goering's wedding in the Berlin Cathedral, but does not give any reason why the titular organist, Fritz Heitmann, did not play.

moved my regular organ concerts there."[15] These organ concerts promoted early music and were sponsored by an artistic society known as the Glaubensgemeinde Ugrino, which was founded by Jahnn and two colleagues to promote an idealistic philosophy based on a utopian balance between art, religion and social order, a philosophy that was beautifully mirrored in the many symbiotic relationships of the baroque organ. The first of Ramin's recitals for Ugrino took place on 11 April 1922, including works by Buxtehude and Lübeck. The series ended five years later with Ramin's twenty-sixth recital, which included music for organ by J. S. Bach. But lest one imagine that Ramin's acquaintance with the Jacobi organ turned him into a zealot for "authentic" performance practice, his definition of the "organ problem" makes clear that he was very much a disciple of Straube: "The great problem in organ building reform consists in creating an instrument which, by uniting the tonal advantages of the classical organ with other technical achievements of our day . . . gives the possibility to bring to life both music composed before Bach and also the great works of Max Reger."[16] For Ramin, Bach and Reger constituted two pillars in the history of organ music, and the modern organ had to navigate successfully around both. This attitude would inform Linder's collaboration for the eclectic design of the new Marcussen organ in Oscar's Church and would greatly affect his way of exploiting organ sound in the performance of early music.

Linder was fascinated by the neo-baroque registrations to which he was exposed during his studies in Germany, as reported in the anonymous program notes to his Bach recording for the Proprius label in 1977:

> Of the D Major Prelude and Fugue (BWV 532), which is included in this album, Alf Linder himself says: "When I made my debut recital, in the Gustaf Vasa Church in Stockholm in 1933, I had included this work in my program, and I performed it in the way in which Bach was performed at that time. When I came to Günther Ramin in Leipzig, I played the D Major Fugue for him, almost as I had played it at my debut recital in Stockholm (five years earlier). After that, Ramin played the same piece his way, in a light and airy manner with only 8', 4' and 1' registers. It was a completely new experience for me, both in terms of sound and technique."[17]

Thus, Linder's work with Ramin led him to cultivate a way of registering organ music different from the approach that was current in Sweden at that time. Otto Olsson did not approve of the new registrational style and wrote a letter admon-

---

15. Günther Ramin, foreword to *Gedanken zur Klärung des Orgelproblems* (Kassel: Bärenreiter, 1929), 3.

16. Ramin, "Wege und Ziele der heutigen Orgelmusikpflege," *Zeitschrift für Kirchenmusiker* (1 July 1926): 42; reproduced in *Gedanken*, 37. [For Heitmann's similar opinion, see chapter 19.]

17. *Bach-Musikanten: Alf Linder spelar på Oscarskyrkans orgel i Stockholm*; Proprius LP 7780, 1977.

ishing his former student for his light, sparkling registrations and reiterating the importance of creating depth in the sound through the use of 16′ pitch. But Linder was very much a man of his time, and he brought the new "German" style across the Baltic, where he created a revitalization of organ playing through his fresh approach to registration.

Linder's Recordings

Especially significant in this regard were Linder's recordings of the complete organ works of Buxtehude on the neo-baroque organ in Skänninge, of which seven of a projected eleven volumes were released by Westminster in 1957. These represent some of the earliest efforts at understanding the relationship between German baroque music and the sound world for which it was destined. The independence of the contrapuntal lines is brought out on sharply contrasting timbres, and the sectional nature of many pieces is enhanced through performance on different divisions of an instrument constructed according to the *Werkprinzip*. Linder replaces the gradual yet constant dynamic and color fluctuations of late romanticism with terraced dynamics and the bright sounds of the neo-baroque organ. The novelty of his approach was criticized in the American press:

> His registration is not always happy. Linder evidently knows that compared to the southern instruments, the North German organs, with their clear reeds, were very brilliant, but he does not assign enough weight to the bass, which is often pale and lacking in assertiveness. . . . He likes to couple four- and two-foot stops to everything which sometimes entirely eliminates the feeling for the eight-foot register, thereby making the part-writing hazy. At times the middle parts, assigned to stops that get under way with difficulty, sound quite flutey; the pft-pft on every tone making the music a bit asthmatic.[18]

These remarks refer as much to the neo-baroque voicing of the Marcussen organ in Skänninge as they do to Linder's interpretation, and they reveal the ways in which the neo-baroque sound ideal deviated from the smoother speech and rich lower foundations of the late-romantic organs upon which this repertoire was usually performed at that time.

Aspects of romantic performance practice are heard alongside the clear touch and use of strong upperwork in Linder's Buxtehude recordings. He exhibits a tendency toward culminating every large work with a bombastic crescendo, and the registration changes are much more frequent than subsequent research into early performance practices advises for this music. This is exemplified in the C-

18. Paul Henry Lang, review of *Buxtehude: Complete Organ Works*; Alf Linder, organ. 7 LPs. Westminster XWN 18117, 18149, 18193, 18221, 18507, 18689, 18777. *Musical Quarterly* 45, no. 3 (July 1959): 424–25.

Minor Chaconne at Skänninge, where from a subdued opening the piece progresses into ever-louder registrations, occasionally interrupted by typically neo-baroque diversions and echoes. Nevertheless, Linder's interpretation represents a marked departure from the prevalent approach to Buxtehude's ostinato works in the 1950s, as reflected in Lang's review: "The dreaminess of the passacaglias and ciaconas escapes him, and the pauses between the variations are at times too deliberate, diminishing the dramatic cumulative effect of the ostinato."[19] A more romantic rendering of the C-Minor Chaconne would produce a seamless blending of the sections, with subtle color changes and a more gradual sense of crescendo than Linder's clear delineations of the work's sectional structure through registration and timing.

In 1971, Linder made a recording of Bach on the eighteenth-century Cahman organ in Leufsta Bruk. His performance of the Trio Sonata no. 1 (CD tracks 8–10) demonstrates the neo-baroque approach to color when applied to a historical instrument. The first movement features flutes at 8′, 4′, and 2⅔′ pitches in the right hand against a Quintadena in the left, creating contrasts of both pitch and timbre. Differences of color are heightened in the second movement, where the Quintadena is juxtaposed with a short-resonator reed, changing hands between the sounds for the repeated sections. The registration for the final movement is made brilliant by the inclusion of a mixture in one hand against 8′, 4′, and 2⅔′ in the other, again changing the timbres between the hands for the repeats. These highly contrasted registrations, with their use of reeds and high-pitched mutations, are typical of the neo-baroque movement, and they clearly date Linder's recording to the sound ideals of the 1960s and 1970s.

Articulation and Phrasing

The articulation and rhythmic control exhibited in these recordings are surprisingly in keeping with current performance practice. Here Linder's scrupulous clarity of touch and innate musicality instill in these interpretations a timeless quality. Although he never codified his views on articulations in any published description or method, Linder's students universally recall his reference to *fingerspel* (finger playing), or using a leggiero touch in order to make their playing clear. (The master often warned his students not to "burn their fingers on the keys.") Releasing each note before the next is played enables each pitch to be heard cleanly, without any blurring from the release of the previous note or overlapping onto the attack of the following note. The brilliance and clarity that result from finger playing are heard in Linder's many recordings, and though it seems as if he made little distinction between performing early music and ro-

19. Lang, review, 424.

mantic music, the small articulations are especially apparent in his renditions of music by Bach and Buxtehude. Each note is clearly released before the next is depressed, producing great clarity in the execution of the polyphonic lines. Judith Linder feels that many contemporary organists have misunderstood her husband's touch at the organ. "They think that he played everything staccato, but this isn't right. He had a unique way of playing the organ—fantastic hands that could do anything."[20] Probably this exaggeration is due to the great difference between Linder's articulation and the prevailing legato style of late romanticism that characterized the Bach and Buxtehude performances of Linder's Danish counterpart, Finn Viderø. It is easy to understand how Linder's clearly articulated polyphony may have sounded completely detached to ears that were accustomed to the smooth, not to say thick, touch of this relentlessly legato style of playing.

There is no concrete evidence for the origin of the *fingerspel* technique in Linder's studies. He greatly admired Olsson's brilliant executions on the organ in Gustaf Vasa Church, and he may have developed *fingerspel* to emulate him. It is also possible that Linder learned the technique from his greatly admired piano teacher at the Royal Academy in Stockholm, Lennart Lundberg. One of the first assignments Linder set for Hambraeus during the mid-1940s was to play Bach's two- and three-part inventions on the piano with the light *fingerspel* touch, and Erik Boström, who studied with Linder from 1967 to 1975, recalls that Linder frequently compared organ and piano technique, considering them to be the same. Perhaps Heitmann advocated this type of approach in his careful articulations of Bach's music. Linder felt that Ramin and Heitmann inhabited two very different worlds: Ramin's was one of temperament and emotion, while Heitmann was concerned with detail and clarity.[21] This is very much in keeping with what we know of each man's influence on Linder, Ramin evoking the *Affekt* of each work through greatly contrasted registrations, and Heitmann performing the large Bach collections for organ with analytical precision.

Whatever its origins, the *fingerspel* technique was especially revolutionary for organ playing in Sweden in the 1940s, because it went against the dictates of modern legato, developed during the course of the nineteenth century, where no note in a melodic line is released until the next note is played, creating a smooth passage from the attack of one note to the attack of the next without the small decrescendo that results from hearing each note's release. Historical documents suggest that over time an increasingly close articulation between notes was used, so that techniques akin to Linder's *fingerspel* are documented in early sources. Surviving sixteenth-century treatises suggest that the usual touch allowed the attacks and releases of each note to be heard. Santa María explains in *L'arte de tañer fantasia*:

20. Telephone interview with Judith Linder, 6 January 2000.
21. Erik Boström's reminiscence; telephone interview, 10 January 2000.

In the striking of the fingers on the keys, one should always lift the finger that has first struck before striking with the one immediately following, both ascending and descending. And one should always proceed thus, for otherwise the fingers will overtake one another, and with this overtaking of the fingers, the tones will overlap and cover one another as if one were striking 2nds. From such overlapping and covering up of one tone by another, it follows that whatever one plays will be muddy and slovenly, and neither purity nor distinctness of tones is achieved.[22]

This concern with clarity is echoed through the centuries, but rarely is the desirable relationship between notes so explicitly stated. Each note is fully released before the next is played; this seems to have been the predominant articulation to be used in music composed before the nineteenth century.

Of course Linder was not trained in musicology, as the disciplines of academic music history and practical musical performance were pursued in separate academic institutions in Sweden (and indeed throughout Europe) until the 1980s, and the basis for much of Linder's playing was an intuitive desire for clarity and musical phrasing rather than historical sources on performance practice. Indeed, he seemed calmly indifferent to the possibilities for performance practice that were suggested by musicological inquiry. In a review of Linder's Buxtehude recordings at Skänninge, Hambraeus was critical of the way in which the sectional forms in the Buxtehude praeludia were interpreted, without bringing out the symmetrical structures and their relationship to the *Werkprinzip* plans of northern German instruments.[23] "Linder—who was no musicologist, and may not even have read the writings of classical theorists—just remarked, after having read my article: 'Yes, of course that is a possible alternative to what I did.' "[24] To be fair, Hambraeus was one of the first to identify the chiasmus as a constitutional formal structure in the North German *Werkorgel* repertoire,[25] but Linder does not appear to have been interested in staying abreast of new analyses of the repertoire that he performed or theories of interpretation resulting from these. He was the consummate performer of the time, who made decisions intuitively according to an overarching musical aesthetic that had been instilled, at least partly, from his studies with Olsson, Ramin and Heitmann.

Instead of citing historical texts to describe articulation at the organ, Linder urged his students to think of orchestral instruments when phrasing the various voices in a Bach work. Hambraeus remembers his comparing the Bach G Major

22. Tomás de Santa María, *Libro llamada arte de tañer fantasia* (Valladolid, 1565; facsimile ed., Heppenheim: Gregg, 1972), fol. 38v; translated by Almonte C. Howell and Warren E. Hultberg as *The Art of Playing the Fantasia* (Pittsburg: Latin American Review, 1991), 97.

23. Bengt Hambraeus, "Buxtehudes Orgelmusik i Noter och Toner," *Musikrevy* 12, no. 1 (1957): 25–26.

24. Fax letter to the author from Bengt Hambraeus, 18 December 1999.

25. Bengt Hambraeus, "Preludium-Fuga-Toccata-Ciacona: en studie kring några formproblem i Buxtehudes orgelmusik," *Svensk tidskrift för musikforskning* 39 (1957): 89–113.

Example 22-1. Dieterich Buxtehude, Praeludium in F♯ Minor (BuxWV 146), mm. 14–16 and 24–26

Prelude and Fugue, BWV 541, to the G Major Brandenburg Concerto, so that the student would imitate at the organ the type of articulation that was heard in the string parts.[26] Linder often equated pedal lines to the bassoon, and suggested that they should be rendered sometimes legato and sometimes staccato. According to Hambraeus, a typical imitation of bassoon articulation occurred in Linder's performance of the spirited pedal part in Bach's chorale *Herr Jesu Christ, dich zu uns wend*, BWV 655. When the pedal line changes to long notes that carry the chorale in bar 52, Linder added a Clairon 4', which was removed for the last three bars, when the pedal line returns to its former motion and figuration.

This orchestral way of thinking is a musical axiom that has informed many different schools of organ playing, and Linder used it to help his students bring out individual contrapuntal voices clearly. Although he did not make many indications in the scores of his students, he always spoke of the importance of enhancing the musical line through careful phrasing. A rare example of his notation of phrasing occurs in the chordal section (bars 14–16 and 24–26) of Buxtehude's F♯ Minor Praeludium, where the dovetailed phrasings between the right and left hands create clarity in the predominantly homophonic texture (example 22-1).[27]

Except in places such as this where he advocated different phrasings to accentuate independent voices, Linder typically phrased through to the downbeat of a bar, rather than adhering strictly to the hierarchy of the beat. (In the repeated sections of Bach's D Minor Fugue, this even affected his manual changes.) Playing through to the downbeat often produces a nice "swing" in his playing, which is sometimes attributed to his work as a pianist in the 1930s with the famous Swedish jazz band led by Frank Vernon. Linder needed the income from this in order to keep himself solvent while living in Stockholm, and after his German and Swedish successes as an organist in the 1940s he never played jazz again

26. Telephone interview with Bengt Hambraeus, 14 December 1999.

27. Linder wrote this phrasing into Bengt Hambraeus's score of the Buxtehude F♯ Minor Praeludium; this was the only specific phrasing of any import revealed in my interviews with former students.

professionally. It is difficult to be specific about how this early experience in the popular realm might have influenced his rhythmic development as an organist. Certainly, his playing of Bach and Buxtehude often exhibits a spontaneity and rhythmic elasticity characteristic of jazz, and students fondly remember experiencing Linder's lighter side when he improvised jazz for relaxation at home or in social settings. He sometimes referred to the role of a double-bass player in the 1930s swing style to help his students achieve a sense of momentum when playing Bach.

Given his intuitive approach to performing early music, it is not surprising that Linder seems to have determined his phrasing and articulation based upon the rhythmic and intervallic structure of the music, rather than according to the hierarchy of the beat. This is heard clearly in the way that he articulated Bach's fugue subjects. In the A Minor Fugue, BWV 543, the subject is rendered as a singing melodic line, played in long phrases with *fingerspel* and detached upbeats. His phrases always transcend the microarticulations of each bar to produce a forward momentum in the music.[28] In the G Minor Fugue, BWV 542, the upbeats are slightly detached, as are the intervals in the descending arpeggios of the subject. The *fingerspel* here produces a clear line that is marked by slight detachments to highlight points of rhythmic and intervallic interest. A very different effect is heard in the subject to the B Minor Fugue, BWV 544, where the conjunct motion of the eighth notes is shaped by rhythmic motion rather than articulation. The lack of detachment in the subject produces a feeling of calm lyricism that contrasts with the more dancelike quality of the G Minor Fugue. A consistently clean touch brings out the melodic contours, while Linder moves ever so slightly toward each downbeat to create rhythmic fluidity.

These qualities of articulation and rhythmic placement are immediately apparent in his performance of the Trio Sonata no. 1 at Leufsta Bruk, where the neo-baroque registrations highlight the clean touch and lilting rhythm. As in the Bach fugue subjects discussed above, the articulations are determined by size of interval and the metric placement of motives. The opening arpeggiations in the first movement (CD track 8) are more detached than the conjunct scale passages following them, highlighting the lively exchange of the motif as it is passed between hands later in the movement. The large intervals in the cadential formulae are similarly detached to delineate the section endings. The articulations are generally tighter for both large and small intervals in the second movement (CD track 9), producing a more lyrical sound that is well adjusted to the incisive speech of the reed registration. In keeping with the brilliant mixture and mutation registrations of the third movement (CD track 10), Linder uses a more

---

28. Erik Boström recalls that Linder suggested to his students that they play only "one beat in a bar"; telephone interview, 10 January 2000.

aggressive touch, with strong attacks and some very sharp releases, creating a sense of great rhythmic drive. These movements are a perfect demonstration of the close relationship between touch and timbre in Linder's organ playing, where the approach to articulation is subtly crafted to bring out the intrinsic qualities in each type of organ sound.

Champion of the New and Respecter of the Old

The musicality and commitment of this style of playing remain compelling today, despite a total upheaval in the concept of organ sound since these recordings were made. This style of playing was an ideal match for the strong, not to say harsh, sounds of the Marcussen organ that was installed in Oscar's Church in 1949, and as such both instrument and performance style are mirrors of an epoch only dimly remembered by young organists today. As shown in the preceding chapter by Bengt Hambraeus, at the time of its installation the Marcussen represented a completely new sound for Swedish audiences, and the public reception was enthusiastic, even if privately some of the critical experts found the voicing to be too direct and forceful. Linder thrived on the new organ, which accommodated his eclectic repertoire. A privileged position for assessing Linder's playing on the new instrument was accorded to Hambraeus, who studied with him as a private organ student from 1944 to 1948 and was later actively involved as a registrant and producer for his recordings until he moved to Canada to take up a teaching position at McGill University in 1972.

Surprisingly, Hambraeus noticed no real change in his teacher's interpretations after the Marcussen was installed.[29] It was as if Linder's approach to playing the organ had already been developed, either in his mind as a musical ideal or as a response to the instruments he had encountered during his studies in Germany. The mechanical action and distinct timbres of the new Marcussen organ at Oscar's Church were perfectly suited to registrations based on the new neo-baroque aesthetic, the action permitting greater control over the articulation and the bright sounds fulfilling the desire for clarity through registration.[30] The novelty of the organ and Linder's approach to playing had great impact on the organ community in Stockholm, who felt that something very strange and new was going on at Oscar's Church. Even while the old Åkerman & Lund organ was in use during Linder's first years as organist there, other organists in the city sometimes warned their students against being influenced by Linder's approach to

29. Telephone interview with Bengt Hambraeus, 23 December 1999.

30. Linder did not approve of Dupré's methods and discouraged his students from practicing on electropneumatic actions; telephone interview with Erik Boström, 10 Jan. 2000.

articulation and registration.[31] This situation gradually changed as the new style was assimilated by younger organists. The impact of the new organ was strengthened by Linder's crucial role as a teacher. He had been appointed to the prestigious position as professor of organ at the Academy of Music in 1945, the same year he became titular organist at Oscar's Church. From this time on, almost every serious young Swedish organist was required to study with him, and the Marcussen organ thus obtained a place of privilege in the training of Swedish church musicians.

Yet Linder was not swept away by the success of the new movement to the extent that he wanted to make every organ in Sweden imitate the Marcussen at Oscar's Church. A close friend of the Swedish organologist Einar Erici, he recognized the need to preserve old organs without altering them to suit changing trends in organ design and construction. As described in Lewenhaupt's anecdote at the beginning of this chapter, Linder said very little, but when he did voice an opinion, his words bore the weight of authority. In addition to saving the pneumatic organs in Småland, he helped to rescue much older organs from modification by performing on them to demonstrate their innate beauty and musical value. Some of these were one-manual instruments that were deemed inadequate for modern use by the propaganda of the 1930s. Linder played concerts on these organs and showed local organists and their congregations that under the right hands, small historical organs could rival and even surpass the musical charms of much larger instruments. Linder's performance of Bach's G Major Fantasy on the one-manual organ at Målilla in 1949 was one of his most inspired performances of that work, and it was vital in saving that instrument.[32]

Even when confronted with the late-romantic organ from 1905 in the St. Petri Church, Västervik, Linder defended the importance of maintaining the instrument in its original state. During the 1960s this type of organ was very frequently "modernized" in an attempt to bring the sonorities in line with the prevailing neo-baroque aesthetic. Yet although the style of the Västervik organ was neither popular nor one that appealed directly to the playing technique or interests of Alf Linder, he was its savior in 1964, when he accompanied Axel Unnerbäck of the National Board of Antiquities on a trip to examine the instrument. With an almost prescient insight into the need to preserve the integrity of old organs despite intervening changes in musical taste, Linder argued that the old instrument should be moved intact to another gallery and that a completely new organ be built to satisfy the congregation. His suggestion was fol-

31. Hambraeus remembers Eric Ericson making this remark; telephone interview with Bengt Hambraeus, 14 December 1999.

32. Anecdote related by Axel Unnerbäck on 8 January 2000 to participants of GOArt's January symposium, Göteborg.

lowed, and now, thanks to Alf Linder, the romantic organ, in its original state, is greatly appreciated in that church.[33]

While zealously preserving the organ's past, Linder was also keenly aware of the need for change and innovation to keep the instrument alive in today's society. Although his own work with contemporary music did not encompass the avant-garde of the Darmstadt school and its disciples, he urged his students to stay abreast of developments in organ repertoire. Despite his perfect accord with the instrument he helped to design, he understood the importance of altering its design to make it more flexible for the next generation, as stated in his report to the parochial committee of Oscar's Church in 1976 (see chapter 21). This document, written when Linder was sixty-nine years of age, reflects his view of the organ as an ever-changing instrument, designed to mirror the changing musical needs of society at large, rather than the whims and dictates of any one individual or musical aesthetic. Perhaps more than any specific aspect of his own playing, it is this enlightened commitment to furthering the organ as a vital representative of the larger musical world that marks him as a true innovator.

33. Unnerbäck, anecdote.

23

FROM DARMSTADT TO STOCKHOLM: TRACING THE SWEDISH CONTRIBUTION TO THE DEVELOPMENT OF A NEW ORGAN STYLE

MARTIN HERCHENRÖDER

IT IS 4 MAY 1962. IN A STUDIO OF THE BROADCASTING STATION OF RADIO BREMEN, seven young men (figure 23-1) are bowing to an audience that has been listening to the first performances of some new compositions, among them three organ pieces: *Interferenser* by Bengt Hambraeus, *Improvisation ajoutée* by Mauricio Kagel, and *Volumina* by György Ligeti. The audience senses it has witnessed a historic event. As the music critic Wolf-Eberhard von Lewinski stated some weeks later, the young composers' approach to the organ was "really new—much more revolutionary than anything Messiaen has attempted in this field."[1]

One of the most striking novelties was a new compositional material: clusters, dense masses of tones without any melodic outline, often sounding like electronic music or even noise. In order to realize these clusters the organist had to change his playing technique into a spectacular use of palms, fists, hands, and arms. Another innovation was the use of reduced wind pressure—*Volumina*, for example, dies away in a long, seemingly never-ending diminuendo of a sustained cluster after the fan motor has already been turned off. There was also the occasional transfer of the action from the keys to the register stops: while tones, chords or clusters were sustained on the manuals, vivid register tremolos or a slight shifting from one flute to another changed their colors.

Indeed, the Bremen concert has since been recognized as the beginning of a new era of organ composition. In order to understand this, it is useful to look briefly at the development of organ music during the decades before and after 1945.

1. Wolf-Eberhard von Lewinski, "Die Orgel als Elefant oder Königin," *Christ und Welt* 15, no. 22 (1962): 20.

Figure 23-1. Radio Bremen concert, 4 May 1962; left to right, Hans Otte, Mauricio Kagel, György Ligeti, Bengt Hambraeus (composers); Karl-Erik Welin (organist), Bo Nilsson, Giuseppe G. Englert (assistants). Printed with kind permission of Bengt Hambraeus.

Organ Music between 1916 and 1961

With only a few exceptions, organ music since the time of Max Reger had lost its connection to the general development of advanced music—most of the innovative and important composers had not written any solo compositions for the instrument. Several factors contributed to this, one of which seems to have been the close connection of the organ to the church (as a room and therefore as an institution). Since the Enlightenment, the ties between artists and the church had gradually loosened, but most organs were still located in churches. So composers without a personal interest in religion had no alternative but to avoid the instrument if they wanted also to avoid connotations of religion in their works.

Meanwhile, specific historical developments in France and in Germany (both of them with effects on other European countries) had produced styles of organ music that had no relation to advanced contemporary music. In France, where organ composers mostly were organists and therefore pupils of the preceding generation of organist-composers (such as Alexandre Guilmant, Charles-Marie Widor, and Marcel Dupré), new compositions were for a long time conceived in the late-romantic, symphonic organ style; the works of Charles Tournemire, Maurice Duruflé, and even the early pieces of Olivier Messiaen show this quite clearly. In Germany, the organ reform movement, which had rediscovered the tonal beauty and technical quality of baroque and Renaissance organs, at the same time ideologically favored the opinion that new organ compositions, in order to be organ music at all, had to be oriented toward a quasi-baroque tonal and contrapuntal style. A neo-baroque, historicizing organ music consequently evolved and led the instrument into what Werner Jacob has called a "contrapuntal ghetto,"[2] without any connection to the advanced music composed at the same time.

One very important reason for the extensive lack of advanced organ music during the first half of the twentieth century, however, was the organ itself—mainly the fact that every change of registers affects a whole manual with all voices and chords, making it impossible to change sound, timbre, and dynamics gradually and independently from one another. Such restrictions made György Ligeti, referring to his motivation for composing *Volumina*, compare the instrument to a "gigantic artificial limb" with which he wanted to "learn to walk again."[3] Arnold Schoenberg had already complained that on the organ it was impossible to change the volume of a single tone or a musical phrase gradually, as on a violin or a flute. This lack of flexibility became crucial after 1950, when the postwar musical avant-garde came together in the German city of Darmstadt every summer and formulated a new system of aesthetics, compositional technique, and style that today is referred to as serialism. The main idea was that all the relevant elements of a piece of music—the parameters (pitch, rhythm, harmony, dynamics, timbre, density of events, etc.)—should be organized on the basis of the same series, a set of predetermined relations between musical events, generally expressed by rows of numbers. The method was derived from Schoenberg's twelve-tone technique, which arranges the twelve pitches of the equal-tempered octave by a pitch row comprising all twelve tones in a defined order[4] that determines the melodic and harmonic outline of a composition. If all the parameters of a piece are organized by the same row, they become structurally linked to each other, so that such a composition results in an extremely coherent network of relations. The effect of this procedure can be that the determination of every parameter changes from tone to tone, meaning that the performer has to realize a new degree of intensity and a new color for each musical event. It

---

2. Werner Jacob, "Der Beitrag von Bengt Hambraeus zur Entwicklung der neuen Orgelmusik," in *Orgel im Gottesdienst Heute: Drittes Colloquium der Walcker-Stiftung 1974*, ed. H. H. Eggebrecht (Stuttgart: Musikwissenschaftliche Verlagsgesellschaft mbH., 1975), 97.

3. György Ligeti, "Die Orgel sprengt die Tradition," *Melos* 33 (1966): 311.

4. For example, if one counts upward from C (= 1), the first four tones of a twelve-tone row beginning with the famous B-A-C-H motive are expressed by the numbers 11–10–1–12 (in German, B is the term for B♭ and H is the term for B♮.

is clear that the organ, in which changes of volume are coupled to changes of timbre, is not an adequate instrument for this method, and so almost none of the serial composers, such as Pierre Boulez and Karlheinz Stockhausen, were interested in it. In fact, Stockhausen made this explicit in one of his letters to me some years ago: "My organ pieces are written for synthesizer."

Olivier Messiaen

Composers were inspired to use the serial technique to organize musical elements other than pitch by the revolutionary approach to rhythm developed in the 1930s and 1940s by the French composer Olivier Messiaen. His analysis of rhythmical structures in works of Igor Stravinsky and research on Greek and Hindu rhythms led him to an astonishing and innovative variety of rhythmical techniques based on the addition of small values to larger ones to form rhythmical proportions of high complexity, a mathematical procedure ready to be used for serial purposes. In his piano etude *Mode de valeurs et d'intensités*, written and performed for the first time during his stay at Darmstadt in the summer of 1949, Messiaen applied quasi-serial methods to pitch, rhythm, volume, and attack, thus creating a composition that worked as a catalyst for serial music. He himself, however, never became a purely serial composer—in all of his pieces there is some use, often extensive, of freely invented and combined elements, such as transcribed bird calls or passages of tonal or modal harmony.

Unlike most other avant-garde composers, Messiaen was an organist and thus very interested in the organ and in trying to apply new compositional techniques to his instrument. He contributed many interesting works to the organ repertoire, written in a very personal and undogmatic musical language. His most innovative pieces date from the early 1950s; the cycles *Messe de la Pentecôte* (1950) and *Livre d'orgue* (1951) experiment with new rhythmical techniques (among them quasi-serial ones), several methods of pitch organization (among them non–serially organized twelve-tone complexes), and unusual registrations. In the long period between Reger's death and the Radio Bremen concert, Messiaen's organ works are almost the only ones that demonstrate close contact with contemporary advanced music.

He did not consistently pursue the path he had begun in these two cycles, however; his next organ works (beginning with *Verset pour la Fête de la Dédicace*, 1961) mix advanced compositional techniques with elements of the more traditional musical language from his earlier works. And as no organ pieces by other composers evoked any remarkable public interest until 1962, Wolf-Eberhard von Lewinski's statement suggesting that there was no direct connection between Messiaen's organ works of the 1950s and the compositions performed for the first time on 4 May 1962 seemed to be an adequate description of the situation.

Example 23-1. Bengt Hambraeus, *Permutations and Hymn*, twelve-tone row

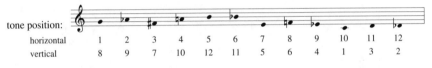

tone position:												
horizontal	1	2	3	4	5	6	7	8	9	10	11	12
vertical	8	9	7	10	12	11	5	6	4	1	3	2

Bengt Hambraeus

Today, looking back, we can see that there are indeed links between *Livre d'orgue* and *Volumina*, but the language of organ music was changing in the shadow of the rapid and exciting development of avant-garde music as a whole, so the process was difficult to observe. This change is related to Oscar's Church in Stockholm and to Marcussen organs in Sweden.

In 1944 a young man began to study with Alf Linder, the organist at Oscar's Church in Stockholm: Bengt Hambraeus, at that time sixteen years old. By 1948, when Hambraeus left Stockholm and his teacher in order to study musicology at Uppsala University, he had not only become acquainted with a great variety of baroque and romantic organ music but had also composed some of his own pieces, inspired by the old Åkerman & Lund organ in Oscar's Church, where some of them had their first performances—a sonata, a toccata with fugue, a chorale partita, a trio, and several other works. During his Linder years his compositional style had changed from a late-romantic idiom to a contrapuntal, tonal, and sometimes modal but more dissonant Hindemith-oriented language, which became harmonically richer and more and more independent in the following years.

But Hambraeus wanted to know more about the actual development of contemporary music. So in 1951 he decided to travel to one of the focal points of contemporary music of those years and attend the Darmstadt summer courses for the first time, returning each summer for the next four years. There, in 1952 he met Olivier Messiaen. His experiences at the center of the avant-garde had a direct influence on his compositional style; he began to experiment with serial techniques, and as a consequence, works written in those years are very close to the mainstream of Darmstadt aesthetics—for example, *Spectrogram* for soprano and three instruments (1953) and *Giuoco del cambio* for chamber ensemble (1954).

The new approach had an effect on Hambraeus's organ style, too; one can see this in his first completed organ work after his initial contact with Darmstadt, *Permutations and Hymn (Nocte surgentes)*, a piece he wrote in 1953. Its beginning is based on a twelve-tone row (example 23-1). The characteristics of this row can be determined by two series of numbers: one shows the horizontal order in which the tones appear (line 1), while the other shows the vertical position of every tone on the chromatic scale (line 2; C = 1). The melodic outline of the

Example 23-2. Bengt Hambraeus, *Permutations and Hymn*, first permutation

Example 23-3. Bengt Hambraeus, *Permutations and Hymn*, second permutation

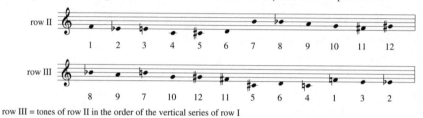

row III = tones of row II in the order of the vertical series of row I

tone row is mirrored in the second series, in which the difference between two consecutive numbers reflects the size of the corresponding interval. In order to generate further material for longer musical developments, Hambraeus applied a procedure of permutations to his row: by reading the tones of the original row (I) in the order of the vertical series instead of the horizontal one, he generated a new horizontal order for the twelve tones in row II (example 23-2). If one renumbers this new row II from 1 to 12 as a horizontal series, one can repeat the same procedure of permutations, thus getting a third row (example 23-3), from the third a fourth one, and so on, for as long as one likes, guaranteeing coherence and variation at the same time. It is this permutation technique that Hambraeus uses for *Permutations and Hymn*, as one can see even in its opening measures (figure 23-2). Here the original row (I) appears in the pedals (doubled as in organum, starting from C♯ and G simultaneously) combined with the first permutation (= row II) in the right hand and the second permutation (= row III) in the left.

The permutation technique used in this organ piece shows a direct Darmstadt influence: It applies the compositional system of "interversion" used by Olivier Messiaen in two sections of his piano etude *Île de Feu II*, which the composer had explained to his Scandinavian student during the summer course in 1952. But there is an interesting difference: as in *Mode de valeurs et d'intensités*, Messiaen applies the procedure of permutation also to the rhythm (namely twelve "chromatic" durations of a length from one to twelve sixteenths), the dynamics (five degrees), and the attacks (four nuances), thus creating quasi-serial passages. Hambraeus, however, restricts the serial organization in his organ piece to the

Figure 23-2. Bengt Hambraeus, *Permutations and Hymn* (manuscript, 1953), beginning. Printed with kind permission of the composer.

pitches. Instead of composing a network of serial relations between different parameters, he introduces, in a second part, a tonal cantus firmus: an old hymn, *Nocte surgentes*, contrapuntally accompanied as in a traditional chorale prelude by further twelve-tone complexes. Twelve-tone method and serial permutation technique are only tools, working together in a context comprising modern and historical material and techniques. If the composition *Permutations and Hymn* reflects Hambraeus's Darmstadt experience, it also shows that the young Swedish composer had kept his artistic independence and a genuine curiosity; in *Nocte surgentes* he experiments with the combination of heterogeneous material in order to find an answer to the question of how to integrate advanced contemporary compositional techniques with the demands of liturgy. It was this independence and curiosity that proved fruitful in a field that became his main focus of interest and artistic research at that time, one that was to open a new dimension for organ composition: his interest in sound.

While writing *Permutations and Hymn,* Hambraeus began to experiment with the possibilities of organ timbres. Although he did not complete further organ compositions before 1958, two fragments have survived from those years: *Etude pour orgue* (1952) and *Composizione per organo* (1953). Here we find pitch permutation techniques comparable to those in *Permutations and Hymn,* but the pieces also try out new sound combinations and new techniques of sound organization by means of unconventional register combinations, mainly *Spaltklang* or gap registrations, such as 16′ + 2′, 16′ + 1′, or 32′ + 2′, and colorful new mixture combinations such as 8′, 5⅓′, 2′, 1⅓′. Two sources of inspiration can

Figure 23-3. Bengt Hambraeus, *Etude pour orgue* (manuscript, 1956), beginning. Printed with kind permission of the composer.

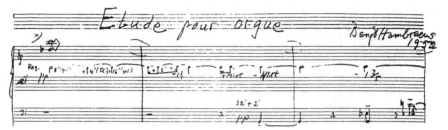

be identified for these registrations—the sometimes exquisite colors in Messiaen's works, especially the organ cycles of the early 1950s, and, perhaps even more important, the influence of Ernst Karl Rössler, a German clergyman and organ scholar who had developed a theory about organ sound and registration during the 1940s.[5] But another innovation is of greater importance: *Etude pour orgue* begins with a sustained manual cluster that changes its color in a determined rhythm (see figure 23-3). This idea was revolutionary because it marks the emancipation of timbre, in two respects. First, the use of a manual cluster as compositional material was new to the field of organ music. It goes beyond what Messiaen employed in his two avant-garde organ cycles, although the compositional aim is comparable to Messiaen's concept of complex chords generating specific sound colors. But beyond that, the registration of this sustained cluster changes according to a determined rhythm, and one can understand this as a completely original application of Schoenberg's idea of *Klangfarbenmelodie* to the organ. It is also a radical interpretation of the independence of musical elements propagated in the aesthetics of serialism. The parameter of timbre was not only treated independently from the other parameters; for several moments it was the only parameter to be treated at all. However, Hambraeus's method was not at this point a serial one. So today, as clearly as we see the Darmstadt influence in these fragments, we recognize at the same time that the composer had begun to pursue his own artistic aims.

Hambraeus's research on sound was not abstract mathematical speculation; these fragments reflect his concrete experience with a specific instrument. This instrument was the organ in the Göteborg Concert Hall, built in 1936–37 by the Danish organ-building firm of Marcussen & Søn. Hambraeus writes about it some forty-five years later: "In those years, the Göteborg Concert Hall organ had unique possibilities for acoustical experiments and was the only instrument in Sweden that would permit more advanced sonorities to be developed in a new

5. Ernst Karl Rössler, *Klangfunktion und Registrierung* (Kassel: Bärenreiter, 1952).

organ style and repertoire; it also featured some of the advanced criteria in the major organs built by Cavaillé-Coll in the middle of the nineteenth century."[6]

These possibilities comprised first the vast diversity of stops from 32' to 1', then the sonic balance, the possibility of producing nearly unlimited combinations between linguals and labials, fundamentals, overtone mutations, and mixtures. Already showing a slight touch of the organ reform movement while still strongly oriented toward a sonic ideal close to that of Cavaillé-Coll's later organs, the instrument integrated characteristics of different aesthetics in an organic whole. This feature seems to have been typical of the Marcussen organs in Sweden built in the first half of this century, among them the new instrument built in the Stockholm Oscar's Church, for which Hambraeus had written in 1949 the compositions *Introitus et Triptychon* and *Partita in Tempore Adventus*.

Six years after his first experiments at the Göteborg organ, Hambraeus conceived a new organ piece where all the experiences reflected in the two fragments came together: *Constellations I*. This composition, joining several short parts in a kaleidoscopic form, is clearly determined by the predominance of sound: complex, colorful chords and registrations are to be heard, sometimes almost sounding like electronic music; the listener witnesses the change of color of a sustained tone (as in *Etude pour orgue*); two asynchronously moving swell pedals shift the sonic components of a chord combined of stops from two different manuals. The change in aesthetic paradigms could not have been clearer; the composer no longer predetermined or organized the sonic material, but analyzed, by means of musical form, its possibilities and characteristics. Serialism had changed to sound composition.

György Ligeti

One year later, in the summer of 1959, Bo Wallner presented *Constellations I*, which Hambraeus meanwhile had recorded on tape, during a special "Swedish Evening" at the Darmstadt summer courses.[7] In the audience was a young Hungarian composer who had left his country after the revolt in the autumn of 1956 and who since then had lived in Germany and Austria: György Ligeti (b. 1923). One year before, Ligeti had published a detailed and critical analysis of Boulez's serial piece *Structure Ia*[8] that contributed to his reputation as a brilliant analyst in questions of contemporary aesthetics and compositional technique. During

6. Bengt Hambraeus, *Aspects of Twentieth Century Performance Practice: Memories and Reflections* (Stockholm: Royal Swedish Academy of Music, 1997), 121.

7. Gunnar Valkare, "Schwedens Leitstern im Neue-Musik-Mekka," in *Von Kranichstein zur Gegenwart: 50 Jahre Darmstädter Beiträge zur Musik*, ed. Rudolf Stephan, Lothar Knessl, Otto Tomek, Klaus Trapp, and Christopher Fox (Stuttgart: Daco-Verlag, 1996), 289–94.

8. György Ligeti, "Pierre Boulez: Entscheidung und Automatik in der *Structure Ia*," *Die Reihe* 4 (1958): 38–63.

this summer Ligeti developed close contacts with the Swedish group of Darmstadt travelers, and as a result he was invited to give a composition class at the
Stockholm Conservatory. His first lecture took place in April 1961, and it was
such a success that he was asked to return regularly.[9] Of course, during his visits
he came in contact with the Swedish musical avant-garde. Among this group
was Bengt Hambraeus, whose *Constellations I* Ligeti had heard in Darmstadt and
whom he had come to know a year before at the International Society for Contemporary Music festival in Cologne.

When Hans Otte, then head of the contemporary music department of Radio
Bremen, asked Ligeti and Hambraeus to contribute new organ works for a concert to take place in 1962 as part of the Radio Bremen series *pro musica nova*,
they came together and discussed new possibilities of organ composition. It must
have been a fascinating meeting. Ligeti had just left the Darmstadt mainstream
with his two sensational pieces *Apparitions* (1958–59) and *Atmosphères* (1961),
two orchestral compositions that consist mainly of elaborately varied clusters.
Hambraeus had meanwhile continued working on the *Constellations* material,
and two new pieces had come into being: the tape composition *Constellations II*
(1959), which used the recording Hambraeus had made of the first piece as
basic material to combine with electronic music, and *Constellations III* (1961).
This work combines the tape of *Constellations II* with a new layer of organ music
to be performed live, making it the first piece in the history of organ music to
combine organ and prerecorded tape. The piece employs sustained and moving
clusters as well. Ligeti could make use of the results Hambraeus had achieved
during his research in the 1950s to help solve the problem of transferring his
own sonic ideas to the specific possibilities of the organ. Ligeti points to this
fact when he writes with respect to *Volumina* that he had been "stimulated by
Constellations I, which is pioneering for the creation of a new organ style."[10]

Karl-Erik Welin and Bo Nilsson

Hambraeus had been asked to play the first performances of the new compositions for Radio Bremen, but for various reasons he had to refuse. He suggested
a young colleague to take his place: Karl-Erik Welin (1934–92). Welin—a pianist
and organist, a former organ student of Alf Linder, and at that time working
closely with Hambraeus at the Swedish Broadcasting Corporation—had been
deeply impressed by the unconventional and virtuoso piano technique of David
Tudor, one of the most influential personalities of the new music scene of that
time. Consequently he had devoted himself, like Tudor, to the interpretation and

9. Wolfgang Burde, *György Ligeti* (Zürich: Atlantis, 1993), 73.
10. Ligeti, "Die Orgel sprengt," 311.

propagation of contemporary music. Together with Hambraeus he had developed new playing techniques for the organ, especially for the performance of clusters. The great importance of Welin's research for the development of a new organ style can be seen as well in his early collaboration with Bo Nilsson (b. 1937).

Nilsson was one of the Swedish composers who had traveled several times to Darmstadt during the late 1950s and probably the only one other than Hambraeus who had won high international acclaim. In 1956, encouraged by Hambraeus, he wrote a three-minute piece for organ, *Spiralen und Kulissen*, which proved to be unsuitable for the instrument, as it went beyond its ambitus and demanded nineteen dynamic nuances as well as crescendi and diminuendi from *ffff* to *pppp* with unchanged registrations both in manuals and pedals. Some years later Karl-Erik Welin, while elaborating an organ adaptation of Nilsson's piano piece *Quantitäten* (1958),[11] asked Nilsson to write a new organ work for him, "a work such as up to now only I have been able to play, with the same notation system as Stockhausen uses in *Zyklus*"[12] Nilsson sent him the score of *Stenogramme*, a piece originally written for percussion on a commission for the South German radio station Südwestfunk but rejected because of its graphic notation.[13] Welin specialized in the interpretation of graphic scores, and in 1960 he elaborated Nilsson's work on the organ with fireworks of clusters. In August of the same year, in a concert at Visby Cathedral, he played the first performance.

Whereas the manuscript of Nilsson's piece seems to be lost,[14] Welin's interpretation (or perhaps one should say one of Welin's interpretations) has survived on a recording from 1965.[15] The recording shows the completely developed cluster technique that was necessary to perform works such as *Volumina* and *Interferenzen*. This recording makes it clear that Welin, too, could advise Ligeti on how to realize his ideas.[16]

11. The composition is regarded as serial; cf. Hanspeter Krellmann, "Unmögliches als Höchstmaß des Möglichen: Der vergessene Avantgardist Bo Nilsson," *Musica* 28 (1974): 329–32. Welin performed his organ version for the first time on 3 Jan. 1960 during a concert he gave in St. Petri Church, Malmö.

12. According to Gunnar Valkare, *Det audiografiska fältet: Om musikens förhållande till skriften och den unge Bo Nilssons strategier*, Skrifter från Musikvetenskapliga avdelningen, no. 49 (Göteborg: Göteborg University, 1997), 205. Concerning *Spiralen und Kulissen*, see also 241–43.

13. The term "graphic notation" generally refers to a type of score that does not use musical symbols (e.g., notes, rests, etc.) or any other signs referring to concrete musical events, but graphic elements meant to evoke musical situations in the reader's mind and stimulate the performer's musical actions.

14. See Hambraeus, *Aspects*, 181. Nilsson was so enthusiastic about Welin's interpretation that he allowed only him to perform the piece, and he buried the score in a coffin in order to prevent other performers from playing it, according to Louis Christensen, "A Swedish School of New Organ Music," *NUMUS West* 1 (Apr. 1972): 17.

15. Artist LP 102; reissued in 1997 on the Phono Suecia, PSCD 105–2; there the piece is spelled *Stenogramm*.

16. Ligeti mentions Welin's contribution to the preparation of *Volumina* in "Die Orgel sprengt," 311.

A "New Organ Style"

When the works commissioned by Radio Bremen were presented to the public in May 1962, almost nobody knew (or could know) that the new organ style had developed over a ten-year period from Messiaen's experiments of the early 1950s. Today we can identify a bridge between *Livre d'orgue* and *Improvisation ajoutée, Interferenzen*, and *Volumina*. We can see that the revolution in organ music had already been prepared, that indeed it had begun earlier; it had been a step-by-step revolution (or perhaps an evolution) beginning in the work of Bengt Hambraeus and later worked out further between Hambraeus, Ligeti, and Welin.

In any event, the process had finally resulted in an important and prominent change of aesthetics and compositional technique, a shift from serial (or quasi-serial) composition to sound composition; the step from Darmstadt to Stockholm had generated a new organ style. It must have been this outstanding change of paradigms that the audience noticed immediately. Comparing the beginning (Messiaen) with the end (Hambraeus, Mauricio Kagel, and Ligeti) of the process, the public believed that they had witnessed a revolution.[17]

Although this "revolution" has perceptible roots, it was indeed the beginning of a new era of enthusiasm for the organ, and the beginning therefore of a new era of organ composition. There are several reasons for this. First of all, the concert mirrored the generally growing interest in the nature of sound that had already been present in Ligeti's preceding orchestral works and that was to become one of the most important fields of research and experimentation in the music of the 1960s. The concert, in a sense, signaled a general paradigmatic shift; composers became interested in the organ as they became interested, for example, in the treble recorder, the harpsichord, the accordion, or electronic music, because it promised to be an as-yet unexploited terrain of immense sound possibilities. A second reason was certainly the radio's mass audience; the Bremen pieces were preserved on tape and could be broadcast everywhere in Europe.

Much of the immediate public interest in the Bremen concert may also have to do with the fact that it was accompanied by a spectacular scandal: the broadcasting station had planned, together with the Protestant community, for the concert to take place in Bremen Cathedral. A few days before the agreed-upon date, the church authorities, anxious that the music might create a scandal in the cathedral, vetoed the concert. As the Bremen broadcasting station did not

---

17. The most specific contribution of *Improvisation ajoutée* to the advanced organ music is the addition of vocal sounds (coughing, laughing, whistling, etc.), thus enlarging the range of (and at the same time questioning) the organ sound; for this typical Kagel idea there seem to be no models.

come up with another suitable venue, the pieces had to be recorded on tape in order to be presented in a room of the broadcasting house, and Hambraeus, who was working as a producer for the Swedish Broadcasting Corporation, arranged a recording session in the Göteborg Concert Hall. But when Welin tried to play the tremendous beginning of *Volumina*—a *fff* cluster covering the whole manual and some pedal keys—on the old Marcussen organ, some vital fuses blew and the organ was rendered completely unusable; the recording project had to be transferred to Stockholm, where it was realized in two churches, St. John and Gustaf Vasa. The rumor that the piece had "burned down" the Göteborg organ, kindled further by Ligeti's ironic comments in the introduction to his composition during the concert, made the new pieces famous overnight: the avant-garde had made the organs burn![18]

Finally, one very important reason for the vivid impact of this concert seems to have been the zeal with which Karl-Erik Welin[19] promoted the new organ pieces. Welin played the Bremen compositions over and over again, and more recordings followed. Many composers began to hear about the new organ style and got an impression of the newly discovered sonic possibilities. The immense and international impact of Welin's engagement is reflected in a considerable number of compositions connected with his name. Among the works dedicated to him are Giuseppe G. Englert (Switzerland/France), *Palaestra 64 pro organo* (1964); Bengt Hambraeus (Sweden), *Interferenzen* (1961–62) and *Shogaku* (1967); Erhard Karkoschka (West Germany), *hinter einem marschrhythmus* (1971); György Ligeti (Hungary/Austria), *Volumina* (1961–62); and Tomás Marco (Spain), *Astrolabio* (1969–70).

Jan W. Morthenson

Welin's importance for the development of a new organ style becomes obvious in the interesting and inventive early organ works of the Swedish composer Jan W. Morthenson (b. 1940). Two of them, namely *Some of these . . .* (1961, rev. 1963) and *Encores* (1962, rev. 1973), are written in an action notation that leaves a great amount of freedom to the organist. Welin, at that time perhaps the only specialist in the interpretations of such scores on the organ, was the ideal performer, and it was for him that Morthenson had conceived them. The perfor-

18. For a detailed description and analysis of the story and its variants described by different sources, see Martin Herchenröder, *Struktur und Assoziation: György Ligetis Orgelwerke* (Schönau: Österreichisches Orgelforum, 1999), 29–33.

19. Later he was followed by other organists, including Gerd Zacher, Werner Jacob, Zsigmond Szathmáry, and Friedemann Herz in Germany, William Albright in the United States, Bernard Foccroulle, in Belgium, Xavier Darasse in France, and Erik Boström, Hans-Ola Ericsson, and Hans Hellsten in Sweden.

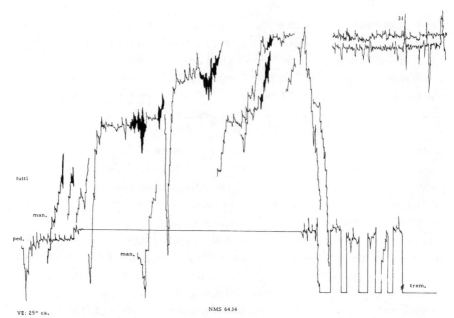

Figure 23-4. Jan W. Morthenson, *Encores*, p. VII. From his *New Organ Music,* ©
1974 AB Nordiska Musikförlaget, Stockholm. Printed by permission of Ehrlingförlagen
AB, Stockholm.

mance of Morthenson's *Encores* (figure 23-4) makes it necessary to change
quickly between cluster play with fists and palms (black-colored spots) and finger
play (oscillating black lines).

Morthenson's compositions *Pour Madame Bovary* (1962, rev. 1973) and *Éternes* (1964, rev. 1973) venture into the unknown land of disturbed sound. They
are both written for organs with mechanical stop action and are performed mainly
with the register stop knobs, while the keys are held down with weights, wedges,
or tape and change only over long intervals of time. The stop knobs have to be
pulled fully or partially, according to a scale from A (fully drawn stop, normal
sound) to E (stop pushed back, no sound), with B, C, and D indicating different
degrees of disturbed intonation. Often, this procedure leads to complex sounds,
mixtures of overtones, and noiselike components. In addition, in *Éternes* the wind
pressure is differentiated so that the air supply of the organ varies—a technique
that radically affects intonation and produces sounds that resemble electronic
music.

Morthenson was no organist; it is highly probable that these ideas were developed in close collaboration with Karl-Erik Welin, who played both premieres
(*Pour Madame Bovary* on 13 October 1962, Great Church [Storkyrkan], Stock-

Figure 23-5. Bengt Hambraeus. Photograph by Michael Hambraeus, 1990.

holm; *Éternes* on 16 June 1964, Uppsala Cathedral).[20] And it may even be that through Welin the sonic ideas realized here found their way to György Ligeti, whose first organ etude, *Harmonies* (1967), also uses reduced wind pressure, thus deforming the harmonic process of the piece into a foggy sound mass.[21]

Back to Oscar's Church

It is perhaps no coincidence that both Karl-Erik Welin and Bengt Hambraeus took their first steps on the organ in Oscar's Church, Stockholm, with the same teacher, Alf Linder. Together they contributed the main elements to the development of a new organ style. And while Welin continued performing and through his performances inspired various composers, Hambraeus continued composing (see figure 23-5). Over the following decades and up until his death in 2000 he integrated new elements into his repertoire of compositional means and enlarged the resources available for advanced contemporary organ music. In *Shogaku*, for instance, Hambraeus opens organ music to Japanese influence (the *sho* is the Japanese mouth organ used in the courtly music known as *gagaku*). *Nebulosa* (1969) and *Extempore* (1975) experiment with mobile and open forms; *Extempore* and *Toccata: Monumentum per Max Reger* (1973) include, to a major degree, music of other periods; and *Triptyque pour orgue avec MIDI* (1994) combines the organ with sounds generated from a MIDI keyboard.

A large number of Hambraeus's recent works are written for a specific kind

---

20. In a personal correspondence to me dated 8 Oct. 1998, Bengt Hambraeus assumes that "probably the whole idea goes back to Welin, who performed many of Morthenson's pieces."

21. Concerning the relations between *Harmonies* and *Éternes* (and also *Volumina*), see Herchenröder, *Struktur und Assoziation*, 91.

Figure 23-6. Bengt Hambraeus, *Ricercare per organo,* p. 13. © 1979 AB Nordiska Musikförlaget, Edition Wilhelm Hansen Stockholm. Printed by permission of Ehrling-förlagen AB, Stockholm, and the composer.

of organ, a tribute to the pluralistic situation of the current organ scene all over the world. *Icons* (1974–75), for instance, was conceived for the late-romantic 112-stop instrument in St. Paul's Anglican Church, Toronto. The forty-eight-piece cycle *Livre d'orgue* (1980–81) analyzes the sonic characteristics of the organ in Redpath Hall at McGill University in Montreal, a classical French organ built in 1981 by the Canadian organ builder Hellmuth Wolff, which follows in nearly every detail the principles of Dom Bédos; and *Organum Sancti Jacobi* (1993) presents the rediscovered original sound of the restored Arp Schnitger organ in St. Jacobi, Hamburg, in a new compositional perspective.

Among the pieces Hambraeus composed for a specific organ are two for the instrument in Oscar's Church: *Ricercare,* a Swedish Radio commission composed in 1974, played for the first time on 15 February 1975 by Erik Lundkvist; and *Riflessioni,* commissioned by the congregation of Oscar's Church for the fiftieth anniversary of the organ, written in 1999 and premiered on 5 September of the same year by Erik Boström, to whom the work is dedicated (CD track 12).

Hambraeus's *Ricercare* is a study in dynamics and sonorities, exploring the possibilities of the instrument just as an early baroque ricercar does. It is exper-imental with respect to the very differentiated synthesis of sound and thus com-parable to the Radio Bremen piece *Interferenzen,* with which it also shares score notation on separate systems, referring to the manual and pedal divisions of the organ. The four-part score of *Ricercare* (see figure 23-6), like the compositional technique—changing the timbre of a chord played simultaneously on different divisions—and, of course, the registration, show that *Ricercare* accentuates the

Werkprinzip character of the Marcussen organ. The various sections of the piece, clearly separated by different registrations and settings, can be interpreted as reflections of the spatially separated and sonically differentiated divisions of the original organ.

Riflessioni reacts to changes made to the Oscar's Church organ after the composition of *Ricercare*. In 1980 the organ-building firm Bruno Christensen & Sønner added a register crescendo and a set of 240 digital free combinations, thus enabling organists and composers to achieve fast and gradual dynamic developments with almost imperceptible register changes and sudden switches between completely different registrations. *Riflessioni* makes significant use of these new possibilities, so the composition contrasts sharply with the *Werkprinzip*-based *Ricercare*; its enormous crescendi and diminuendi form a piece of Reger-like character.

The Reger allusion is not restricted to the dynamics; the whole piece is populated by characteristic quotations from organ compositions of the past—Dieterich Buxtehude, Nicolaus Bruhns, J. S. Bach, and Julius Reubke, but above all Reger, and these Reger quotations form a sort of hidden cantus firmus. All of the quotations refer to Alf Linder, Hambraeus's organ teacher and the organist of Oscar's Church who initiated the new Marcussen organ built in 1949. Fragments of Linder's repertoire emerge in flashes from the stream of this music and are condensed, linked together, and blended by means of combination, arrangement, and variation. Let us examine a characteristic passage midway through the piece (figure 23-7).

The subito adagio (CD track 12 at 08:25) leads to a quotation from mm. 35–38 of Bach's Fantasy in G Minor (BWV 542), transposed from E to A minor and slightly varied with respect to the rhythm of the pedal part; the other voices, and thus the harmony, are identical to the original. The passage stops at the end of the second system on a diminished-seventh chord, which serves as a bridge to the following fragment of Reger's Fantasy in D Minor, op. 135b, beginning also with a diminished-seventh chord at m. 39.[22] This leads into the subito vivace,[23] where Reger's original music (Fantasy, mm. 40–41) is cut into pieces (rest at the end of the third system), rhythmically varied (*swinging*, triplet at the end of the last system), and altered with respect to the octave level of single tones (last system). The continuation of this varied quotation (on the next page;

22. Printed score ([Berlin]: Simrock, 1916); in the manuscript, which is longer than the printed version, the second part of the passage appears in m. 49. Hambraeus's notation, in longer durations than in the original, does not really alter Reger's rhythm; it is only a kind of exact transcription of what an organist (perhaps Linder?) does when playing these chords (including the articulation, for instance, of the rest between the two octaves in the left hand before the subito vivace begins).

23. Reger: quasi vivace.

Figure 23-7. Bengt Hambraeus, *Riflessioni* (manuscript, 1999), p. 14. Printed with kind permission of the composer.

not included in the example) blends into a long allusion to Reger's fugue, the two themes of which are presented in a rather altered way to form an almost newly composed, no longer tonal exposition of the themes.

Because Hambraeus's quotation methods change from page to page, and because the piece contains dozens of examples from Linder's repertoire, the description of this passage can only provide a first hint of the composer's techniques, which range from exact quotation through variation of the original music and blending of styles by bridge chords to new composition with transferred material from historical music. But this page further serves as a key passage to the entire composition in its juxtaposition of Bach and Reger. Like several other passages, page 14 offers an homage to Bach. In the Reger quotation, Bach is present not only in his Fantasy in G Minor but even in his name. The initial notes of the third to the sixth four-note group in the last system (right hand) form a transposed B-A-C-H motive (D♭–C–E♭–D). This foreshadows a large B-A-C-H passage in the last section of *Riflessioni*, where fragments from *Contrapunctus XI* and the unfinished fugue of Bach's *The Art of Fugue* are combined. Both of them are based on the four notes forming Bach's name.

Reger's Fantasy and Fugue in D Minor (op. 135b) can be interpreted as a kind of guide through the labyrinth of quotations, appearing several times and serving as a quarry from which musical material is mined—even for the beginning of *Riflessioni,* which is derived from the beginning of Reger's Fantasy. There Reger's first four notes are transposed to E minor and composed to a five-tone ostinato, which serves as a harmonic basis (right hand); the other tones of Reger's figuration appear gradually, but freely combined rhythmically, in the left hand and the pedals.

The Organ as a Mirror of Its Time

In hindsight, one can attribute an almost symbolic character to both *Ricercare* and *Riflessioni;* these two pieces have brought back to Oscar's Church a movement that one could say truly began here, the development of a new organ style. The roots of this style emerged in the early 1960s and are closely linked to the names of Karl-Erik Welin and Bengt Hambraeus, both pupils of Alf Linder in this church, both intimately familiar with its Marcussen organ.

While *Ricercare* can be interpreted as a summary of experiences in the field of experimental sound composition in the 1960s and 1970s, *Riflessioni* mirrors the increasingly pluralistic situation of stylistic approaches during the 1980s and 1990s to which Hambraeus had contributed important impulses very early, since the mid-1960s. The great stylistic, formal, and sonic differences between the two pieces very clearly show the immense flexibility of the Marcussen organ, which could become the source of inspiration for experiments with sound synthesis and contrast and help to generate a Reger-like fantasy with quasi—late romantic dynamic developments. The organ in Oscar's Church, already linked to the pre-history of advanced contemporary organ music, has been a source of inspiration for important and highly characteristic organ pieces of the last decades and has therefore mirrored, for over fifty years, the fundamental compositional tendencies of its time.

24

THE ORGAN AS SCRYING GLASS: IMAGES FROM THE
ORGAN REFORM MOVEMENT

JOEL SPEERSTRA

IN THE FIRST HALF OF THE TWENTIETH CENTURY, BEFORE OUR CURRENT CULTURE
of organ historicism, historical organs were regarded so variously that, to add
another mirror metaphor to this volume's collection of mirrors, the organ functioned almost as a scrying glass. The scrying glass was a traditional northern
European instrument of divination. A simple mirror could be used, and the scryer
learned to focus beyond the reflection on the surface and allow imagination and
inspiration to create its own pictures. The meaning of those pictures could be
interpreted in almost any way that suited the scryer. People often chose to see
exactly what they wanted to see reflected in the organ's surface. Albert Schweitzer saw the Holy Trinity manifest in the Hauptwerk, the Rückpositiv, and the
Schwellwerk; Hans Henny Jahnn saw a way to connect directly with the substance of past pagan cultures. At the same time, the organ reform movement
truly was divining some of the secrets of the historical organ-building tradition
and began more and more to be influenced by what it perceived in that dim
glass.

The scope of this chapter is too limited to discuss all that now falls under
the rubric of "organ reform movement," but a brief outline begins with Albert
Schweitzer's criticism of "factory-built organs" and his advocacy, as early as 1906,
of the Alsatian Silbermann organ as the ideal resource for the music of Bach.
In a parallel development, a new interest in the baroque organ type began in the
1920s with the restoration of the Schnitger organ in Hamburg's St. Jacobi
Church and the influential but highly compromised Praetorius Organ built by
Walcker in Freiburg, based only on the descriptions of model organ dispositions
given in Praetorius's *Syntagma Musicum*. Although the new organ movement that
grew up around these two influential projects often cited Schweitzer as its initiator, Schweitzer himself saw the "fullblooded horse" of the monumental

Cavaillé-Coll organs as a culmination of the Silbermann ideal and wrote privately in 1950 that the new "so-called baroque organs" were like riding a pony: "German organ builders and theorists from the middle of the '20s often wrongly suggested that I was the initiator of this organ type. Nothing could be further from the truth. But I have so far chosen not to oppose the German Organ Reform Movement openly."[1]

The German neo-baroque organ builders who experimented with historical organs as a resource for information and inspiration were handicapped both by the interruption of World War II and the impossibility of obtaining high-quality materials directly after it. The scene of greatest creativity shifted to Denmark, where high-quality materials and a developed sense of functional design led to a Danish version of the organ reform movement that reached a peak of development in the 1950s.[2] But here, too, a fundamental handicap eventually curtailed further development. The movement prided itself on avoiding stylistic copies, in part because one of its fundamental tenets was to create something "living" and functional, but in part also because there simply was not enough historical pipe material left in Denmark from which to learn anything new by copying. After 1970, with a wave of proper restorations of important historical organs in North Germany, the focus of greatest creativity shifted once again to the historical models as new sources of inspiration for tonal design. Primarily through the restoration work of the German organ workshop of Ahrend and Brunzema, the recognition of the international value of the Schnitger building tradition in particular created a new breakthrough, and the whole current culture of organ historicism can be said to have truly begun. The key event that led to this breakthrough was the Groningen (Netherlands) conference on Arp Schnitger in 1969. It was followed shortly thereafter by a similar conference on the historical organ in Stockholm in 1970.

The interview material in this chapter traces three manifestations of the organ reform movement. The discussion progresses from the extraordinary early figure of Hans Henny Jahnn (1894–1959), the expressionist author and organ expert, followed by scenes from the development of the Danish organ reform movement, and concludes with a parallel development in Sweden, spearheaded by Einar Erici (1885–1965), the doctor and organ enthusiast from Stockholm who single-handedly preserved countless historical organs in the first half of the twentieth century.

1. Albert Schweitzer, letter to the American organists J. B. Jamison and Carl Weinrich, published in Harald Schützeichel, *Die Orgel im Leben und Denken Albert Schweitzers*, vol. 2, *Quellenband* (Freiburg im Breisgau, 1995), 358. See also Sverker Jullander, "Albert Schweitzer om den tyska orgelrörelsen," *Orgelforum* 2 (1999): 60–63.

2. For a classic statement of the tenets of the organ reform movement in Denmark, see Poul-Gerhard Andersen, *Organ Building and Design* (London: George Allen and Unwin, 1969), 301–22.

The people interviewed in this chapter are three of the most influential late-twentieth-century figures for the northern European organ scene. Each of them has played an important role in moving us toward our current culture of organ historicism, a culture that values the high quality of historical organ sound and seeks to understand and preserve the organs themselves for future generations. The first two helped greatly to create the conditions for the Groningen conference, and the third organized the Stockholm conference in direct response to it. Harald Vogel spoke with me in the fireplace room of Steinhaus Bunderhee, the early-eighteenth-century house with a fifteenth-century tower that has served as the center of his activities as the director of the North German Organ Academy since its founding in 1972. Cor H. Edskes, a world-renowned expert on the historical organ, lives in the Schnitger capital of the world, Groningen. He spoke with me in the Kosterij Café tucked into the tower of the Martinikerk, home of one of the city's three famous Arp Schnitger organs, an instrument which he helped recently to restore. Axel Unnerbäck and I talked at his home in Stockholm, full of historical keyboard instruments and warm afternoon sunlight reflected from the water of one of the city's many harbors. Unnerbäck, of Sweden's National Antiquities Board, is responsible for the preservation and protection of Sweden's many historical churches, including their historical organs.

The act of interviewing itself is also not far removed from the act of scrying. The interviewer has the pleasure of watching one scene after another form and disappear, and then afterward is left alone to divine the meaning and relationship of these disjointed tableaux. The excerpts that follow present the interview subjects' own words, edited slightly for grammatical smoothness and, in the case of Unnerbäck, translated from the original Swedish.

We begin with Hans Henny Jahnn. There is an often-repeated story that Jahnn discovered, almost by accident on a walk in Hamburg in 1919, that the St. Jacobi organ was about to be removed from the church rather than restored, and Jahnn began a concerted campaign to have the instrument saved.[3]

Harald Vogel on Hans Henny Jahnn

Hans Henny Jahnn was one of the most important expressionistic authors in the German language—in fact, one of the most important authors of the German language of the twentieth century. Unfortunately, you cannot translate him because it has to do so much with how he uses language to create atmosphere.

3. See Walter Musch, *Gespräche mit Hans Henny Jahnn* (Frankfurt/M.: Europäische Verlagsanstalt, 1967), 144. The date of the organ's rediscovery and subsequent use for concerts has been called into question by Christopher Anderson in "Schnitger, Ramin, Jahnn, and the 'Organ Problem' of the 1920s," a paper delivered at the 2000 meeting of the Göteborg International Organ Academy. A more probable date is 1923.

He was also interested in organs as a child. He and his friend Gottlieb Harms ran away from home and went on a tour of all the old Hanseatic cities, to Stralsund and Rostock and Lübeck. It was a real initiation into the Hanseatic culture. They became mesmerized by these fabulous old towns and churches and organs, and later they edited all of the important first complete published works of Scheidt and of Buxtehude and Gesualdo and Lübeck and Bruhns.

They worked very hard, of course, but they were also living a sort of dandy life in the 1920s, because they were friends with a shipping magnate who paid for everything. They had plans for a new cult center called the Ugrino Center. In a little place near Hamburg they wanted to erect a series of temples: one Babylonian, one Egyptian, Greek, Roman. And in each of these temples they would have a Babylonian organ, an Egyptian organ, a Greek organ, and they described how the organs should be built. All of these outrageous ideas are in their writings.

Günther Ramin, who followed Karl Straube as the cantor of St. Thomas in Leipzig, was the most gifted German organist of his generation. Ramin and Jahnn became friends after meeting at a premiere of one of Jahnn's dramas in Leipzig. Jahnn invited Ramin to play in a series of concerts in St. Jacobi, Hamburg, to raise funds for the organ restoration and the new façade pipes. Ramin was also at the 1925 conference set up by Jahnn and Harms, performing a program of historical organ music: Schlick and Cabezon, Scheidt, Buxtehude, and the large E-Minor Prelude and Fugue by Bach.

Even though it wasn't completely restored until 1930, the organ was in full playing condition in 1925, because they had raised money through the Ugrino concerts, and so Ramin and the best German organists of the day played for this conference, which was the real starting point of the Orgelbewegung—a sort of waking up to the appreciation of Schnitger and pre-Schnitger German master organ builders.

Hans Henny Jahnn had to leave Germany because the Nazis could not swallow his extremely wild expressionism. It was not terribly focused, but very individualistic and dared to express things that people would not dream of expressing at that time in public. Jahnn really belonged to the scene of the 1920s, and the tragedy is that when he came back to Germany from Denmark in the 1950s, the intense focus on individual expression in art had passed. But Jahnn was also a clever propagandist. His article about the superiority of the slider chest was the starting point for organ builders to begin to build them again.[4] What he states in the article is not completely correct, but the effect of the article was electrifying. He had the gift for creating propaganda for the right thing at the right time.

He had this funny system of male and female registers, and he carried this out

---

4. The article Vogel refers to is Hans Henny Jahnn, "Bemerkungen zur Schleiflade (zu den Aufsätzen des Herrn Gattringer über Schleifladen)," *Zeitschrift für Instrumentenbau* 48 (1927–28): 886.

even as to how the stops were arranged at the console: one side was male and one side was female. At the Lichtwark School in Hamburg, now the Heinrich Hertz School, there is an organ where he carried this idea out completely. Jahnn and Harms not only developed these kinds of ideas, but they realized them.

The idea behind the cult of Ugrino was to build bridges to the substance of the past—a "back to the roots" movement typical of art generally in the early twentieth century, even in musicology. We would say today that their work with historical music manuscripts was an attempt to preserve an endangered "cultural heritage," but it was also an unrealistic attempt to revive the cultural substance of a time. For instance, they planned to build temples for specific times, and the idea of the organ for the Babylonian temple was that the pipes would be made of copper, the Egyptian organ would be made of silver. In the Egyptian organ, the pipes had the shape of an equilateral triangle because of the shapes of the pyramids. Jahnn's preface to the complete works of Vincent Lübeck is an art in itself. It is an expressionistic program hooked onto the personality of Vincent Lübeck:

> *By virtue of justice and duty the upper realms have spoken out for the canonization of the works of Vincent Lübeck, that not only for the ritual of the Protestant Church, not only through the craftsmanship of the compositions, not alone through the greatness of the musical thoughts, which are in an abstract sense of the highest importance, but much more for the sake of the goal which they strive to achieve, their most sublime artistic vocation to acquire an ulterior greatness, that they in reaching such a goal form a Unity with the works of Palestrina, Scheidt, Buxtehude, Bach and those of the same power.[5]*

Such a sentence. And the book is fabulously produced. There are extra blank pages everywhere. It is full of beautiful Jugendstil *designs, and the notation is the most beautiful notation of Vincent Lübeck's organ music ever produced. They even include a facsimile page from the* Clavierübung *of 1728 and include critical commentary. Nobody could afford to do this now.*

In the scrying glass of the Hamburg St. Jacobi organ, Jahnn must have felt as though he were contacting the substance of Hamburg's past. Perhaps he was trying to recapture the revelatory experience of his first youthful "initiation" into Hanseatic culture. Jahnn left Germany in the 1930s and after traveling in Scandinavia settled on the island of Bornholm in Denmark. During this period, his ideas were highly influential, especially for the Frobenius organ workshop. The most important project from a historical standpoint was the restoration and reconstruction of the historic Genarp organ in the Malmö museum in 1940. Cor Edskes takes up the story of the development of the internationally influential

---

5. From the introduction to *Vincent Lübeck Musikalische Werke*, ed. Gottlieb Harms (Klecken: Ugrino Abteilung Verlag, 1921), [i].

Danish organ reform movement, which would find its focus not around the Frobenius firm, but in its rival, the Marcussen firm, founded in 1806 by Jürgen Marcussen. Under the leadership of his great-great-grandson Sybrand Zachariassen from the beginning of the 1920s until his death in 1960, the firm broke new ground in the twentieth century with instruments that returned to mechanical action and slider windchests.

Cor Edskes on the Danish Organ Reform Movement

There was a Dutch organist called Johannes Legêne whose father was Danish. He knew a great deal about the organ reform movement in Denmark and we learned about it through him. He said that the organs in Denmark were already much better than those in Holland, and many of us went to Denmark to see for ourselves. I visited Denmark for the first time in 1946 and made a tour of organs with Finn Viderø, who was convinced that they were as good as the old organ in St. Jakobi, Lübeck. It was not true, of course, but it was a little bit in that direction.

Organ builders often said that it was not possible to capture the historical sound, that the pipes sounded so good because they were old. They were still using the techniques of the romantic organ-building tradition. You saw nicking in pipes, and pipe feet that were almost closed, but the scaling was already much better. The Marcussen firm had a fantastic archive with many annotations about old organs, and Sybrand Zachariassen had visited many organs in Germany, especially the organs in Lübeck. He began to make these annotations already as a young man. Until 1920 the land in Apenrade (Åbenrå) where the workshop stood was German, and when it came back to Denmark, the firm had to make a completely new start. He was operating in a new market and made a conscious decision to build in a completely different style than the typical Danish firms.

The most important developments in organ building were always motivated by economics. The firm had to make a new start, and they visited Germany. Zachariassen picked up new ideas, and he was the first to make these ideas reality. The ideas of the Orgelbewegung in Germany then could only really be seen in the change of stop names, not in changes in actual building techniques.

So this Dutch organist whom I mentioned, Johannes Legêne, also invited Zachariassen and Poul-Gerhard Andersen to Holland to see the old instruments, because in Denmark almost no old instruments were preserved. Only the Compenius organ. Poul Gerhard and Zachariassen had measured the whole Compenius organ during the war and knew many things about it, but almost all the other historical material in Denmark had been lost.

When they came to Holland after the war, we went to see Schnitger organs in Uithuizen and in Groningen, in the Aa kerk and also the important instruments in Amsterdam and Haarlem and Alkmaar, and they saw open pipe feet everywhere and were convinced enough to go home and try it themselves. But the problem was, they didn't understand that it was not only the open foot holes. That was a very good time for the firm, because Sybrand Zachariassen and the voicer Adolf Wehding made a very good team. Zachariassen was also very interested in scalings when he made his trip to Holland, but he overlooked many things. They examined the old pipes, but said things like "this soldering is not so exact" and so on. They had at the time many old stops in their shop, but they didn't study them. I think they were convinced that they were already making much better organs than the old ones. It was also a general tenet of belief that after the war everything was being made better than before, that they were making all things technically and functionally better than they did in the sixteenth and seventeenth centuries. The actions at first were made just like Cavaillé-Coll's. Before the Marcussen firm built their first big mechanical action organ in Copenhagen in the Nikolai Church in 1931, they studied the Cavaillé-Coll organ in the Jesus Church in Copenhagen (see chapter 14). Actually you can also find this balanced action occasionally in the old instruments too.

In Germany, some organ builders made real neo-baroque organs, like von Beckerath and Paul Ott, but the technical quality was bad, and the materials were bad. Many pipes were made of zinc. I believe the general quality of the Danish instruments was much better. The Danish have a good feeling for quality in general. And in Germany after the war, it was impossible to get good materials. In Denmark it was not a problem. They had very good wood and so forth. During the war Marcussen had to start making the shallots for reeds themselves. They had imported them from Germany before. They went back to the nineteenth-century Marcussen practice of building them in wood. First they used ebony, using the upper keys of old keyboards.

So they tried this open-toe pipe foot in the Oscar's Church organ in Stockholm, and it was a real neo-baroque instrument. It was a totally different concept for its time and therefore many organists were convinced by it (see chapter 21). Then they started building pipes with open feet and totally without nicking. It was a little bit like the army. First you shoot too far, and then you shoot too short, and then eventually you reach the target.

In 1956 there was a 150th anniversary jubilee for the Marcussen firm, and Anton Heiller was there, as well as many people from Sweden: Josef Hedar, Gotthard Arnér, and Alf Linder. The whole Scandinavian and North German organ world was there. It was then that people from Germany became interested in the Danish organ type.

The jubilee was in Åbenrå. For three days we didn't sleep at all. It was a wonderful moment. There were concerts in the cathedral in Haderslev, and Linder and Walter Kraft from Lübeck played. This jubilee really marked the beginning of Danish organ-building influence over all of Europe. The firm could invite many important people, because it was the jubilee. Almost all of the important organists and advisors of the Danish organ reform movement were there.

After the jubilee year, an event like it was organized every two years for a time. Marie-Claire Alain first visited Denmark at the next Organ Week in 1958, and it was her first experience with the Orgelbewegung. *She was astonished that the action of the organ was so good. The instruments technically played much better than the organs in France, and she was just electrified by this neo-baroque sound. It was totally unknown in France. And then afterward, Marie-Claire made many recordings on Danish organs. There was a very big discussion about the further development of the Danish organ, and some people said that we must have some stops in our organs that you only find in France—cornets and cromhornes and so on. Then in came Doctor Åge Andersen, who was almost always drunk, carrying a bottle of aquavit in his hand, and he said, "We have spent the whole afternoon discussing whether to put French cromhornes in Danish organs. But I say to you, why not Danish krummhorns in French organs?"*

Harald Vogel Recalls a Visit to the Compenius Organ

During the 1960 Organ Week there was also a memorable scene at Frederiksborg Castle, where the local organist (Jens Jacobsen Laumann) had been playing since 1926. He was about seventy years old and he was the watchdog of the Compenius organ. And we mentioned to him that this very talented young French organist named Marie-Claire Alain was here and maybe she would like to play a little bit. But we had to physically drag the old organist a little bit to the side of the organ bench. He did not leave the organ bench. So he was at one end of the organ bench and Marie-Claire was balancing precariously on the other end playing Sweelinck. It was sort of like a time machine in Denmark: it seemed to us that the war had not happened there at all. It was as if in Denmark there had somehow been complete continuity.

By the Organ Week in 1960 it was clear that this was the swan song of the Danish superiority. Because we knew that the organs of the young organ builders Ahrend and Brunzema were already better than the Marcussen and Frobenius organs of that time. They had reached a peak, but at the same time the Ahrend and Brunzema firm had outraced them. This was clear to most of the people there who knew the Ahrend and Brunzema organs, including the Dutch people, so it was a sort of strange atmosphere. These organ weeks didn't continue for very long because there was so much controversy about many things. There was controversy between Viderø and Marcussen and between Marcussen and Frobenius and somehow they paralyzed one another, so that this flourishing situation in the 1940s and early 1950s did not continue.

The major mistake that happened in Denmark is that the most talented organist, Finn Viderø, didn't get the teaching job at the conservatory in Copenhagen. This was a sort of intrigue. And if he had gotten this job, he would have attracted the best students from all over the world. But he got very bitter about it and simply didn't continue his fabulous career. I can remember one of the first memories of the organ I had was on the Danish radio. I heard Viderø playing in the early 1950s. I simply could not believe how fabulous his playing was. Danish radio had many programs a week, recordings really on the cutting edge (see chapter 4).

Cor Edskes Continues . . .

These weeks were important international meeting places. I spoke to Ahrend and Brunzema a great deal about what was happening in Denmark. I said they were doing a good job in Denmark, but I wasn't in complete agreement with their methods. Ahrend and Brunzema were working in the Ott workshop in the early 1950s, and I said to them that they needed to create a firm of their own and make a product just like the old organs. And they were very interested and opened an organ-building firm in Leer in June of 1954 and toured all over Europe.

In Holland most organists still had much respect for the old sound, because people could still hear it. In Denmark there were almost no antique organs preserved. That was the point. There wasn't a lack of respect for the old sound, but a lack of contact with it. For instance, Walther Frobenius, during the restoration of the organ in Roskilde in 1956, revoiced the old pipes of the Rückpositiv, and I asked him what he was doing. He said, "Well, we work as long as we have to in order to get these old pipes to sound exactly like our new pipes."

Frobenius threw out most things from the 1924 restoration and moved it in the modern Danish direction with a new action, and in the process melted down many old pipes, or used them to repair other pipes, by just cutting them off and soldering them onto another pipe. The situation in that respect was always much better in Holland, because there was much more of the tradition preserved. Almost all of the big organs are old ones. And the organists who came from abroad always asked where the electric stop action was.

The Danish Organ Weeks were organized by an organ enthusiast from Denmark called Count Hans Schack, who worked in cooperation with Danish radio. They had good contacts with the big Danish breweries, which gave the money to support the event, and so we almost were obligated to visit a brewery during these organ weeks. We came to the Tuborg firm, and we had a little talk with the director, and then Schack gave a little speech himself and concluded with "and now may I offer you a beer," and he pulled a Carlsberg out of his jacket pocket and said, "Have you tried this kind?" and the director said "No, no we don't know that one at all."

Count Schack was Danish, but his family was German from 1864 to 1920, until the border between Germany and Denmark was redrawn, leaving their house and lands in Denmark. I met him first in Hannover, where there was an organ congress around the inauguration of the new organ in the Market Church made by von

Beckerath and Hammer. Count Hans Schack lived in a big white castle in the southern part of Jutland on the border with Germany. He was a real organ enthusiast. I was often there in his castle. We talked about organs, but it was always a little bit comical. There was also something theatrical about these meetings. One evening Zachariassen and I were at a party at Count Schack's. We had a dinner and conversation and there was a little positive in the castle made by Paul Ott. Schack bought it in Germany. He said he wanted to have such a little organ in the castle, but it turned out to be such a bad instrument. Around one o'clock in the morning the guests assembled around this positive and poured glasses of aquavit into it, and then it really was destroyed. And Schack said, "The organ doesn't work properly. I will have to send it back to Paul Ott." And he got a refund!

But he also did many things for the Danish organ-building scene. He was interested in Anton Heiller and Marie-Claire Alain and was the first to bring them to Denmark. Schack also played a bit, and you could find him everywhere in Germany when there was an organ week or an organ inauguration. He was always there. He was a real character. One of the sons of the queen of Denmark is now living in his castle.

He had an organ himself in the Castle Church from 1679, restored by von Beckerath. He had a great deal of money in Germany, but after the war he could not get it to Denmark. So he had to spend it in Germany and decided to have his organ restored by a German organ builder. Von Beckerath restored it and added a new Rückpositiv and a new pedal and damaged the whole thing. It's possible that this instrument was made by Hans Henrich Cahman, who was at that time an organ builder in Flensburg and afterward came to Sweden (see chapter 10).

The long-term success of the Danish organ reform seems to have been hampered by the fact that there was no longer any living tradition of historical organ sound in Denmark, as opposed to the Netherlands, where the enormous number of surviving organs from the seventeenth and eighteenth centuries made the tradition of listening to historical organ sound unbroken. In Sweden, more historical material survived as well, but not without a great deal of struggle, and especially not without a particular character, Einar Erici—a doctor by trade and organ researcher by vocation, who understood and valued the sound of the historical organs and knew how to fight to keep them. Edskes met Erici when he came to the Netherlands on a study trip. He arrived with Åge Andersen, a village doctor and organ enthusiast in Gørding, near Esbjerg, who owned a grand piano from the collection of Kaiser Wilhelm and drove a fantastic prewar sports car. Like Count Schack, Åge Andersen too had money that had been left in Germany before the war, and he chose to spend it on a Maybach, which could only be sold under contract that one also guaranteed employment for a chauffeur for ten years. The chauffeur also had intimate knowledge of the car, and so one got a live-in mechanic for the same price. On this occasion, however, the Danish entourage arrived in Groningen sans chauffeur.

Cor Edskes Recalls Einar Erici's Visit to Holland

Åge Andersen knew the organ historian Einar Erici from Sweden because he was also a medical doctor. I met Erici when they came to Holland on an organ tour. Andersen drove the enormous Maybach with sixteen cylinders, and with it we made a grand tour, Erici and Åge Andersen and I. Erici wanted to see all the old organs here in Holland. When we came to Utrecht to visit Lambert Erné (1917–71), the tireless organ expert who dominated the Dutch organ scene in the 1950s and 1960s, we were to stay at a very famous hotel, the best hotel in Utrecht. But Erici had not brought a suitcase and instead had packed all of his clothes in a pillowcase, a white one. And when he came into the best hotel in Utrecht with his white pillowcase over his shoulder, they threw him out.

Axel Unnerbäck Remembers Einar Erici

People talked about him quite often out in the churches. Whenever you came to an old church with a good organ, you almost always heard, "Here Dr. Erici comes to play the organ." (See figure 24-1.) When I became aware that he had already written quite a lot about old organs and began to be interested in the topic seriously, I collected all of his various articles. Eventually I thought it would be great if I could get in contact with him, and one day I just got out the telephone book and called him. I thought I would need some kind of excuse for calling, so I thought up a reason: they were planning to rebuild an organ from 1835 in Östergötland, and I thought I would try to talk to him about saving this organ. I gave him a call, and when he picked up the phone he didn't answer with the number, which was the strict custom of the time, he just said "Hallo" in this really thick Östergötland dialect. That's where I'm from too. I began telling him about this project, and suddenly we had talked almost an hour.

He said that I should come up and visit and drink a little tea and talk. He made it plain that he wasn't terribly well, but it would be nice to meet. A couple of weeks later I called again and we set a time. He said I was welcome, but he didn't feel terribly well, so it couldn't go on "into the wee hours." At seven o'clock I arrived and was asked to take off my shoes. He offered me a pair of completely worn out slippers that he told me he had bought during his student days. He was still so alive and agile and talked and moved so quickly. He was so clear mentally, and he forgot almost immediately that he had said we oughtn't to talk so late. I don't think I came home until almost one o'clock in the morning. That was such an important moment for me, to meet someone who was so passionately interested and knew so much about

Figure 24-1. Dr. Einar Erici at the Nordström organ in Nykil Church. Photograph by Axel Unnerbäck, 1960.

Swedish organs. As we exchanged experiences about instruments that we both knew well, we discovered that we had a very similar understanding of the sound world of the old instruments. It was also a shocking meeting for me, because I thought that the old organs out in the churches were all basically quite safe, but Erici told story after story about how many battles he had fought to preserve one historical organ after another.

In those days there was an organization called the Organ Council of the Friends of Hymn Singing, founded in the 1930s, that had a very great influence. Three organists sat on this board: Henry Weman, who was the cathedral organist in Uppsala; Waldemar Åhlen, who was the organist here in St. Jacob's Church in Stockholm; and Gotthard Arnér, who was the cathedral organist in Stockholm. What Erici had to fight against was this organ council. Their idea was that every church should have a good organ with the "resources" to play liturgically. For Weman and Åhlen, that meant an instrument with two manuals and a separate pedal. Arnér was much more aware of the possibilities of the old one-manual organ. Almost all of the old organs were one manual with pull-down pedal. Many organists were often really unsatisfied that they had such small instruments, and the organ council gave them support to rebuild them. Erici's idea was that an organ with two manuals and pedal was totally unnecessary if the historical one had worked for a hundred years. Erici himself went out and played for a service sometimes in order to show that a single-manual organ with pull-down pedal worked perfectly well, and he also organized concerts with organists such as Alf Linder, Gotthard Arnér, and Finn Viderø to show that great music could be played on them. Erici made a great difference because he was goal-oriented, and the goal was that the best old organs must be saved and that the organ sound was important to protect, because even the organ reform movement instruments had not yet achieved this level of sound quality.

The organ council was also involved with restorations of old organs, which were almost always disastrous. Erici thought that Åhlen and Weman had no understanding of the old instruments and of historical organ sound, and they helped destroy so many organs that it is almost impossible to describe. Gotthard Arnér was part of the newer generation and had more positive interactions with Erici. I was really shocked by Erici's stories of how many catastrophes had already occurred and how many were avoided only at the very last moment, thanks mostly to Erici himself with the help of some of the friends he had among the professional organists, especially Alf Linder. I had had no idea there were so many problems. So when I left Erici's that first evening, I was completely wired. It was very late and there wasn't much traffic, and I didn't take the bus or the tram. I remember that I was so excited about the meeting and at the same time shocked by what he had told me that I couldn't even walk—I had to run.

Now the National Antiquities Board has more power to protect historical organs from intrusive restorations or damage, but that only happened through the long *process of the 1964 Cahman organ restoration in Leufsta Bruk. A colleague of mine interested in organs was able to clarify the law that had already given us authority to protect the organ façades because they were part of the decoration of the church and officially extend that authority to cover the organs behind the façades as well, giving us the power to stop the rebuilding of the action and protect the original wind system.*

After that first meeting we had very close contact. He called often, sometimes almost every night and normally several times a week, and sometimes the conversations were very long. I was about twenty, and he was seventy at the time.

When I met Erici I had a sort of general enthusiasm for organs. I was still really enthusiastic about the new organ reform movement organs that had been built and often played them together with my friends from school. We thought they were fantastic, because they had Rückpositivs and all mechanical action. All the other new organs were pneumatic, and we thought the construction and the sound was incredibly boring, so we found it totally magical to play these instruments with mechanical action and a sound that had freshness and vitality. The organs from the 1930s and 1940s were all pale and unfocused by comparison.

Erici's lifelong work, an inventory of Swedish organs, was already written in a typed manuscript in 1946, and I made a revised publication for the first time in 1965. A humanities research grant made it possible.[6] The first edition of the book was finished the same day that Erici celebrated his eightieth birthday in 1965. The bookbindery had to work the whole night in order for me to be able to take the first copy of the book with me to the birthday party. His health was already quite poor, and he didn't live more than a year after that, but he was able to see the final result printed.

Erici was personal friends with Albert Schweitzer. When Schweitzer was at Gammalkil, he stayed with his good friends the Lagerfelts, who owned a manor nearby, and he gave concerts on the 1806 Pehr Schiörlin organ, the largest and most famous of the seventy organs Schiörlin had built. I actually was there at his last concert in 1951 and met Schweitzer. I was only thirteen, not old enough to really understand who he was, but it's nice to remember that I actually met him.

So that was one of Erici's contacts with the continent. Erici himself told me about how he and Albert Schweitzer and Waldemar Åhlen (who was also very impressed with Albert Schweitzer) walked in the gardens of Lagerfelt's manor talking about organs, and suddenly they stopped and took one another by the hand and said together: "Eine Orgel muβ schön klingen" [an organ must sound beautiful]. They were all agreed that the sound was the most important thing, but Erici thought that Waldemar Åhlen really didn't have any understanding of organ sound, that those

---

6. Einar Erici and R. Axel Unnerbäck, *Orgelinventarium: bevarade klassiska kyrkorglar i Sverige,* [new, rev. ed.] (Stockholm: Proprius, 1988).

were really just empty words to him. Erici had a story about Åhlen, that he had a plan to rebuild an old organ; Erici said that he asked, "How is it going with the sound? That instrument sounded so good," and Åhlen answered, "Sound. You can't bother yourself about trying to preserve that." Erici used that as an example of how hopeless he was.

Of the seventeenth- and eighteenth-century organs in Stockholm, only the Finnish Church organ has survived. The plan was to pneumaticize it and rebuild it with a second manual. The organ expert for the project was Oskar Lindberg, a very well known professor, and he was a very good friend of Erici's. He also happened to be a patient of Erici's. Quite by accident, at about the same time, Lindberg developed a problem with his ear, and he was very worried about losing his hearing. Erici told Lindberg that he could certainly try to make sure he didn't lose his hearing in that ear, but he made Lindberg promise first to work to save the organ in the Finnish Church. "Yes" he said, "of course, I promise." There was in fact nothing wrong with his hearing; he just had a completely normal plug of wax, but that old organ survived, and they built a pneumatic organ behind it instead. About ten years ago it was restored, and the pneumatic organ behind it was taken away.

Erici, Champion of Historical Organs

Alf Linder had a real sensitivity toward sound and was very inspired when he played historical instruments. He often supported Erici. Swedish radio began doing recordings in the 1940s of old Swedish organs and used them mostly on a weekly Saturday afternoon radio program. First there were historical bells at six o'clock, ringing from a church in Sweden, and then a Bible text, and then music on a historical Swedish organ, with younger talented organists such as Alf Linder (CD tracks 8–10) and Gotthard Arnér. Erici helped to record these organs.

His oft-mentioned vision was that the old Swedish organs should serve as inspirational models for a revival of sound as an ideal in organ building. In 1956–57 he received support from Gotthard Arnér and the Moberg brothers to realize his vision with the first consistently carried out reconstruction of a historical organ: the only preserved Wistenius organ, from 1751, in Åtvid Church.

Erici was known mostly through his travels while researching his organ inventory. He would come to country churches and sit and play for hours. And he also went out to organs when it was clear that they were threatened. It could be dangerous for an instrument when the organ council became involved, and then Erici often felt that he also needed to become an active participant. Erici wrote popular articles in daily periodicals and organized jubilees when organs were to celebrate a hundred-year birthday. Finn Viderø, one of his friends, played on the organ in Konungsund in 1953 for its hundred-year jubilee, and Erici held a lecture in the church in which he talked about the organ builder and the organ's history. People thought this sort of thing was so interesting, to hear and see the original "old graybeard" and hear a talented organist play and show what a fantastic spectrum an old organ had. Erici understood in a modern way how to do public relations for something valuable. After such a peak-experience concert it just didn't work to say to a congregation that this instrument was deadly dull and needed to be thrown out. The organ was saved.

There are enough stories from the three people interviewed for this chapter to fill many books, but these few are offered as a brief oral history to compliment the other kinds of information in the present volume. The story of the twentieth-century organ reform movement in northern Europe is the story of a journey that begins with almost total fragmentation and leads back, through increased international postwar contact and the efforts of many individual visionaries, to an almost homogenous organ scene stretching from Stockholm to Amsterdam, not unlike the seventeenth-century international organ culture explored at the very beginning of this book. With hindsight it is easy to wonder why there was not more scientific curiosity about recreating the organ sound, and why only certain steps of a historical process were adopted while others were ignored. But within that process, every step was a revelation and also a trap. Every step forward that the organ reform took, from changing the names on the stop labels through rebuilding slider chests to studying the actual construction of the pipes themselves, represented a place that could become an ending in itself. Einar Erici is the real prototype of what has come afterwards: an enthusiast who was not willing to accept the concept that antique sound developed automatically when materials aged, and who was willing to fight to preserve historical information for future generations. In his scrying glass, Erici saw an image not of the past, but of the future, where the historical organs would once again become material and inspiration for a new wave of organ building. A new generation now stands with him and reaffirms, "Eine Orgel muß schön klingen."

ℙOSTLUDIUM

25

A NEW ORGAN FOR A NEW MILLENNIUM

KERALA J. SNYDER

WE HAVE SEEN IN THE PRECEDING CHAPTERS SOME OF THE MYRIAD WAYS IN WHICH an organ can reflect the time when it was built. But any organ that has survived its own time, as the six organs featured here have done, also has a story to tell about the times through which it has lived. With a few recent exceptions, church organs are looked upon not as historic artifacts that must be protected, but as instruments of the liturgy that must adapt to current needs or be replaced. Only the Compenius organ has emerged virtually intact, because it has been considered a museum piece from the very beginning. And even this instrument was retuned to suit contemporary taste when it was moved from Frederiksborg (Hillerød) to Fredericksberg Castle (Copenhagen) in 1791.

Some of the changes that have been made to these organs turned out quite successfully. The addition of a general crescendo pedal and digital combination system to the Marcussen organ in Oscar's Church has greatly expanded the repertory that can be played on it without destroying its ability to function as a *Werkprinzip* instrument for the performance of baroque music. And the two stops added to the St. Jacobi, Hamburg, organ in 1761 by the organ builder Johann Jakob Lehnert—Viola da Gamba 8′ in the Hauptwerk and Trommet 8′ in the Rückpositiv, in place of Schnitger's Gedackt 8′ (in Kammerton) and Schallmey 4′ respectively—had become so much a part of the organ that they were retained in Jürgen Ahrend's 1993 restoration, whose goal was otherwise to return it to the state in which Arp Schnitger had left it in 1693.[1]

The Leufsta Bruk organ suffered the most extreme accomodation to changing taste when the pipework of its Rückpositiv was removed to make space for a harmonium early in the twentieth century (see chapter 12). Some of its

---

1. Jürgen Ahrend, "Die Restaurierung der Arp Schnitger-Orgel von St. Jacobi in Hamburg," in *Die Arp Schnitger-Orgel der Hauptkirche St. Jacobi in Hamburg*, ed. Heimo Reinitzer (Hamburg: Christians Verlag, 1995), 130.

pipes were damaged or lost in the process, but fortunately they were stored away, not discarded, so they could be restored to their proper place in 1933. Their removal represented a shift from a classic to a romantic aesthetic, and as the generations turned, the Jesus Church organ nearly fell victim to the organ reform movement. In 1947 an organ consultant made the serious recommendation that the Cavaillé-Coll organ be moved from the Jesus Church to a YMCA hall or school auditorium, to be replaced by a "real" organ at the west end of the church.[2] It had already lost one of its most characteristic stops, the Voix céleste in the Récit, in favor of a Bordun 8'. But taste changed once again, the organ remained in place, and the Voix céleste was reconstructed in 1963 (see chapter 15).

The most serious damage to one of these organs was inflicted not by changing taste but by war. The St. Jacobi organ had to sacrifice its tin façade pipes to World War I, and its original case, bellows, and console were destroyed by the bombs of World War II. But its pipework and windchests had been safely stored away, so that despite these grave misfortunes it still contains most of its original pipes. With Ahrend's reconstructed case and façade pipes, this grand Hanseatic organ once again shines resplendently on the west wall of St. Jacobi Church in Hamburg.

Not all of the organs mentioned in the preceding chapters have fared so well. Of Schnitger's organ for the Lübeck Cathedral, only the keydesk and stop name plates remain, at the nearby St. Annen Museum.[3] A new Walcker organ was installed behind its façade in 1893, and all of this fell victim to the bombs of 1942. The façade of the magnificent organ that Heinrich Julius commissioned from David Beck for the church of his Gröningen bishop's residence—renovated under Andreas Werckmeister's direction, as described in chapter 7—still partially exists, but in two separate places. The entire organ was moved in 1770 from Gröningen Castle to St. Martini Church in Halberstadt (where Werckmeister had served as organist), but after a subsequent rebuilding in 1838 the case for the Rückpositiv was given to the village church in nearby Harsleben. The remaining pipes of the Beck organ were removed from behind the Hauptwerk façade in 1902, when a Röver-Hausneidorf pneumatic organ was installed behind it; this façade was preserved even after the church became a concert hall in 1954 and the organ was sold.[4]

---

2. Jørgen Haldor Hansen and Ole Olesen, *Jesuskirkens Orgler* (Copenhagen: Jesuskirkens Koncerter, 1993), 48–49.

3. An inscription on a positive in private possession claims that its 8' wooden stop came from the Brustwerk of the Cathedral organ (see Dietrich Wölfel, *Die wunderbare Welt der Orgeln: Lübeck als Orgelstadt* [Lübeck: Schmidt-Römhild, 1980], 214), but this stop most likely dates from a time later than Schnitger (information kindly supplied by Hans Davidsson).

4. Wolf Hobohm, "Zur Geschichte der David-Beck-Orgel in Gröningen," in *Bericht über das 5. Symposium zu Fragen des Orgelbaus im 17./18. Jahrhundert*, ed. Eitelfriedrich Thom (Blankenburg/Michaelstein: Die Kultur-und Forschungsstätte, 1985), 64–66. This article contains pictures of the two façades.

The seventeenth-century organ from the German Church in Stockholm suffered a similar fate—being moved to a different church and having its Rückpositiv severed from the main organ—but in this case the story has a happy ending. As a Hanseatic city, Stockholm had a large German population, and the congregation got its first organ from Paulus Müller of Spandau in 1607. After the third enlargement, in 1651, the organ had become the largest in all of Sweden, with 35 stops on three manuals and pedal. The organist at this time was Andreas Düben (c. 1597–1662), a Sweelinck student who served concurrently as chapel master to the king of Sweden. His son Gustaf (c. 1628–90) succeeded to both positions and assembled the large music collection (now at Uppsala) that preserved the vocal works of Franz Tunder and Dieterich Buxtehude, among others. Under the Dübens and their successors the organ served the German Church congregation until 1779, when they sold it to the village church of Övertorneå, in the far north of Sweden on the River Torne, which forms the boundary between Sweden and Finland.

On its way northward, the German Church organ lost its pedal division, and even so it was too big for the small village church, so its Hauptwerk and Oberwerk were installed in Övertorneå with a new pull-down pedal, while its Rückpositiv was converted into a one-manual organ for the neighboring village of Hedenäset. Over the next two centuries the Övertorneå organ was played, repaired, retired, and partially restored, but always viewed with respect. When Hans-Ola Ericsson became professor of organ at the music conservatory of nearby Piteå, he recognized the enormous potential for cultural and educational enrichment that this organ offered and initiated the Övertorneå Project. Under this program, an international team of experts thoroughly documented the two parts of the organ in 1992–93. On the basis of this information, together with a wealth of archival documents, Grönlunds Orgelbyggeri of Gammelstad (near Luleå) reconstructed the German Church organ in Norrfjärden Church, close to Piteå, and it was inaugurated in 1997.[5] There it serves both the church in its worship and the music school in its teaching. Only after this stage had been completed, with the experience gained through the building process, did the Övertorneå organ receive a thorough restoration, which was completed in 1999.[6] This project, with its progression from documentation to reconstruction and only then to restoration, shines like a beacon into the twenty-first century as a model for the preservation of our inheritance of historic musical instruments.

5. See Lena Weman Ericsson, ed., *Övertorneåprojektet: Om dokumentationen av orgeln i Övertorneå och rekonstruktionen av 1684 års Orgel i Tyska kyrkan* (Piteå: Musikhögskolan, 1997). A second reconstruction will be installed in the German Church in Stockholm.
6. See Lena Weman Ericsson, ed., *Övertorneåprojektet: Om restaureringen av orgeln i Övertorneå* (Piteå: Musikhögskolan, 1999).

The North German Organ in Örgryte New Church, Göteborg (2000)

The North German Organ Research Project in Göteborg had as its goal not the reconstruction of a particular *organ*, as in the Övertorneå Project, but of a particular organ *sound*: that of a large organ for a Hanseatic city, in the style of Arp Schnitger, tuned in pure quarter-comma meantone. In the process, it sought to uncover and replicate lost seventeenth-century building techniques and to answer the question: why do historic organ pipes generally sound better than new ones? This ambitious plan resulted from the vision of one man, Hans Davidsson, and could only be carried out within the context of a major university research project, with extensive government and foundation support. Two universities in fact collaborated in its realization: Göteborg University, which set up the organ research workshop in which the organ was built, and Chalmers University of Technology, in whose laboratories some of those secrets were uncovered. The home for the new organ would be in Örgryte New Church, where it could serve the needs of both the congregation and the music school of the university.

The preliminary research for the North German organ benefited enormously from the fact that the pipework of the organ in St. Jacobi, Hamburg, had already been thoroughly documented by Cor H. Edskes while it was disassembled for its recent restoration.[7] This provided a point of departure, but other organs had to be studied as well before a plan for the new organ could be drafted, because St. Jacobi's façade would not fit in Örgryte Church, and it was missing its original keydesk and wind system. The design of the Örgryte organ was eventually based mainly on prototypes from St. Jacobi for its disposition (see specification 2-2) and pipework, from Lübeck Cathedral for its façade (see figure 1-4) and keydesk, from the Great Church (Grote Kerk) in Zwolle for the bellows, and from St. Laurents Church in Alkmaar for its key action.

Meanwhile, experiments in the laboratories at Chalmers were uncovering important information for the building process. Analysis of seventeenth-century pipe metal at the Department of Metallurgy revealed traces of sand, proving that the metal had been cast onto a bed of sand, not of cloth, as in modern times. This would change the cooling speed of the metal and consequently its degree of hardness, but the North European technology of casting pipe metal on sand had been lost since the eighteenth century. Its reconstruction in the organ research workshop proved to be the most significant breakthrough in the entire project. The Department of Applied Acoustics studied tone generation, made important recommendations for acoustical adjustments to Örgryte Church, and performed psychoacoustical experiments comparing the sounds of old and new

---

7. Summarized as "Das Pfeifenwerk," in *Die Arp Schnitger-Orgel der Hauptkirche St. Jacobi in Hamburg*, 186–96.

Figure 25-1. The North German organ (2000) in Örgryte New Church, Göteborg. Photograph © Ulf Celander@swipnet.se, 2000.

organ pipes. The Department of Fluid Dynamics set up a full-scale model of an organ wind system in its laboratory as well as computer simulations, by means of which an interchangeable system of wind channels was devised for the Örgryte organ that permits ongoing experiments with three different wind systems.

The interaction between research and organ-building craft continued throughout the construction of the organ, which was built by an international team consisting of Henk van Eeken, who produced the design and technical drawings; Munetaka Yokota, who was responsible for the research, production, and voicing of the pipework; and Mats Arvidsson, who supervised the entire building process, including the reconstruction of the case from two extant photographs. Every step in the process has been thoroughly documented and will be published. The organ was inaugurated on 12 August 2000 (see Figure 25-1).

SPECIFICATION 25-1.
Örgryte New Church, Göteborg, North German Organ, 2000

Werck (Manual 2)	Rück Positiv (Manual 1)	Ober Positiv (Manual 3)
CDEFGA-c‴	CDE-c‴	CDEFGA-c‴
Principal 16′	Principal 8′	Principal 8′
Quintaden 16′	Quintadena 8′	Hollfloit 8′
Octav 8′	Gedact 8′	Rohrfloit 8′
Spitzfloit 8′	Octav 4′	Octav 4′
Octav 4′	Blockfloit 4′	Spitzfloit 4′
Super Octav 2′	Octav 2′	Nassat 3′
Rauschpfeiff II	Quer Floit 2′	Octav 2′
Mixtur VI–VIII	Sieffloit 1½′	Gemshorn 2′
Trommet 16′	Sexquialt II	Scharff VI
	Scharff VI–VIII	Cimbel III
	Dulcian 16′	Trommet 8′
	Bahrpfeiff 8′	Vox Humana 8′
		Zincke 8 (from f)

Brust Positiv (Manual 4)	Pedal	
CDEFGA-c‴	CD-d′	
Principal 8′	Principal 16′	
Octav 4′	SubBass 16′	
Hollfloit 4′	Octav 8′	
Waltfloit 2′	Octav 4′	
Sexquialter II	Rauschpfeiffe III	
Scharff IV–VI	Mixtur VI–VIII	
Dulcian 8′	Posaunen 32′ (from F)	
Trechter Regal 8′	Posaunen 16′	
	Dulcian 16′	
	Trommet 8′	Cimbelstern
	Trommet 4′	Vogelgesang
	Cornet 2′	Trommel

Couplers: OP/W, BP/W
Sperrventile: W, RP, OP, BP, Pedal; Hauptsperrventil
Tremulant, Tremulant RP, Tremulant Pedal
Temperament: ¼ syntonic-comma meantone
Subsemitones in all manuals: eb/d♯, g♯/ab, eb′/d♯′, g♯′/ab′, eb″/d♯″; in RP, add: bb/a♯,
bb′/a♯′, g♯″/ab″; Pedal: eb/d♯, g♯/ab
12 bellows of 4′ × 8′; three interchangeable wind systems
Pitch: a′ = 465 Hz

Recording and Registration

CD track 13: Hans Davidsson playing Matthias Weckmann, *Es ist das Heil uns kommen her*, versus 7
　　Werck: Principal 16', Octav 8', Octav 4', Super Octav 2', Mixtur, Rauschpfeiff;
　　Brust Positiv: Principal 8', Octav 4', Scharff;
　　Ober Positiv: Principal 8', Octav 4', Octav 2', Scharff;
　　Pedal: Posaune 16', Trommet 8', Trommet 4', Octave 8', Octave 4', Rauschpfeiffe, Mixtur.
　　Ober Positiv, Werk, and Brust Positiv coupled together

Selected Literature

Carlsson, Anders, et al., eds. *Tracing the Organ Masters' Secrets*. Göteborg: GOArt, 2000.
Davidsson, Hans. "The North German Organ Project." *Svensk tidskrift för musikforskning* 75 (1993): 7–27.
The North German Organ Research Project at Göteborg University, edited by Joel Speerstra (in preparation).

The Örgryte organ presents one more manifestation of a cultural phenomenon that we have witnessed throughout this book: the remarkable exchange of people, goods, ideas, and music across boundaries that have at times been rather strongly guarded but are now rapidly falling as the European Union becomes a reality and globalization increases. The initial vision for this organ (by Hans Davidsson) came from Sweden, as well as its location and most of its funding. Its models in Hamburg and Lübeck, its chief consultant (Harald Vogel), and its wood carvers (Christiane and Harald Sandler) are German. An international team from the Netherlands, Sweden, and Japan (Henk van Eeken, Mats Arvidsson, and Munetaka Yokota) built it out of oak from Switzerland (donated by the organ builder Oskar Metzler). An Iraqi furniture maker (Moufak Failli) built the complex moldings of its towers, and a Hungarian organ builder (Endre Kerekes) reconstructed the Lübeck keyboards. And organists have come from all over the world to play it. But the seventeenth-century building process that the research surrounding it has uncovered is basically German.

We saw the importation to Sweden of German organ-building techniques earlier in this book with the immigration in the 1680s of Hans Henrich Cahman, whose son built the Leufsta Bruk organ. Through his apprenticeship with Hans Christoph Fritzsche, who had renovated the organ at St. Jacobi, Hamburg, Hans Henrich Cahman brought to Sweden knowledge gleaned from the very same organ that inspired the North German organ at Örgryte.

Three of the organs discussed here were exported across national boundaries. The movement of the Cavaillé-Coll organ from France to Denmark and of the

Marcussen from Denmark to Sweden came purely as the result of business transactions, while the Compenius organ traveled from Germany to Denmark as a gift within a family. Its sounds, played by Finn Viderø and broadcast by Danish Radio, crossed back over that border to inspire the young Harald Vogel.

Some of these boundaries moved during the lifetime of the Compenius organ. The Danish province of Scania, where Dieterich Buxtehude spent his earliest years, became Swedish in 1658, the year he returned to Helsingborg to take up his first position as organist. The Marcussen firm has had its shop in the same place—Åbenrå, Denmark—since 1830, but in 1864 the border between Germany and Denmark shifted northward, and Åbenrå, Denmark, became Apenrade, Germany. It returned to Danish sovereignty in 1920.

Despite nationalistic differences that have raged furiously at times, the unifying force of the Baltic Sea has encouraged the movement of organ culture across boundaries throughout these four centuries. The organ of St. Jacobi, Hamburg, stands as a monument of North German organ craft, from Arp Schnitger and before to Jürgen Ahrend in the present time. With the building of the North German organ in Göteborg, this highly prized local culture has truly become international.

BIBLIOGRAPHY

Åberg, Mats, and Herwin Troje. "The Choir Organ in the Kristine Church, Falun." *British Institute of Organ Studies* 7 (1983): 50–58.

Anderson, Christopher. "Schnitger, Ramin, Jahnn, and the 'Organ Problem' of the 1920s." Paper delivered at the Biannual Meeting of the Göteborg International Organ Academy, Göteborg, Sweden, August 2000.

Andersen, Poul-Gerhard. "Orgelromantik i Danmark." *Orglet* 1 (1974): 4–14.

Anfält, Tomas. "Offentlighet och privatliv: Om livet på Leufsta herrgård på 1700-talet." In *Herrgårdskultur och salongsmiljö*, edited by Erik Kjellberg. Uppsala: Uppsala University Institutionen för musikvetenskap, 1997.

Baron, John. *Scudamore Organs, or Practical Hints Respecting Organs for Village Churches and Small Chancels, on Improved Principles*. London: Bell & Daldy, 1862.

Bédos de Celles, Francois. *L'art du facteur d'orgues*. 1770. Facsimile reprint edited by Christhard Mahrenholz. Kassel: Bärenreiter, 1965.

Belotti, Michael. "Die Choralfantasien Heinrich Scheidemanns in den Pelpliner Orgeltabulaturen." *Schütz-Jahrbuch* 14 (1992): 90–107.

Bepler, Jill. *Ferdinand Albrecht Duke of Braunschweig-Lüneburg (1636–1687): A Traveller and His Travelogue*. Wolfenbütteler Arbeiten zur Barockforschung, vol. 16. Wiesbaden: Otto Harrassowitz, 1988.

Beschreibung der Münster-Orgel zu Ulm. Ludwigsburg: Walcker, 1900.

Bicknell, Stephen. *The History of the English Organ*. Cambridge: Cambridge University Press, 1996.

Blomberg, Göran. *"Liten och gammal—duger ingenting till": Studier kring svensk orgelrörelse och det äldre svenska orgelbeståndet ca 1930–1980/83*. Göteborg: Swedish Science Press, 1986.

Blomberg, Göran, and Mads Kjersgaard. "Bälingeorgelns restaureringsfråga." Unpublished report, 1990. Stockholm, Antikvarisk-Topografiska Arkivet.

Boalch, Donald H. *Makers of the Harpsichord and Clavichord, 1440–1840*. 3d ed. Oxford: Oxford University Press, 1995.

Boström, Erik. *Marcussenorgeln i Oscarskyrkan Stockholm: Historik och beskrivning till 50-års jubileet 1999*. Stockholm: Oscars församling, 1999.

Bouchard, Antoine. "Canada's Oldest Organbuilding Firm." *Tracker* 43, no. 2 (1999): 9–20.

Bracker, Jörgen, ed. *Bauen nach der Natur—Palladio: Die Erben Palladios in Nordeuropa*. Ostfildern: Gerd Hatje, 1997.

Brunner, Otto, Werner Conze, and Reinhart Koselleck, eds. *Geschichtliche Grundbegriffe*. Stuttgart: Klett-Cotta, 1987–92.

Bunjes, Paul G. *The Praetorius Organ*. St. Louis, Mo.: Concordia, 1966.

Bunners, Christian. *Kirchenmusik und Seelenmusik: Studien zu Frömmigkeit und Musik im Luthertum des 17. Jahrhunderts*. Göttingen: Vandenhoeck und Ruprecht, 1966.

Burde, Wolfgang. *György Ligeti*. Zürich: Atlantis, 1993.

Burg, Joseph, and Hans-Otto Jakob. "Cavaillé-Coll et Francfort-sur-le-Main: Notes sur un échange artistique." *L'Orgue* 193 (1985): 6–21.

Burney, Charles. *The Present State of Music in Germany, the Netherlands, and the United Provinces*. London: T. Beckett, 1775.

Busch, Hermann J. "L'influence d'Aristide Cavaillé-Coll sur la facture d'orgues en Allemagne dans la deuxième moitié du XIXe siècle." *Cahiers et mémoires de l'orgue* 48, no. 2 (1992): 89–96.

———. "Zwischen Tradition und Fortschritt: Zu Orgelbau, Orgelspiel, und Orgelkomposition in Deutschland im 19. Jahrhundert." In *Mundus Organorum*, ed. Alfred Reichling. Berlin: Merseberger, 1978.

Buszin, Walter. "Luther on Music." *Musical Quarterly* 32 (1946): 80–97.

Butler, Gregory. "The Fantasia as Musical Image." *Musical Quarterly* 60 (1974): 602–15.

Butt, John. *Music Education and the Art of Performance in the German Baroque*. Cambridge: Cambridge University Press, 1994.

Carlsson, Anders, et al., eds. *Tracing the Organ Masters' Secrets*. Göteborg: GOArt, 2000.

Catalog von E. F. Walcker & Cie. in Ludwigsburg. Stuttgart: Stuttgarter Vereins-Buchdruckerei, 1874.

Cavaillé-Coll, Cécile, and Emmanuel Cavaillé-Coll. *Aristide Cavaillé-Coll*. Paris: Librairie Fischbacher, 1929.

Choral-Psalmbok a Cant: & Bass: skrifwen af John: Everhardt. Scara: n.p., 1744.

Colding, Torben Holck. "Carl Jacobsen." In *Dansk Biografisk Leksikon*. 3d. ed., edited by Sven Cedergreen Bech. Vol. 7. Copenhagen: Gyldendal, 1981.

Cöllen, Lucas van. *Dedicatio Templi S. Gertrudis Hamburgiensis*. Hamburg, n.p., 1609.

Cuveland, Helga de. *Der Gottorfer Codex von Hans Simon Holtzbecker*. Worms: Wernersche Verlagsgsellschaft, 1989.

David, Hans T., and Arthur Mendel, eds. *The New Bach Reader*. Revised and enlarged by Christoph Wolff. New York: Norton, 1998.

Davidsson, Hans. *Matthias Weckmann: The Interpretation of His Organ Music*. Skrifter från Musikvetenskapliga Institutionen, vol. 22. Göteborg:Gehrmans Musikförlag, 1991.

———. "The North German Organ Project." *Svensk tidskrift för musikforskning* 75 (1993): 7–27.

De Geer, Charles. *Mémoires pour servir à l'histoire des insectes*. 7 vols. Stockholm: L. L. Grefing, 1752–78.

Delamare, Nicolas. *Traité de la police*. Vol. 1. Paris: n.p., 1705.

Ditlevsen, Fin, and Finn Viderø, eds. *Orgelmusik*, Bd. I, *Praeludier og Koralbearbejdelser fra det 17de Aarhundrede*. Copenhagen: Engstrøm & Sødring, 1938.

———. *Orgelmusik*, Bd. II Copenhagen: Engstrøm & Sødring, 1963.

Dirksen, Pieter. *The Keyboard Music of Jan Pieterszoon Sweelinck*. Utrecht: Koninklijke Vereniging voor Muziekgeschiedenis, 1997.

Dollinger, Philippe. *Die Hanse*. Stuttgart: Alfred Kröner, 1966.

Douglass, Fenner. "Cavaillé-Coll and Electricity in Organ Building." In *Visitatio Organorum*. Buren, the Netherlands: Frits Knuf, 1980.

———. *Cavaillé-Coll and the Musicians*. Raleigh, N.C.: Sunbury, 1980.

Douhan, Bernt. "Louis De Geer." In *Vallonerna*, edited by Tomas Anfält. Uppsala: Stiftelsen Leufstabruk, 1996.

Dufourcq, Norbert, ed. "A propos du Cinquantenaire de la mort de Cavaillé-Coll 1899–1949: Lemmens et Cavaillé-Coll (Publications de lettres)." *L'Orgue* 67 (1953): 59–61.

Dunning, Albert. "Die De Geer'schen Musikalien in Leufsta: Musikalische schwedisch-niederländische Beziehungen im 18. Jh." *Svensk tidskrift för musikforskning* 48 (1966): 187–210.

Eckhardt, Karin. *Christian Precht: Ein Hamburger Bildhauer in der zweiten Hälfte des 17. Jahrhunderts.* Beiträge zur Geschichte Hamburgs, vol. 32. Hamburg: Verein für Hamburgische Geschichte, 1987.

Ekstrand, Viktor. *Svenska landtmätare, 1628–1900: Biografisk förteckning.* Stockholm: Sveriges lantmätarefören,} 1896–1903.

Edler, Arnfried. *Der nordelbische Organist: Studien zu Sozialstatus, Funktion, und kompositorischer Produktion eines Musikberufes von der Reformation bis zum 20. Jahrhundert.* Kieler Schriften zur Musikwissenschaft, vol. 23. Kassel: Bärenreiter, 1982.

———. "The Social Status of Organists in Lutheran Germany from the Sixteenth through the Eighteenth Century." In *The Social Status of the Professional Musician from the Middle Ages to the Nineteenth Century,* edited by Walter Salmen, translated by Herbert Kaufman and Barbara Reisner. New York: Pendragon Press, 1983.

Eickhölter, Manfred, and Rolf Hammel-Kiesow, eds. *Ausstatungen Lübecker Wohnhäuser: Raumnutzungen, Malereien, und Bücher im Spätmittelalter und in der frühen Neuzeit.* Häuser und Höfe in Lübeck, vol. 4. Neumünster: Karl Wachholtz, 1993.

Eller, Povl. "Compenius-orglets historie." *Dansk årbog for musikforskning* 17 (1986): 7–51.

Elvin, Laurence. *Forster & Andrews, Organ Builders.* Lincoln, Neb.: Elvin, 1968.

———. *Organ Blowing: Its History and Development.* Lincoln, Neb.: Elvin, 1971.

Erici, Einar, and R. Axel Unnerbäck. *Orgelinventarium: Bevarade klassiska kyrkorglar i Sverige.* [New, rev. ed.] Stockholm: Proprius, 1988.

Ericsson, Lena Weman, ed. *Övertorneåprojektet: Om dokumentationen av orgeln i Övertorneå och rekonstruktionen av 1684 års orgel i Tyska kyrkan.* Piteå: Musikhögskolan, 1997.

———. *Övertorneåprojektet: Om restaureringen av orgeln i Övertorneå.* Piteå: Musikhögskolan, 1999.

Falsjö, Mark. "Alf Linder—en av 1900-talets stora orgelkonstnärer." *Kyrkomusikernas tidning* 65, no. 4 (1999): 4–11.

Festskrift vid Oscars-kyrkans Motettaftnars 10-årsjubileum den 10 december 1919. Stockholm: Oscarskyrkan, 1919.

Fischer, Johannes. *Das Orgelbauergeschlecht Walcker: Die Menschen. Die Zeiten. Das Werk.* Kassel: Bärenreiter, 1966.

Fock, Gustav. *Arp Schnitger und seine Schule: Ein Beitrag zur Geschichte des Orgelbaues im Nord- und Ostseeküstengebiet.* Kassel: Bärenreiter, 1974.

———. *Hamburg's Role in Northern European Organ Building.* Edited and translated by Lynn Edwards and Edward Pepe. Easthampton, Mass.: Westfield Center, 1997.

Forchert, Arno. "Von Bach zu Mendelssohn: Vortrag bei den Bach-Tagen Berlin 1979." In *Bachtage Berlin: Vorträge 1970 bis 1981,* edited by Günther Wagner. Neuhausen-Stuttgart: Hänssler-Verlag, 1985.

Forkel, J. N. *Über Johann Sebastian Bachs Leben, Kunst, und Kunstwerke.* Edited by Claudia Maria Knispel. Berlin: Henschel Verlag, 2000.

Forsius, Sigfrid Aronus. *Physica (cod. Holm. D 76), Uppsala universitets årsskrift 1952*, no. 10. Edited by Johan Nordström. Uppsala: Lundequistska bokhandeln, 1952.

Foss, Julius. *Organist- og kantorembederne i København og de danske købstæder og sammes indehavere i 1905.* Copenhagen: G.E.C. Gad, 1906.

Franz, Carl. "Einige Beobachtungen über den Orgelbau und die musikalischen Zustände in Paris." *Die Orgelbauzeitung* 2 (1880): 145–48.

Franzén, Olle. "Hülphers." In *Svenskt biografiskt lexikon.* Vol. 19. Örebro: N. M. Lindhs boktryckeri, 1857.

Freie Orgelwerke des norddeutschen Barocks. Edited by Klaus Beckmann. Wiesbaden: Breitkopf & Härtel, 1984.

Friborg, Flemming. "Carl Jacobsens helligdomme." In *Carl Jacobsens helligdomme,* edited by A. M. Nielsen. Copenhagen: Ny Carlsberg Glyptotek, 1998.

Gable, Frederick. *Dedication Service for St. Gertrude's Chapel, Hamburg, 1607.* Madison, Wisc.: A-R Editions, 1998.

———. "The Polychoral Motets of Hieronymus Praetorius." Ph.D. diss., University of Iowa, 1966.

Geck, Karl Wilhelm. *Sophie Elisabeth Herzogin zu Braunschweig und Lüneburg (1613– 1676) als Musikerin.* Saarbrücker Studien zur Musikwissenschaft, n. F., vol. 6. Saarbrücken: Saarbrücker Druckerei, 1992.

Gehrmann, Hermann, ed. *Die Compositions-Regeln.* Vol. 10 of *Werken van Jan Pieterszoon Sweelinck.* Leipzig: Breitkopf & Härtel, 1901.

Gerber, Ernst Ludwig. *Historisch-Biographisches Lexikon der Tonkünstler.* Edited by Othmar Wesseley. Graz: Akademische Druck- u. Verlagsanstalt, 1977.

Gerhardt, Paul, and Max Reger, eds. *Album nordischer Komponisten für Orgel.* Copenhagen: Wilhelm Hansen, 1921.

Gerkens, Gerhard. *Das fürstliche Lustschloß Salzdahlum und sein Erbauer Anton Ulrich von Braunschweig-Wolfenbüttel.* Quellen und Forschungen zur Braunschweigischen Geschichte, vol. 22. Braunschweig: Geschichtsverein, 1974.

Gilloch, Graeme. *Myth and Metropolis: Walter Benjamin and the City.* Cambridge: Polity Press, 1996.

Glamann, Kristof. *Bryggeren J. C. Jacobsen på Carlsberg.* [Copenhagen]: Gyldendal, 1990.

Glamann, Kristof. *Carlsbergsfondet.* [Copenhagen:] Rhodos, 1976.

Glamann, Kristof. *Øl og marmor.* [Copenhagen]: Gyldendal, 1995.

Godwin, Jocelyn. "Athanasius Kircher and the Occult." In *Athanasius Kircher und seine Beziehungen zum gelehrten Europa seiner Zeit,* edited by John Fletcher. Wiesbaden: Otto Harrassowitz, 1988.

Göransson, Harald. "Koralpsalmboken 1697: Studier i svensk koralhistoria." Ph.D. diss., Uppsala University, 1992.

Gorenstein, Nicolas. "Le tutti: Une registration qui n'existe pas." *L'Orgue* 236 (1995): 3– 27.

Gottschalg, A. W. "Die moderne Orgel in orchestraler Behandlung." *Urania* 44 (1887): 99–106.

Graßmann, Antjekathrin. "David Gloxin." In *Lübecker Lebensläufe aus neun Jahrhunderten,* edited by Alken Bruns. Neumünster: Karl Wachholtz, 1993.

The Great Organ in the Boston Music Hall. Boston: Ticknor & Fields, 1866.

Gudewill, Kurt. "Die Gottorfer Musikkultur." In *Gottorfer Kultur im Jahrhundert der Uni-*

versitätsgrundung: Kulturgeschichtliche Denkmäler und Zeugnisse des 17. Jahrhunderts aus der Sphäre der Herzöge von Schleswig-Holstein-Gottorf, edited by Ernst Schlee. Kiel: Christian-Albrechts-Universität, 1965.

Gurlitt, Wilibald. "Die Frankfurter Paulskirchen-Orgel von 1827." *Zeitschrift für Instrumentenbau* 60 (1940): 89ff.

Hambraeus, Bengt. *Aspects of Twentieth Century Performance Practice: Memories and Reflections.* Kungliga musikaliska akademiens skriftserie, vol. 86. Stockholm: Royal Swedish Academy of Music, 1997.

———. "Buxtehudes orgelmusik i noter och toner." *Musikrevy* 12, no. 1 (1957): 25–26.

———. "Preludium-Fuga-Toccata-Ciacona: En studie kring några formproblem i Buxtehudes orgelmusik." *Svensk tidskrift för musikforskning* 39 (1957): 89–113.

Hansen, Jørgen Haldor, and Ole Olesen. *Jesuskirkens orgler.* Valby: Valby sogns menighedsråd, 1976.

Hart, Gunter. "Daniel Meyer: Orgelmacher zu Göttingen." *Acta Organologica* 11 (1977): 119–34.

Hartmann, Günter. *Karl Straube und seine Schule: "Das Ganze ist ein Mythos."* Bonn: Verlag für systematische Musikwissenschaft, 1991.

Hassler, Hans Leo. *Canzonen für Orgel oder andere Tasteninstrumente.* Edited by Alfred Reichling. Berlin: Merseburger, 1975

Hedin, Sven. *Ett varningsord.* Stockholm: Bonnier, 1912.

———. *Andra varningen.* Stockholm: Kungl. Boktryckeriet, 1914.

Heine, Heinrich. "Reisebilder, Dritter Teil, 1829–30: Reise von München nach Genua." In *Sämtliche Werke,* vol. 5, edited by Hans Kaufmann. München: Kindler Taschenbücher, 1964.

Heinrich, Christoph. *Georg Hinz: Das Kunstkammerregal.* Hamburg: Hamburger Kunsthalle, 1996.

Herchenröder, Martin. *Struktur und Assoziation: György Ligetis Orgelwerke.* Schönau: Österreichisches Orgelforum, 1999.

Hess, Joachim. *Dispositien der merkwaardigste Kerk-Orgelen.* Gouda: Johannes vander Kloss, 1774.

Hetsch, Gustav. "Orglet." *Hvar 8. Dag.* [1904–16?]. Photocopy in the Danish Organ Registry, Museum of Music History, Copenhagen.

Hinton, J. W. *Story of the Electric Organ.* London: Simpkin, Marshall, 1909.

Hobohm, Wolf. "Zur Geschichte der David-Beck-Orgel in Gröningen." In *Bericht über das 5. Symposium zu Fragen des Orgelbaus im 17./18. Jahrhundert,* edited by Eitelfriedrich Thom. Blankenburg/Michaelstein: Die Kultur- und Forschungsstätte, 1985.

Hopkins, Edward J., and Edward F. Rimbault. *The Organ: Its History and Construction.* London: Robert Cocks, 1855.

Hortschansky, Klaus. "The Musician as Music Dealer in the Second Half of the Eighteenth Century." In *The Social Status of the Professional Musician,* edited by Walter Salmen, translated by Herbert Kaufman and Barbara Reisner. New York: Pendragon Press, 1983.

Hülphers, Abrah. Abrah:s Son. *Historisk Afhandling om Musik och Instrumenter.* 1773. Facsimile edition with an English introduction by Thorild Lindgren and a note on the organs by Peter Williams. Amsterdam: Frits Knuf, 1971.

Huybens, Gilbert. *Aristide Cavaillé-Coll: Liste des travaux exécutés*. Lauffen am Neckar: Rensch, 1985.

Irwin, Joyce L. *Neither Voice nor Heart Alone: German Lutheran Theology in the Age of the Baroque*. New York: Peter Lang, 1993.

Jaacks, Gisela. *Abbild und Symbol: Das Hamburger Modell des Salomonischen Tempels*. Hamburg-Porträt, vol. 17. Hamburg: Museum für Hamburgische Geschichte, 1982.

―――. " 'Eitler Pomp' oder 'Hamburger Anstand'? Zu Kleidungssitten im hamburgischen Toten- und Trauerbrauchtum des 17. und 18. Jahrhunderts." *Beiträge zur deutschen Volks- und Altertumskunde* 24 (1985): 19–30.

―――. *Hamburg zu Lust und Nutz: Bürgerliches Musikverständnis zwischen Barock und Aufklärung (1660–1760)*. Veröffentlichungen des Vereins für Hamburgische Geschichte, vol. 44. Hamburg: Verein für Hamburgische Geschichte, 1997.

Jaacks, Gisela, and Silke Beiner-Büth. *Decken- und Wanddekoration in Hamburg vom Barock zum Klassizismus*. Hamburg-Porträt, vol. 28. Hamburg: Museum für Hamburgische Geschichte, 1997.

Jahnn, Hans Henny. "Bemerkungen zur Schleiflade (zu den Aufsätzen des Herrn Gattringer über Schleifladen)." *Zeitschrift für Instrumentenbau* 48 (1927–28): 886.

Jacob, Werner. "Der Beitrag von Bengt Hambraeus zur Entwicklung der neuen Orgelmusik." In *Orgel im Gottesdienst Heute: Drittes Colloquium der Walcker-Stiftung 1974*, edited by H. H. Eggebrecht. Stuttgart: Musikwissenschaftliche Verlags-Gesellschaft, 1975.

Jeffery, Peter. *Re-Envisioning Past Musical Cultures: Ethnomusicology in the Study of Gregorian Chant*. Chicago: University of Chicago Press, 1992.

Johnson, Cleveland. *Vocal Compositions in German Organ Tablatures, 1550–1650: A Catalogue and Commentary*. Outstanding Dissertations in Music from British Universities. New York: Garland, 1989.

Jullander, Sverker. "Matthison-Hansen, dansk organistdynasti, Del I: Hans Matthison-Hansen." *Orgelforum* 21, no. 4 (1999): 174–81.

―――. "French and German Influences in the Organ Music of Otto Olsson." In *Proceedings of the Göteborg International Organ Academy, 1994*, edited by Hans Davidsson and Sverker Jullander. Skrifter från Musikvetenskapliga avdelningen, no. 39. Göteborg: Göteborg University, 1995.

―――. *Rich in Nuances: A Performance-Oriented Study of Otto Olsson's Organ Music*. Skrifter från Musikvetenskapliga avdelningen, no. 50. Göteborg: Göteborg University, 1997.

Jurine, Michel. *Joseph Merklin, facteur d'orgues européen: Essai sur l'orgue français au XIXe siècle*. Paris: Aux Amateurs de livres, 1991.

Kaufmann, Michael Gerhard. *Orgel und Nationalsozialismus*. Kleinblittersdorf: Musikwissenschaftliche Verlags-Gesellschaft, 1997.

Kepler, Johannes. *The Harmony of the World*. Translated by E. J. Aiton, A. M. Duncan, and J. V. Field. Philadelphia: American Philosophical Society, 1997.

Kirnberger, Johann Philipp. *The Art of Strict Musical Composition*. Translated by David Beach and Jurgen Thym. New Haven: Yale University Press, 1982.

Kircher, Athanasius. *Musurgia Universalis sive Ars Magna Consoni et Dissoni*. 1650. Facsimile reprint edited by Ulf Scharlau. Hildesheim: Georg Olms Verlag, 1970. Abbreviated German translation by Andreas Hirsch, 1662. Facsimile reprint edited by Wolfgang Goldhan, Kassel: Bärenreiter, 1988.

Kite-Powell, Jeffrey T. *The Visby (Petri) Organ Tablature: Investigation and Critical Edition.* Wilhelmshaven: Heinrichshofen, 1979.

Klaiber, Karl Friedrich. "Orgelbauer Walcker von Ludwigsburg." *Daheim* 5 (1869): 411–15.

Klais, Hans Gerd. "War die Kegellade ein Irrtum?" In *Mundus Organorum,* edited by Alfred Reichling. Berlin: Merseberger, 1978.

Knight, A.H.J. *Heinrich Julius, Duke of Brunswick.* Oxford: Basil Blackwell, 1948.

Koselleck, Reinhart. "Volk, Nation, Nationalismus, Masse." In *Geschichtliche Grundbegriffe.* Edited by Otto Brunner, Werner Conze, and Reinhart Koselleck. Vol. 7. Stuttgart: E. Klett, 1972–.1992.

Krellmann, Hanspeter. "Unmögliches als Höchstmaß des Möglichen: Der vergessene Avantgardist Bo Nilsson." *Musica* 28 (1974): 329–32.

Krüger, Liselotte. *Die hamburgische Musikorganisation im XVII. Jahrhundert.* Sammlung Musikwissenschaftlicher Abhandlung herausgegeben unter Handlung von Karl Nef. Strassburg: Heitz, 1933.

———. "Johann Kortkamps Organistenchronik: Eine Quelle zur hamburgischen Musikgeschichte des 17. Jahrhunderts." *Zeitschrift des Vereins für Hamburgische Geschichte* 33 (1933): 188–213.

Kyhlberg, Bengt. "Kring Hans Heinrich Cahmans orgelbygge i Växjö domkyrka 1688–1691." In *Kronobergsboken. Hyltén-Cavalliusföreningens årsbok.* Växjö: Kronobergs läns hembygdsförbund, 1964.

La Vopa, Anthony. *Grace, Talent, and Merit: Poor Students, Clerical Careers, and Professional Ideology in Eighteenth Century Germany.* Cambridge: Cambridge University Press, 1988.

Ladegast, Walter. *Friedrich Ladegast, der Orgelbauer von Weissenfels.* Stockach am Bodensee: Weidling, 1998.

Lang, Paul Henry. Review of *Buxtehude: Complete Organ Works,* performed by Alf Linder, organist. *Musical Quarterly* 45, no. 3 (July 1959): 424–25.

[Lewenhaupt, Carl-Gustaf]. *Dokumentation av Cahmanorgeln i Leufsta bruks kyrka.* Uppsala: Länsstyrelsens meddelandeserie, 1998.

Lewinski, Wolf-Eberhard von. "Die Orgel als Elefant oder Königin." *Christ und Welt* 15, no. 22 (1962): 20.

Lietzmann, Hilda. *Herzog Heinrich Julius zu Braunschweig und Lüneburg (1564–1613): Persönlichkeit und Wirken für Kaiser und Reich.* Braunschweig: Braunschweigischen Geschichtsvereins, 1993.

Ligeti, György. "Die Orgel sprengt die Tradition." *Melos* 33 (1966): 311–13.

———. "Pierre Boulez: Entscheidung und Automatik in der Structure Ia." *Die Reihe* 4 (1958): 38–63.

Lilliestam, Lars. "On Playing by Ear." *Popular Music* 15, no. 2 (1996): 195–216.

Linde, Koos van de, Jeroen Deriemaeker, and Gerard Pels. *Het Schijvenorgel van de Kathedraal te Antwerpen.* Antwerpen: Antwerpse Kathedraalconcerten, 1988.

Lindemann, Mary. *Patriots and Paupers: Hamburg, 1712–1830.* New York: Oxford University Press, 1990.

Lindley, Mark. "A Quest for Bach's Ideal Style of Organ Temperament." In *Stimmungen im 17. Und 18. Jahrhundert: Vielfalt oder Konfusion?* edited by Günter Fleischhauer et al. Michaelstein: Stiftung Kloster Michaelstein, 1997.

Lynge, Gerhardt. *Danske Komponister i det 20. Aarhundredes Begyndelse.* Aarhus: Erik H. Jung, 1917.

Locke, Ralph P. "Paris: Centre of Intellectual Ferment." In *Music and Society: The Early Romantic Era.* Englewood Cliffs, N.J.: Prentice Hall, 1990.

Lord, Albert. *Epic Singers and Oral Tradition.* Ithaca, N.Y.: Cornell University Press, 1991.

———. *The Singer of Tales.* Cambridge: Harvard University Press, 1964.

Lübeck, Vincent. *Vincent Lübeck, Musikalische Werke.* Edited by Gottlieb Harms. Klecken: Ugrino Abteilung Verlag, 1921.

Lueders, Kurt. "Reflections on the Esthetic Evolution of the Cavaillé-Coll Organ." In *Charles Brenton Fisk: Organ Builder: Essays in His Honor,* edited by Fenner Douglass, Owen Jander, and Barbara Owen. Easthampton, Mass.: Westfield Center, 1986.

Mactaggart, Peter, and Ann Mactaggart, eds. *Musical Instruments in the 1851 Exhibition.* London: Mac & Me, 1986.

Maison A. Cavaillé-Coll, *Orgues de tous modèles.* 1889. Facsimile reprint published as *Maison A. Cavaillé-Coll: Paris 1889,* edited by Alfred Reichling. Documenta Organologica, vol. 2. Berlin: Merseburger, 1977.

Mannerheim, Augustin. "Min hemorgel: Bruno Christensens mästarprov." *Orgelforum* 4, no. 2 (1982): 37–41.

Marshall, Kimberly, ed. *Historical Organ Techniques and Repertoire.* Vol. 3, *Late-Medieval before 1460.* Colfax, N.C.: Wayne Leupold Editions, 2000.

Mattheson, Johann. *Grundlage einer Ehren-Pforte.* 1740. Facsimile reprint edited by Max Schneider. Berlin: Leo Liepmannssohn, 1910.

———. *Der vollkommene Capellmeister.* 1739. Fascimile reprint edited by Margarete Reimann. Kassel: Bärenreiter, 1954.

McClelland, Charles. *State, Society, and University in Germany, 1700–1914.* New York: Cambridge University Press, 1980.

Meine-Schawe, Monika. "Neue Forschungen zum Mausoleum in Stadthagen." In *"Uns und unseren Nachkommen zu Ruhm und Ehre": Kunstwerke im Weserraum und ihre Auftraggeber.* Materialien zur Kunst-und Kulturgeschichte in Nord- und Westdeutschland, vol. 6. Marburg: Jonas, 1992.

Melodeyen Gesangbuch, darinn D. Luthers und ander Christen gebreuchlichsten Gesenge, jhren gewöhnlichen Melodeyen nach, durch Hieronymum Praetorium, Joachimum Deckerum, Jacobum Praetorium, Davidem Scheidemannum. Musicos und verordnete Organisten in den vier Caspelkirchen zu Hamburg in vier stimmen ubergesetzt begriffen sindt. Hamburg: Samuel Rüdinger, 1604.

Metzler, Wolfgang. *Romantischer Orgelbau in Deutschland.* Ludwigsburg: Verlag E. F. Walcker, 1962.

Modée, Reinhold Gustaf. *Utdrag Utur alle ifrån den 7. Decemb. 1817. utkomne Publique Handlingar, Placater, Förordningar, Resolutioner Ock Publikationer &c. Vol. 1 till 1730.* Stockholm: n.p., 1742.

Monié, Vilhelm. *Minnen från Leufstabruk, 1900–1927.* Edited by Karin Monié. Stockholm: Karin Monié, 2000.

Moosmann, Ferdinand, and Rudi Schäfer. *Eberhard Friedrich Walcker (1794–1872)*. Kleinblittersdorf: Musikwissenschaftliche Verlagsgesellschaft, 1994.

Morin, Gösta. "Bidrag till sjuttonhundratalets svenska koralhistoria." *Svensk tidskrift för musikforskning* 26 (1944): 119–49.

Möseneder, Karl. *Zeremoniell und monumentale Poesie: Die "Entrée solennelle" Ludwigs XIV. 1660 in Paris*. Berlin: Gebr. Mann, 1983.

Musch, Walter. *Gespräche mit Hans Henny Jahnn*. Frankfurt am Main: Europäische Verlagsanstalt, 1967.

Nagy, Gregory. *Poetry as Performance*. Cambridge: Cambridge University Press, 1996.

Neidhardt, Johann George. *Beste und leichteste Temperatur des Monochordi, vermittelst welcher das heutiges Tages bräuchliche Genus Diatonico-Chromaticum eingerichtet wird, daß alle Intervalla, nach gehöriger Proportion, einerley Schwebung überkommen, und sich daher die Modi regulares in alle und iede Claves, in einer angenehmen Gleichheit, transponiren lassen. . . .* Jena: Bey Johann Bielcken, 1706.

———. *Gäntzlich erschöpfte, Mathematische Abtheilungen des Diatonisch-Chromatischen, temperirten canonis monochordi*. Königsberg: Christoph Gottfried Eckart, 1732.

———. *Sectio canonis harmonici, zur vollen Richtigkeit der generum modulandi*. Königsberg: Christ. Gottfr. Eckart, 1724

Niedt, Friedrich Erhard. *Musicalische Handleitung*. 2d ed. Edited by Johann Mattheson. 1721. Translated by Pamela L. Poulin and Irmgard C. Taylor as *The Musical Guide*. Oxford: Clarendon, 1989.

Nielsen, Anne Marie. "Jesuskirken og den oldkristne basilika." In *Carl Jacobsens helligdomme*. Edited by A. M. Nielsen. Copenhagen: Ny Carlsberg Glyptotek, 1998.

Ochse, Orpha. *The History of the Organ in the United States*. Bloomington: Indiana University Press, 1975.

Olsson, Birger. *Olof Hedlund Orgelbyggare: Levnad, verksamhet, orgelverkens öden*. Skrifter från Institutionen för Musikvetenskap, no. 55. Göteborg: Göteborg University, 1998.

Les Orgues de Cavaillé-Coll en leur temps. Saint-Geniès-des-Mourgues: Editions de Bérange, 1999.

Owen, Barbara. *The Registration of Baroque Organ Music*. Bloomington: Indiana University Press, 1997.

Padgham, Charles A. *The Well-Tempered Organ*. Oxford: Positif Press, 1986.

Palsgård, André. *Orgelsagen i Højby Kirke 1906*. Søborg: Andre Palsgård, 1997.

Panetta, Vincent J. Jr. "Praetorius, Compenius, and Werckmeister: A Tale of Two Treatises." In *Church, Stage, and Studio: Music and Its Contexts in Seventeenth-Century Germany*, edited by Paul Walker. Ann Arbor: UMI, 1990.

Panetta, Vincent J., Jr. "An Early Handbook for Organ Inspection: The 'Kurzer Bericht' of Michael Praetorius and Esaias Compenius." *Organ Yearbook* 21 (1991): 5–33.

Pape, Uwe. *Die Buchholz-Orgel in der Stadtkirche zu Kronstadt*. Berlin: Pape, 1998.

Persson, Per Inge, Adrian C. Pont, and Verner Michelsen. "Notes on the Insect Collection of Charles De Geer, with a Revision of his Species of Fanniidae, Anthomyiidae, and Muscidae (Diptera)." *Entomologica Scandinavica* 15 (1984): 89–95.

Petzoldt, Richard. "The Economic Conditions of the Eighteenth-Century Musician." In *The Social Status of the Professional Musician from the Middle Ages to the Nineteenth Century*, edited by Walter Salmen, translated by Herbert Kaufman and Barbara Reisner. New York: Pendragon Press, 1983.

Porter, William. "Sweelinck's Fingering?" *Courant* 1, no. 1 (1983): 34–36.

Poulsen, Frederik. "Jacobsen, Carl." In *Dansk Biografisk Leksikon*, edited by Povl Engel-stof. Vol. 11. Copenhagen: J. H. Schultz, 1937.

Praetorius, Michael. *Syntagma Musicum*. 3 vols. 1615–19. Facsimile reprint, ed. Wilibald Gurlitt. Kassel: Bärenreiter, 1958–59.

———. *Syntagma Musicum II, De Organographia: Parts I and II*, translated and edited by David Z. Crookes. Oxford: Clarendon, 1986

Praetorius, Michael, and Esaias Compenius. *Orgeln Verdingnis*, edited by Friedrich Blume. Kieler Beiträge zur Musikwissenschaft, no. 4. Wolfenbüttel: Kallmeyer, 1936.

Ramin, Günther. *Gedanken zur Klärung des Orgelproblems*. Kassel: Bärenreiter, 1929.

Reed, T. J. *The Classical Center: Goethe and Weimar, 1775–1832*. Totowa, N.J.: Barnes and Noble, 1980.

Reifenberg, Peter. "Abriß der Geschichte der Cavaillé-Coll-Orgel von St. Bernhard, Mainz-Bretzenheim." In the program of the International Symposium "Reformer-Genie-Visionär: Internationales Symposium zum 100. Todestag des französischen Or-gelbauers Aristide Cavaillé-Coll (1811–1899)." Mainz, 1999.

Reimer, Emil, "Johan Gottfred Matthison-Hansen, Professor, Orgelvirtuos og Komponist." Parts 1–3. *Medlemsblad för dansk organist- og kantorforening* 6, no. 11 (1909): 149–51; 7, no. 6 (1910): 205–8; 7, no. 7 (1910): 216–17.

Reimer, Erich. *Die Hofmusik in Deutschland, 1500–1800: Wandlungen einer Institution*. Wilhelmshaven: Florien Noetzel Verlag, 1991.

Reimers, Holger. *Ludwig Münstermann: Zwischen protestantischer Askese und gegenrefor-matorischer Sinnlichkeit*. Materialien zur Kunst- und Kulturgeschichte in Nord- und Westdeutschland, vol. 8. Marburg: Jonas Verlag, 1993.

Reinitzer Heimo, ed. *Die Arp Schnitger-Orgel der Hauptkirche St. Jacobi in Hamburg*. Hamburg: Christians Verlag, 1995.

Rist, Johann. *Das AllerEdelste Leben der gantzen Welt / Vermittelst eines anmuthigen und erbaulichen Gespräches / Welches ist dieser Ahrt Die Ander / und zwahr Eine Hornungs-Unterredung*. Hamburg: Johann Naumanns Buchhandlung, 1663.

Roepstorff, Sylvester. "Jesuskirkens teologi." In *Carl Jacobsens helligdomme*, edited by A. M. Nielsen. Copenhagen: Ny Carlsberg Glyptotek, 1998.

Rochelle, Mercedes. *Mythological and Classical World Art Index*. Jefferson, N.C.: Mc-Farland, 1991.

Rochlitz, Friedrich. "Die Verschiedenheit der Urtheile über Werke der Tonkunst." *All-gemeine Musikalische Zeitung* 1, no. 32 (8 May 1799): 497–506.

Rössler, Ernst Karl. *Klangfunktion und Registrierung*. Kassel: Bärenreiter, 1952.

Roth, Dietrich, ed. *Das Moller-Florilegium des Hans Simon Holtzbecker*. Kultur Stiftung der Länder-Patrimonia, vol. 174. Berlin: Kulturstiftung Ossietzky, 1999.

Ruhnke, Martin. *Beiträge zu einer Geschichte der deutschen Hofmusikkollegien im 16. Jahrhundert*. Berlin: Merseburger, 1963.

Rupp, Emile. "Die Orgel der Zukunft." *Zeitschrift für Instrumentenbau* 27 (1906): 91–92.

Salmen, Walter. "The Social Status of the Musician in the Middle Ages." In *The Social Status of the Professional Musician from the Middle Ages to the Nineteenth Century*, edited by Walter Salmen, translated by Herbert Kaufman and Barbara Reisner. New York: Pendragon Press, 1983.

Sambucus, Johannes. "Emblemata et Aliquot nummi Antiqui Operis Ioan. Sambuci." In

Emblemata: Handbuch zur Sinnbildkunst des XVI und XVII Jahrhunderts. Stuttgart: J. B. Metzler, 1967.

Sandström-Hanngren, Marianne. "Brukets historia." In *Brukseminariet: Kompendium nr. 5.* Uppsala: Uppsala University, [1981].

Santa María, Tomás de. *Libro llamada arte de tañer fantasia.* 1565. Facsimile reprint, edited by Rudesindo F. Soutelo. Madrid: Arte Tripharia, 1982. Also published as *The Art of Playing the Fantasia*, edited by Gregg Heppenheim, translated by Almonte C. Howell and Warren E. Hultbert. Pittsburg: Latin American Review, 1991.

Sayer, Michael. "Industrialized Organ-Building: A Pioneer." *Organ Yearbook* 7 (1976): 90–100.

Schiødte, Erik. "Jesuskirken i Valby." *Tidsskrift for kunstindustri* 8 (1892): 1–14. Reprinted as *Jesuskirken i Valby: Festskrift på 100 års dagen 15. november 1991.* Copenhagen: Valby Sogns Menighedsråd, 1991.

Scheidt, Samuel. *Tabulatura Nova.* Vol. 2. Edited by Harald Vogel. Wiesbaden: Breitkopf & Härtel, 1999.

Schlee, Ernst. *Das Schloß Gottorf in Schleswig.* Kunst in Schleswig-Holstein, vol. 15. Flensburg: Christian Wolff, 1965.

Schlick, Arnolt. *Spiegel der Orgelmacher und Organisten.* 1511. Facsimile reprint edited and translated by Elizabeth Berry Barber. Buren: Frits Knuf, 1980.

Schröder, Dorothea. *Christina von Schweden in Hamburg: "Die Stunden dauern hier Ewigkeiten . . ."* Hamburg: Kurt Saucke, 1997.

Schulze, Hagen. *The Course of German Nationalism: From Frederick the Great to Bismarck, 1763–1867.* Cambridge: Cambridge University Press, 1991.

Schützeichel, Harald. *Die Orgel im Leben und Denken Albert Schweitzers.* Vol. 2, *Quellenband.* Freiburg im Breisgau, 1995.

Schwab, Heinrich W. "The Social Status of the Town Musician." In *The Social Status of the Professional Musician from the Middle Ages to the Nineteenth Century*, edited by Walter Salmen, translated by Herbert Kaufman and Barbara Reisner. New York: Pendragon Press, 1983.

Schwarzwälder, Herbert. *Geschichte der Freien Hansestadt Bremen.* Vol. 1, *Von den Anfängen bis zur Franzosenzeit (1810).* Hamburg: Hans Christians, 1985.

Sheehan, James. *German History, 1770–1866.* Oxford: Clarendon Press, 1989.

Shuster-Fournier, Carolyn. "Les orgues de salon d'Aristide Cavaillé-Coll." *Cahiers et mémoires de l'orgue* 57–58 (1997): 25–40.

Siegele, Ulrich. "Bach and the Domestic Politics of Electoral Saxony." In *The Cambridge Companion to Bach*, edited by John Butt. Cambridge: Cambridge University Press, 1997.

Simond, Charles. "Cent Ans de Paris: 1800–1900." In *Paris de 1800 à 1900: d'après les estampes et les mémoires du temps.* Paris: Librairie Plon, 1901

Smets, Paul, ed. *Orgeldispositionen: Eine Handschrift aus dem XVIII. Jahrhundert.* Kassel: Bärenreiter, 1931.

Smith, Gregory Eugene. "Homer, Gregory, and Bill Evans? The Theory of Formulaic Composition in the Context of Jazz Piano Improvisation." Ph.D. diss., Harvard University, 1983.

Smith, Rollin. *Playing the Organ Works of César Franck.* New York: Pendragon Press, 1997.

Snyder, Kerala J. *Dieterich Buxtehude: Organist in Lübeck*. New York: Schirmer, 1987.

Söderberg, N. J. *Orgelverk i domkyrkan*. Studier till Uppsala domkyrkas historia, vol. 2. Uppsala: Almqvist & Wiksell, 1936.

Soliday, Gerald Lyman. *A Community in Conflict: Frankfurt Society in the Seventeenth and Early Eighteenth Centuries*. Hanover, N.H.: University Press of New England, 1974.

Speerstra, Joel. "The Compenius Organ: An Alchemical Wedding of Sound and Symbol." Paper presented at the meeting of the Swedish Society for Musicology, June 2001.

Sponheuer, Bernd. *Musik als Kunst und Nicht-Kunst: Untersuchungen zur Dichotomie von 'hoher' und 'niederer' Musik im musikästhetischen Denken zwischen Kant und Hanslick*. Kassel: Bärenreiter Verlag, 1987.

———. "Reconstructing Ideal Types of the 'German' in Music." In *Music and German National Identity*, ed. Celia Applegate and Pamela Potter. Chicago: University of Chicago Press, 2002.

Steblin, Rita. *A History of Key Characteristics in the Eighteenth and Early Nineteenth Centuries*. Ann Arbor: UMI Research Press, 1983; reprint, Rochester: University of Rochester Press, 1996.

Steinhaus, Hans. "Deutsche Orgeln im Urteil von Aristide Cavaillé-Coll." *Acta Organologica* 14 (1980): 215–26.

Sumner, William Leslie. *Father Henry Willis, Organ Builder*. London: Musical Opinion, 1955.

———. *The Organ: Its Evolution, Principles of Construction, and Use*. 4th ed. London: St. Martin's Press, 1973.

Sweelinck, Jan Pieterszoon. *Opera omnia*. 2d ed. Edited by Gustav Leonhardt. Amsterdam: Vereniging voor Nederlandse Muziekgeschiedenis, 1974.

Theissen, Andrea. "Die Neubürgerpolitik der Stadt Braunschweig im Rahmen ihrer Finanz- und Wirtschaftspolitik vom Ende des 15. Jahrhunderts bis zum Dreißigjährigen Krieg." In *Stadt im Wandel: Kunst und Kultur des Bürgertums in Norddeutschland 1150–1650*, vol. 4, edited by Cord Meckseper. Braunschweig: Braunschweigisches Landesmuseum, 1985.

Thistlethwaite, Nicholas. *Birmingham Town Hall Organ*. Birmingham: Birmingham City Council, 1984.

Thöne, Friedrich. *Wolfenbüttel: Geist und Glanz einer alten Residenz*. München: F. Bruckmann, 1963.

Töpfer, Johann Gottlob. *Die Theorie und Praxis des Orgelbaues*. 2d ed. Edited by M. Allihn. Weimar: B. F. Voigt, 1888.

Treitler, Leo. "Homer and Gregory: The Transmission of Epic Poetry and Plainchant." *Musical Quarterly* 60, no. 3 (July 1974): 333–72.

Unnerbäck, R. Axel. "Domkyrkans orglar från Cahman till Setterquist." In *Linköpings domkyrka III*, Sveriges kyrkor, 225. Stockholm: Riksantikvarieämbedet, 2001.

———. *Leufsta bruks kyrka*. 3d rev. ed. Upplands kyrkor, vol. 141 (Uppsala: Ärkestiftets stiftsråd, 1977).

———. "Orgelbyggare, tjänsteman och köpman: Ett bidrag till Johan N. Cahmans biografi." Parts 1 and 2. *Orgelforum* 6, no. 2 (1984): 17–24; 7, no. 1 (1985): 14–19.

Upham, Jabez B. "Narration of My Organ Tour: Remarks at a Meeting of the Harvard

Music Association, January 1858." In "Methuen," part 1. *The American Organist* 45, no. 3 (March 1962), 14.

Ussing, Henry. *Min Livsgerning som jeg har forstaaet den.* Copenhagen: n.p., 1939.

Valkare, Gunnar. *Det audiografiska fältet: Om musikens förhållande till skriften och den unge Bo Nilssons strategier.* Skrifter från Musikvetenskapliga avdelningen, no. 49. Göteborg: Göteborg University, 1997.

———. "Schwedens Leitstern im Neue-Musik-Mekka." In *Von Kranichstein zur Gegenwart: 50 Jahre Darmstädter Beiträge zur Musik,* edited by Rudolf Stephan, Lothar Knessl, Otto Tomek, Klaus Trapp and Christopher Fox. Stuttgart: Daco-Verlag, 1996.

Viderø, Finn. "Orgelbevaegelsen og Norden." In *Strengen er av gull: Festskrift Rolf Karlsen,* edited by Ove Kr Sundberg. Oslo: Universitetsforlaget, 1981.

Vier Bedencken Fürnehmen Theologischen und Juristischen Facultäten, Wie auch Herrn Doct. Johann Friedrich Mayers / P. P. und Königl. Schwedischen Ober=Kirchen=Raths / Was doch von denen so genandten Operen zu halten. Frankfurt am Main: n.p., 1693.

Vogel, Harald. "North German Organ Building of the Late Seventeenth Century: Registration and Tuning." In *J. S. Bach as Organist: His Instruments, Music, and Performance Practices,* edited by George Stauffer and Ernest May. Bloomington: Indiana University Press, 1986.

———. "Zur Spielweise der Musik für Tasteninstrumente um 1600." In *Tabulatura Nova,* Teil II, edited by Harald Vogel. Wiesbaden: Breitkopf & Härtel, 1999.

Vogt, Franz-Josef. "Die Walcker-Orgel der kath. Pfarrkirche Herz-Jesu und St. Florian zu Poznan-Jezyce (Posen-Jersitz)." *Ars Organi* 48 (2000): 159–62.

Vretblad, Patrik. *Orgelregistren: Uppslagsbok för organister, orgelbyggare, och orgelns vänner.* Stockholm: C. E. Fritzes Kungl. Hovbokhandel, 1932.

Wade, Mara. *Triumphus nuptialis Danicus: German Court Culture and Denmark: The "Great Wedding" of 1634.* Wolfenbütteler Arbeiten zur Barockforschung, vol. 27. Wiesbaden: Harrassowitz, 1996.

Walker, Daniel Pickering. "Kepler's Celestial Music." *Journal of the Warburg and Courtauld Institutes* 30 (1967): 228–50.

Walker, Mack. *German Home Towns: Community, State, and General Estate, 1648–1871.* Ithaca, N.Y.: Cornell University Press, 1971.

Walker, Paul. "From Renaissance 'Fuga' to Baroque Fugue: The Role of the 'Sweelinck Theory Manuscripts'." *Schütz-Jahrbuch* 7–8 (1986): 93–104.

Walker, Paul Mark. *Theories of Fugue from the Age of Josquin to the Age of Bach.* Rochester: University of Rochester Press, 2000.

Warncke, Johannes. *Handwerk und Zünfte in Lübeck.* Lübeck: Gebrüder Borchers, 1912.

Wedgwood, J. I. "Was Barker the Inventor of the Pneumatic Lever?" *Organ* 14 (July 1934): 49–52.

Werckmeister, Andreas. *Erweiterte und verbesserte Orgel-Probe.* 1698. Facsimile reprint edited by Dietz-Rüdiger Moser. Kassel: Bärenreiter, 1970.

———. *Organum Gruningense redivivum.* Quedlinburg: Struntz, 1705.

———. *Orgelprobe . . . Benebenst einem kurtzen jedoch gründlichen Unterricht, Wie . . . ein Clavier wohl zu temperiren und zu stimmen sey, damit man nach heutiger Manier alle modos fictos in einer erträglichen und angenehmen harmoni vernehme.* Frankfurt: Calvisius, 1681.

Wester, Bertil. *Kristine kyrkas orgel: Orglar i Rättviks tingslag samt en exkurs över Oscars-*

kyrkans orgel, Stockholm. Stockholm: Generalstabens Litografiska Anstalts Förlag, 1946.

Whaley, Joachim. *Religiöse Toleranz und sozialer Wandel in Hamburg, 1529–1819*. Hamburg: Friedrich Wittig, 1992.

Whitworth, Reginald. *The Electric Organ*. London: Musical Opinion, 1948.

Williams, Peter. *The European Organ, 1450–1850*. London: Batsford, 1966.

Wölfel, Dietrich. *Die wunderbare Welt der Orgeln: Lübeck als Orgelstadt*. Lübeck: Schmidt-Römhild, 1980.

Wolff, Christoph. *Johann Sebastian Bach: The Learned Musician*. New York: W. W. Norton, 2000.

Wolschke, Martin. *Von der Stadtpfeiferei zu Lehrlingskapelle und Sinfonieorchester*. Regensburg: Gustav Bosse Verlag, 1981.

Zanker-v. Meyer, Dorothea. *Die Bauten von J. C. und Carl Jacobsen: Zur Bautätigkeit einer Industriellenfamilie in Dänemark*. Berlin: Deutscher Kunstverlag, 1982.

Compiled by John Sheridan

Copenhagen, Denmark, Jesus Church, Marcussen Organ (1890)

Hansen, Jørgen Haldor. *Jesuskirkens Orgler*. Pheasant Records, PHRCD 9801, 1997.

Göteborg, Sweden, Örgryte New Church, North German Organ (2000)

Davidsson, Hans. *Gelobet seist Du: Christmas in Lübeck 1705*. Intim Musik IMCD 078, 2001.

Porter, William. Music of Heinrich Scheidemann and Jacob Praetorius. Forthcoming on Loft Recordings.

Ruiter-Feenstra, Pamela. Music of Tunder. Forthcoming on Loft Recordings.

Vogel, Harald. Music of Hieronymus and Michael Praetorius, Hans Leo Hassler, Scheidemann, and Steffens. Forthcoming on Organeum.

Hamburg, Germany, St. Jacobi Church, Schnitger Organ (1693)

Biggs, E. Power. *Johann Sebastian Bach: Toccata (and Fugue) in D Minor: Played . . . on Fourteen Notable European Organs of the Past Five Centuries*. Columbia ML 5032, 1953.

Koopman, Ton. *Bach Organ Works, vols. 3–4*. Teldec 4509944602, 4509984432, 1995.

Leonhardt, Gustav. *The Arp Schnitger Organ in the Jacobi Church at Hamburg*. Sony Classical SK 66262, 1994.

Reymaier, Konstantin. *Konstantin Reymaier plays the Arp Schnitger Organ of St. Jacobi, Hamburg*. Priory Records PRCD 607, 1999.

Vogel, Harald. *Dietrich Buxtehude, Orgelwerke, vol. 7*. Dabringhaus & Grimm MD+GL 3427, 1993.

Wunderlich, Heinz. *Bach and the King of Instruments*. Oryx OR-EX71.

———. *Bach Organ Music*. Oryx 3C304.

———. *Bach Organ Works*. Cantate 610702, 1970. Also issued as Nonesuch H 71252.

———. *Bach, Toccata und Fuge, d-moll, BWV 565*. Cantate 653321, 1961.

———. *Max Reger, Orgelwerke*. Arp-Schnitger-Records ASR 21, 22, 23, 24, 25, 1979–81.

———. *Norddeutsche Orgelmeister*. Schwann (Musica Sacra) AMS2586, 1970.

———. *Die Orgel in Jahrhunderten und ihre Stilepochen*. Pelca PSR40520, 1978. Also issued as MHS1604/1605.

Hillerød, Denmark, Frederiksborg Castle, Compenius Organ (1610)

Biggs, E. Power. *The Art of the Organ*. Philips ABL3066. Reissued as Columbia SL-219/ML 4971–72, 1953.

Chapelet, Francis. *Frederiksborg*. Orgues historiques 16, 1967.

———. *Historic Organs of Europe*. Oryx ORYX502, 1966. Reissued as Odyssey 32160067–68. Some tracks reissued on Oryx EXP5.

Frandsen, Per Kynne. *The Historic Organ*. Dacapo 8.224057, 1996.

Laumann, Jens. *Chorale Preludes*. HMV X4975, 1945.

Tramnitz, Helmut. *Orgelmusik der Schütz-Zeit*. DG (Archive) 198350, 1962–64. Reissued as Arc 3250.

———. *Deutsche Barockmusik*. Archiv APM14350, 1964.

Viderø, Finn. *Buxtehude, Prelude and Fugue in G Minor*. HMV DB5248, 1936.

———. *Chorale Preludes*. HMV DA5262, 1939.

———. *Les Cloches*. HMV DA5207, 1939.

———. *Compenius Organ Album*. HMV GSC 47, 48, 49, 50, 51, 52, 1951.

———. *Frescobaldi, Sonata sopra i pedali; Sweelinck, Echo Fantasy no. 10*. HMV DB5214, 1951.

———. *Music on the Historic Compenius Organ in Frederiksborg Castle*. Odeon MOAK 9, n.d. Reissued as *Musique pour orgue sacrée et profane des XVI et XVIIèmes siècles*, Valois MB 17, 1959.

———. *Scheidt, Da Jesu an dem Kreuze Stund*. HMV DB5213, 1956.

Vogel, Harald. *Portrait einer fürstlichen Orgel*. Organa ORA 3002, 1972.

Leufsta Bruk, Sweden, Leufsta Bruk Church, Cahman Organ (1728)

Biggs, E. Power. *The Art of the Organ*. Columbia SL-219, [1955].

Blomberg, Göran. *Göran Blomberg spelar på orgeln i Leufsta Bruks Kyrka*. Bluebell BELL133, 1981.

———. *Orgeln i Leufstabruks Kyrka*. ARR CD 03, 1988–90.

Ericsson, Hans-Ola. *Organo con forza: Contemporary Organ Music*. Phono Suecia PSCD31, 1987.

Fagius, Hans. *Bach, The Complete Organ Music, vol. 2*. Bis CD-308, 309, 1985.

Jacobsen, Lena. *The Bachs, According to Old Rules of Rhetoric*. Prophone PROP 7773–75, 1977.

———. *Georg Muffat, Apparatus musico-organisticus*. Musical Heritage Society, 1975.

Kraft, Walter. *Bach Organ Music, Volume 3*. Vox SVBX5443, 1964.

———. *Chorale Preludes for the Christmas Season*. Vox TV340848, 1967.

Stockholm, Sweden, Oscar's Church, Marcussen Organ (1949)

Biggs, E. Power. *The Art of the Organ*. Philips ABL3066. Reissued as Columbia SL-219/ML 4971–72, 1953.

———. *Johann Sebastian Bach: Toccata (and Fugue) in D Minor: Played . . . on Fourteen Notable European Organs of the Past Five Centuries*. Columbia ML 5032, 1953.

Boström, Erik. *Olivier Messiaen: The Complete Organ Works, vol. 6–7*. Proprius PRCD9014–15, 1989.

———. *The Oscar Church Organ*. Proprius PRCD 9002, 1988.

Ericsson, Hans-Ola. *Organo con forza: Contemporary Organ Music*. Phono Suecia PSCD31, 1987.

Linder, Alf. *Bach-Musikanten: Alf Linder spelar på Oscarskyrkans orgel i Stockholm*. Proprius LP 7780.

Stenholm, Rolf. *Lar oss betanka. . . .* Proprius PROP9932, 1984.

Compiled by David Knight

INDEX